【英汉对照全译本】

AN INQUIRY INTO THE NATURE AND CAUSES OF THE WEALTH OF NATIONS
国民财富的性质与原理

［英］亚当·斯密 著

赵东旭 丁 毅 译

（一）

中国社会科学出版社

图书在版编目(CIP)数据

国民财富的性质与原理/[英]亚当·斯密著;赵东旭,丁毅译.—北京:中国社会科学出版社,2007.8
(西方学术经典译丛)
ISBN 978-7-5004-6293-4

Ⅰ.国… Ⅱ.①亚…②赵…③丁… Ⅲ.政治经济学 Ⅳ.F0

中国版本图书馆 CIP 数据核字(2007)第 097622 号

出版策划	曹宏举
责任编辑	丁玉灵
责任校对	周 昊
技术编辑	李 建

出版发行	中国社会科学出版社		
社　　址	北京鼓楼西大街甲 158 号	邮　编	100720
电　　话	010—84029450(邮购)		
网　　址	http://www.csspw.cn		
经　　销	新华书店		
印　　刷	北京京晟纪元印刷有限公司		
版　　次	2007 年 8 月第 1 版		
印　　次	2007 年 8 月第 1 次印刷		
开　　本	630×970　1/16		
印　　张	128.25		
字　　数	1372 千字		
定　　价	245.00 元		

凡购买中国社会科学出版社图书,如有质量问题请与本社发行部联系调换

版权所有　侵权必究

出版说明

为了进一步促进中西文化交流,构建全新的西学思想平台,我们出版了这套《西方学术经典译丛》(英汉对照全译本)。本译丛精选西方学术思想流变中最有代表性的部分传世名作,由多位专家学者选目,内容涵盖了哲学、宗教学、政治学、经济学、心理学、法学、历史学等人文社会科学领域,收录了不同国家、不同时代、不同体裁的诸多名著。

本译丛系根据英文原著或其他文种的较佳英文译本译出,在国内第一次以英汉对照的形式出版。与以往译本不同的是,本译丛全部用现代汉语译出,尽量避免以往译本时而出现的文白相间、拗口难懂的现象;另外出于尊重原作和正本清源的目的,本译本对原作品内容一律不做删节处理,全部照译。以往译本由于时代和社会局限,往往对原作品有所删节,因此,本译本也是对过去译本的补充和完善。

为加以区别,原文中的英文注释,注释号用①、②……形式表示;中文译者注释则以〔1〕、〔2〕……形式表示。至于英译本中出现的原义页码和特殊索引等问题,中文译者在"译者后记"中将予以解释、说明。另外,在英文原著或原英译本中,有一些表示着重意义的斜体或大写等字体,考虑到读者可以在英汉对照阅读中注意到,在本译文中没有照样标出,还望读者理解。

中国社会科学出版社

An Inquiry Into The Nature
And Causes Of The Wealth Of Nations
By *Adam Smith*

本书根据 Methuen &Co. Ltd. 1930 年版本译出

CONTENTS

目 录

（一）

Introduction And Plan Of The Work ················ 2

绪论及全书设计 ················ 3

BOOK I Of The Causes Of Improvement In The Productive Powers Of Labour, And Of The Order According To Which Its Produce Is Naturally Distributed Among The Different Ranks Of The People ······ 10

第一篇 论劳动生产力提高的原因以及劳动产品在社会不同阶层间的自然分配顺序 ········ 11

CHAPTER I Of The Division Of Labour ················ 10

第一章 论劳动分工 ················ 11

CHAPTER II Of The Principle Which Gives Occasion To The Division Of Labour ················ 34

第二章 论劳动分工的原因 ················ 35

CHAPTER Ⅲ　That The Division Of Labour Is Limited

　　　　　　By The Extent Of The Market ················· 44

第三章　论分工受到市场范围的限制················· 45

CHAPTER Ⅳ　Of The Origin And Use Of Money ········· 54

第四章　论货币的起源和效用················· 55

CHAPTER Ⅴ　Of The Real And Nominal Price Of Commodities, Or Of

　　　　　　Their Price In Labour, And Their Price In Money ········· 70

第五章　论商品的真实价格及名义价格，

　　　　或论用劳动表示的商品价格和

　　　　用货币表示的商品价格················· 71

CHAPTER Ⅵ　Of The Component Parts Of The Price Of Commodities ············ 110

第六章　论商品价格的组成部分················· 111

CHAPTER Ⅶ　Of The Natural And Market Price Of Commodities ········· 126

第七章　商品的自然价格和市场价格················· 127

CHAPTER Ⅷ　Of The Wages Of Labour ················· 146

第八章　劳动工资论················· 147

CHAPTER Ⅸ　Of The Profits Of Stock ················· 198

第九章　论资本利润················· 199

CHAPTER Ⅹ　Of Wages And Profit In The Different Employments of

　　　　　　Labour And Stock ················· 224

第十章　工资、利润随劳动与资本用途的

　　　　不同而不同················· 225

— 2 —

（二）

CHAPTER XI　Of The Rent Of Land ……………………………… 336
第十一章　论地租 …………………………………………… 337
Conclusion Of the Chapter ……………………………………… 566
本章的结论 …………………………………………………… 567
BOOK II　Of The Nature, Accumulation, And Employment Of Stock ………… 604
第二篇　论资财的性质及其蓄积和用途 …………… 605
INTRODUCTION ……………………………………………… 604
绪　论 ………………………………………………………… 605
CHAPTER I　Of The Division Of Stock ………………………… 610
第一章　论财货的划分 ……………………………………… 611

（三）

CHAPTER II　Of Money Considered As A Particular Branch Of The
　　　　　　General Stock Of The Society, Or Of The Expence Of
　　　　　　Maintainng The National Capital ……………… 628
第二章　论作为社会总资财的一部分或作为
　　　　维持国民资本的费用的货币 ……………… 629
CHAPTER III　Of The Accumulation Of Capital, Or Of Productive And
　　　　　　Unproductive Labour …………………………… 724
第三章　论资本积累，并论生产性和
　　　　非生产性劳动 …………………………… 725

CHAPTER IV　Of Stock Lent At Interest ················· 766

第四章　论贷出取息的财货 ························ 767

CHAPTER V　Of The Different Employment Of Capitals ········ 786

第五章　论资本的各种用途 ························ 787

BOOK III　Of The Different Progress Of Opulence In Different Nations ········· 820

第三篇　论不同国家财富的不同途径 ········ 821

CHAPTER I　Of The Natural Progress Opulence ············ 820

第一章　论财富的自然增长 ························ 821

CHAPTER II　Of The Discouragement Of Agriculture In The Ancient State

　　　　Of Europe After The Fall Of The Roman Empire ········· 832

第二章　论罗马帝国衰落后农业在欧洲

　　　　过去状态下受到的压制 ··················· 833

CHAPTER III　Of The Rise And Progress Of Cities And Towns, After The

　　　　Fall Of The Roman Empire ················· 862

第三章　论罗马帝国衰落后城镇的勃兴

　　　　与发展 ··························· 863

CHAPTER IV　How The Commerce Of The Towns Contributed To The

　　　　Improvement Of The Country ··············· 886

第四章　城镇商业怎样对农村的改良做出贡献 ······ 887

BOOK IV　Of Systems Of Political Economy ············· 914

第四篇　论政治经济学体系 ················ 915

INTRODUCTION ···························· 914

引　言 ································· 915

— 4 —

CHAPTER I　Of The Principle Of The Commercial Or Mercantile System ········ 916
第一章　论商业体系或贸易体系的原理 ············· 917

（四）

CHAPTER II　Of Restraints Upon The Importation From Foreign Countries Of
　　　　　　Such Goods As Can Be Produced At Home ············· 968
第二章　论对从外国进口的、在国内能生
　　　　产的货物的限制 ······························ 969
CHAPTER III　Of The Extraordinary Restraints Upon The Importation Of
　　　　　　Goods Of Almost All Kinds, From Those Countries With
　　　　　　Which The Balance Is Supposed To Be Disadvantageous ········· 1010
第三章　论把与那些国家之间发生的贸易差额
　　　　看作是不利的而对那些国家的各种
　　　　货物的进口所施加的特别限制 ·············· 1011
CHAPTER IV　Of Drawbacks ··· 1064
第四章　退　税 ··· 1065
CHAPTER V　Of Bounties ··· 1078
第五章　津　贴 ··· 1079
CHAPTER VI　Of Treaties Of Commerce ····························· 1158
第六章　论通商条约 ·· 1159
CHAPTER VII　Of Colonies ·· 1182
第七章　论殖民地 ·· 1183

— 5 —

（五）

CHAPTER Ⅷ　Conclusion Of The Mercantile System ……… 1356

第八章　关于重商主义的结论 ……………………… 1357

CHAPTER Ⅸ　Of The Agricultural Systems, Or Of Those Systems Of Political Economy, Which Represent The Produce Of Land As Either The Sole Of The Principal Source Of The Revenue And Wealth Of Every Country ………… 1398

第九章　论重农主义即政治经济学中把土地的生产物视为各国赋税及财富的唯一来源或主要来源的学派 ………… 1399

BOOK Ⅴ　Of The Revenue Of The Sovereign Or Commonwealth ……… 1448

第五篇　论君主或者国家的收入 ……………… 1449

CHAPTER Ⅰ　Of The Expences Of The Sovereign Or Commonwealth ………… 1448

第一章　君主或国家的费用 ……………………… 1449

（六）

CONCLUSION …………………………………… 1702

结　论 …………………………………………… 1703

CHAPTER Ⅱ　Of The Sources Of The General Or Public Revenue Of The Society ……………………………… 1706

第二章　论社会一般收入或公共收入的来源 ……… 1707

— 6 —

Appendix To Articles I And II ·················· 1804
第一项和第二项的附录 ·················· 1805
CHAPTER III　Of Public Debts ·················· 1920
第三章　论公债 ·················· 1921
APPENDIX ·················· 2012
附　录 ·················· 2013
译者后记 ·················· 2018

Introduction And Plan Of The Work

<small>The produce of annual labour supplies annual consumption,</small>   The annual① labour of every nation is the fund which originally supplies it with all the necessaries and conveniencies of life② which it annually consumes, and which consist always either in the immediate produce of that labour, or in what is purchased with that produce from other nations.

<small>better or worse according to the proportion of produce to people,</small>   According therefore, as this produce, or what is purchased with it, bears a greater or smaller proportion to the number of those who are to consume it, the nation will be better or worse supplied with all the necessaries and conveniencies for which it has occasion. ③

But this proportion must in every nation be regulated by two different circumstances; first, by the skill, dexterity, and judgment with which its labour is generally applied; and, secondly, by the proportion between the number of those who are employed in useful labour,

---

    ① [This word, with 'annually' just below, at once marks the transition from the older British economists' ordinary practice of regarding the wealth of a nation as an accumulated fund. Following the physiocrats, Smith sees that the important thing is how much can be produced in a given time.]

    ② [Cp. with this phrase Locke, *Some Considerations of the Consequences of the Lowering of Interest and Raising the Value of Money*, ed. of 1696, p. 66, 'the intrinsic natural worth of anything consists in its fitness to supply the necessities or serve the conveniencies of human life.']

    ③ [The implication that the nation's welfare is to be reckoned by the average welfare of its members, not by the aggregate, is to be noticed.]

绪论及全书设计

一个国家国民每年①的劳动,是供给他们每年消费的一切生活必需品和便利品②的源泉。这种必需品和便利品,或者是由本国国民劳动的直接产品构成,或者是由利用这些直接产品从外国购进来的产品构成。

〔每年劳动的产品供给每年的消费,〕

这类产品或用这类产品从外国购进来的产品,对于消费者人数来说要么有着较大的比例,要么有着较小的比例。所以一个国家国民所需要的全部必需品和便利品供给情况的好坏,就取决于这一比例的大小。③

〔供给的好坏取决于产品和人数的比例,〕

但是,对于所有国家的国民来说,这一比例都受着这两种情况的约束:第一,一个国家国民总体上使用劳动的熟练程度,技巧

---

① "每年"一词,当即就展现了老一代英国经济学家普遍做法的转变:他们将国民财富看作是一种"积累的资源"(accumulated fund)。根据重农主义者观点,斯密认为重要的是一个时期内可以生产的产量。

② "生活便利品"(conveniencies of life),洛克在《降低利率和提高货币价值的后果之思考》(1696年,第66页)中用到了这个词:任何事物的内在价值,都是由它适于供给人类生活的必需品或者适于人类生活的便利服务构成的。

③ 应该注意到这种含义:一个国家的财富是用其成员的平均福利来计算的,而不是用总额来计算的。

<small>which proportion is regulated by the skill, etc., of the labour and the proportion of useful labourers,</small>
and that of those who are not so employed.① Whatever be the soil, climate, or extent of territory of any particular nation, the abundance or scantiness of its annual supply must, in that particular situation, depend upon those two circumstances.

<small>and more by the skill, etc., than by the proportion of useful labourers, as is shown by the greater produce of civilised societies,</small>
The abundance or scantiness of this supply too seems to depend more upon the former of those two circumstances than upon the latter. Among the savage nations of hunters and fishers, every individual who is able to work, is more or less employed in useful labour, and endeavours to provide, as well as he can, the necessaries and conveniencies of life, for himself, or such of his family or tribe as are either too old, or too young, or too infirm to go a hunting and fishing. Such nations, however, are so miserably poor, that from mere want, they are frequently reduced, or, at least, think themselves reduced, to the necessity sometimes of directly destroying, and sometimes of abandoning their infants, their old people, and those afflicted with lingering diseases, to perish with hunger, or to be devoured by wild beasts. Among civilized and thriving nations, on the contrary, though a great number of people do not labour at all, many of whom consume the produce of ten times, frequently of a hundred times more labour than the greater part of those who work; yet the produce of the whole labour of the society is so great, that all are often abundantly supplied, and a workman, even of the lowest and poorest order, if he is frugal and industrious, may enjoy a greater share of the necessaries and conveniencies of life than it is possible for any savage to acquire.

<small>The causes of improvement and natural distribution are the subject of Book I.</small>
The causes② of this improvement, in the productive powers of labour, and the order, according to which its produce is naturally distributed among the different ranks and conditions of men in the society, make the subject of the First Book of this Inquiry.

Whatever be the actual state of the skill, dexterity, and judg-

---

① [This second circumstance may be stretched so as to include the duration and intensity of the labour of those who are usefully employed, but another important circumstance, the quantity and quality of the accumulated instruments of production. is altogether omitted.]

② [Only one cause, the division of labour, is actually treated.]

和判断力;第二,从事有用劳动的人数和那些不从事有用劳动的人数的比例。① 无论一个特定国家的土壤、气候和国土面积如何,其国民每年供给丰富或者欠缺,必然取决于这两种情况。

然而,一个国家国民每年这种供给的情况,似乎前者比后者所起的决定作用更大。在那些尚未开化的渔猎国家中,任何一个能够从事劳动的人都或多或少地从事有用劳动,尽力为自己或其家人或族人中老弱病残而不能渔猎的人提供各种生活必需品和便利品。但是,这些未开化的国家生活极端贫困,以至于常常因为贫困迫不得已,或者至少自认为沦落到了这种地步,有时迫不得已直接杀害自己的幼儿、老人以及长期患病的人;有时则抛弃这些人,任其饿死或被野兽吞食。与此不同的是,在那些文明和繁荣的国家里,尽管有大量的人根本不从事劳动,而且这些人所消费的劳动生产物,往往比大多数从事劳动的人的消费要高出十倍乃至上百倍。但由于整个社会的劳动产品数量如此巨大,以至于这个社会中所有的人常常都能得到充足的供给,甚至就连处于社会最底层的最贫穷的一个劳动者,只要他勤俭节约,也能享受比任何一个未开化的人所能得到的更多的生活必需品和便利品。

劳动力改进的原因,②劳动产品按照怎样的顺序自然地在社会各阶层中分配,是本书第一篇的主题。

不管一个国家国民在进行劳动时所表现出来的技能、熟练程度和判断能力怎样,在这种劳动状态持续不变的情况下,该国国

---

① 第二种情况可以扩展到包括从事有用劳动的劳动持续时间和劳动强度,但是另一种重要情况,即累积的生产工具的数量和质量,则完全被忽略不计。

② 实际上只谈了一个原因,即劳动分工。

| 国民财富的性质与原理

<small>Capital stock, which regulates the proportion of useful labourers, is treated of in Book II.</small> ment with which labour is applied in any nation, the abundance or scantiness of its annual supply must depend, during the continuance of that state, upon the proportion between the number of those who are annually employed in useful labour, and that of those who are not so employed. The number of useful and productive① labourers, it will hereafter appear, is every where in proportion to the quantity of capital stock which is employed in setting them to work, and to the particular way in which it is so employed. The Second Book, therefore, treats of the nature of capital stock, of the manner in which it is gradually accumulated, and of the different quantities of labour which it puts into motion, according to the different ways in which it is employed.

<small>The circumstances which led Europe to encourage the industry of the towns and discourage agriculture are dealt with in Book III.</small> Nations tolerably well advanced as to skill, dexterity, and judgment, in the application of labour, have followed very different plans in the general conduct or direction of it; and those plans have not all been equally favourable to the greatness of its produce. The policy of some nations has given extraordinary encouragement to the industry of the country; that of others to the industry of towns. Scarce any nation has dealt equally and impartially with every sort of industry. Since the downfal of the Roman empire, the policy of Europe has been more favourable to arts, manufactures, and commerce, the industry of towns; than to agriculture, the industry of the country. The circumstances which seem to have introduced and established this policy are explained in the Third Book.

<small>The theories to which different policies have given rise are explained in Book IV.</small> Though those different plans were, perhaps, first introduced by the private interests and prejudices of particular orders of men, without any regard to, or foresight of, their consequences upon the general welfare of the society; yet they have given occasion to very different theories of political œconomy; of which some magnify the importance of that industry which is carried on in towns, others of that which is carried on in the country. Those theories have had a considerable influence, not only upon the opinions of men of learning, but upon the public conduct of princes and sovereign states. I have endeavoured,

---

① [This word slips in here as an apparently unimportant synonym of 'useful,' but subsequently ousts 'useful' altogether, and is explained in such a way that unproductive labour may be useful.]

民每年的国民供给状况,必然取决于该国中每年从事有用劳动的人数与不从事有用劳动的人数的比例。随后将要看到,在任何场合有用的生产性①劳动者人数,都与用来推动劳动的资本量的大小以及资本的具体使用情况成比例。因此在本书的第二篇中,将要讨论资本的性质、资本逐步积累的方式、资本的不同用途以及由此所导致的劳动量也不同等问题。

<small>第二篇中将讨论资本(它规定着有用劳动者比例)的情况。</small>

在那些劳动生产过程中劳动技能、熟练程度和判断力方面比较先进的国家,对于劳动的一般管理或指导,都采取了非常不同的计划。这些计划,并不同等地有利于一国生产产品的增加。有些国家的政策,特别鼓励农村的产业;而另一些国家的政策则比较鼓励城市的产业。很少有一个国家能够对于所有的产业都采取不偏不倚的政策而使其产业得到平均发展。自罗马帝国灭亡以来,欧洲国家的政策都比较有利于城市产业即工艺、制造业和商业的发展,而不利于农村产业即农业的发展。本书第三篇中将说明在何种情况下人们采用和确立的这种政策。

<small>第三篇中讨论导致欧洲各国鼓励城市产业而不鼓励农村产业的情况。</small>

虽然最初这些计划的实行是源于某些特殊阶级的私利与偏见,他们并未考虑或者预见这些计划将如何影响整个社会的福利,可是这些计划却导致了极不相同的经济学说。有人认为城市产业比较重要;而有些人则认为农村产业更为重要。这些不相同的学说,不仅对学者们的意见产生了巨大的影响,而且对于君王制度和国家的公共政策也产生了重大影响。我将在第四篇中

<small>第四篇中将阐述各种政策引起不同理论的因而不同的情况。</small>

---

① "生产性"一词在这里只是随意提到的,它是作为"有用的"一词的根本不重要的同义词。但后来则完全舍弃了"有用的"一词,认为不生产的劳动同样也可以是有用的。

| 国民财富的性质与原理

The expenditure, revenue and debts of the sovereign are treated of in Book V.

in the Fourth Book, to explain, as fully and distinctly as I can, those different theories, and the principal effects which they have produced in different ages and nations.

To explain in what has consisted the revenue of the great body of the people, or what has been the nature of those funds, which, in different ages and nations, have supplied their annual consumption, is the object of these Four first Books. The Fifth and last Book treats of the revenue of the sovereign, or commonwealth. In this book I have endeavoured to show; first, what are the necessary expences of the sovereign, or commonwealth; which of those expences ought to be defrayed by the general contribution of the whole society; and which of them, by that of some particular part only, or of some particular members of it: secondly, what are the different methods in which the whole society may be made to contribute towards defraying the expences incumbent on the whole society, and what are the principal advantages and inconveniencies of each of those methods: and, thirdly and lastly, what are the reasons and causes which have induced almost all modern governments to mortgage some part of this revenue, or to contract debts, and what have been the effects of those debts upon the real wealth, the annual produce of the land and labour of the society. ①

---

① [Read in conjunction with the first two paragraphs, this sentence makes it clear that the wealth of a nation is to be reckoned by its *per capita* income.]

力图详尽明确地阐释这些不同学说，并说明这些学说在不同时代和不同国家中所产生的主要影响。

总之，本书前四篇的目的就在于说明一个国家广大人民的收入是怎样构成的，并说明不同时代和不同国家供给其国民每年消费的那些资源的性质。本书最后一篇第五篇所要讨论的是君主或国家的收入。在这一篇里，我将尽力说明以下几点：第一，什么是君主或国家的必要开支，其中哪些开支应该用整个社会的赋税来支付？哪些开支应该由社会某个特殊阶级或成员的特殊赋税来支付？第二，募集整个社会赋税以应对社会支出的各种不同方法以及每种方法的利弊如何？第三，导致近代几乎所有政府都把收入中的一部分作为担保用以发行公债的原因，以及使用这种公债对于实际财富即对于社会的土地和劳动的年产物的影响如何。[1]

君主或者国家的开支、收入和公债将在第五篇中予以讨论。

① 参见前两段，这句话清楚地表示了一个国家的财富是根据该国的人均收入来度量的。

BOOK I

Of The Causes Of Improvement In The Productive Powers Of Labour, And Of The Order According To Which Its Produce Is Naturally Distributed Among The Different Ranks Of The People.

CHAPTER I
Of The Division Of Labour[1]

<small>Division of labour is the greatest cause of its increased powers,</small>

The greatest improvement in the productive powers of labour,

[1] [This phrase, if used at all before this time, was not a familiar one. Its presence here is probably due to a passage in Mandeville, *Fable of the Bees*, pt. ii. (1729), dial. vi., p. 335: 'CLEO. . . . When once men come to be governed by written laws, all the rest comes on apace . . . No number of men, when once they enjoy quiet, and no man needs to fear his neighbour, will be long without learning to divide and subdivide their labour. HOE. I don't understand you. CLEO. Man, as I have hinted before, naturally loves to imitate what he sees others do, which is the reason that savage people all do the same thing: this hinders them from meliorating their condition, though they are always wishing for it: but if one will wholly apply himself to the making of bows and arrows, whilst another provides food, a third builds huts, a fourth makes garments, and a fifth utensils, they not only become useful to one another, but the callings and employments themselves will, in the same number of years, receive much greater improvements, than if all had been promiscuously followed by every one of the five. HOR. I believe you are perfectly right there; and the truth of what you say is in nothing so conspicuous as it is in watch-making, which is come to a higher degree of perfection than it would have been arrived at yet, if the whole had always remained the employment of one person; and I am persuaded that even the plenty we have of clocks and watches, as well as the exactness and beauty they may be made of, are chiefly owing to the division that has been made of that art into many branches.' The index contains, 'Labour, The usefulness of dividing and subdividing it'. Joseph Harris, *Essay upon Money and Coins*, 1757, pt. i., § 12, treats of the 'usefulness of distinct trades,' or 'the advantages accruing to mankind from their betaking themselves severally to different occupations,' but does not use the phrase 'division of labour'.]

第一篇 论劳动生产力提高的原因以及劳动产品在社会不同阶层间的自然分配顺序

第一章 论劳动分工①

劳动生产力的最大的改进,以及在劳动力运作或应用过程中

> 劳动分工是劳动效率提高的主要原因,

---

① "分工"一词即便以前曾经有人使用过,也不是很常见的。它用于此处,可能是源于孟德维尔《蜜蜂的寓言》第 2 卷(1729 年)第 6 章第 335 页中的一段话:克利奥……当某些人受到书面法律的管辖时,其他人很快也会遇到类似情况……如果人类全都喜欢安宁,并且不需要担忧别人时,人类就永远不再需要学习劳动分工与劳动再分工。豪尔:我不明白你指什么?克利奥:正如我上面所暗示的,人类天生地喜欢模仿他人的所作所为,这也是那些未开化的人类同样如此施为的原因。尽管他们非常渴望能够改善他们的境遇,但这种行为却限制了他们。但是如果一个人完全投入于制造弓箭,另一个人专门提供食物,第三个人专门建造房屋,第四个人专门制作衣服,第五个人制造生产器具,这样他们不仅变得对其他人有利,而且可以集中和运用他们自身的能力。在相同的年度里,相比于大家混乱一团的没有分工而言,他们可以得到更多的改进。豪尔:你说的情况完全正确,但我想你所说的事实在制表行业是更为明显,在那里通过分工可以达到如果不分工的话根本无法达到的程度。这点可以从我们拥有的大量钟表以及他们的精确度和美丽的外表来看到,它们都主要是因为制造它们的劳动被分成许多部门来分工完成才有此效果。这个索引包括"分工与再分工的好处",约瑟夫·哈里斯在他的《论货币与硬币》(1757 年,第 1 部分第 12 节)中采用的说法是"不同职业的好处"或"人类置身于不同的分工而给自身增加的好处",而没有采用"劳动分工"这个说法。

and the greater part of the skill, dexterity, and judgment with which it is any where directed, or applied, seem to have been the effects of the division of labour.

<small>as may be better understood from a particular example,</small> The effects of the division of labour, in the general business of society, will be more easily understood, by considering in what manner it operates in some particular manufactures. It is commonly supposed to be carried furthest in some very trifling ones; not perhaps that it really is carried further in them than in others of more importance: but in those trifling manufactures which are destined to supply the small wants of but a small number of people, the whole number of workmen must necessarily be small; and those employed in every different branch of the work can often be collected into the same workhouse, and placed at once under the view of the spectator. In those great manufactures, on the contrary, which are destined to supply the great wants of the great body of the people, every different branch of the work employs so great a number of workmen, that it is impossible to collect them all into the same workhouse. We can seldom see more, at one time, than those employed in one single branch. Though in such manufactures, therefore, the work may really be divided into a much greater number of parts, than in those of a more trifling nature, the division is not near so obvious, and has accordingly been much less observed.

To take an example, therefore,① from a very trifling manufacture; but one in which the division of labour has been very often taken notice of, the trade of the pin-maker; a workman not educated to this business (which the division of labour has rendered a distinct trade),② nor acquainted with the use of the machinery employed in it (to the invention of which the same division of labour has probably given occasion), could scarce, perhaps, with his utmost industry, make one pin in a day, and certainly could not make twenty. But

---

① [Another and perhaps more important reason for taking an example like that which follows is the possibility of exhibiting the advantages of division of labour in statistical form.]

② [This parenthesis would alone be sufficient to show that those are wrong who believe Smith did not include the separation of employ-ments in 'division of labour'.]

所体现的大部分技能、熟练性和判断力,似乎都是劳动分工的结果。

通过考察个别制造业的劳动分工状况,就可以更加容易得理解社会一般劳动分工所产生的结果。人们普遍认为,某些微不足道的制造业,分工最为细致。但实际上,这些不重要的制造业的分工,并不比重要制造业的分工更为周密。原因就在于不重要的制造业目的只在于供给少数人的小量需求,其雇用的劳动者人数必然很少,而且每个不同工作部门中工作的工人常常可以集中在一个工厂内,使观察者一眼就能看到。反之,那些大型制造业,要满足大多数人的大量需求,每个不同的工作部门都雇用了大量的劳动者,所以要把这许许多多工人集合在一个工厂中是不可能的。在同一时间里我们能看到的只能是其中一个部门所雇用的工人。因此,与那些微小的制造业相比,虽然在这种大型制造业中工作被划分成了更多的部门,但由于这种划分不如小型制造业的划分那么明显,所以很少有人注意到。

> 可以从一个具体的例子中更好地了解劳动分工对于提高效率的作用。

制针业虽然极其微小,但其劳动分工却常常引起人们的注意。因此,我在这里用它作为例子。① 如果一个工人没有受过相应的职业(劳动分工已经使制针业成为一个专门的职业)②训练,又不知道怎么样使用这种职业的机器(这种机器的发明恐怕也正是劳动分工才使其成为现实),那么即使他竭力工作,也许一天连一枚针都制造不出,更谈不上制造20枚针。但是按照目前这个

---

① 引出下面一个例子的另一个更为重要的原因是要以统计的形式来展现劳动分工好处的可能性。

② 仅仅括号里面的内容就足以证明那些认为斯密的"劳动分工"中没有包括"工作分离"的错误之处了。

in the way in which this business is now carried on, not only the whole work is a peculiar trade, but it is divided into a number of branches, of which the greater part are likewise peculiar trades. One man draws out the wire, another straights it, a third cuts it, a fourth points it, a fifth grinds it at the top for receiving the head; to make the head requires two or three distinct operations; to put it on, is a peculiar business, to whiten the pins is another; it is even a trade by itself to put them into the paper; and the important business of making a pin is, in this manner, divided into about eighteen distinct operations, which, in some manufactories, are all performed by distinct hands, though in others the same man will sometimes perform two or three of them. ① I have seen a small manufactory of this kind where ten men only were employed, and where some of them consequently performed two or three distinct operations. But though they were very poor, and therefore but indifferently accommodated with the necessary machinery, they could, when they exerted themselves, make among them about twelve pounds of pins in a day. There are in a pound upwards of four thousand pins of a middling size. Those ten persons, therefore, could make among them upwards of forty-eight thousand pins in a day. Each person, therefore, making a tenth part of forty-eight thousand pins, might be considered as making four thousand eight hundred pins in a day. But if they had all wrought separately and independently, and without any of them having been educated to this peculiar business, they certainly could not each of them have made twenty, perhaps not one pin in a day; that is, certainly, not the two hundred and fortieth, perhaps not the four thousand eight hundredth part of what they are at present capable of performing, in consequence of a proper division and combination of their different operations.

such as pinmaking.

In every other art and manufacture, the effects of the division

---

① [In Adam Smith's *Lectures*, p. 164, the business is, as here, divided into eighteen operations. This number is doubtless taken from thè *Encyclopè die*, tom. v. (published in 1755), *s. v.* Epingle. The article is ascribed to M. Delaire, 'qui décrivait la fabrication de lèpingle dans les ateliers meme des ouvriers,' p. 807. In some factories the division was carried further. E. Chambers, *Cyclopœdia*, vol. ii. , 2nd ed. , 1738, and 4th ed. , 1741, *s. v.* Pin, makes the number of separate operations twenty-five.]

行业的制造方式,不仅整个工作都已经成为专门的职业岗位,而且这种行业所分成的许多部门的大部分也已经成为了专门的职业。第一个人抽铁线,第二人将其拉直,第三个人将其截断,第四个人将铁线一端削尖,第五个人磨光另一端,以便安装针头。以下要做针头,要进行两到三个不同的操作工序。装针头是一个专门的职业,将针头涂白色是另一个专门的职业,甚至于连装进纸盒都是专门的职业。这样,制针这个重要的行业就大约被分为18种不同的工序。在有些工厂,这18种工序分别由18个不同的工人来担任。当然,在另外一些工厂中有时由一人兼任两三道工序的现象也是存在的。① 我曾经见过一个这样的小工厂,那里只雇用了10个工人,因此在该工厂中,有几个工人分别从事两三种不同的工序。虽然这些工人很贫穷,必要的机器设备也很差,但如果他们全力以赴的话,一天就可以生产出12磅的成针。以每磅中等型号的针有4000枚来计算,这十个工人每天就可以制造出48000千枚针,这样他们每人每天就可以制造出4800枚针。但是如果他们各自独立工作,没受过一种专门的职业训练,那么他们中的任何人,都毫无疑问是无法在一天中制造出20枚针的,甚至可能一天连一枚针也制造不出来。也就是说他们不仅不能完成由适当分工合作之后而制成的1/240的数量,甚至连该数量的1/4800能否制造出来恐怕也尚未可知。

在其他各种工艺和制造业中,虽然有许多行业无法进行这样_{制针业的例子。}

---

① 在亚当·斯密的《关于法律、警察、岁入及军备的演讲》中,这样的职业被分为18个不同的部分。这个数字无疑是取自百科全书中德莱尔的文章(1755年出版),在一些工厂分工进一步细化。钱伯斯的百科全书(1738年第2卷第2版)(1741年第4版)中就分为25道工序。

of labour are similar to what they are in this very trifling one; though, in many of them, the labour can neither be so much subdivided, nor reduced to so great a simplicity of operation. The division of labour, however, so far as it can be introduced, occasions, in every art, a proportionable increase of the productive powers of labour. The separation of different trades and employments from one another, seems to have taken place, in consequence of this advantage. This separation too is generally carried furthest in those countries which enjoy the highest degree of industry and improvement; what is the work of one man in a rude state of society, being generally that of several in an improved one. In every improved society, the farmer is generally nothing but a farmer; the manufacturer, nothing but a manufacturer. The labour too which is necessary to produce any one complete manufacture, is almost always divided among a great number of hands. How many different trades are employed in each branch of the linen and woollen manufactures, from the growers of the flax and the wool, to the bleachers and smoothers of the linen, or to the dyers and dressers of the cloth ! The nature of agriculture, indeed, does not admit of so many subdivisions of labour, nor of so complete a separation of one business from another, as manufactures. It is impossible to separate so entirely, the business of the grazier from that of the corn-farmer, as the trade of the carpenter is commonly separated from that of the smith. The spinner is almost always a distinct person from the weaver; but the ploughman, the harrower, the sower of the seed, and the reaper of the corn, are often the same. The occasions for those different sorts of labour returning with the different seasons of the year, it is impossible that one man should be constantly employed in any one of them. This impossibility of making so complete and entire a separation of all the different branches of labour employed in agriculture, is perhaps the reason why the improvement of the productive powers of labour in this art, does not always keep pace with their improvement in manufactures. The most opulent nations, indeed, generally excel all their neighbours in agriculture as well as in manufactures; but they are commonly more distinguished by their superiority in the latter than in the former. Their lands are in general better cultivated, and having more labour and expence bestowed upon them, produce more in proportion to the extent and natural fertility of the ground.

细密地分工,其操作也不能变得如此之简单,但是劳动分工的效果却总是与这种微不足道的制针业一样。只要能够进行劳动分工,劳动生产力就能相应地成比例地增长。各种不同行业之所以彼此分立,似乎也是由于分工带来的好处的结果。那些具有最发达的产业和劳动生产率改进程度的国家,其劳动分工也最为彻底;在落后社会中一个人所做的工作,在进步社会中则一般都有几个人来分工承担。在那些进步的社会中,农场主一般只是农场主,而制造者就只是一个制造者。而且生产一种完全制成品所必需的劳动,也往往都是由许多劳动者共同完成。仅以麻织业和毛织业为例,从亚麻和羊毛的生产到亚麻布的漂白和烫平,或到呢绒的染色和浆纱,在每一个部门中都有不同的人在处理,各个部门所使用的不同技艺也是如此之多!的确,农业由于其性质,决定了它不能像制造业那样进行细密地分工,各种工作之间也不像制造业那样泾渭分明。一般来说,木匠的职业与铁匠的职业通常是截然分开的,但牧民的工作与农场主的工作,却不能像前者那样完全地分开。纺织工和织布工,几乎都是两个不同的人,但犁地、耙地、播种和收割,通常来说都是由一个人兼任。农业上这些不同的劳作,要随季节的推移而交替,指定一个人专门从事一种劳作的做法是绝不可能的。所以,农业的劳动生产力的提高总跟不上制造业劳动生产力的提高程度的主要原因,就与农业不可能对所有不同的劳作进行完全彻底地实现劳动分工有关。现在最富裕的国家,固然在农业和制造业上一般都超过了邻国,但其在制造业方面的优势,必定要大于农业方面的优势。富裕国家的土地,一般都耕耘得比较好,投在土地上的劳动与费用也比较多,生产出来的产品的数量按照土地面积与肥沃的程度的比例来说也

But this superiority of produce is seldom much more than in proportion to the superiority of labour and expence. In agriculture, the labour of the rich country is not always much more productive than that of the poor; or, at least, it is never so much more productive, as it commonly is in manufactures. The corn of the rich country, therefore, will not always, in the same degree of goodness, come cheaper to market than that of the poor. The corn of Poland, in the same degree of goodness, is as cheap as that of France, notwithstanding the superior opulence and improvement of the latter country. The corn of France is, in the corn provinces, fully as good, and in most years nearly about the same price with the corn of England, though, in opulence and improvement, France is perhaps inferior to England. The corn-lands of England, however, are better cultivated than those of France, and the cornlands of France are said to be much better cultivated than those of Poland. But though the poor country, notwithstanding the inferiority of its cultivation, can, in some measure, rival the rich in the cheapness and goodness of its corn, it can pretend to no such competition in its manufactures; at least if those manufactures suit the soil, climate, and situation of the rich country. The silks of France are better and cheaper than those of England, because the silk manufacture, at least under the present high duties upon the importation of raw silk, does not so well suit the climate of England as that of France. But the hard-ware and the coarse woollens of England are beyond all comparison superior to those of France, and much cheaper too in the same degree of goodness. ① In Poland there are said to be scarce any manufactures of any kind, a few of those coarser household manufactures excepted, without which no country can well subsist.

<small>The effect is similar in all trades and also in the division of employments.</small>

---

① [In *Lectures*, p. 164, the comparison is between English and French 'toys,' *i.e.*, small metal articles.]

比较多；但是富裕国家在这种产量上的优势，很少在比例上大大超过其花在劳动和费用投入的优势上。在农业方面，富裕国家的劳动生产力未必就比贫困国家的劳动生产力大得多，起码来说不像制造业方面的差距那么明显。因此，如果品质一样的话，富裕国家的谷物在市场上的销售价格，未必就比贫困国家的价格低廉。就富裕程度和劳动力的进步程度来说，法国要远强于波兰，但波兰谷物的价格，却与同样质量的法国小麦价格同样低廉。而与英格兰比较，法国在富裕方面和劳动力的进步程度或许要稍逊一筹，但在法国生产谷物的省份生产出来的谷物，与品质同样优良的英格兰谷物相比，在大多数年头中两者的价格也大致是相同的。然而，英格兰的谷地耕种得比法国好，而法国的谷地据说也耕种得比波兰好得多。因此贫穷国家在耕种上尽管不及富国，但某种程度上贫穷国家生产的谷物却能在品质的优良及售价的低廉方面与富裕国家竞争。但是，在制造业上贫穷国家是不能和富裕国家进行这种竞争的，至少如果富裕国家发展这类制造业的土壤、气候和地理位置得天独厚时，贫穷国家是不能和富裕国家竞争的。法国丝绸之所以比英国丝绸又好又便宜，就是因为丝绸业，至少是在目前对生丝进口课以高关税的情况下，英国不像法国那样有完全适合的气候。但英国的五金器具和粗毛织物却远胜于法国，而且在品质同样优良的情况下在价格上也比法国低廉得多。① 据说，在波兰除了少数几个国家可以生产所必需的粗糙的家用制品外，几乎就没有什么其他制造品了。

---

① 在《关于法律、警察、岁入及军备的演讲》第164页中，作了关于英、法"玩具"，也就是小金属器件的比较。

The advantage is due to three circumstances, This great increase of the quantity of work, which, in consequence of the division of labour, the same number of people are capable of performing, is owing to three different circumstances; first, to the increase of dexterity in every particular workman; secondly, to the saving of the time which is commonly lost in passing from one species of work to another; and lastly, to the invention of a great number of machines which facilitate and abridge labour, and enable one man to do the work of many.

(1) improved dexterity, First, the improvement of the dexterity of the workman necessarily increases the quantity of the work he can perform; and the division of labour, by reducing every man's business to some one simple operation, and by making this operation the sole employment of his life, necessarily increases very much the dexterity of the workman. A common smith, who, though accustomed to handle the hammer, has never been used to make nails, if upon some particular occasion he is obliged to attempt it, will scarce, I am assured, be able to make above two or three hundred nails in a day, and those too very bad ones. [1] A smith who has been accustomed to make nails, but whose sole or principal business has not been that of a nailer, can seldom with his utmost diligence make more than eight hundred or a thousand nails in a day. I have seen several boys under twenty years of age who had never exercised any other trade but that of making nails, and who, when they exerted themselves, could make, each of them, upwards of two thousand three hundred nails in a day. [2] The making of a nail, however, is by no means one of the simplest operations. The same person blows the bellows, stirs or mends the fire as there is occasion, heats the iron, and forges every part of the nail: In forging the head too he is obliged to change his tools. The different operations into which

---

[1] [In *Lectures*, p. 166, ' a country smith not accustomed to make nails will work very hard for three or four hundred a day and those too very bad. ']

[2] [In *Lectures*, p. 166, ' a boy used to it will easily make two thousand and those incomparably better. ']

这种由于有了劳动分工,所导致同样数量的劳动者能够完成比过去多得多的工作量的现象,可归因于三种不同的方面:第一,由于每个劳动者的熟练程度的提高;第二,由于节约了从一种工作转到另一种工作的时间,而这种转移通常要损失不少时间;第三,由于大量机器的发明便利和简化了劳动,使一个人能干许多人的工作。

第一,劳动者熟练程度的改进,势必使他所能完成的工作量增加。劳动分工的结果,使得各个劳动者的劳动局限到某种简单的操作,并使这种简单操作成为他终生唯一的职业,当然可以使劳动者的熟练程度得到大大提高。一个习惯于使用铁锤却从来不曾练习制铁钉的普通铁匠,如果一旦有必要让他制钉时,我确信,他一天至多只能做出二三百枚钉来,而且其质量还很差。① 即使一个惯于制钉但却不以制钉为唯一的或主要职业的铁匠,他如果尽其所能,也很难一天制造出 800 枚或 1000 枚以上的钉子来。我曾经看到过几个不到 20 岁的专门以制钉为职业的年轻人,当他们尽力工作时,每人每天都可以制造 2300 多枚钉子。② 然而,制造一枚钉子绝非一件最简单的操作。如果是同一劳动者来做,他要鼓炉、要适时搅动或调整火力,要把铁烧热来捶打钉子的每一部分,而且当打制钉头时还得调换他的工具。一枚针或者制造

---

① 在《关于法律、警察、岁入及军备的演讲》第 166 页中写道:"一个不惯于制钉的工匠一天非常努力的话只可以制造三四百枚钉子,而且质量还非常差。"

② 在《关于法律、警察、岁入及军备的演讲》第 166 页中写道:"一个习惯于制钉的男孩一天很容易制造 2000 多枚质量相对较高的钉子。"

the making of a pin, or of a metal button,① is subdivided, are all of them much more simple, and the dexterity of the person, of whose life it has been the sole business to perform them, is usually much greater. The rapidity with which some of the operations of those manufactures are performed, exceeds what the human hand could, by those who had never seen them, be supposed capable of acquiring.

(2) saving of time,

Secondly, the advantage which is gained by saving the time commonly lost in passing from one sort of work to another, is much greater than we should at first view be apt to imagine it. It is impossible to pass very quickly from one kind of work to another, that is carried on in a different place, and with quite different tools. A country weaver,② who cultivates a small farm, must lose a good deal of time in passing from his loom to the field, and from the field to his loom. When the two trades can be carried on in the same workhouse, the loss of time is no doubt much less. It is even in this case, however, very considerable. A man commonly saunters a little in turning his hand from one sort of employment to another. When he first begins the new work he is seldom very keen and hearty; his mind, as they say, does not go to it, and for some time he rather trifles than applies to good purpose. The habit of sauntering and of indolent careless application, which is naturally, or rather necessarily acquired by every country workman who is obliged to change his work and his tools every half hour, and to apply his hand in twenty different ways almost every day of his life; renders him almost always slothful and lazy, and incapable of any vigorous application even on the most pressing occasions. Independent, therefore, of his deficiency in point of dexterity, this cause alone must always reduce considerably the quantity of work which he is capable of performing.

---

① [In *Lectures*, p. 255, it is implied that the labour of making a button was divided among eighty persons.]

② [The same example occurs in *Lectures*, p. 166.]

一枚金属纽扣①可划分为许多项操作,这些分工后的操作就要简单得多,而那些终生从事于某项操作的人,其熟练程度通常也就高得多。因此,除非你亲眼看到过,在此类制造品的制造中,某些操作快得几乎都令人无法想像,你无法想像人类的双手会有如此之大的本领。

第二,由于分工所节约的由一种工作转换到另一种工作的时间而带来的好处,要比我们乍看起来所想像的好处大得多。人们不可能很快地从一种工作转入到另一种不同工作地点和不同劳动工具的工作中。以一个要耕种农田的农村织布匠②来说,由织布机到耕地,再由耕地回到织布机,必然会浪费许多时间。当然,如果这两种工序在同一工厂内进行的话那么时间上的损失肯定要少得多,但即便如此,损失还是非常之大。当人们由一种工作转换到另一种工作时,一般都要闲逛一会儿。在其新的工作开始之际,他们很少能够立刻就全神贯注地投入工作;就像他们所说的,总不免有点心不在焉,在一段时间内他们与其说是在工作,倒不如说在浪费时间。每个农村劳动者,他们每隔半小时就要更换一次他们的工作和工具,在其一生中几乎每天都要做二十项不同的工作,他们自然或者甚至说必然会养成闲荡、偷懒、随便的习惯。他们总是懒懒散散,即便在最紧迫的时候,也不能够全力以赴地工作。因此,即便没有熟练程度方面的缺陷,单只这些习惯就会大大地缩减他们所能够完成的工作量。

(2) 时间的节约;

---

① 在《关于法律、警察、岁入及军备的演讲》第255页中写道:此中暗含了金属纽扣的制作在80人之间进行分工的意思。

② 在《关于法律、警察、岁入及军备的演讲》第166页中出现过同样的例子。

国民财富的性质与原理

and (3) application of machinery, invented by workmen,

Thirdly, and lastly, every body must be sensible how much labour is facilitated and abridged by the application of proper machinery. It is unnecessary to give any example. ① I shall only observe, therefore, that the invention of all those machines by which labour is so much facilitated and abridged, seems to have been originally owing to the division of labour. Men are much more likely to discover easier and readier methods of attaining any object, when the whole attention of their minds is directed towards that single object, than when it is dissipated among a great variety of things. But in consequence of the division of labour, the whole of every man's attention comes naturally to be directed towards some one very simple object. It is naturally to be expected, therefore, that some one or other of those who are employed in each particular branch of labour should soon find out easier and readier methods of performing their own particular work, wherever the nature of it admits of such improvement. A great part of the machines made use of in those manufactures in which labour is most subdivided, were originally the inventions of common workmen, who, being each of them employed in some very simple operation, naturally turned their thoughts towards finding out easier and readier methods of performing it. Whoever has been much accustomed to visit such manufactures, must frequently have been shewn very pretty machines, which were the inventions of such workmen, in order to facilitate and quicken their own particular part of the work. In the first fire-engines, a boy was constantly employed to open and shut alternately the communication between the boiler and the cylinder, according as the piston either ascended or descended. One of those boys, who loved to play with his companions, observed that, by tying a string from the handle of the valve which opened this communication to another part of the machine, the valve would open and shut without his assistance, and leave him at liberty to divert himself with his play-fellows. One of the greatest improvements that has been made upon this machine,

---

① [Examples are given in *Lectures*, p. 167: 'Two men and three horses will do more in a day with the plough than twenty men without it. The miller and his servant will do more with the water mill than a dozen with the hand mill, though it too be a machine.']

第一篇　第一章

第三,也即最后,应用适当的机器能够在多大程度上方便和简化劳动这是每个人必然都知道的。无须举例来说明。① 我在此只想说的是,那些发明使劳动变得如此方便和简单的机器的过程,最初似乎也是由于劳动分工。当人们所有的注意力都集中到一个单一的目标,而不是分散到许多不同的事物上时,他们就更加有可能发现更加容易、更加迅速地达到目的的方法。分工的结果,就必然使每个人的全部注意力自然而然的集中在一个简单的事物上。所以,我们可以自然地预期,只要工作的性质上还有改良的余地,在从事每一个具体的劳动部门的劳动者中,不久自会有人发现一些比较容易而且比较迅速的方法来完成他们各自的工作。在分工最为细密的制造业中所使用的机器,最初大部分都是由普通工人发明的。他们每个人都从事最简单的操作,当然会用心发明比较便捷的操作方法。任何常去参观制造厂的人,都会发现一些极为精巧的机械,这些机械就是普通工人为了便利和简化他们担当的那部分工作而发明出来的。最初的蒸汽机操作原需雇用一个儿童,随着活塞的升降,来专门不断地交替开关汽锅与汽缸间的通道。有一个担任此项工作的儿童,因为爱和同伴玩耍,就用一条绳子把开闭这个通道活门的把手系在机器的另一部分,活门这样就可以不需人力而自行开闭了。自从蒸汽机发明

（3）机器的应用：工人发明机器,

---

① 在《关于法律、警察、岁入及军备的演讲》第 167 页中举过这样的例子:"两个人和三匹马比 20 个人没有任何工具劳动成果要多。磨坊主和他的仆人用水磨工作要比 12 个人用手工磨子劳动的成果要多。"

— 25 —

or by ma-chine-makers and philoso-phers.

since it was first invented, was in this manner the discovery of a boy who wanted to save his own labour. ①

All the improvements in machinery, however, have by no means been the inventions of those who had occasion to use the machines. Many improvements have been made by the ingenuity of the makers of the machines, when to make them became the business of a peculiar trade; and some by that of those who are called philosophers or men of speculation, whose trade it is not to do any thing, but to observe every thing; and who, upon that account, are often capable of combining together the powers of the most distant and dissimilar objects. ② In the progress of society, philosophy or speculation becomes, like every other employment, the principal or sole trade and occupation of a particular class of citizens. Like every other employment too, it is subdivided into a great number of different branches, each of which affords occupation to a peculiar tribe or class of philosophers; and this subdivision of employment in philosophy, as well as in every other business, improves dexterity, and saves time. Each individual becomes more expert in his own peculiar branch, more work is done upon

---

① [This pretty story is largely, at any rate, mythical. It appears to have grown out of a misreading (not necessarily by Smith) of the following passage: 'They used before to work with a buoy in the cylinder enclosed in a pipe, which buoy rose when the steam was strong, and opened the injection, and made a stroke; thereby they were capable of only giving six, eight or ten strokes in a minute, till a boy, Humphry Potter, who attended the engine, added (what he called scoggan) a catch that the beam Q always opened; and then it would go fifteen or sixteen strokes in a minute. But this being perplexed with catches and strings, Mr. Henry Beighton, in an engine he had built at Newcastle-on-Tyne in 1718, took them all away, the beam itself simply supplying all much better.'— J. T. Desaguliers, *Course of Experimental Philosophy*, vol. ii., 1744, p. 533. From pp. 469, 471, it appears that hand labour was originally used before the 'buoy' was devised.]

② [In *Lectures*, p. 167, the invention of the plough is conjecturally attributed to a farmer and that of the hand-mill to a slave, while the invention of the water-wheel and the steam engine is credited to philosophers. Mandeville is very much less favourable to the claims of the philosophers: 'They are very seldom the same sort of people, those that invent arts and improvements in them and those that inquire into the reason of things: this latter is most commonly practised by such as are idle and indolent, that are fond of retirement, hate business and take delight in speculation; whereas none succeed oftener in the first than active, stirring and laborious men, such as will put their hand to the plough, try experiments and give all their attention to what they are about.'—*Fable of the Bees*, pt. ii. (1729), dial. iii., p. 151. He goes on to give as examples the improvements in soap-boiling, grain-dyeing, etc.]

以来,最大的改进之一就是由这样一个贪玩的男孩发现的。①

然而,机器的改进并非全部由会使用机器的人发现的。当机器制造成为一个专业的时候,有许多改进是出自机械制造者的聪明才智;还有一些改良,是出自哲学家或思想家的聪明才智。哲学家或思想家的任务不是制造任何实物,而在于观察一切事物,所以他们常常能够结合利用各种完全没有关系而且极不相似的力量。② 随着社会的进步,哲学家或思想家也像其他各种职业那样,成为某 特定阶层人们的主要业务或唯 的行业或职业。也像其他职业那样,哲学分成了许多不同分支,各个分支,又分别成为一种哲学家的行业。哲学上这种分工,像产业上的分工一样,提高了熟练程度,并节省了时间。各人擅长各人的特殊部分的工作,不但增加了全体劳动者的成就,而且大大增加了科学技术的

旁注:机器制造者发明的机器和哲学家发明的机器。

---

① 这个故事很大程度上是虚构的。可能源于对下面故事的误解(不一定是斯密):"以前他们常常在一个封闭管道的圆柱形容器中用浮标工作,当气流很强的时候浮标上升,打开通道造成 次冲程;因此他们 分钟仅能冲击六次、八次或十次。直到后来一个看管机器的名叫波特的小男孩改变了这种状况,他利用一个他称为 scoggan 的钩子使得 Q 轴总是打开,这样一分钟的冲击次数就可以达到十五至十六次。但亨利先生对此表示困惑,1718年他在泰恩河纽卡斯尔(今英国 Nothumberland 郡的首府)设计了一台机器,但是如果把他们全部都拿走,这个轴供给得更好。"Course of Experimental Philosophy(1744 年版第 533 页,第 468~471 页),在浮标设计使用之前最初使用的是手工劳动。

② 在《关于法律、警察、岁入及军备的演讲》第 167 页中,好像是农夫发明了犁,奴隶发明了磨粉机,但是水轮机和蒸汽机的发明却归功于哲学家。孟德维尔不太喜欢有些哲学家这样的主张:他们几乎不是一种类型的人,有些人发明技术改进技术,有些人探究事情的原因。前者大部分都是一些懒惰、散漫者的所为,他们贪图安逸憎恶劳作,喜欢猜测;然而那些经常用犁耕种勤劳忙碌的人,尝试着试验,集中精力于他们准备要做的事情,在行动上却往往没有前者成功。

the whole, and the quantity of science is considerably increased by it. ①

<small>Hence the universal opulence of a well-governed society,</small> It is the great multiplication of the productions of all the different arts, in consequence of the division of labour, which occasions, in a well-governed society, that universal opulence which extends itself to the lowest ranks of the people. Every workman has a great quantity of his own work to dispose of beyond what he himself has occasion for; and every other workman being exactly in the same situation, he is enabled to exchange a great quantity of his own goods for a great quantity, or, what comes to the same thing, for the price of a great quantity of theirs. He supplies them abundantly with what they have occasion for, and they accommodate him as amply with what he has occasion for, and a general plenty diffuses itself through all the different ranks of the society.

<small>even the day-labourer's coat being the produce of a vast number of workmen.</small> Observe the accommodation of the most common artificer or day-labourer in a civilized and thriving country, and you will perceive that the number of people of whose industry a part, though but a small part, has been employed in procuring him this accommodation, exceeds all computation. The woollen coat, for example, which covers the day-labourer, as coarse and rough as it may appear, is the produce of the joint labour of a great multitude of workmen. The shepherd, the sorter of the wool, the wool-comber or carder, the dyer, the scribbler, the spinner, the weaver, the fuller, the dresser, with many others, must all join their different arts in order to complete even this homely production. How many merchants and carriers, besides, must have been employed in transporting the materials from some of those workmen to others who often live in a very distant part of the country ! how much commerce and navigation in particular, how many ship-builders, sailors, sail-makers, rope-makers, must have been employed in order to bring together the different drugs made use of by the dyer,

---

① [The advantage of producing particular commodities wholly or chiefly in the countries most naturally fitted for their production is recognised below, p. 423, but the fact that division of labour is necessary for its attainment is not noticed. The fact that division of labour allows different workers to be put exclusively to the kind of work for which they are best fitted by qualities not acquired by education and practice, such as age, sex, size and strength, is in part ignored and in part denied below. The disadvantage of division of labour or specialisation is dealt with below.]

数量。①

　　由于分工,所有不同行业的产量成倍增长。在一个治理得很好的社会里,普遍富裕的情况可以普及到最下层人民身上。每个劳动者,除自身所需的以外,还有大量产品可以出卖;同时,因为一切其他劳动者的情况也相同,各个人都能以自身生产的大量产品,换得其他劳动者生产的大量产品。换言之,都能换得其他劳动者大量产品的价格。别人所需的物品,他能予以充分地供给;他自身所需的,别人亦能予以充分地供给。于是,社会各阶层都普遍富裕起来。

一个治理好的社会变得普遍富裕起来。

　　通过观察一个文明而又发达的国家的普通工匠或日工的生活用品,你便知道,用他的劳动的一部分来生产这种日用品的人,虽然只是一小部分,数目却是难以计量的。例如,日工所穿的毛织外套,虽然看起来很粗糙,却是许多劳动者联合劳动的产物。为完成这种日常所需的产物,需要有牧羊者、剪羊毛者、梳羊毛者、染工、粗梳工、纺工、织工、漂白工、裁缝工,以及其他许多人,组合不同的工艺来工作。此外,这些劳动者居住的地方,往往相隔很远,把材料从一些工人的手中运至其他工人手中,该需要有多少商人和运输者啊!染匠所用的不同染料,常需购自世界上各个遥远的地方,要把各种染料由各个不同地方收集起来,该需要

日工的大衣甚至是大量劳动人员联合劳动的产物。

---

① 在那些最适合它们产品的国家中生产这些特定商品的优势已经完全地或者基本地都被认识到了(423页),但是劳动分工对于生产这些商品的必要性却没有被意识到。劳动分工允许不同的工人专注于他们各自最适合的工作,他们各自的特性,例如年龄、性别、身高和力量等,并不是通过教育培训来获得的,这个事实部分地被忽略,部分地被下面内容所否定。劳动分工和专业化的劣势在第2卷中将被谈及。

— 29 —

which often come from the remotest corners of the world! What a variety of labour too is necessary in order to produce the tools of the meanest of those workmen! To say nothing of such complicated machines as the ship of the sailor, the mill of the fuller, or even the loom of the weaver, let us consider only what a variety of labour is requisite in order to form that very simple machine, the shears with which the shepherd clips the wool. The miner, the builder of the furnace for smelting the ore, the feller of the timber, the burner of the charcoal to be made use of in the smelting-house, the brick-maker, the brick-layer, the workmen who attend the furnace, the mill-wright, the forger, the smith, must all of them join their different arts in order to produce them. Were we to examine, in the same manner, all the different parts of his dress and household furniture, the coarse linen shirt which he wears next his skin, the shoes which cover his feet, the bed which he lies on, and all the different parts which compose it, the kitchen-grate at which he prepares his victuals, the coals which he makes use of for that purpose, dug from the bowels of the earth, and brought to him perhaps by a long sea and a long land carriage, all the other utensils of his kitchen, all the furniture of his table, the knives and forks, the earthen or pewter plates upon which he serves up and divides his victuals, the different hands employed in preparing his bread and his beer, the glass window which lets in the heat and the light, and keeps out the wind and the rain, with all the knowledge and art requisite for preparing that beautiful and happy invention, without which these northern parts of the world could scarce have afforded a very comfortable habitation, together with the tools of all the different workmen employed in producing those different convenieneies; if we examine, I say, all these things, and consider what a variety of labour is employed about each of them, we shall be sensible that without the assistance and co-operation of many thousands, the very meanest person in a civilized country could not be provided, even according to, what we very falsely imagine, the easy and simple manner in which he is commonly accommodated. Compared, indeed, with the more extravagant luxury of the great, his accommodation must no doubt appear extremely simple and easy; and yet it may be true, perhaps, that the accommodation of an European prince does not always so much exceed that of an industrious and frugal peasant, as the accommodation of the latter

多少商业和航运业，雇用多少造船者、航海人、制帆人和制绳人啊！为生产这些最普通劳动者所使用的工具，又需要多少种类的劳动啊！姑且不谈复杂机械，如水手操作的船、漂白工用的作坊或织工用的织机，单就简单器械如牧羊人剪毛时所用的剪刀来说，其制造就须经过许多种类的劳动。为了生产这一极简单的剪刀，矿工、熔铁炉建造者、伐木工、熔铁厂烧炭工人、制砖者、泥水匠、锅炉工、机械安装工人、铁匠等等，必须把他们不同的技艺结合起来。同样，如果我们用同样的方式来考察一个劳动者的服装和家庭用具，如贴身穿的粗麻衬衣，脚上穿的鞋子，就寝用的床铺和床铺上各种装置，调制食物的厨房炉具，由地下采掘出来而且需要经过水陆运输才能送到手边供其烧饭的煤炭，厨房中一切其他用具，食桌上一切用具，刀子和叉子，盛放食物和分取食物的陶瓷盘子和锡制器皿，制造面包和啤酒所使用的不同原料，那种能透进热气和光线并能遮风避雨的玻璃窗，为了准备玻璃这种使世界北方成为极舒适的居住地的美妙的发明所需要的知识和技艺，以及工人制造这些不同的便利品所用的不同工人手中的工具等等。总之，我们如果考察一下这一切，并考虑到要投在这每样东西上的各种劳动，我们就会知道，没有成千上万的人的帮助和合作，一个文明国家里的最普通的工人，都不可能得到他通常所能得到的（按照我们很错误地想像的是）他一般能够适应的舒服简单方式的日用品。确实，与富人的豪华奢侈相比，他们的生活用品毫无疑问是极其简单而又平常的；但是，这或许又是真的，一个欧洲君主的生活用品不一定大大超过一个俭朴农场主的生活用品，而这个农场主的生活用品却超过了非洲君主的生活用品，这

exceeds that of many an African king, the absolute master of the lives and liberties of ten thousand naked savages. ①

---

① [This paragraph was probably taken bodily from the MS. of the author's lectures. It appears to be founded on Mun, *England's Treasure by Forraign Trade*, chap. iii., at end; Locke, *Civil Government*, §43; Mandeville, *Fable of the Bees*, pt. i., Remark P, and ed., 1723, p. 182, and perhaps Harris, *Essay upon Money and Coins*, pt. i., §12. See Lectures, pp. 161-162 and notes.]

些君主正是数以万计的赤裸野蛮人的生命与自由的绝对主宰啊!①

---

① 这一段全部摘自作者《关于法律、警察、岁入及军备的演讲》的手稿。它出现于孟的《外贸给英格兰带来的财富》,第二章末尾。洛克的《国民政府》第43节;孟德维尔的《蜜蜂的寓言》第1部分1723年出版的第2版评论,第182页,以及哈里斯的《货币与硬币》第1部分第12节。见《关于法律、警察、岁入及军备的演讲》的第161~162页和注解。

CHAPTER II
Of The Principle Which Gives Occasion To The Division Of Labour

The division of labour arises from a propensity in human nature to exchange.

This division of labour, from which so many advantages are derived, is not originally the effect of any human wisdom, which foresees and intends that general opulence to which it gives occasion. ① It is the necessary, though very slow and gradual, consequence of a certain propensity in human nature which has in view no such extensive utility; the propensity to truck, barter, and exchange one thing for another.

This propensity is found in man alone.

Whether this propensity be one of those original principles in human nature, of which no further account can be given; or whether, as seems more probable, it be the necessary consequence of the faculties of reason and speech, it belongs not to our present subject to enquire. It is common to all men, and to be found in no other race of animals, which seem to know neither this nor any other species of contracts. Two greyhounds, in running down the same hare, have sometimes the appearance of acting in some sort of concert. Each turns her towards his companion, or endeavours to intercept her when his companion turns her towards himself. This, however, is not the effect of any contract, but of the accidental concurrence of their passions in the same object at that particular time. Nobody ever saw a dog make a fair and deliberate exchange of one bone for another with another dog. ②

---

① [I. e. , it is not the effect of any conscious regulation by the state or society, like the 'law of Sesostris,' that every man should follow the employment of his father, referred to in the corresponding passage in *Lectures*, p. 168. The denial that it is the effect of individual wisdom recognising the advantage of exercising special natural talents comes lower down.]

② [It is by no means clear what object there could be in exchanging one bone for another.]

第二章 论劳动分工的原因

劳动分工有这么多的好处,其实原本这并非是人类的智慧使然,预见到并想利用它来实现普遍富裕。① 它实际是一种人类倾向所造成的必然结果,这种倾向逐渐地缓慢发展起来,是互通有无、物物交换、互相交易的倾向,没有任何广泛的功利色彩。

<small>人性中交换引向了劳分工。的倾起动</small>

这种倾向,是不是一种不能进一步分析的人类本能,或者更确切地说是不是理性和语言能力的必然结果,这不属于我们现在研究的课题。这种倾向,为人类所共有,在其他各种动物中不存在。其他各种动物,似乎都不知道这种或其他任何一种契约。两只猎犬同时追逐一只兔子的情况,有时也像是一种协同动作。猎犬把兔子赶向其同伴的方向,或在对手把兔子赶到它这边时竭力拦截。不过这种协同动作,只是在那一时刻,是猎犬们欲望对于同一目标的偶然的契合,而并非是契约的结果。我们从来没有见过两只猎犬公平审慎地有意识地交换骨头,②也从未来没有

<small>交换的倾向只人才有。</small>

---

① 也就是说,并非受到任何国家或社会的公之于众的法规例如 Sesostris 法的影响,每个人应该继承其父亲的事业,可以参考《关于法律、警察、岁入及军备的演讲》的相应章节(第 168 页)。受到个人智慧认识到训练特殊自然天赋的好处的影响,这种相反的意见流传了下来。

② 用一根骨头交换另一根的目标也绝非很清楚。

Nobody ever saw one animal by its gestures and natural cries signify to another, this is mine, that yours; I am willing to give this for that. When an animal wants to obtain something either of a man or of another animal, it has no other means of persuasion but to gain the favour of those whose service it requires. A puppy fawns upon its dam, and a spaniel endeavours by a thousand attractions to engage the attention of its master who is at dinner, when it wants to be fed by him. Man sometimes uses the same arts with his brethren, and when he has no other means of engaging them to act according to his inclinations, endeavours by every servile and fawning attention to obtain their good will. He has not time, however, to do this upon every occasion. In civilized society he stands at all times in need of the co-operation and assistance of great multitudes, while his whole life is scarce sufficient to gain the friendship of a few persons. In almost every other race of animals each individual, when it is grown up to maturity, is entirely independent, and in its natural state has occasion for the assistance of no other living creature. But man has almost constant occasion for the help of his brethren, and it is in vain for him to expect it from their benevolence only. He will be more likely to prevail if he can interest their self-love in his favour, and shew them that it is for their own advantage to do for him what he requires of them. Whoever offers to another a bargain of any kind, proposes to do this. Give me that which I want, and you shall have this which you want, is the meaning of every such offer; and it is in this manner that we obtain from one another the far greater part of those good offices which we stand in need of. It is not from the benevolence of the butcher, the brewer, or the baker, that we expect our dinner, but from their regard to their own interest. We address ourselves, not to their humanity but to their self-love, and never talk to them of our own necessities but of their advantages. Nobody but a beggar chuses to depend chiefly upon the benevolence of his fellow-citizens. Even a beggar does not depend upon it entirely. The charity of well-disposed people, indeed, supplies him with the whole fund of his subsistence. But though this principle ultimately provides him with all the necessaries of life which he has occasion for, it neither does nor can provide him with them as he has occasion for them. The greater part of his occasional wants are supplied in the same manner as those of other people,

见过一种动物,以姿势或自然号叫向其他动物表示:这个是我的,那个是你的,我愿意和你交换。一个动物,如果想从一个人或其他动物那里得到什么东西时,除了博得能向它提供东西的人或动物的欢心外,没有别的说服劝诱手段。小犬要吃食,就向母犬摇尾乞怜;长毛垂耳狗要吃食,就做出千姿百态来唤起餐桌上主人的注意。我们人类对于同胞有时也采取这种手段。如果他没有别的其他方法使同胞按照自己的意愿行事时,他会以种种卑劣阿谀的行为,博取他们的欢心。但是他们没有时间每一次都这样做,在文明社会中,一个人在任何时候都需要许多人的合作和帮助,而他的一生也不足以获得几个人的友谊。别的动物长到成年时,几乎全都能够独立,自然状态下不再需要其他动物的帮助。但人类几乎总是需要同胞的帮助,要想仅仅依赖他人的善意,那是一定不行的。他如果能够诉诸他们的利己之心,并告诉他们,给他做事对他们自己有利,那么他就有可能如愿以偿。不论是谁,如果要同他人做交易,都要这样提议:请给我那个我所要的,你也可以获得你所要的。这句话就是交易的意义。我们所需要帮助的绝大部分是依照这个方法取得的。我们每天所需的饭食,不是出自屠户、酿酒师或面包师的恩惠,而是出于他们自利之心。我们从不向他们乞求仁慈,而是通过唤起他们利己之心,我们不谈自己有需要,而说这样对他们有利。社会上,除乞丐外,没有一个人完全靠别人的仁慈过活。而且就连乞丐,也不能一味依赖他人的仁慈。当然,乞丐全部生活资料的供给,都是出于乐善好施人的施舍。虽然这种施舍最后给乞丐提供了他所需要的一切生存资料,但没有也不可能随时随刻都能给他提供他所需要的东西。他的人部分需要也是和其他人用同样的方式得到供给,也是

by treaty, by barter, and by purchase. With the money which one man gives him he purchases food. The old cloaths which another bestows upon him he exchanges for other old cloaths which suit him better, or for lodging, or for food, or for money, with which he can buy either food, cloaths, or lodging, as he has occasion. ①

<small>It is encouraged by self-interest and leads to division of labour,</small>　　As it is by treaty, by barter, and by purchase, that we obtain from one another the greater part of those mutual good offices which we stand in need of, so it is this same trucking disposition which originally gives occasion to the division of labour. In a tribe of hunters or shepherds a particular person makes bows and arrows, for example, with more readiness and dexterity than any other. He frequently exchanges them for cattle or for venison with his companions; and he finds at last that he can in this manner get more cattle and venison, than if he himself went to the field to catch them. From a regard to his own interest, therefore, the making of bows and arrows grows to be his chief business, and he becomes a sort of armourer. Another excels in making the frames and covers of their little huts or moveable houses. He is accustomed to be of use in this way to his neighbours, who reward him in the same manner with cattle and with venison, till at last he finds it his interest to dedicate himself entirely to this employment, and to become a sort of house-carpenter. In the same manner a third becomes a smith or a brazier; a fourth a tanner or dresser of hides or skins, the principal part of the clothing of savages. And thus the certainty of being able to exchange all that surplus part of the produce of his own labour, which is over and above his own consumption, for such parts of the produce of other men's labour as he may have occasion for, encourages every man to apply himself to a particular occupation, and to cultivate and bring to perfection whatever talent or genius he may possess for that particular species of business. ②

　　The difference of natural talents in different men is, in reality,

---

　　① [The paragraph is repeated from *Lectures*, p. 169. It is founded on Mandeville, *Fable of the Bees*, pt. ii. (1729), dial., vi., pp. 421, 422.]
　　② [*Lectures*, pp. 169-170.]

通过契约、交换和买卖。他把一个人给他的金钱去购买食物,把另一个人给他的旧衣服去交换更合身的旧衣服,或交换一些食物或者住所;或者,先把旧衣服换成钱,再用钱随心所欲地购买自己需要的食品、衣服和住所。①

如同我们所需要的相互帮忙,大部分是通过契约、交换和买卖取得的,分工也正是在人类要求互相交换这个倾向中产生的。例如,在狩猎或游牧民族中,有一个人,善于制造弓矢,而且比其他任何人的制造速度要快、也更为熟练。他往往以自己制成的弓矢,与同伴交换家畜或兽肉,结果他发觉,与其亲自到野外捕猎,倒不如与狩猎人交换,因为相比而言交换所得到的要更多。出于他自身的利益考虑,他就以制造弓矢为主要职业,于是他便成为一种专门制造武器的人。另有一个人,擅长建造小茅房或移动房屋的框架和屋顶,他往往用这种方式给邻居提供服务,邻居也以家畜兽肉作为酬劳,于是最终他发觉,完全献身于这一工作符合他自身的利益。同样,第三个人成为铁匠或铜匠,第四个人成为毛皮或皮毛的硝皮者或制革者,皮革是原始人类的主要衣料。这样一来,人人都一定能够用自己消费不了的自己劳动生产物的剩余部分,去交换自己所需要的别人劳动生产物的剩余部分。这就鼓励每个人去专门从事一种特定业务,使他们在各自的业务上培养和完善各自业务的天资或才能。②

不同人的天赋才能实际上并不像我们所想像的有那么大差

<small>交换出自利,并且导致了劳动分工。</small>

① 这一段是转述于《关于法律、警察、岁入及军备的演讲》第 169 页。在孟德维尔的《蜜蜂的寓言》第二部分(1729 年)第 421、422 页出现过。
② 《关于法律、警察、岁入及军备的演讲》,第 169~170 页。

<small>thus giving rise to differences of talent more important than the natural differences,</small>

much less than we are aware of; and the very different genius which appears to distinguish men of different professions, when grown up to maturity, is not upon many occasions so much the cause, as the effect of the division of labour. ① The difference between the most dissimilar characters, between a philosopher and a common street porter, for example, seems to arise not so much from nature, as from habit, custom, and education. When they came into the world, and for the first six or eight years of their existence, they were, perhaps, very much alike, and neither their parents nor playfellows could perceive any remarkable difference. About that age, or soon after, they come to be employed in very different occupations. The difference of talents comes then to be taken notice of, and widens by degrees, till at last the vanity of the philosopher is willing to acknowledge scarce any resemblance. But without the disposition to truck, barter, and exchange, every man must have procured to himself every necessary and conveniency of life which he wanted. All must have had the same duties to perform, and the same work to do, and there could have been no such difference of employment as could alone give occasion to any great difference of talents. ②

---

① [This is apparently directed against Harris, *Money and Coins*, pt. i., § 11, and is in accordance with the view of Hume, who asks readers to 'consider how nearly equal all men are in their bodily force, and even in their mental powers and faculties, ere cultivated by education'. —'Of the Original Contract, in *Essays, Moral and Political*, 1748, p. 291.]

② [*Lectures*, pp. 170-171.]

异。成年人在不同职业上表现出来的非常相同的才能,在大多数场合,与其说是分工的原因,倒不如说是分工的结果。① 拿两个性格极不相同的人的例子来说,一个是哲学家,另一个是街头的挑夫。他们之间的差异,看来并非是天生如此,而是受风俗、习惯与教育的影响。生下来到七八岁以前,他们之间的天性或许非常之相似,他们的父母和朋友也不能在他们两者间看出什么显著的差别。大约在这个年龄,或者此后不久,他们就开始从事于非常不同的职业,于是他们才能的差异渐渐被发现,并且随后逐渐扩大,最后,哲学家为虚荣心所驱使,不肯承认他们之间有任何类似的地方。但是,人类如果没有互通有无、物物交换和互相交易的倾向,每个人都要亲自生产自己需要的生活必需品和便利品,而且每个人的任务和工作都是相同的,那么就不可能存在工作差异所产生的才能的巨大差异了。②

---

① 很明显这是针对哈里斯《货币与硬币》第一篇第十一章和休谟一致的观点,休谟让读者"认为在受到教育得到发展以前,所有人在体力方面,甚至在智力和才能方面,都是差不多的"。见《道德和政治论文集》,1748 年,第 291 页。

② 《关于法律、警察、岁入及军备的演讲》,第 170~171 页。

^{and rendering those differences useful.}　　As it is this disposition which forms that difference of talents, so remarkable among men of different professions, so it is this same disposition which renders that difference useful. Many tribes of animals acknowledged to be all of the same species, derive from nature a much more remarkable distinction of genius, than what, antecedent to custom and education, appears to take place among men. By nature a philosopher is not in genius and disposition half so different from a street porter, as a mastiff is from a greyhound, or a greyhound from a spaniel, or this last from a shepherd's dog. Those different tribes of animals, however, though all of the same species, are of scarce any use to one another. The strength of the mastiff is not in the least supported either by the swiftness of the greyhound, or by the sagacity of the spaniel, or by the docility of the shepherd's dog. The effects of those different geniuses and talents, for want of the power or disposition to barter and exchange, cannot be brought into a common stock, and do not in the least contribute to the better accommodation and conveniency of the species. Each animal is still obliged to support and defend itself, separately and independently, and derives no sort of advantage from that variety of talents with which nature has distinguished its fellows. Among men, on the contrary, the most dissimilar geniuses are of use to one another; the different produces of their respective talents, by the general disposition to truck, barter, and exchange, being brought, as it were, into a common stock, where every man may purchase whatever part of the produce of other men's talents he has occasion for.

交换的倾向使各个行业人的才能产生了巨大的差异,这个倾向也使这种才能的差异变的有用。许多被认为是属于同种族的动物,它们所表现出来天性的天资,比人类在未受教育和未受习俗影响之前所表现出来的资质差异要大得多。就天赋和天性来说,哲学家与街上挑夫的差异,比猛犬与猎狗、比猎狗与长耳狗、长耳狗与牧畜家犬的差异要少得多。但是,这些同种族的不同种类的动物,并没有相互利用的机会。猛犬的力量,绝不能因猎狗的敏速,长耳狗的智巧,牧畜家犬的柔顺而有什么增强。它们因为没有交换交易能力和倾向,所以,不能把这些不同的资质和才能,形成一个共同的财富向同种动物提供幸福和便利。每个动物仍然需要各自独立,各自保卫,而不能享受自然赋予同类的不同才能的好处。人类的情况,就完全不同。他们彼此间,哪怕是最相似的才能也能对彼此有用。他们相依着互通有无、物物交换和互相交易,好像把各自才能所生产的各种不同产品,形成了一个共同财富,每个人都可以从中随意购买到自己所需要的别人生产的产品。

通过分工使才能的差异变的有用。

CHAPTER III
That The Division Of Labour Is Limited By The Extent Of The Market

<small>Division of labour is limited by the extent of the power of exchanging</small>

As it is the power of exchanging that gives occasion to the division of labour, so the extent of this division must always be limited by the extent of that power, or, in other words, by the extent of the market. When the market is very small, no person can have any encouragement to dedicate himself entirely to one employment, for want of the power to exchange all that surplus part of the produce of his own labour, which is over and above his own consumption, for such parts of the produce of other men's labour as he has occasion for.

<small>Various trades cannot be carried on except in towns.</small>

There are some sorts of industry, even of the lowest kind, which can be carried on no where but in a great town. A porter, for example, can find employment and subsistence in no other place. A village is by much too narrow a sphere for him; even an ordinary market town is scarce large enough to afford him constant occupation. In the lone houses and very small villages which are scattered about in so desert a country as the Highlands of Scotland, every farmer must be butcher, baker and brewer for his own family. In such situations we can scarce expect to find even a smith, a carpenter, or a mason, within less than twenty miles of another of the same trade. The scattered families that live at eight or ten miles distance from the nearest of them, must learn to perform themselves a great number of little pieces of work, for which, in more populous countries, they would call in the assistance of those workmen. Country workmen are almost every where obliged to apply themselves to all the different branches of industry that have so much affinity to one another as to be employed about the same sort of materials. A country carpenter deals in every sort of work that is made of wood: a country smith in every sort of work that is made of iron. The former is not only a carpenter, but a joiner, a cabinet maker, and even a carver in wood, as well as a

第三章 论分工受到市场范围的限制

分工起因于交换,分工的范围因此必然要受到交换能力的限制。也就是说要受到市场范围的限制。如果市场过小,那么就不能鼓励人们去专门从事一种职业,因为这样他就无法用超出自己消费的自己劳动生产物的剩余部分去随意换得自己需要的别人劳动生产物品的剩余部分。

有些种类的业务,即便是最低级的业务活动,也只能在大城市中经营。例如搬运工人在其他地方就无法生活。对他而言小村落范围太小了;即便是普通的集市也嫌过小,因为无法使他维持固定职业。散布在荒凉的苏格兰高地一带的荒凉小乡村的非常小的村庄的独居农户,为了他们的家庭生存,他们必须兼当屠夫、面包师和酿酒人。在那种地方,很难找到一个铁匠、木匠或泥瓦匠;在20英里范围内,两个这样的人就更难找到了。相距八九英里的零星散居人家,他们必须学会自己亲自动手来做许多小事情;在比较富裕的地方,那些小事情就必然会请各种工人来帮忙了。在农村几乎所有的工人都是使用同一材料,一个人做很多不同的工作。一个农村木匠要从事利用木材的一切工作;农村铁匠要从事利用铁的一切工作。农村木匠不仅是木匠,同时又是细工木匠、家具帅、雕刻帅、车轮制造者、耕犁制造者,甚至是两轮

国民财富的性质与原理

wheelwright, a ploughwright, a cart and waggon maker. The employments of the latter are still more various. It is impossible there should be such a trade as even that of a nailer in the remote and inland parts of the Highlands of Scotland. Such a workman at the rate of a thousand nails a day, and three hundred working days in the year, will make three hundred thousand nails in the year. But in such a situation it would be impossible to dispose of one thousand, that is, of one day's work in the year.

<small>Water-carriage widens the market.</small>   As by means of water-carriage a more extensive market is opened to every sort of industry than what land-carriage alone can afford it, so it is upon the sea-coast, and along the banks of navigable rivers, that industry of every kind naturally begins to subdivide and improve itself, and it is frequently not till a long time after that those improvements extend themselves to the inland parts of the country. A broad-wheeled waggon, attended by two men, and drawn by eight horses, in about six weeks time carries and brings back between London and Edinburgh near four ton weight of goods. In about the same time a ship navigated by six or eight men, and sailing between the ports of London and Leith, frequently carries and brings back two hundred ton weight of goods. Six or eight men, therefore, by the help of water-carriage, can carry and bring back in the same time the same quantity of goods between London and Edinburgh, as fifty broad-wheeled waggons, attended by a hundred men, and drawn by four hundred horses. ① Upon two hundred tons of goods, therefore, carried by the cheapest land-carriage from London to Edinburgh, there must be charged the maintenance of a hundred men for three weeks, and both the maintenance, and, what is nearly equal to the maintenance, the wear and tear of four hundred horses as well as of fifty great waggons. Whereas, upon the same quantity of goods carried by water, there is to be charged only the maintenance of six or eight men, and the wear and tear of a ship of two hundred tons burthen, together with the value of the superior risk, or the difference of the insurance between land and water-carriage. Were there no other communication between those two places, therefore, but by land-carriage, as no goods could be transported from

---

① [The superiority of carriage by sea is here considerably less than in *Lectures*, p. 172, but is . still probably exaggerated. W. Playfair, ed. of *Wealth of Nations*, 1805, vol. i., p. 29, says a waggon of the kind described could carry eight tons, but, of course, some allowance must be made for thirty years of road improvement.]

四轮运货车制造者。铁匠的工作甚至更为繁杂。在苏格兰高地那样的穷乡僻壤,根本就没有制钉这样一种专门的职业。这样他每天只能制钉 1000 枚,一年劳动 300 天,每年只能制钉 30 万枚。但在这种情况下,一年也不可能卖出他一天的制造数量,即卖不出 1000 枚。

　　相比陆运,水运开辟了宽广得多的市场。所以自古以来各种产业自然的分工改进,自然而然地都发源于沿海沿河一带。这种改进往往经过很长的时间才慢慢推广到内地。一辆宽轮马车由两个人驾驭八匹马拉,载重约四吨货物,往返伦敦和爱丁堡间,大约需要六个星期的日程。然而同样日程,由六人或八人驾驶的一艘货轮,载重 200 吨货物,往返伦敦和利斯之间,日程也大致相同。所以在相同的时间内,需 100 人驾驭 400 匹马拉动 50 辆四轮运货车搬运的货物,可由六人或八人通过水运来完成。而且,把 200 吨货物由伦敦运往爱丁堡,按照最低陆运费计算,也需开支 100 人三个星期的生活费和 400 匹马 50 辆四轮运货车的损耗费。①而水运同样的货物所应负担的,只需开支六人至八人的生活费、载重 200 吨货船的损耗费和较大的保险费以及水运保险费与陆运保险费之间的差额。所以,假若在这两地之间,除陆运以外没有其他交通手段,那么除了与重量相比价格非常昂贵的货物以外,便没有什么其他货物能由一地运至另一地了。这样,两地间的商业,就只有现今的一小部分,而这两地在彼此的产业

水运拓宽市场,

---

① 海上运输的优越性在此远远不如《关于法律、警察、岁入及军备的演讲》(第 172 页)中说的多,但是还是很可能被夸张了。W. 普雷法尔版的《国民财富》(1805 年)第 1 卷第 29 页中描述了这样一种大篷车,可以运输八吨物品,但是当然应该考虑到 30 年的道路改进。

the one to the other, except such whose price was very considerable in proportion to their weight, they could carry on but a small part of that commerce which at present subsists between them, and consequently could give but a small part of that encouragement which they at present mutually afford to each other's industry. There could be little or no commerce of any kind between the distant parts of the world. What goods could bear the expence of land-carriage between London and Calcutta?① Or if there were any so precious as to be able to support this expence, with what safety could they be transported through the territories of so many barbarous nations ? Those two cities, however, at present carry on a very considerable commerce with each other, and by mutually affording a market, give a god deal of encouragement to each other's industry.

and so the first improvements are on the sea-coast or navigable rivers,

Since such, therefore, are the advantages of water-carriage, it is natural that the first improvements of art and industry should be made where this conveniency opens the whole world for a market to the produce of every sort of labour, and that they should always be much later in extending themselves into the inland parts of the country. The inland parts of the country can for a long time have no other market for the greater part of their goods, but the country which lies round about them, and separates them from the sea-coast, and the great navigable rivers. The extent of their market, therefore, must for a long time be in proportion to the riches and populousness of that country, and consequently their improvement must always be posterior to the improvement of that country. In our North American colonies the plantations have constantly followed either the sea-coast or the banks of the navigable rivers, and have scarce any where extended themselves to any considerable distance from both.

for example among the ancient nations on the Mediterranean coast.

The nations that, according to the best authenticated history, appear to have been first civilized, were those that dwelt round the coast of the Mediterranean sea. That sea, by far the greatest inlet that is known in the world, having no tides, nor consequently any waves except such as are caused by the wind only,② was, by the smoothness of its surface, as well as by the multitude of its islands, and the proximity of its neighbouring shores, extremely favourable to the infant navigation of the world; when, from their ignorance of the compass, men were afraid to quit the view of the coast, and from the imperfection

---

① [Playfair, op. cit. , p. 30, says that equalising the out and home voyages goods were carried from London to Calcutta by sea at the same price (12s. per cwt.) as from London to Leeds by land.]

② [This shows a curious belief in the wave-producing capacity of the tides.]

中相互提供的帮助,也只有现今的一小部分。那么在世界上遥远的地区之间,就不可能有多少商业,或者根本没有商业。有什么货物负担得起由伦敦至加尔各答的陆上运费呢?①即使有这种货物存在,那么又有什么运输方式能使货物安然通过处于两地间的许多野蛮民族的领土呢?但是,现今这两个城市之间却相互进行大规模的贸易,相互提供市场,并对彼此的产业发展给予了很大的鼓励。

由于水运有这么大的好处,所以工艺和产业的最初改进就出现在便于使世界开放,可以便利到达的海岸或河流口岸从而成为每一种劳动产品市场的地方,而这种改进总要很久以后才能普及到内地。内地在长期时间内只能在那些将其与海岸和通航的河流隔开的邻国中为自己的大部分货物找到市场。所以,它们的货物销售市场必然和邻近地方的富裕程度与人口数量成比例,它们的改良进步总落后于邻国。在我们北美殖民地,所开发的大种植园经常沿着海岸和河岸,很少扩展到离此很远的地方。

所以,最初的改进发生在海岸或河流,

根据最可靠的历史记载,最早开化的是地中海沿岸各国。地中海是举世闻名的最大内海,没有潮汐,除海风引起的浪涌之外没有惊涛骇浪。②地中海海面平滑,岛屿棋布,与临近海岸接近,对于早期的航海非常合适。那时指南针尚未发明,造船术尚不完

如那些地中海沿岸的古代国家。

---

① 在前述所引用的书中第 30 页,普雷法尔说国外货物运输和国内货物运输是平等的,从伦敦运往加尔各答和从伦敦运往利兹运费是一样的,都是每英担 125 先令。

② 在此表达了一个奇怪的想法:潮汐能够制造波浪。

国民财富的性质与原理

of the art of ship-building, to abandon themselves to the boisterous waves of the ocean. To pass beyond the pillars of Hercules, that is, to sail out of the Streights of Gibraltar, was, in the antient world, long considered as a most wonderful and dangerous exploit of navigation. It was late before even the Phenicians and Carthaginians, the most skilful navigators and ship-builders of those old times, attempted it, and they were for a long time the only nations that did attempt it.

<small>Improvements first took place in Egypt,</small>　Of all the countries on the coast of the Mediterranean sea, Egypt seems to have been the first in which either agriculture or manufactures were cultivated and improved to any considerable degree. Upper Egypt extends itself nowhere above a few miles from the Nile, and in Lower Egypt that great river breaks itself into many different canals,① which, with the assistance of a little art, seem to have afforded a communication by water-carriage, not only between all the great towns, but between all the considerable villages, and even to many farm-houses in the country; nearly in the same manner as the Rhine and the Maese do in Holland at present. The extent and easiness of this inland navigation was probably one of the principal causes of the early improvement of Egypt.

<small>Bengal and China;</small>　The improvements in agriculture and manufactures seem likewise to have been of very great antiquity in the provinces of Bengal in the East Indies, and in some of the eastern provinces of China; though the great extent of this antiquity is not authenticated by any histories of whose authority we, in this part of the world, are well assured. In Bengal the Ganges and several other great rivers form a great number of navigable canals in the same manner as the Nile does in Egypt. In the Eastern provinces of China too, several great rivers form, by their different branches, a multitude of canals, and by communicating with one another afford an inland navigation much more extensive than that either of the Nile or the Ganges, or perhaps than both of them put together. It is remarkable that neither the antient Egyptians, nor the Indians, nor the Chinese, encouraged foreign commerce, but seem all to have derived their great opulence from this inland navigation.

All the inland parts of Africa, and all that part of Asia which lies any considerable way north of the Euxine and Caspian seas, the antient

---

① [It is only in recent times that this word has become applicable especially to artificial channels; see Murray, *Oxford English Dictionary*, s. v.]

善,人都畏惧远离海岸、置身于惊涛骇浪之中。越过海克力斯之柱[1]驶过直布罗陀海峡西航,自古在航海上就被视为最危险最可敬的伟业。就连当时最善于航行的腓尼基人和迦太基人,也是过了许久才敢于尝试。而且在很长时间内他们都是唯一尝试的国家。

在地中海沿岸的所有国家中,在农业和制造业两方面都得到改良的要首推埃及。上埃及在尼罗河两岸数英里内,在下埃及,尼罗河分成许多支流。① 借助一些技术,不仅可以在境内各人城市间、各大村落间,甚至在农村的农舍之间,似乎都提供了一种水上交通的便利,这点与今日荷兰境内的莱茵河和麦斯河几乎一样。内陆航行,如此广泛便利,可能是埃及早期进步的主要原因之一。

进步首先发生在埃及。

在东印度的孟加拉各省,以及中国东部的几个省份,农业和制造业似乎在很早的时候就已有了改进。虽然其古老程度没有得到我们主宰世界这方的有权威的历史学家的确证。印度的恒河及其他大河,形成了大量可通航的支流,与埃及的尼罗河一样。中国东部各省也有几条大河,分成支流和水道,彼此交叉。这种航行范围的广阔,不但远远超过了尼罗河或恒河,甚至比两条大河合在一起还要广阔。但令人奇怪的是,古代埃及人、印度人和中国人,都不鼓励对外贸易,似乎富裕全然都来自于内陆的航行。

孟加拉和中国;

所有非洲内地,黑海和里海以北遥远的亚洲地区,例如古代

---

① 直到近代这个单词才主要用来指人工海峡;见默里的《牛津英文词典》。

〔1〕海克力斯之柱(The killers of Hercules),是直布罗陀海峡东口南北的两岬。

| 国民财富的性质与原理

<small>while Africa, Tartary and Siberia, and also Bavaria, Austria and Hungary are backward.</small> Scythia, the modern Tartary and Siberia, seem in all ages of the world to have been in the same barbarous and uncivilized state in which we find them at present. The sea of Tartary is the frozen ocean which admits of no navigation, and though some of the greatest rivers in the world run through that country,① they are at too great a distance from one another to carry commerce and communication through the greater part of it. There are in Africa none of those great inlets, such as the Baltic and Adriatic seas in Europe, the Mediterranean and Euxine seas in both Europe and Asia, and the gulphs of Arabia, Persia, India, Bengal, and Siam, in Asia, to carry maritime commerce into the interior parts of that great continent: and the great rivers of Africa are at too great a distance from one another to give occasion to any considerable inland navigation. The commerce besides which any nation can carry on by means of a river which does not break itself into any great number of branches or canals, and which runs into another territory before it reaches the sea, can never be very considerable; because it is always in the power of the nations who possess that other territory to obstruct the communication between the upper country and the sea. The navigation of the Danube is of very little use to the different states of Bavaria, Austria and Hungary, in comparison of what it would be if any of them possessed the whole of its course till it falls into the Black Sea.②

---

① [The real difficulty is that the mouths of the rivers are in the Arctic Sea, so that they are separated. One of the objects of the Siberian railway is to connect them.]

② [The passage corresponding to this chapter is comprised in one paragraph in *Lectures*, p. 172.]

的塞西亚，今日的鞑靼[1]和西伯利亚，如同我们现在看到的这样似乎一直都处于野蛮不开化的状态。鞑靼的海是不能通航的冰洋，虽然有些世界著名大河流过鞑靼，但因彼此距离太远，大部分地区不利于贸易和交通。① 在欧洲，有波罗的海与亚得里亚海；在欧亚两大陆间，有地中海与黑海；在亚洲，有阿拉伯、波斯、印度、孟加拉湾及暹罗[2]海湾。但在非洲，没有这样的大内海，境内各大河又相隔太远，因此不能提供大量的内陆航运。此外，纵然在一个国家里有大河流贯其间，但由于并不分成许多支流和行道，其下游又须流经另一国国境入海，两岸仍然不能有大规模的商业，因为上游国家与海洋的交通受下游国家的强力阻止。对巴伐利亚、奥地利和匈牙利各国来说，多瑙河几乎没有用处，但如果该河到流入黑海以前的整个流域都被三国中任何一国所独占的话，情况就会大不相同了。②

而非洲、鞑靼、西伯利亚巴伐利亚奥地利、匈牙利很落后。

---

① 实际的困难是河流的入海口在北冰洋，因此它们分离了。西伯利亚铁路的目标之一就是连接它们。
② 与本章相对应的段落包含在《关于法律、警察、岁入及军备的演讲》第172页中的一段中。
〔1〕 鞑靼(Tartary)，包括东欧及亚洲的一广大地区，中古时期鞑靼人曾入侵并定居于此。
〔2〕 暹罗(Siam)，泰国的旧称。

CHAPTER IV
Of The Origin And Use Of Money

<small>Division of labour being established, every man lives by exchanging.</small>   When the division of labour has been once thoroughly established, it is but a very small part of a man's wants which the produce of his own labour can supply. He supplies the far greater part of them by exchanging that surplus part of the produce of his own labour, which is over and above his own consumption, for such parts of the produce of other men's labour as he has occasion for. Every man thus lives by exchanging, or becomes in some measure a merchant, and the society itself grows to be what is properly a commercial society.

<small>Difficulties of barter lead to the selection of one commodity as money,</small>   But when the division of labour first began to take place, this power of exchanging must frequently have been very much clogged and embarrassed in its operations. One man, we shall suppose, has more of a certain commodity than he himself has occasion for, while another has less. The former consequently would be glad to dispose of, and the latter to purchase, a part of this superfluity. But if this latter should chance to have nothing that the former stands in need of, no exchange can be made between them. The butcher has more meat in his shop than he himself can consume, and the brewer and the baker would each of them be willing to purchase a part of it. But they have nothing to offer in exchange, except the different productions of their respective trades, and the butcher is already provided with all the bread and beer which he has immediate occasion for. No exchange can, in this case, be made between them. He cannot be their merchant, nor they his customers; and they are all of them thus mutually less serviceable to one another. In order to avoid the inconveniency of such situations, every prudent man in every period of society, after the first establishment of the division of labour,

— 54 —

第四章 论货币的起源和效用

分工一旦完全确立,一个人自己劳动的产品,只能满足自己需要的极小部分。他的绝大部分需要,都要用超过自己消费的剩余部分来交换自己所需要的别人劳动产品的剩余部分来满足。这样,每个人都要依赖交换而生活,或者说,在一定程度上,每个人都成为了商人,而社会本身也成为真正的商业社会。

<small>分工一旦确立,每个人都靠交换来生活。</small>

但在刚开始分工的时候,这种交换能力的作用,往往遇到种种阻碍和困难。假设一个人持有某种商品,超过了自己的消费,而另一个人所持有的这种物品却不够自己消费。这时,前者当然愿意出卖剩余的部分,后者当然愿意购买前者手中剩余物品的一部分。但若后者手中,目前恰好没有持有前者所需要的物品,他们之间的交易,仍然无法进行。比如,屠户把超过自己消费部分的肉放在店内,酿酒师和面包师都愿意购买自己所需要的一份肉,但这时,假设他们除了各自行业的不同制造品外,没有别的可供交换的物品,而屠户现在需要的全部面包和啤酒已经得到了供给,在这种情况下,他们彼此之间无法进行交易。屠户不能成为酿酒师和面包师的商人,而酿酒师和面包师也不能成为屠户的顾客。这样,他们就不能互相提供服务。然而自最初的分工确立以后,在社会的每个时期那些聪明的人,为了避免这种不便,便除了

<small>交换困难导致选用某种商品作为货币。</small>

国民财富的性质与原理

must naturally have endeavoured to manage his affairs in such a manner, as to have at all times by him, besides the peculiar produce of his own industry, a certain quantity of some one commodity or other, such as he imagined few people would be likely to refuse in exchange for the produce of their industry. ①

_{for example, cattle, salt, shells, cod, tobacco, sugar, leather and nails.} Many different commodities, it is probable, were successively both thought of and employed for this purpose. In the rude ages of society, cattle are said to have been the common instrument of commerce; and, though they must have been a most inconvenient one, yet in old times we find things were frequently valued according to the number of cattle which had been given in exchange for them. The armour of Diomede, says Homer, cost only nine oxen; but that of Glaucus cost an hundred oxen. Salt is said to be the common instrument of commerce and exchanges in Abyssinia; ② a species of shells in some parts of the coast of India; dried cod at Newfoundland; tobacco in Virginia; ③ sugar in some of our West India colonies; hides or dressed leather in some other countries; and there is at this day a village in Scotland where it is not uncommon, I am told, for a workman to carry nails instead of money to the baker s shop or the ale-house. ④

In all countries, however, men seem at last to have been determined by irresistible reasons to give the preference, for this employment, to metals above every other commodity. Metals can not only

---

① [The paragraph has a close resemblance to Harris, *Money and Coins*, pt. i, § § 19, 20.]

② [Montesquieu, *Esprit des lois*, liv. xxii. , chap i. , note.]

③ [W. Douglass, *A Summary Historical and Political of the First Planting, Progressive Improvements and Present State of the British Settlements in North America*, 1760, vol. ii. , p. 364. Certain law officers' fees in Washington were still computed in tobacco in 1888. —J. J. Lalor, *Cyclopædia of Political Science*, 1888, s. v. Money, p. 879.]

④ Playfair ed of *Wealth of Nations*, 1805 vol. i. ,p. 36, says the explanation of this is that factors furnish the nailers with materials, and during the time they are working give them a credit for bread, cheese and chandlery goods, which they pay for in nails when the iron is worked up. The fact that nails are metal is forgotten at the beginning of the next paragraph in the text above.]

自己劳动产品以外,身边都随时随地携带一定数量的某种物品,他们想用这种物品去和任何人交换劳动产品时,就不会遭到拒绝。①

为了达到这一目的而被人们先后想到并用过的物品可能有很多。在社会未开化时期,据说曾以牲畜作为商业上的通用媒介。虽然牲畜是一种很不方便的交换媒介,但我们却发现古代常常用交换的牲畜头数来决定一些物品的价值。荷马曾说:迪奥米德的铠甲仅值九头牛,而格罗卡斯的铠甲却值100头牛。据说,阿比西尼亚[1]以盐为商业和交换的媒介;②印度沿海某些地方,以某种贝壳为媒介;弗吉尼亚用烟草;③纽芬兰用干鳕鱼;英国西印度殖民地用砂糖;其他若干国家则用兽皮或皮革。据我所闻,直到今日,苏格兰还有个乡村,那里的工人还用铁钉而不是货币来交换面包师的面包或是啤酒店的啤酒。④

然而,在任何国度,由于种种不可抗拒的理由,人们似乎都最终决定使用金属作为交换的媒介,行使货币的职能。金属比起任

例如,牲畜、盐、贝壳、鳕鱼、烟草、糖、皮革和铁钉。

---

① 这一段与哈里斯的《货币与硬币》第1部分第19、20页内容非常相似。

② 孟德斯鸠(Montesquieu):《论法的精神》第22章第1节注解。

③ W. 道格拉斯1760年版本的《不列颠北美殖民地的最初种植、后续改良和现状的历史和政治概述》第2卷第364页中。华盛顿某些法官的费用仍然计算在1888年的烟草中。——J. J. 拉乐,1888年的《政治学百科全书》第879页。

④ 普雷法尔版的《国家财富》(1805年)第1卷第36页中这样解释:这就是工人提供制钉的材料,在制钉期间他们通过信用来获得面包、奶酪和杂货商品,这些是他们用制好的钉子来交换的。钉子还是一种材料,这个事实在上述文字中的开始时被忘记了。

[1] 阿比西尼亚(非洲东部国家,首都 Addis Ababa)。

Metals were eventually preferred because durable and divisible. be kept with as little loss as any other commodity, scarce any thing being less perishable than they are, but they can likewise, without any loss, be divided into any number of parts, as by fusion those parts can easily be reunited again; a quality which no other equally durable commodities possess, and which more than any other quality renders them fit to be the instruments of commerce and circulation. The man who wanted to buy salt, for example, and had nothing but cattle to give in exchange for it, must have been obliged to buy salt to the value of a whole ox, or a whole sheep, at a time. He could seldom buy less than this, because what he was to give for it could seldom be divided without loss; and if he had a mind to buy more, he must, for the same reasons, have been obliged to buy double or triple the quantity, the value, to wit, of two or three oxen, or of two or three sheep. If, on the contrary, instead of sheep or oxen, he had metals to give in exchange for it, he could easily proportion the quantity of the metal to the precise quantity of the commodity which he had immediate occasion for.

Iron, copper, gold and silver, Different metals have been made use of by different nations for this purpose. Iron was the common instrument of commerce among the antient Spartans; copper among the antient Romans; and gold and silver among all rich and commercial nations.

were at first used in unstamped bars, Those metals seem originally to have been made use of for this purpose in rude bars, without any stamp or coinage. Thus we are told by Pliny,① upon the authority of Timæus, an antient historian, that, till the time of Servius Tullius, the Romans had no coined money, but made use of unstamped bars of copper, to purchase whatever they had occasion for. These rude bars, therefore, performed at this time the function of money.

and afterwards stamped to show quantity and fineness; The use of metals in this rude state was attended with two very considerable inconveniencies; first with the trouble of weighing; and, secondly, with that of assaying them. In the precious metals, where a small difference in the quantity makes a great difference in the value, even the business of weighing, with proper exactness, requires at least very accurate weights and scales. The weighing of gold in particular is an operation of some nicety. In the coarser metals, in-

---

① Plin. Hist. Nat. lib. 33. cap. 3.

何别的东西来都要不易磨损一些,而且它还能任意分割,分割以后也可很容易再熔成原形。这种性质却为一切其他有耐久性商品所没有。金属的这一特性,使金属成为合适的商业流通媒介。例如,假设只有牲畜而没有别的物品可以交换盐,想购买食盐的人,一次所购价值,必然要一次性买进相当于整头牛或整头羊价值相当的盐。他所购买的价值不能低于这个限度,因为他用以购买食盐的牲畜不能分割,分割了就要受到损失。如果他想购买更多的食盐,同样不得不购入两倍或三倍多的盐,这些相当于两三头牛或羊的价值。反之,假如他用以交易的物品不是牛羊而是金属,他就能很容易按照他目前的需要,精确支付相当分量的金属来购买价值相当的商品。

> 金属因其耐久和易于分割而最终被采用。

各国为此目的而使用了不同的金属。古斯巴达人用铁,古罗马人用铜,而一切富裕商业国家则使用金银。

> 铁、铜、金和银。

最初用于交换目的的金属,似乎都是粗条,未加任何印记未经任何铸造。普林尼①告诉我们,根据古代历史学家蒂米阿斯的话说,直到瑟维阿斯·图利阿斯时代为止,罗马人还没有铸造的货币,他们使用没有刻印记的铜条购买需要的物品。因此,这些粗条就是当时当作货币使用的东西。

> 最初使用的金属都是没有印记的金属条块。

使用这种粗条的金属有两种极大的不便。第一是称量的困难;第二是化验的困难。贵金属在分量上的微小差异会造成在价值的很大差别。但要十分准确称量这类金属,至少需有极精密的砝码和天平。金的称量,尤其是一种极其精密的操作。当然,较粗糙的金属称量存在微小的误差,在价值上不会发生大的影响,

> 以后加盖印记,表明重量和纯度;

---

① 普林尼:《自然史》第33编,第3章。

deed, where a small error would be of little consequence, less accuracy would, no doubt, be necessary. Yet we should find it excessively troublesome, if every time a poor man had occasion either to buy or sell a farthing's worth of goods, he was obliged to weigh the farthing. The operation of assaying is still more difficult, still more tedious, and, unless a part of the metal is fairly melted in the crucible, with proper dissolvents, any conclusion that can be drawn from it, is extremely uncertain. Before the institution of coined money, however, unless they went through this tedious and difficult operation, people must always have been liable to the grossest frauds and impositions, and instead of a pound weight of pure silver, or pure copper, might receive in exchange for their goods, an adulterated composition of the coarsest and cheapest materials, which had, however, in their outward appearance, been made to resemble those metals. To prevent such abuses, to facilitate exchanges, and thereby to encourage all sorts of industry and commerce, it has been found necessary, in all countries that have made any considerable advances towards improvement, to affix a public stamp upon certain quantities of such particular metals, as were in those countries commonly made use of to purchase goods. Hence the origin of coined money, and of those public offices called mints; institutions exactly of the same nature with those of the aulnagers and stampmasters of woollen and linen cloth. All of them are equally meant to ascertain, by means of a public stamp, the quantity and uniform goodness of those different commodities when brought to market.

<small>stamps to show fineness being introduced first,</small> The first public stamps of this kind that were affixed to the current metals, seem in many cases to have been intended to ascertain, what it was both most difficult and most important to ascertain, the goodness or fineness of the metal, and to have resembled the sterling mark which is at present affixed to plate and bars of silver, or the Spanish mark which is sometimes affixed to ingots of gold, and which being struck only upon one side of the piece, and not covering the whole surface, ascertains the fineness, but not the weight of the metal. Abraham weighs to Ephron the four hundred shekels of silver which he had agreed to pay for the field of Machpelah.① They are said however to be the current money of the merchant, and yet are received by weight and not by tale, in the same manner as ingots of gold and bars of silver are at present. The revenues of the antient Saxon

---

① [Genesis xxiii. 16.]

没有必要十分精确地去称重。但若一个穷人,买卖值一个法新[1]的货物,每次也需称量这一个法新的重量,这是一件多麻烦的事情啊。化验金属的工作更为困难、更为烦琐。除非把金属的一部分放在坩埚里,用适当的熔剂将其完全熔化,否则检验的结果都很不可靠。然而在铸币制度建立以前,除非通过这种又困难又烦琐的过程,否则人们就很容易受到极大的欺骗。他们售卖货物的所得一镑纯银或纯铜混有许多最粗劣最低贱的金属,只是表面上看来和银铜一样。因此,为避免此种弊害、促进交易、鼓励各种工商业,都认为有必要在普遍用以购买货物的一定分量的特定金属上加盖官印。于是就出现了铸币制度和称为造币厂的国家机构。这种制度的性质,类似麻布、呢绒检察官制度。这些制度都是为了通过加盖公印,确定这市场上各种商品的数量并且划一它们的品质。

最初盖在货币金属上的公印,其目的似乎都在于确定金属的品质或纯度,这种保证又是最难最重要的;当时的刻印,与现今银盘或银条上所刻的纯度标记很相似。在金条上刻印,只附在金属一边而不盖住金属全面的西班牙式标记,亦与此相似。用来确定金属的纯度而非金属的重量。传载,"亚伯拉罕称银子400谢克尔[2]给以弗伦,作为支付麦比拉的田价"。[①] 据说银子是当时商人流通的货币。可是,和现在的金条和银块一样,都不论个数只论重量。在古代,英格兰的撒克逊国王们,其收入据说不是征收货

首先采用公章来表明纯度,

---

① 《创世记》第23篇,第16页。
[1] 法新(farthing)是英国从前使用的铜币,值一便士的1/4。
[2] 谢克尔,古希伯来或巴比伦的衡量单位(和钱币)。

kings of England are said to have been paid, not in money but in kind, that is, in victuals and provisions of all sorts. William the Conqueror introduced the custom of paying them in money. This money, however, was, for a long time, received at the exchequer, by weight and not by tale. ①

and coinage to show weight later.

The inconveniency and difficulty of weighing those metals with exactness gave occasion to the institution of coins, of which the stamp, covering entirely both sides of the piece and sometimes the edges too, was supposed to ascertain not only the fineness, but the weight of the metal. Such coins, therefore, were received by tale as at present, without the trouble of weighing.

The names of coins originally expressed their weight.

The denominations of those coins seem originally to have expressed the weight or quantity of metal contained in them. In the time of Servius Tullius, who first coined money at Rome, the Roman As or Pondo contained a Roman pound of good copper. It was divided in the same manner as our Troyes pound, into twelve ounces, each of which contained a real ounce of good copper. The English pound sterling in the time of Edward I., contained a pound, Tower weight, of silver of a known fineness. The Tower pound seems to have been something more than the Roman pound, and something less than the Troyes pound. This last was not introduced into the mint of England till the 18th of Henry VIII. The French livre contained in the time of Charlemagne a pound, Troyes weight, of silver of a known fineness. The fair of Troyes in Champaign was at that time frequented by all the nations of Europe, and the weights and measures of so famous a market were generally known and esteemed. The Scots money pound contained, from the time of Alexander the First to that of Robert Bruce, a pound of silver of the same weight and fineness with the English pound sterling. English, French, and Scots pennies too, contained all of them originally a real pennyweight of silver, the twentieth part of an ounce, and the two-hundred-and-fortieth part of a pound. The shilling too seems originally to have been the denomination of a weight. *When wheat is at twelve shillings the quarter*, says an antient statute of Henry Ⅲ. *then wastel bread of a farthing shall*

---

① [Lowndes, *Essay*, p. 4.]

币而是征收实物,即各种食物和饮料。征服者威廉一世运用了以货币纳税的习惯。不过纳入国库的货币,在很长的一段时期里,是按重量而不按个数缴纳的。①

称量金属的麻烦和困难引起了铸币制度的产生。金属块的两面完全被铸币的刻印盖住,有时它的边缘也被盖住,这不但要确保金属的纯度,还要确保它的重量。于是,铸币就像现在的一样,全以个数流通,没有了称重量的麻烦。<small>后来通过铸造表明重量。</small>

那些铸币的名称,最初是要表明内含金属的重量或数量。瑟维阿斯·图利阿斯开始在罗马铸造货币,他那个时代,当时罗马币阿斯(AS)或庞多(Pondo)包含一罗马镑纯铜。阿斯或庞多像我们的特洛伊镑那样,分为12盎司,每盎司含有一盎司十足的纯铜。在爱德华一世时代,一英镑含有一陶尔镑纯银。一陶尔镑似比一罗马镑重,而比一特洛伊镑轻。特洛伊镑直到亨利八世十八年,才被英格兰造币厂采用。特洛伊是法国东北部香槟省的一个集市,当时欧洲各国人常去那里,大家因此都熟知并推崇这个有名的市场度量衡。在查理曼大帝时代,一法定货币里弗(Livre)含纯银一特鲁瓦镑。自亚历山大一世至布鲁斯时代止,苏格兰币都含有与英镑一镑相同重量相同纯度的白银。英国、法国和苏格兰一便士的货币,最初都含有十足一便士的白银,即一盎司的1/20,一镑的1/240。先令最初似乎也是一个重量名称。亨利三世当时的法律规定:小麦售价1夸特20先令时,则每块售价一法新的上<small>铸币的名称最早代表的是重量。</small>

---

① 朗兹:《论银币(增补版)》,第4页。

weigh eleven shillings and four pence. ① The proportion, however, between the shilling and either the penny on the one hand, or the pound on the other, seems not to have been so constant and uniform as that between the penny and the pound. During the first race of the kings of France, the French sou or shilling appears upon different occasions to have contained five, twelve, twenty, and forty pennies. Among the antient Saxons a shilling appears at one time to have contained only five pennies, ② and it is not improbable that it may have been as variable among them as among their neighbours, the antient Franks. From the time of Charlemagne among the French, ③ and from that of William the Conqueror among the English, ④ the proportion between the pound, the shilling, and the penny, seems to have been uniformly the same as at present, though the value of each has been very different. For in every country of theworld, I believe, the avarice and injustice of princes and sovereign states, abusing the confidence of their subjects, have by degrees diminished the real quantity of metal, which had been originally contained in their coins. The Roman As, in the latter ages of the Republic, was reduced to the twenty-fourth part of its original value, and, instead of weighing a pound, came to weigh only half an ounce. The English pound and penny contain at present about a third only; the Scots pound and penny about a thirty-sixth; and the French pound and penny about a sixty-sixth part of their original value. ⑤ By means of those operations the princes and sovereign states which performed them were enabled, in appearance, to

---

① [The Assize of Bread and Ale, 51 Hen. Ⅲ., contains an elaborate scale beginning, 'When a quarter of wheat is sold for xii d. then wastel bread of a farthing shall weigh vi l. and xvi s.' and goes on to the figures quoted in the text above. The statute is quoted at second-hand from Martin Folkes' *Table of English Silver Coins* with the same object by Harris, *Essay upon Money and Coins*, pt. i., § 29, but Harris does not go far enough in the scale to bring in the penny as a weight.]

② [Hume, *History of England*, ed. of 1773, i., p. 226. Fleetwood, *Chronicon Preciosum*, 1707, p. 30. These authorities say there were 48 shillings in the pound, so that 240 pence would still make £ r.]

③ [Harris, *Money and Coins*, pt. i., § 29.]

④ ['It is thought that soon after the Conquest a pound sterling was divided into twenty shillings.'—Hume, *History of England*, ed. of 1773, vol. i,. p. 227.]

⑤ [Harris, *Money and Coins*, p. i., § 30, note, makes the French livre about one seventieth part of its original value.]

等小麦面包应重11先令4便士。① 但是,先令与便士或先令与镑的比例,似乎不像便士与镑的比例那么稳定划一。法兰西前几位国王在位时期,法国的苏(Sou)或先令,不同的情况下含五便士,12便士,或含20乃至40便士。在古代撒克逊人中间,一先令有的时候似只含五便士,②其含量的变动可能与其邻国人法兰克人的先令变动相类似。自查理曼大帝时代以来的法国,③自征服王威廉第一时代以来的英格兰,④镑、先令或便士的价值,似乎和现今一样,没有多大变动,尽管每一种价值有很大变动。我相信,世界上各国,君主和国家的贪婪不公使他们背弃臣民,逐渐削减货币最初所含金属的真实数量。在罗马共和国后期的各个时期,罗马的阿斯,减到原来价格的1/24,名义含量的一镑实际上只有半盎司。英格兰的镑和便士,现今价值大约相当于原价的1/3;苏格兰的镑和便士,大约相当于原价的1/36;法国的镑和便士仅相当于原价的1/66。⑤ 君王和国家通过采用这些办法就能以比原来要求较小量的白银偿还债务履行各种契约。实际上,表面上是这样

---

① 亨利三世的面包啤酒法令,包含了一个精确刻度的开始:如果一夸特小麦交换12先令,那么一法新面包将重4.16六升。与哈里斯《货币与硬币》(第1部分,第29节)的目的相同,这个法令摘自于马丁·福克斯的《英国银币法》的二手资料。但是哈里斯没有将便士作为重量将其进一步引入。

② 休谟的《英格兰史》(1773年)第226页,弗利特伍德的 Chronicon Preciosum(1707年)第30页。这些权威人士说一镑包含48先令,因此240便士将仍然是一镑。

③ 哈里斯:《货币与硬币》第1部分,第29页。

④ 在征服不久之后,一镑被认为可以分成20先令。——休谟:《英格兰史》(1773年)第1卷,第227页。

⑤ 哈里斯:《货币与硬币》第1部分第30页注解,规定法国里弗大约相当于其原始价值的1/70。

pay their debts and to fulfil their engagements with a smaller quantity of silver than would otherwise have been requisite. It was indeed in appearance only; for their creditors were really defrauded of a part of what was due to them. All other debtors in the state were allowed the same privilege, and might pay with the same nominal sum of the new and debased coin whatever they had borrowed in the old. Such operations, therefore, have always proved favourable to the debtor, and ruinous to the creditor, and have sometimes produced a greater and more universal revolution in the fortunes of private persons, than could have been occasioned by a very great public calamity. ①

It is in this manner that money has become in all civilized nations the universal instrument of commerce, by the intervention of which goods of all kinds are bought and sold, or exchanged for one another. ②

The next inquiry is what rules determine exchangeable value.

What are the rules which men naturally observe in exchanging them either for money or for one another, I shall now proceed to examine. These rules determine what may be called the relative or exchangeable value of goods.

Value may mean either value in use or value in exchange.

The word VALUE, it is to be observed, has two different meanings, and sometimes expresses the utility of some particular object, and sometimes the power of purchasing other goods which the possession of that object conveys. The one may be called "value in use;" the other, "value in exchange." The things which have the greatest value in use have frequently little or no value in exchange; and on the contrary, those which have the greatest value in exchange have frequently little or no value in use. Nothing is more useful than water: but it will purchase scarce any thing; scarce any thing can be had in exchange for it. A diamond, on the contrary, has scarce any value in

---

① [The subject of debased and depreciated coinage occurs again below, pp. 36, 37, 194; vol. ii. , pp. 51-57, 415-418. One of the reasons why gold and silver became the most usual forms of money is dealt with below, pp. 172, 173. See Coin and Money in the index.]

② [In *Lectures*, pp. 182-190, where much of this chapter is to be found, money is considered 'first as the measure of value and then as the medium of permutation or exchange'. Money is said to have had its origin in the fact that men naturally fell upon one commodity with which to compare the value of all other commodities. When this commodity was once selected it became the medium of exchange. In this chapter money comes into use from the first as a medium of exchange, and its use as a measure of value is not mentioned. The next chapter explains that it is vulgarly used as a measure of value because it is used as an instrument of commerce or medium of exchange.]

的,他们的债权人因此被剥夺了应收账款的一部分。政府允许国内一切其他债务人享有和君王相等的特权,他们同样能以新的贬值货币来偿还货币改铸前的旧债。因此,这种手段证明常有利于债务人,而很不利于债权人,比起一场非常大的公共灾祸,有的时候它所带来的私人财产上革命造成的灾难更为巨大、普遍。①

货币通过这种方式,成为一切文明国普遍的商业媒介。所有货物通过这些媒介,都能进行买卖,相互交换。②

我现在要考察人们在以货物交换货币或用货物交换货物的过程中遵循的自然规则。这些法则决定着所谓的货物的相对价值或交换价值。接下来考察决定交换价值的规则。

应当注意,价值(value)一词含有两个不同的意义:有时表示特定物品的效用;有时则表示由于占有该物品而带来的对他种物品的购买力。前者可被称为使用价值,后者可被称为交换价值。价值可分为使用价值和交换价值。具有很大使用价值的东西,往往具有交换价值极小,甚至根本没有;反言之,具有的交换价值很大的东西,往往使用价值极小或根本没有。没有什么比水的用途更大,但我们不能用它购买任何东西,也不会拿任何东西去与水交换。反之,钻石的使用价值几乎

---

① 贬值的货币制度这一主题在以下第 36、37、194 页(第 2 卷第 51~57 页,第 415~418 页)中再次出现。金银成为最通用的货币形式的原因之一在下面第 172、173 页中将会涉及。见《货币与硬币》索引。

② 在《关于法律、警察、岁入及军备的演讲》第 182~190 页中(这章很多都能在这里找到),货币首先被认为是价值的衡量尺度,然后才被认为是交换媒介。据说货币的起源出自这样一个事实:人类必然地发现一种可以和其他所有商品相比较的商品。在本章中,货币最开始被用作交换媒介,作为价值尺度的作用却没有提及。下一章解释普遍用作价值尺度是因为被用作价值尺度或交换媒介。

	use; but a very great quantity of other goods may frequently be had in exchange for it. ①
Three questions,	
(1) wherein consists the real price of commodities,	In order to investigate the principles which regulate the exchangeable value of commodities, I shall endeavour to shew,

First, what is the real measure of this exchangeable value; or, wherein consists the real price of all commodities. |
(2) what are the different parts of this price,	Secondly, what are the different parts of which this real price is composed or made up.
(3) why the market price sometimes diverges from this price,	And, lastly, what are the different circumstances which sometimes raise some or all of these different parts of price above, and sometimes sink them below their natural or ordinary rate; or, what are the causes which sometimes hinder the market price, that is, the actual price of commodities, from coinciding exactly with what may be called their natural price.
will be answered in the next three chapters.	I shall endeavour to explain, as fully and distinctly as I can, those three subjects in the three following chapters, for which I must very earnestly entreat both the patience and attention of the reader: his patience in order to examine a detail which may perhaps in some places appear unnecessarily tedious; and his attention in order to understand what may, perhaps, after the fullest explication which I am capable of giving of it, appear still in some degree obscure. I am always willing to run some hazard of being tedious in order to be sure that I am perspicuous; and after taking the utmost pains that I can to be perspicuous, some obscurity may still appear to remain upon a subject in its own nature extremely abstracted.

---

① [*Lectures*, p. 157. Law, *Money and Trade*, 1705, ch. i. (followed by Harris, *Money and Coins*, pt. i., §3), contrasts the value of water with that of diamonds. The cheapness of water is referred to by Plato, *Euthydem*. 304 B., quoted by Pufendorf, *De jure nature et gentium*, lib. v., cap. i., §6; cp. Barbeyrac's note on §4.]

没有,但往往能够交换到大量其他货物。①

我尽力阐明以下三点用以探讨支配商品交换价值的原则:

第一,什么是交换价值的真实尺度,或者说,构成一切商品真实价格的是什么?

第二,构成真实价格的不同部分,究竟是什么?

第三,什么情况使真实价格的某一部分或全部,有时高于有时又低于他们自然或普通的价格比率? 或者说,有时阻碍商品实际价格,使其不能与其自然价格刚好一致的原因是什么?

关于这三个问题,我将在以下三章内尽可能详细地清楚说明。不过,某些地方看来似乎是不必要的赘述需要读者的耐心;某些地方我已经尽力充分详尽地说明,但难免仍然不够清楚。为了读者弄清楚,请读者细心体会,我往往愿意啰唆赘述以确保读者能充分理解我所想表达的;但对一个本身极其抽象的问题,在我尽力说得明白无误之前,可能仍难免有些晦涩不清的地方。

三个问题:
(1)什么是商品的真实价格?
(2)哪些是真实价格的不同部分?
(3)什么市场价格有时偏离真实价格?

后面三章回答上述问题。

---

① 《关于法律、警察、岁入及军备的演讲》,第 157 页,《法律、货币和贸易》(1705 年)第 5 章(哈里斯的《货币与硬币》第 1 部分第 3 节随后),将水的价值和钻石的价值相比。水的廉价可以参考柏拉图的 Euthydem 304,Pufendorf 的 De jure natura et gentium 第 1 章第 6 节;Barbeyrac 的注解第 4 节。

CHAPTER V

Of The Real And Nominal Price Of Commodities, Or Of Their Price In Labour, And Their Price In Money

Labour is the real measure of exchangeable value, Every man is rich or poor according to the degree in which he can afford to enjoy the necessaries, conveniencies, and amusements of human life. But after the division of labour has once thoroughly taken place, it is but a very small part of these with which a man's own labour can supply him. The far greater part of them he must derive from the labour of other people, and he must be rich or poor according to the quantity of that labour which he can command, or which he can afford to purchase. The value of any commodity, therefore, to the person who possesses it, and who means not to use or consume it himself, but to exchange it for other commodities, is equal to the quantity of labour which it enables him to purchase or command. Labour, therefore, is the real measure of the exchangeable value of all commodities.

and the first price paid for all things. The real price of every thing, what every thing really costs to the man who wants to acquire it, is the toil and trouble of acquiring it. What every thing is really worth to the man who has acquired it, and who wants to dispose of it or exchange it for something else, is the toil and trouble which it can save to himself, and which it can impose upon other people. What is bought with money or with goods is purchased by labour,① as much as what we acquire by the toil of our

---

① ['Everything in the world is purchased by labour.' —Hume, ' Of Commerce,' in *Political Discourses*, 1752, p. 12.]

第五章　论商品的真实价格及名义价格,或论用劳动表示的商品价格和用货币表示的商品价格

一个人是穷是富,要看他享受人生生活的必需品、便利品和娱乐的程度怎么样。但分工一旦完全确立以后,各人所需要的这些东西,只有很小的一部分由自己的劳动来提供,绝大部分需要由他人的劳动来提供。所以,他是贫是富,要看他支配或者购买得起的他人劳动的多少。对于一个占有某货物但又不愿自己消费而愿用来交换其他商品的人说来,该物的价值等于使他能购买或支配的劳动数量。因此,劳动是衡量一切商品交换价值的真实尺度。劳动是交换价值的真实尺度,

任何一个东西的真实价格,即要取得这件东西的人实际上所付出的代价,是为了获得它而付出的辛苦和麻烦。对于已经得到这件东西而想处理它或者想用来交换其他东西的人来说,占有它而能自己节省并转移到别人身上去的辛苦和麻烦便是它的真正价值。以货币或货物购买物品就像我们用自己的辛苦取得的一样,都是用劳动购来的。① 这些货币或货物,使我们能够节省相当的也是购买一切东西的最初价格。

---

① 世界上所有的东西都是用劳动来购买的。——休谟《政治演讲录》(1752 年)第 12 页中的《关于商业》。

own body. That money or those goods indeed save us this toil. They contain the value of a certain quantity of labour which we exchange for what is supposed at the time to contain the value of an equal quantity. Labour was the first price, the original purchase-money that was paid for all things. It was not by gold or by silver, but by labour, that all the wealth of the world was originally purchased; and its value, to those who possess it, and who want to exchange it for some new productions, is precisely equal to the quantity of labour which it can enable them to purchase or command.

<small>Wealth is power of purchasing labour.</small>   Wealth, as Mr. Hobbes says, is power. ① But the person who either acquires, or succeeds to a great fortune, does not necessarily acquire or succeed to any political power, either civil or military. His fortune may, perhaps, afford him the means of acquiring both, but the mere possession of that fortune does not necessarily convey to him either. The power which that possession immediately and directly conveys to him, is the power of purchasing; a certain command over all the labour, or over all the produce of labour which is then in the market. His fortune is greater or less, precisely in proportion to the extent of this power; or to the quantity either of other men's labour, or, what is the same thing, of the produce of other men's labour, which it enables him to purchase or command. The exchangeable value of every thing must always be precisely equal to the extent of this power which it conveys to its owner. ②

But though labour be the real measure of the exchangeable value of all commodities, it is not that by which their value is commonly estimated. It is often difficult to ascertain the proportion between two different quantities of labour. The time spent in two different sorts of work will not always alone determine this proportion. The different degrees of hardship endured, and of ingenuity exercised, must likewise

---

① ['Also riches joined with liberality is Power, because it procureth friends and servants: without liberality not so, because in this case they defend not but expose men to envy as a prey.'—*Leviathan*, I., x.]

② [This paragraph appears first in Additions and Corrections and ed. 3.]

劳动,但它们含有一定数量的劳动价值,因此我们可以交换其他当时被认为含有同样劳动价值量的物品。劳动是用以购买一切货物的最初代价,是首次支付的购买货币。世界全部财富,原来不是用金银购买而是用劳动购买的。财富的价值,对于占有它并愿用以交换一些新产品的人来说,恰好等于它使他们能够购买或支配的劳动数量。

霍布斯先生曾说,财富就是权力。① 但获得或承继一大笔财产的人,未必能获得或承继任何政治权力,不管是民政上的还是军政上的。他的财产或许可以给他提供一种获得民政和军政两种权力的手段,但只有财产他未必就能获得这两种政权。财产能直接给他提供购买权力,是对于当时市场上所有劳动或所有劳动产品的支配权。他的财产的多少与这种权力的大小精确成比例,也就是说,财产的多少,与他所能购买和所能支配的他人劳动数量即他人劳动生产物数量的大小精确地成比例。一件东西的交换价值,一定正好等于这物品给其所有者所带来的劳动支配权的大小。②

财富就是购买劳动的权力。

虽然劳动是所有商品交换价值的真实尺度,但商品的价值通常却不是按劳动衡量的。确定两种不同的劳动量的比例往往是一件很困难的事。单单化在两种不同工作上的时间是不能决定这种比例的。工作时的不同艰难程度和所用的不同技巧,也需要

———————

① 富人和慷慨就是力量,因为它能取得朋友和仆人;如果没有慷慨就不是这样,因为在这种条件下他们仅仅将他们作为嫉妒的对象。——霍布斯《利维坦》第一篇,第十章。

② 这一段首先出现在附录和修正以及第3版中。

But value is not commonly estimated by labour, because labour is difficult to measure, be taken into account. There may be more labour in an hour's hard work than in two hours easy business; or in an hour's application to a trade which it cost ten years labour to learn, than in a month's industry at an ordinary and obvious employment. But it is not easy to find any accurate measure either of hardship or ingenuity. In exchanging indeed the different productions of different sorts of labour for one another, some allowance is commonly made for both. It is adjusted, however, not by any accurate measure, but by the higgling and bargaining of the market, according to that sort of rough equality which, though not exact, is sufficient for carrying on the business of common life. ①

and commodities are more frequently exchanged for other commodities, Every commodity besides, is more frequently exchanged for, and thereby compared with, other commodities than with labour. It is more natural therefore, to estimate its exchangeable value by the quantity of some other commodity than by that of the labour which it can purchase. The greater part of people too understand better what is meant by a quantity of a particular commodity, than by a quantity of labour. The one is a plain palpable object; the other an abstract notion, which, though it can be made sufficiently intelligible, is not altogether so natural and obvious.

especially moneys which is therefore more frequently used in estimating value. But when barter ceases, and money has become the common instrument of commerce, every particular commodity is more frequently exchanged for money than for any other commodity. The butcher seldom carries his beef or his mutton to the baker, or the brewer, in order to exchange them for bread or for beer; but he carries them to the market, where he exchanges them for money, and afterwards exchanges that money for bread and for beer. The quantity of money which he gets for them regulates too the quantity of bread and beer which he can afterwards purchase. It is more natural and obvious to him, therefore, to estimate their value by the quantity of money, the commodity for which he immediately exchanges them, than by that of bread and

---

① [The absence of any reference to the lengthy discussion of this subject in chap. x, is curious.]

考虑进去。每小时的困难工作，比同样时间完成的容易工作也许包含有更多劳动量；需要十年学习才能掌握的工作做一小时，比普通业务工作一个月包含可能更多的劳动量。但是，艰难程度和技巧的衡量尺度不容易找到。诚然，在不同劳动的不同产品之间进行交换时，通常都会考虑到上述困难程度和技巧程度。但是，不是按任何准确尺度来调整的，而是通过市场上的讨价还价来进行调整的，这虽然不精确，但它是一种能够满足日常生活的商业行为。①

另外，商品频繁地与商品交换，而不是与劳动交换，因此是与其他商品比较而不是跟劳动进行比较。所以，它的交换价值更加自然的以其所能购得的其他商品数量，而不是它所能购买的其他劳动数量来衡量。一定数量的某种商品，比起一定量的某种劳动更容易被大多数人理解。因为，商品数量是一个可以看得见摸得着的东西，而劳动数量却是一个抽象的概念。即使人们能够充分理解它，但是它也不像具体物那样明显自然。

但是，当物物交换已经停止了，货币成为商业上被普遍接受的交换媒介的时候，商品就更多与货币交换而不是与其他商品交换。屠户并不是把牛肉或羊肉直接拿到面包店或酒店去交换自己需要的面包或啤酒，却是先把牛肉或羊肉拿到市场，用肉去换取货币，然后用货币交换面包或啤酒。他售卖牛羊肉所能换取的货币量，决定着他后来所能购买的面包和啤酒的多少。因此，更明显更自然的是货币的数量，也就是用肉直接换来的商品数量，

---

① 关于这个话题冗长的讨论在第十章中不存在，是一个很奇怪的现象。

beer, the commodities for which he can exchange them only by the intervention of another commodity; and rather to say that his butcher's meat is worth threepence or fourpence a pound, than that it is worth three or four pounds of bread, or three or four quarts of small beer. Hence it comes to pass, that the exchangeable value of every commodity is more frequently estimated by the quantity of money, than by the quantity either of labour or of any other commodity which can be had in exchange for it.

But gold and silver vary in value, sometimes costing more and sometimes less labour, whereas equal labour always means equal sacrifice to the labourer, Gold and silver, however, like every other commodity, vary in their value, are sometimes cheaper and sometimes dearer, sometimes of easier and sometimes of more difficult purchase. The quantity of labour which any particular quantity of them can purchase or command, or the quantity of other goods which it will exchange for, depends always upon the fertility or barrenness of the mines which happen to be known about the time when such exchanges are made. The discovery of the abundant mines of America reduced, in the sixteenth century, the value of gold and silver in Europe to about a third of what it had been before. As it cost less labour to bring those metals from the mine to the market, so when they were brought thither they could purchase or command less labour; and this revolution in their value, though perhaps the greatest, is by no means the only one of which history gives some account. But as a measure of quantity, such as the natural foot, fathom, or handful, which is continually varying in its own quantity, can never be an accurate measure of the quantity of other things; so a commodity which is itself continually varying in its own value, can never be an accurate measure of the value of other commodities. Equal quantities of labour, at all times and places, may be said to be of equal value to the labourer. In his ordinary state of health, strength and spirits; in the ordinary degree of his skill and dexterity,① he must always lay down the same portion of his ease, his liberty, and his happiness. The price which he pays must always be the same, whatever may be the quantity of goods which he receives in return for it. Of these, indeed, it may sometimes purchase a greater and sometimes a smaller quantity; but it is their value which varies, not that of the labour which purchases them. At all times and

---

① [The words from 'In his ordinary state of health' to 'dexterity' appear first in ed. 2.]

来估计牛羊肉价值,而不是面包和啤酒的数量,也就是用肉直接换来的商品数量。宁可说屠夫拥有的肉每磅值三便士或四便士,而不愿意说值三镑或四镑面包,或值三夸特或四夸特淡啤酒。所以,事情这样出现:一个商品的交换价值,更频繁的按货币量计算,而不是按这商品所能换得的劳动量或其他任何商品量计算。

然而,像所有其他商品一样,金银的价值也是变动的,有时便宜有时昂贵,有时购买也有难有易。特定数量的金银所能购买或所能支配的劳动量,或所能交换的其他商品数量,往往取决于当时已发现的著名金银矿山出产的富饶或是贫瘠。美洲16世纪发现了丰富的金银矿山,于是欧洲的金银价值几乎降至原价的1/3。由于这些金属从矿山送到市场所花费的劳动较少,所以送到市场以后所能支配或购买的劳动也同比减少。这虽然也许是金银价值在历史上变动最大的一次,但是据记载着并非是独一无二的一次。人的一步之长,伸开两臂合抱,或是一手之所握,这些本身就会不断变动的数量尺度,不可能作为精确测量其他物品的标准尺度。同样地,本身价值不断变化地商品,不可能作为测量其他商品的准确尺度。对于劳动者而言,等量的劳动在任何时间、任何地点都具有同等的价值。依照劳动者普遍具有的健康状况、精力和熟练与技巧程度,①他必然牺牲等额的舒适安逸、自由与幸福。无论他得到的回报如何,他所支付的价格总是相同的。当然,他的劳动能够买得到的货物有时多有时少,但这只是货物价值变动,而不是购买货物的劳动价值发生了变动。无论在任何地方,

旁注:但金银的价值是变动的,有时候更有时候更值的,有时候少劳动却等于同等劳动的牺牲,

---

① "依照劳动者普遍具有的健康状况、精力和熟练与技巧程度"这些文字首先出现在第2版中。

places that is dear which it is difficult to come at, or which it costs much labour to acquire; and that cheap which is to be had easily, or with very little labour. Labour alone, therefore, never varying in its own value, is alone the ultimate and real standard by which the value of all commodities can at all times and places be estimated and compared. It is their real price; money is their nominal price only.

<small>although the employer regards labour as varying in value.</small> But though equal quantities of labour are always of equal value to the labourer, yet to the person who employs him they appear sometimes to be of greater and sometimes of smaller value. He purchases them sometimes with a greater and sometimes with a smaller quantity of goods, and to him the price of labour seems to vary like that of all other things. It appears to him dear in the one case, and cheap in the other. In reality, however, it is the goods which are cheap in the one case, and dear in the other.

<small>So regarded, labour has a real and a nominal price.</small> In this popular sense, therefore, labour, like commodities, may be said to have a real and a nominal price. Its real price may be said to consist in the quantity of the necessaries and conveniencies of life which are given for it; its nominal price, in the quantity of money. The labourer is rich or poor, is well or ill rewarded, in proportion to the real, not to the nominal price of his labour.

<small>The distinction between real and nominal is sometimes useful in practice.</small> The distinction between the real and the nominal price of commodities and labour, is not a matter of mere speculation, but may sometimes be of considerable use in practice. The same real price is always of the same value; but on account of the variations in the value of gold and silver, the same nominal price is sometimes of very different values. When a landed estate, therefore, is sold with a reservation of a perpetual rent, if it is intended that this rent should always be of the same value, it is of importance to the family in whose favour

那些很难得到的或是要花费很多劳动才能得到的东西价格就昂贵;那些很容易得到的或是花费很少劳动就能得到的东西价格就低廉。因此,只有本身价值绝不变动的劳动,才是最终的真实的标准,这个标准可以在任何时间任何地方来估量和比较所有商品的价值。劳动是商品的真实价格,货币仅仅只是商品的名义价格。

不过,等量的劳动对于劳动者而言,总是具有同样的价值,但在雇用他的人看来,它的价值却有时大一些有时小一些。对于这些同等数量的劳动,雇主有时需用多量有时只需用少量的货物去购买;因而,对他而言,劳动的价格与其他所有物品价格一样常常在变化。在他认为,有些时候劳动的价格昂贵,有的时候劳动的价格低廉。但实际上,只是有的时候货物是廉价的;有的时候货物是昂贵的。

尽管雇主把劳动看作变化的。

所以,按照一般而言,劳动也像商品一样,可以说是有真实价格与名义价格的。所谓的真实价格就是劳动可以交换回的一定数量的生活必需品和便利品的数量。所谓名义价格,就是劳动可换回的一定数量的货币。劳动者是贫穷还是富裕,所得劳动报酬是低还是高,不是与其劳动的名义价格成比例,而是与劳动的真实价格成比例的。

如此看来,劳动具有真实价格义价格。

商品与劳动的真实价格与名义价格的区别,不仅仅是纯理论问题,有时在实践上更有用处。相同的真实价格总是具有相同的价值;但是由于金银价值的变化,相同的名义价格,其价值有时很不相同。但相同的名义价格的价值,却往往因金银价值变动而具有很不同的价值。所以,假设一份地产要以保留永久租佃为条件来售卖,要是他打算让地租的价值永远不变,那么就不该把地租

真实价格和名义价格的区分,有时在实践上有用。

it is reserved, that it should not consist in a particular sum of money. ① Its value would in this ease be liable to variations of two different kinds; first, to those which arise from the different quantities of gold and silver which are contained at different times in coin of the same denomination; and, secondly, to those which arise from the different values of equal quantities of gold and silver at different times.

<small>since the amount of metal in coins tends to diminish,</small> Princes and sovereign states have frequently fancied that they had a temporary interest to diminish the quantity of pure metal contained in their coins; but they seldom have fancied that they had any to augment it. The quantity of metal contained in the coins, I believe of all nations, has, accordingly, been almost continually diminishing, and hardly ever augmenting. Such variations therefore tend almost always to diminish the value of a money rent.

<small>and the value of gold and silver to fall.</small> The discovery of the mines of America diminished the value of gold and silver in Europe. This diminution, it is commonly supposed, though I apprehend without any certain proof, is still going on gradually, and is likely to continue to do so for a long time. Upon this supposition, therefore, such variations are more likely to diminish, than to augment the value of a money rent, even though it should be stipulated to be paid, not in such a quantity of coined money of such a denomination (in so many pounds sterling, for example), but in so many ounces either of pure silver, or of silver of a certain standard.

The rents which have been reserved in corn have preserved their value much better than those which have been reserved in money, even where the denomination of the coin has not been altered. By the 18th of Elizabeth② it was enacted, That a third of the rent of all col-

---

① ['Be above all things careful how you make any composition or agreement for any long space of years to receive a certain price of money for the corn that is due to you, although for the present it may seem a tempting bargain.' — Fleetwood, *Chronicon Preciosum*, p. 174.]

② [C. 6, which applies to Oxford, Cambridge, Winchester and Eton, and provides that no college shall make any lease for lives or years of tithes, arable land or pasture without securing that at least one-third of 'tholde' (presumably the whole not the old) rent should be paid in coin. The Act was promoted by Sir Thomas Smith to the astonishment, it is said, of his fellow-members of Parliament, who could not see what difference it would make. 'But the knight took the advantage of the present cheapness; knowing hereafter grain would grow dearer, mankind daily multiplying, and licence being lately given for transportation. So that at this day much emolument redoundeth to the colleges in each university, by the passing of this Act; and though their rents stand still, their revenues do increase.' —Fuller, *Hist. of the University of Cambridge*, 1655, p. 144, quoted in Strype, *Life of the learned Sir Thomas Smith*, 1698, p. 192]

规定为一定数额的货币。① 货币的价值可能受到两种不同的变动的影响:第一,在不同的时代,同一铸币所含的金银分量不同;第二,在不同的时代,同一分量金银价值也各不相同。

君王和国家常常想通过减少铸币所含的纯金属的量来获得暂时的利益,但他们很少想过增加铸币内所含纯金属的数量。所以,我相信,各国铸币内所含的纯金属量都一直在减少,而从来没有增加。因此,这种变动常在逐步促使货币地租的价值降低。<small>因为铸币所包含的金属数量不断地减少。</small>

美洲金银矿山的发现降低了欧洲黄金白银的价值。大家普遍推测,金银价值一直在逐渐下降,而且在长时期内大概会持续下去,虽然我不清楚这是否有确凿的证据。所以,按照这种推测,这种变动只会降低而不是增加货币地租的价值,这样即使地租不规定为某一数量的某一单位铸币支付,那也要规定为多少盎司纯银或某种成色的白银若干盎司来支付。<small>金银价值也在下降。</small>

谷物地租,即使在铸币单位没有发生变化的时候,也比货币地租更能保持地租的价值。伊丽莎白十八年②颁布了这样的法

---

① 当心以上所有的事情,在比较长的一段时间里你怎样获得一个稻米的特定价格的合同由你来决定,不管目前这个价格看起来是多么诱人。——弗利特伍德的 *Chronicon Preciosum*,第174页。

② 第6章应用于牛津、剑桥、温彻斯特和伊顿,规定所有的学院都必须交纳生活租金或什一税(什一税:自愿交付或作为税收应当交付的个人年收入的十分之一,特别是用于供养教士或教会),可耕种土地或牧场至少能够确保出售的(可能是全部而非旧的)三分之一的牧场租金要用现金支付。据说这个法令可能是由托马斯·史密斯先生提出,使他的国会议员感到惊奇的是,他们也看不出这将有什么区别。但是议员们知道以后的稻谷将变得越来越昂贵,人类也将成倍增长,运输的执照也将发放,所以他们充分利用目前的低廉价格。如果有一天这个法令得以通过,在那时每个大学学院的报酬都将提高;尽管他们的租金不变,他们的利润将增加。

<small>English rents reserved in money have fallen to a fourth since 1586,</small> lege leases should be reserved in corn, to be paid, either in kind, or according to the current prices at the nearest public market. The money arising from this corn rent, though originally but a third of the whole, is in the present times, according to Doctor Blackstone, commonly near double of what arises from the other two-thirds. ① The old money rents of colleges must, according to this account, have sunk almost to a fourth part of their ancient value; or are worth little more than a fourth part of the corn which they were formerly worth. But since the reign of Philip and Mary the denomination of the English coin has undergone little or no alteration, and the same number of pounds, shillings and pence have contained very nearly the same quantity of pure silver. This degradation, therefore, in the value of the money rents of colleges, has arisen altogether from the degradation in the value of silver.

<small>and similar Scotch and French rents almost to nothing.</small> When the degradation in the value of silver is combined with the diminution of the quantity of it contained in the coin of the same denomination, the loss is frequently still greater. In Scotland, where the denomination of the coin has undergone much greater alterations than it ever did in England, and in France, where it has undergone still greater than it ever did in Scotland, some ancient rents, originally of considerable value, have in this manner been reduced almost to nothing.

<small>Corn rents are more stable than money rents,</small> Equal quantities of labour will at distant times be purchased more nearly with equal quantities of corn, the subsistence of the labourer, than with equal quantities of gold and silver, or perhaps of any other commodity. Equal quantities of corn, therefore, will, at distant times, be more nearly of the same real value, or enable the possessor to purchase or command more nearly the same quantity of the labour of other people. They will do this, I say, more nearly than equal quantities of almost any other commodity; for even equal quantities of corn will not do it exactly. The subsistence of the labourer, or the real price of labour, as I shall endeavour to show hereafter, is very diffe-

---

① [*Commentaries*, 1765, vol, ii. ,p. 322]

令:国内各学院地租,其中 1/3 要纳谷物为地租,或以实物按照当时最近市场上的谷价折合成货币。由谷物折合货币的部分,最初不过占全部地租的 1/3,但现在按照布莱克斯顿博士的统计,却已将近于其他 2/3 地租的两倍了。① 据此算法,各学院的货币地租几乎已经减到原来价值的 1/4 了,或者说是其原来所值谷物的 1/4 了。但是,自菲利普和玛丽在位时期迄今,英国铸币单位几乎没有什么变化;同一数量的英镑、先令或便士,所含的纯银几乎具有完全相同的分量。由此可以见得,各学院货币地租价值的降低,完全是由于白银价值的下降。

<small>自 1586 年来,英国用规定地租的货币地租已经下降到 1/4,</small>

如果白银价值下降的同时,铸币内所含的纯银量又同时减少,那么货币地租的损失就更大了。苏格兰铸币含银量的变动比英格兰经历了更大的变化,而法兰西铸币又比苏格兰的变化大得更多。所以,这两国昔日具有很大价值的地租,现在几乎一文不值。

<small>同样,苏格兰和法兰西国规定地租几乎消失始尽。</small>

在两个相隔较远的时期里,购买同等数量的劳动,更可能的是用同等数量的谷物(即劳动者的生活资料)而不是同等数量金银或其他货物来完成。所以,等量谷物在两个相隔很远的时期里,更有可能保持差不多相同的真实价值,或者可以这样说,持有谷物者更可能以等量谷物购买或支配他人的等量劳动。我是说,等量谷物比等量的几乎其他商品更可能购买或支配等量的劳动,因为即使是同等数量的谷物,也不可能完全等量地购买或支配劳动。劳动者的生活资料,也就是劳动的真实价格,正如我在后面章节所要说的,在不同的场合是大不相同的。劳动者所享有的生

<small>谷物地租比货币地租更为稳定,</small>

---

① 《传记》(1765 年)第 2 卷,第 322 页。

rent upon different occasions; more liberal in a society advancing to opulence, than in one that is standing still; and in one that is standing still, than in one that is going backwards. Every other commodity, however, will at any particular time purchase a greater or smaller quantity of labour in proportion to the quantity of subsistence which it can purchase at that time. A rent therefore reserved in corn is liable only to the variations in the quantity of labour which a certain quantity of corn can purchase. But a rent reserved in any other commodity is liable, not only to the variations in the quantity of labour which any particular quantity of corn can purchase, but to the variations in the quantity of corn which can be purchased by any particular quantity of that commodity.

<small>but liable to much larger annual variations,</small> Though the real value of a corn rent, it is to be observed however, varies much less from century to century than that of a money rent, it varies much more from year to year. The money price of labour, as I shall endeavour to show hereafter, does not fluctuate from year to year with the money price of corn, but seems to be every where accommodated, not to the temporary or occasional, but to the average or ordinary price of that necessary of life. The average or ordinary price of corn again is regulated, as I shall likewise endeavour to show hereafter, by the value of silver, by the richness or barrenness of the mines which supply the market with that metal, or by the quantity of labour which must be employed, and consequently of corn which must be consumed, in order to bring any particular quantity of silver from the mine to the market. But the value of silver, though it sometimes varies greatly from century to century, seldom varies much from year to year, but frequently continues the same, or very nearly the same, for half a century or a century together. The ordinary or average money price of corn, therefore, may, during so long a period, continue the same or very nearly the same too, and along with it the money price of labour, provided, at least, the society continues, in other respects, in the same or nearly in the same condition. In the mean time the temporary and occasional price of corn may frequently be double, one year, of what it had been the year before, or fluctuate, for example, from five and twenty to fifty shillings the quarter. But when corn is at the latter price, not only the nominal, but the real value of a corn rent will be double of what it is when at the former,

活资料,在迈向富裕的社会比在停滞不前的社会要多;在停滞不前的社会又要比退步的社会多。在某一时间内,每一种除谷物以外的商品所能购得的劳动数量,必定与该商品当时所能购得的生活资料量成比例。所以,一定分量谷物所能购买的劳动量的变动会影响谷物地租。但用其他任何商品来衡量的地租,不但要受一定数量的谷物所能购买的劳动数量变动的影响,而且还要受一定数量该种商品所能交换到的谷物数量变动的影响。

但是我们应当注意到这样一点,就一个世纪时间而言,谷物地租真实价值的变动,要比货币地租真实价值的变动少得多,然而从每一年的情况来说,却比货币地租真实价值的变动多得多。正如后面章节我所要说的,劳动的货币价格,并不逐年随谷物的货币价格波动而发生变化。在任何地方,它似乎不与谷物暂时的或偶然的价格相适应,而与谷物平均的或普通的价格相适应,而且谷物的平均或普通价格,就这一点在以后章节的论述,受白银价格以及矿山提供白银数量大小的支配,同时还要受到运输白银到市场所必须使用的劳动量的支配,还有所必须消费的谷物数量的支配。就一个世纪而言,银价有时虽有很大变动,但就每一年而言,却很少有很大变动,往往在半个世纪甚至一个世纪内,常常具有不变的价值。因此,谷物也在这么长的一个时期内,具有不变或几乎不变的平均或普通货币价格。而与之相同,劳动货币价格保持不变,只要在社会其他方面不发生什么变动或没有变动的情况是这样。不过,在此期间,谷物的暂时或偶然价格,常常出现今年比去年高一倍的状况,例如,每夸特的价格从今年的25先令上涨到明年的50先令。可是,当谷物每夸特涨到了50先令时,谷物地租的名义价值和真实价值就比以前高一倍,或者说能

但谷物价格引起的每年变化确实很大,

or will command double the quantity either of labour or of the greater part of other commodities; the money price of labour, and along with it that of most other things, continuing the same during all these fluctuations.

<small>so that labour is the only universal standard.</small> Labour, therefore, it appears evidently, is the only universal, as well as the only accurate measure of value, or the only standard by which we can compare the values of different commodities at all times and at all places. We cannot estimate, it is allowed, the real value of different commodities from century to century by the quantities of silver which were given for them. We cannot estimate it from year to year by the quantities of corn. By the quantities of labour we can, with the greatest accuracy, estimate it both from century to century and from year to year. From century to century, corn is a better measure than silver, because, from century to century, equal quantities of corn will command the same quantity of labour more nearly than equal quantities of silver. From year to year, on the contrary, silver is a better measure than corn, because equal quantities of it will more nearly command the same quantity of labour. ①

But though in establishing perpetual rents, or even in letting very long leases, it may be of use to distinguish between real and nominal

---

① ['In England and this part of the world, wheat being the constant and most general food, not altering with the fashion, not growing by chance: but as the farmers sow more or less of it, which they endeavour to proportion, as near as can be guessed to the consumption, abstracting the overplus of the precedent year in their provision for the next; and *vice versa*, it must needs fall out that it keeps the nearest proportion to its consumption (which is more studied and designed in this than other commodities) of anything, if you take it for seven or twenty years together: though perhaps the scarcity of one year, caused by the accidents of the season, may very much vary it from the immediately precedent or following. Wheat, therefore, in this part of the world (and that grain which is the constant general food of any other country) is the fittest measure to judge of the altered value of things in any long tract of time: and therefore wheat here, rice in Turkey, etc., is the fittest thing to reserve a rent in, which is designed to be constantly the same for all future ages. But money is the best measure of the altered value of things in a few years: because its vent is the same and its quantity alters slowly. But wheat, or any other grain, cannot serve instead of money: because of its bulkiness and too quick change of its quantity.' —Locke, *Some Considerations of the Consequences of the Lowering of Interest and Raising the Value of Money* ed. of 1696, pp. 74, 75.]

够支配比以前大一倍的劳动量或其他货物量,但在这所有的变动中,劳动的货币价格和大多数其他商品的货币价格却仍旧不变。

由此可以很清楚地看出,劳动才是唯一通用而且精确的价值尺度,也可以这样说,劳动才是能在一切时代和一切地方比较各种商品价值的唯一标准。我们不能用一种物品所能换得的银量来估定这物品从一个世纪到另一个世纪的真实价值;我们不能用一种物品所能换得的谷物量来估定这物品从一年到另一年的真实价值。但是无论从一个世纪到另一个世纪还是一年到另一年,我们都可以用劳动量极其准确地来估定这个物品的真实价值。就一个世纪到一个世纪而言,谷物作为尺度比白银更适合,因为等量谷物比等量白银更有可能支配等量的劳动。反之,就从一年到一年而言,白银比谷物来说作为衡量尺度更优,因为在这种情况下,等量白银比等量谷物更能支配等量劳动。①

因此,劳动是唯一的普遍标准。

但是,虽然真实价格与名义价格的区分对签订永久地租或缔

---

① 在英格兰和世界的上一些地方,小麦是一种固定的最为普遍的食品。不随潮流而改变,也不会偶然上升;但是由于农夫会努力保持一个比例来决定种植的数量,扣除前一年多余的作为库存为下一年准备的部分,几乎刚好可以满足消费;反之亦然,如果你从事这种预算有7年或者20年,就发现它必须要保持和消费(这种比其他任何商品的计算和研究更多)最为接近的比例;但是可能由于季节的偶然因素某些年份会出现稀缺,可能和最近的前一年和紧挨的下一年很不相同。因此,小麦在世界上这个地区(稻谷在世界上其他国家地区是最稳定和最为普遍接受的食品)是最适合判断在很长一段时间中出现价值变化的物品的尺度;因此小麦在这里,稻米在土耳其等是最适合保存的物品,它在以后所有的年份中将保持不变。但是货币是衡量多年价值出现变化的商品的最佳尺度,因为它的口径是最统一的,数量变化是最慢的。但小麦或其他谷物,是不可能替代货币的,因为它们的体积太大,数量变化太快。——洛克,《关于降低利率、提高货币价值后果的一些思考》,1696年版,第74、75页。

_{But in ordinary transactions money is sufficient, being perfectly accurate at the same time and place.} price; it is of none in buying and selling, the more common and ordinary transactions of human life.

At the same time and place the real and the nominal price of all commodities are exactly in proportion to one another. The more or less money you get for any commodity, in the London market, for example, the more or less labour it will at that time and place enable you to purchase or command. At the same time and place, therefore, money is the exact measure of the real exchangeable value of all commodities. It is so, however, at the same time and place only.

_{and the only thing to be considered in transactions between distant places.} Though at distant places, there is no regular proportion between the real and the money price of commodities, yet the merchant who carries goods from the one to the other has nothing to consider but their money price, or the difference between the quantity of silver for which he buys them, and that for which he is likely to sell them. Half an ounce of silver at Canton in China may command a greater quantity both of labour and of the necessaries and conveniencies of life, than an ounce at London. A commodity, therefore, which sells for half an ounce of silver at Canton may there be really dearer, of more real importance to the man who possesses it there, than a commodity which sells for an ounce at London is to the man who possesses it at London. If a London merchant, however, can buy at Canton for half an ounce of silver, a commodity which he can afterwards sell at London for an ounce, he gains a hundred per cent. by the bargain, just as much as if an ounce of silver was at London exactly of the same value as at Canton. It is of no importance to him that half an ounce of silver at Canton would have given him the command of more labour and of a greater quantity of the necessaries and conveniencies of life than an ounce can do at London. An ounce at London will always give him the command of double the quantity of all these, which half an ounce could have done there, and this is precisely what he wants.

结长期租地契约的情况可能会有用处,但是对日常生活中的普通交易却毫无作用。

在相同的时间和相同的地点,任何商品的真实价格与名义价格都保持一定比例。例如,在伦敦市场上售卖一种商品所换回多少货币,那么它就在当时当地能购买或能支配多少的劳动量。因此,在同一时间和地方,货币是所有商品的真实交换价值的准确尺度。但是,这样的情况只发生在同一时间和同一地点。

> 在中币能够在时间和地点完全准确的。但是在普通交易中就够了,同一时间和地点,货币尺度是完全准确的。

位于相隔很远的两个地方的商品,其真实价格与货币价格之间不一定成比例,而在两地之间往来贩运货物的商人只考虑商品的货币价格,也就是说,他所考虑的只是购买商品所支付的白银数量和出卖商品可以换回的白银数量之间的差额。中国广州的半盎司白银可支配的劳动量或生活必需品和便利品的数量,也许要多于伦敦一盎司白银所可支配的这些商品数量。所以,在中国的广州[1]以半盎司白银出售的一种商品,对于在该地拥有某一商品的人来说,比在伦敦拥有该种商品并且售价一盎司白银的人来说,实际上也许更有价值,更为重要。但是,如果伦敦商人以半盎司白银在广州购买某一商品并且后来能以一盎司白银的价格在伦敦出卖,通过这笔交易,他就获得了百分之百的利益,好像一盎司白银在伦敦和广州具有完全相同的银价。这个商人好像并不关心广州半盎司白银比伦敦一盎司白银能够支配更多劳动或更多生活必需品和便利品这个情况。他所关心的是,在伦敦一盎司白银使他能够支配的劳动量和生活必需品与便利品量,总是两倍于半盎司白银。

> 唯一要考虑的是不同地点之间的交易。

---

　　[1] Canton,广州(旧称)。

国民财富的性质与原理

So it is no wonder that money price has been more attended to   As it is the nominal or money price of goods, therefore, which finally determines the prudence or imprudence of all purchases and sales, and thereby regulates almost the whole business of common life in which price is concerned, we cannot wonder that it should have been so much more attended to than the real price.

In this work corn prices will sometimes be used.   In such a work as this, however, it may sometimes be of use to compare the different real values of a particular commodity at different times and places, or the different degrees of power over the labour of other people which it may, upon different occasions, have given to those who possessed it. We must in this case compare, not so much the different quantities of silver for which it was commonly sold, as the different quantities of labour which those different quantities of silver could have purchased. But the current prices of labour at distant times and places can scarce ever be known with any degree of exactness. Those of corn, though they have in few places been regularly recorded, are in general better known and have been more frequently taken notice of by historians and other writers. We must generally, therefore, content ourselves with them, not as being always exactly in the same proportion as the current prices of labour, but as being the nearest approximation which can commonly be had to that proportion. I shall hereafter have occasion to make several comparisons of this kind. ①

Several metals have been coined, but only one is used as the standard, and that usually the one first used in commerce,   In the progress of industry, commercial nations have found it convenient to coin several different metals into money; gold for larger payments, silver for purchases of moderate value, and copper, or some other coarse metal, for those of still smaller consideration. They have always, however, considered one of those metals as more peculiarly the measure of value than any of the other two; and this preference seems generally to have been given to the metal which they happened first to make use of as the instrument of commerce. Having once begun to use it as their standard, which they must have done when they had no other money, they have generally continued to do so even when the necessity was not the same.

The Romans are said to have had nothing but copper money till

---

① [Below, chap. xi *passim*.]

由于商品的名义价格或货币价格最终决定一切买卖行为的适当与否,并且调节日常生活中几乎所有涉及价格的交易,所以不足为奇的是,人们大都注意名义价格而不注意真实价格。

> 因此,价格受到的大意不足为奇。

但是,在这本书中,比较某种特定商品在不同时间和不同地方的不同真实价值,也就是,比较某一特定商品在不同时期带给其所有者的不同的支配他人劳动的能力,这种做法是很有益的。在此,我们所要比较的,并非是出售特定商品通常可换回的不同白银数量,而是不同数量白银所能买得的不同劳动数量。但是,人们往往无从准确知道不同时间不同地方,劳动的即时价格如何。对于谷物时价的正式记录虽然不多,但对于谷物时价,人们一般比较清楚掌握,并且历史学家和其他作家也常常注意谷物时价。所以,一般而言,我们相当满意地用谷物时价来作比较,这不是因为它和劳动时价总是具有完全相同的比例,而是因为二者一般总是以最近似的比例涨落。我在下面要作几个这种比较。①

> 在本书中,有时要使用谷物价格。

随着产业的进步,商业国家发现了将几种金属铸币同时使用很方便:黄金用于巨额支付;白银用于中等价值交易的支付;铜币或比铜币更贱的金属铸币用于更小交易的支付。在这三种金属中,总是有一种被人们认定作为主要的价值尺度。而他们所选择的那种,似乎都是最先用作商业媒介的金属。当他们没有其他货币时,一旦开始使用它们作为本位货币,一般就会被继续使用,哪怕当初的这种必要性已经消失了。

> 有几种货币充当商业活动的作用,但首先使用那种为本位货币。

据说,在第一次古迦太基战争之前的五年内,罗马才开始铸

---

① 下面,第十一章,经常出现。

国民财富的性质与原理

<small>as the Romans used copper,</small> within five years before the first Punic war,① when they first began to coin silver. Copper, therefore, appears to have continued always the measure of value in that republic. At Rome all accounts appear to have been kept, and the value of all estates to have been computed, either in *Asses* or in *Sestertii*. The *As* was always the denomination of a copper coin. The word *Sestertius* signifies two *Asses* and a half. Though the *Sestertius*, therefore, was originally a silver coin, its value was estimated in copper. At Rome, one who owed a great deal of money, was said to have a great deal of other people's copper. ②

<small>and modern European nations silver.</small> The northern nations who established themselves upon the ruins of the Roman empire, seem to have had silver money from the first beginning of their settlements, and not to have known either gold or copper coins for several ages thereafter. There were silver coins in England in the time of the Saxons; but there was little gold coined till the time of Edward III. nor any copper till that of James I. of Great Britain. In England, therefore, and for the same reason, I believe, in all other modern nations of Europe, all accounts are kept, and the value of all goods and of all estates is generally computed in silver: and when we mean to express the amount of a person's fortune, we seldom mention the number of guineas, but the number of pounds sterling which we suppose would be given for it.

<small>The standard metal originally was the only legal tender,</small> Originally, in all countries, I believe, a legal tender of payment could be made only in the coin of that metal, which was peculiarly considered as the standard or measure of value. In England, gold was not considered as a legal tender for a long time after it was coined into money. The proportion between the values of gold and silver money was not fixed by any public law or proclamation; but was left to be settled by the market. If a debtor offered payment in gold, the creditor might either reject such payment altogether, or accept of it at such a valuation of the gold as he and his debtor could agree upon. Copper is not at present a legal tender, except in the change of the smaller silver coins. In this state of things the distinction between the

---

① Pliny, lib. xxxiii. c. 3. [This note is not in ed. 1.]
② [Habere aes alienum.]

造银币;在这之前,罗马只有铜币。① 所以,罗马共和国似乎一直以铜币作为价值尺度。在罗马,一切账簿的记录,一切不动产价值,似乎都是以若干阿斯或若干塞斯特斯[1]计算。阿斯是铜币名称。而塞斯特斯一词即表示为两个半阿斯,所以塞斯特斯虽然本是一种银币,但它的价值常常以铜币计算。所以,在罗马,对于负债很多的人,人们都说,他欠了别人很多的铜。②

例如,罗马人使用铜。

那些在罗马帝国废墟上建立起来的北方各国,似乎在定居之初只有银币,在此后的多个世纪中都不知道金币,也没有铜币。在撒克逊时代的英格兰也只有银币。爱德华三世之前的时代,大不列颠没有什么金币。在詹姆士一世之后才有铜币。因此,在英格兰,在近代欧洲的其他各国,出于同样的理由,我相信,一切账簿的记录以及一切货物与一切财产价值的计算都用白银。当要表示一个人的财产数量是多少时,我们不说它值多少几尼,[2]而说它值多少英镑。

现代欧洲各国用银。

最初在所有的国家,我相信各国法定的支付手段,只是使用被特别认为是价值标准或尺度的那种金属铸成的货币。在英格兰,黄金在铸币后很久还不曾取得法定货币资格。金币与银币的比价,不是由法律或公告来规定的,而是完全取决于市场。在这种情况下,债务人如果用金币偿债,债权人完全是可以拒绝的。也可以按照双方同意的金价计算。在今日,铜币已经不是法定货币了,只用以作为小额银币的零头。在这种情况下,本位金属货

本位金属最初是唯一的法定货币,

---

① 普林尼:《自然史》第33篇,第3章。第一版中没有这个脚注。
② 债务权利。
[1] 塞斯特斯(Sestertius),古代罗马的货币单位。
[2] Guinea,几尼,英国的旧金币。

metal which was the standard, and that which was not the standard, was something more than a nominal distinction.

In process of time, and as people became gradually more familiar with the use of the different metals in coin, and consequently better acquainted with the proportion between their respective values, it has in most countries, I believe, been found convenient to ascertain this proportion, and to declare by a public law① that a guinea, for example, of such a weight and fineness, should exchange for one-and-twenty shillings, or be a legal tender for a debt of that amount. In this state of things, and during the continuance of any one regulated proportion of this kind, the distinction between the metal which is the standard, and that which is not the standard, becomes little more than a nominal distinction. ②

In consequence of any change, however, in this regulated proportion, this distinction becomes, or at least seems to become, something more than nominal again. If the regulated value of a guinea, for example, was either reduced to twenty, or raised to two-and-twenty shillings, all accounts being kept and almost all obligations for debt being expressed in silver money, the greater part of payments could in either case be made with the same quantity of silver money as before; but would require very different quantities of gold money; a greater in the one case, and a smaller in the other. Silver would appear to be more invariable in its value than gold. Silver would appear to measure the value of gold, and gold would not appear to measure the value of silver. The value of gold would seem to depend upon the quantity of silver which it would exchange for; and the value of silver would not

---

① [The Act, 19 Hen. VII. , c. 5, ordered that certain gold coins should pass for the sums for which they were coined, and 5 and 6 Ed. VI. prescribed penalties for giving or taking more than was warranted by proclamation. The value of the guinea was supposed to be fixed by the proclamation of 1717, for which see *Economic Journal*, March, 1898. Lead tokens were coined by individuals in the reign of Elizabeth James I. coined copper farthing tokens, but abstained from proclaiming them as money of that value. In 1672 copper halfpennies were issued, and both halfpennies and farthings were ordered to pass as money of those values in all payments under sixpence. —Harris, *Money and Coins*, pt. i. , § 39; Liverpool, *Treatise on the Coins of the Realm*, 1805, pp. 130, 131.]

② [I. e. , if 21 pounds may be paid with 420 silver shillings or with 20 gold guineas it does not matter whether a 'pound' properly signifies 20 silver shillings or $\frac{20}{21}$ of a gold guinea.]

币与非本位金属货币的区别,已不仅仅是名义上的区别了。

随着时间的推移,人们逐渐习惯于同时使用各种不同的金属铸币,而且了解各种铸币之间的价值比例;我相信,在那时候,大多数国家感到了确定这比例很便利,于是用法律①来规定。例如,特定纯度和重量的一个几尼应该兑换21先令,或可用它作为支付债务法定货币偿付。在此情况之下,在法定比例继续有效期间内,本位金属币与非本位金属币的区别,只是名义上的区别了。②

不过,这种法定比例会发生变动,本位金属币与非本位金属币的区别又成为、至少似乎成为不仅仅是名义上的了。例如,在一切账目都以银币表示,一切债务都以同一数量的银币支付的场合,如果一几尼金币的法定价值落至20先令,或升至22先令,以银币偿还旧债,和以前的没有什么不同;但是如果用金币来偿还的话,数量就大不相同了。在一几尼落至20先令的时候,所需要的金币数量就多一些;在一几尼升至22先令的时候,所需要的金币数量就少一些。在这种情况下,银价似乎相对于金价而言不易于变动。这时,好像是黄金的价值依存于得以换回的白银数量,而白银的价值似乎并不依存于它所能换回的黄金数量。但这种差

旁注:以后两种金属之间的比例均由法律规定,为法定货币,它们的区别不再重要了。

旁注:除了在法定比例发生变化的时候。

---

① 亨利七世的法令第19篇第5章规定,一定的金币应当超过它们被锻铸的数量,第5版、第6版描述了多于或少于公布的必需的数量的惩罚。几尼的价值认为被1717年的公告固定了下来,参见1898年3月的《经济杂志》。在伊丽莎白在位期间个人锻造铜币,詹姆斯一世时锻造铜法新(farthing)代币,但是用公告来规定它们可以获得货币一样的价值。在1672年发行了半便士的铜币,半便士铜币和半便士的法新被规定为和六便士货币拥有同样的价值。——哈里斯《货币与硬币》,第1部分第39节;利物浦《于国货币条约》(1805年)第103、131页。

② 也就是说如果21镑与420先令银币价值相当,或20几尼金币相当,一镑是否刚好意味着等于20先令银币或$\frac{20}{21}$几尼金币就无所谓了。

seem to depend upon the quantity of gold which it would exchange for. This difference, however, would be altogether owing to the custom of keeping accounts, and of expressing the amount of all great and small sums rather in silver than in gold money. One of Mr. Drummond's notes for five-and-twenty or fifty guineas would, after an alteration of this kind, be still payable with five-and-twenty or fifty guineas in the same manner as before. It would, after such an alteration, be payable with the same quantity of gold as before, but with very different quantities of silver. In the payment of such a note, gold would appear to be more invariable in its value than silver. Gold would appear to measure the value of silver, and silver would not appear to measure the value of gold. If the custom of keeping accounts, and of expressing promissory notes and other obligations for money in this manner, should ever become general, gold, and not silver, would be considered as the metal which was peculiarly the standard or measure of value.

During the continuance of a regulated proportion, the value of the most precious metal regulates the value of the whole coinage, as in Great Britain,　　In reality, during the continuance of any one regulated proportion between the respective values of the different metals in coin, the value of the most precious metal regulates the value of the whole coin. ① Twelve copper pence contain half a pound, avoirdupois, of copper, of not the best quality, which, before it is coined, is seldom worth seven-pence in silver. But as by the regulation twelve such pence are ordered to exchange for a shilling, they are in the market considered as worth a shilling, and a shilling can at any time be had for them. Even before the late reformation of the gold coin of Great Britain, ② the gold, that part of it at least which circulated in London

---

① [This happens to have been usually, though not always, true, but it is so simply because it has usually happened that the most precious metal in use as money has been made or become the standard. Gold was already the standard in England, though the fact was not generally recognised; see Harris, *Money and Cains*, pt. ii., § § 36, 37, and below, vol. ii.]

② [In 1774.]

异,完全起因于记账的习惯,所有数额的大小多用银币而不是金币来表示。例如,德拉蒙先生的一张期票,账面金额为 25 几尼或 50 几尼金币,在法定比例发生变动以后,仍可像以前那样用同等数量的金币支付债务。但是如果用白银支付的话,则所需白银数量必定随法定比例的变动而有很大的不同。这张期票兑现的时候,黄金的价值与银价比较又似乎不易于变动。这时,又好像是在用黄金的价值来衡量白银的价值,而不是以白银的价值来衡量黄金的价值了。所以,如果账簿的记录以及期票、债券上的款额全都习惯以金币来表示,并且被普遍接受,则被认为作为价值标准或价值尺度的特定金属,就应当是黄金而不是白银了。

实际上,在不同金属铸币的各自的价值中,如果有个法定比例持续不变,那么所有铸币的价值就又是最昂贵的那种金属的价值来支配的。① 英国 12 便士的铜币包含了常衡(16 盎司为一镑)铜半镑,而由于铜质不是最好的,在没有被铸成铜币之前还不值银币 7 便士。但是,法律这样规定了,这样的铜币 12 便士可以兑换一先令,在市场上被普遍接受这种认识,于是值一先令,并随时都能兑换成一先令。在英国②最近的金币改革以前,英国金币与

法定比例继续有效时,所有铸币的价值,如在大不列颠,最重贵金属的价值所支配。

---

① 当然这是很常见的但不是很频繁,但是这是多么简单啊,因为往往用作货币的是最珍贵的金属被锻造成为标准。金已经成为英格兰的标准,尽管这个事实还没有普遍被认识到。见哈里斯的《货币与硬币》第 2 部分第 36 节,见下面第 2 卷。

② 在 1774 年。

and its neighbourhood, was in general less degraded below its standard weight than the greater part of the silver. One-and-twenty worn and defaced shillings, however, were considered as equivalent to a guinea, which perhaps, indeed, was worn and defaced too, but seldom so much so. The late regulations① have brought the gold coin as near perhaps to its standard weight as it is possible to bring the current coin of any nation; and the order, to receive no gold at the public offices but by weight, is likely to preserve it so, as long as that order is enforced. The silver coin still continues in the same worn and degraded state as before the reformation of the gold coin. In the market, however, one-and-twenty shillings of this degraded silver coin are still considered as worth a guinea of this excellent gold coin.

<small>where the reformation of the gold coin has raised the value of the silver coin.</small>

The reformation of the gold coin has evidently raised the value of the silver coin which can be exchanged for it.

In the English mint a pound weight of gold is coined into forty-four guineas and a half, which, at one-and-twenty shillings the guinea, is equal to forty-six pounds fourteen shillings and six-pence. An ounce of such gold coin, therefore, is worth $3l.\ 17s.\ 10\frac{1}{2}d.$ in silver. In England no duty or seignorage is paid upon the coinage, and he who carries a pound weight or an ounce weight of standard gold bullion to the mint, gets back a pound weight or an ounce weight of gold in coin, without any deduction. Three pounds seventeen shillings and tenpence halfpenny an ounce, therefore, is said to be the mint price of gold in England, or the quantity of gold coin which the mint gives in return for standard gold bullion.

Before the reformation of the gold coin, the price of standard gold bullion in the market had for many years been upwards of 3l. 18s. sometimes 3l. 19s. and very frequently 4l. an ounce; that sum, it is probable, in the worn and degraded gold coin, seldom containing more than an ounce of standard gold. Since the reformation of the gold coin, the market price of standard gold bullion seldom exceeds 3l. 17s. 7d. an ounce. Before the reformation of the gold coin, the market price was always more or less above the mint price. Since that reformation, the market price has been constantly below the mint price. But that market price is the same whether it is paid in gold or

---

① [These regulations, issued in 1774, provided that guineas should not pass when they had lost a certain portion of their weight, varying with their age. —Liverpool, *Coins of the Realm*, p. 216, note.]

大部分银币不同,一般地说,都不会低劣到标准重量以下,至少在伦敦及其附近流通的金币是这样的。可是,21先令的被磨损的银币仍被视为一几尼的金币,但是金币的磨损不像银币那样严重。英国最近的法律①规定,并且英政府已采取措施,金币可以像别的国家的现行铸币可能做到的那样尽量接近于标准重量,但政府部门只能依重量计算来收受金币的命令,在这命令继续有效执行的期间内,可以使金币的标准重量保持不变,而银币仍然和金币改革以前那样处于磨损剥蚀状态。可是在市场上仍然这样认为:磨损了的银币21先令等价于优良的金币一几尼。

这样,金币的改革显然抬高了能和金币兑换的银币的价值。

在英国的造币厂,把一磅金铸成44个半几尼,按一几尼兑换21先令来计算,就等于46镑14先令6便士。因此,一盎司这样重的金币,价值银币3镑17先令10便士半。铸币税的征收在英格兰向来都不存在,一磅重或一盎司标准金块送往造币厂以后,可以丝毫无损地换回重一磅或一盎司的铸币。所以,每盎司3镑17先令10便士半,就成为英格兰所谓金的造币厂价格,也就是造币厂支付给标准金块的金币数量。

在金币改革前,市场上标准金块的价格多年以来都保持在每盎司3镑18先令以上,有时为3镑19先令,还有时为4镑。但在磨损剥蚀的4镑金币里,可能很少含有一盎司以上的标准金。金币改革以后,每盎司标准金块的市价很少超过3镑17先令7便士。金币改革之前的市场价格总是或多或少地超过造币厂价格;改革后的市场价格一直低于造币厂价格。但支付手段不论是金币还是银币,市场价格总是相同的。所以,最近金币的改革,提高的不仅仅是金币的价值,而且还提高了银币和金块,

在该国,金币改革提高了银币的价值。

---

① 这些1774年发布的改革规定,根据年代的不同,当几尼失去了其重量的一部分之后就不应该继续流通。——利物浦:《王国货币》,第216页注解。

in silver coin. The late reformation of the gold coin, therefore, has raised not only the value of the gold coin, but likewise that of the silver coin in proportion to gold bullion, and probably too in proportion to all other commodities; though the price of the greater part of other commodities being influenced by so many other causes, the rise in the value either of gold er silver coin in proportion to them, may not be so distinct and sensible.

In the English mint a pound weight of standard silver bullion is coined into sixty-two shillings, containing, in the same manner, a pound weight of standard silver. Five shillings and two-pence an ounce, therefore, is said to be the mint price of silver in England, or the quantity of silver coin which the mint gives in return for standard silver bullion. Before the reformation of the gold coin, the market price of standard silver bullion was, upon different occasions, five shillings and four-pence, five shillings and five-pence, five shillings and six-pence, five shillings and seven-pence, and very often five shillings and eight-pence an ounce. Five shillings and seven-pence, however, seems to have been the most common price. Since the reformation of the gold coin, the market price of standard silver bullion has fallen occasionally to five shillings and three-pence, five shillings and four-pence, and five shillings and five-pence an ounce, which last price it has scarce ever exceeded. Though the market price of silver bullion has fallen considerably since the reformation of the gold coin, it has not fallen so low as the mint price.

<small>Silver is rated below its value in England.</small> In the proportion between the different metals in the English coin, as copper is rated very much above its real value, so silver is rated somewhat below it. In the market of Europe, in the French coin and in the Dutch coin, an ounce of fine gold exchanges for about fourteen ounces of fine silver. In the English coin, it exchanges for about fifteen ounces, that is, for more silver than it is worth according to the common estimation of Europe.[①] But as the price of copper in bars is not, even in England, raised by the high price of copper in English coin, so the price of silver in bullion is not sunk by the low rate of silver

---

① [Magens, *Universal Merchant*, ed. Horsley, 1753, pp. 53-55, gives the proportions thus: French coin, 1 to $\frac{5803}{12279}$, Dutch, 1 to $\frac{32550}{164426}$, English, 1 to $\frac{14295}{68200}$.]

以及银币和一切其他货物对比的价值。不过,金币和银币价值的上升和大部分其他货物的价格相比并不是那么明显,因为他们还受许多其他原因的影响。

英格兰造币厂把一镑重的标准银块铸成 62 先令银币,两者所含的标准银都为一镑。因此,一盎司合 5 先令 2 便士就成为了英格兰所谓白银造币厂价格,也就是造币厂交换标准银块所给付的银币数量。在金币改革以前,在不同的场合下一盎司标准银块的市场价格出现过一些以下的兑换情况:5 先令 4 便士,5 先令 5 便士,5 先令 6 便士,5 先令 7 便士,5 先令 8 便士。不过,5 先令 7 便士好像是为最普通的交换比价。自金币改革以后,一盎司标准银块的市场价格时常降到 5 先令 3 便士、5 先令 4 便士或 5 先令 5 便士,并且很少超过 5 先令 5 便士。可是,虽然金币改革以来银块的市场价格大幅度下降,但始终没有降到像造币厂的价格那么低。

在英格兰货币的不同金属之间的比价中,铜的评价远远超过其真实价值,而银的评价略低于其真实价值。在欧洲市场上的法国、荷兰铸币,一盎司纯金大约兑换纯银 14 盎司;英格兰的铸币比价,一盎司纯金却能兑换约 15 盎司纯银。就是说,银在英格兰要低于欧洲的普通估算。① 但是,即使在英格兰,铜块的价格也没有因为铸币中铜的比价提高而增高;与此同样的是,银块价格,也

<small>在英格兰,白银评价低于其价值。</small>

---

① 马根斯著,霍斯利编辑的《环球商人》(1753 年)第 53~55 页给出这样的比例:一单位法国铸币相当于 $14\frac{5803}{12279}$ 盎司,一单位荷兰铸币 $\frac{32550}{164423}$ 盎司,英格兰铸币相当于 $\frac{14259}{68200}$ 盎司。

国民财富的性质与原理

in English coin. Silver in bullion still preserves its proper proportion to gold; for the same reason that copper in bars preserves its proper proportion to silver. ①

<small>Locke's explanation of the high price of silver bullion is wrong.</small>

Upon the reformation of the silver coin in the reign of William III. the price of silver bullion still continued to be somewhat above the mint price. Mr. Locke imputed this high price to the permission of exporting silver bullion, and to the prohibition of exporting silver coin. ② This permission of exporting, he said, rendered the demand for silver bullion greater than the demand for silver coin. But the number of people who want silver coin for the common uses of buying and selling at home, is surely much greater than that of those who want silver bullion either for the use of exportation or for any other use. There subsists at present a like permission of exporting gold bullion, and a like prohibition of exporting gold coin; and yet the price of gold bullion has fallen below the mint price. But in the English coin silver was then, in the same manner as now, under-rated in proportion to gold; and the gold coin (which at that time too was not supposed to require any reformation) regulated then, as well as now, the real value of the whole coin. As the reformation of the silver coin did not then reduce the price of silver bullion to the mint price, it is not very probable that a like reformation will do so now.

<small>If the silver coin were reformed, it would be melted.</small>

Were the silver coin brought back as near to its standard weight as the gold, a guinea, it is probable, would, according to the present proportion, exchange for more silver in coin than it would purchase in bullion. The silver coin containing its full standard weight, there would in this case be a profit in melting it down, in order, first, to sell the bullion for gold coin, and afterwards to exchange this gold coin for silver coin to be melted down in the same manner. Some alteration in the present proportion seems to

---

① [Full weight silver coins would not remain in circulation, as the bullion in them was worth more reckoned in guineas and in the ordinary old and worn silver coins than the nominal amount stamped on them.]

② [Locke, *Further Considerations Concerning Raising the Value of Money*. 2nd ed., 1695, pp. 58-60. The exportation of foreign coin (misprinted 'kind' in Pickering) or bullion of gold or silver was permitted by 15 Car. Ⅱ., c. 7, on the ground that it was 'found by experience that' money and bullion were 'carried in greatest abundance (as to a common market) to such places as give free liberty for exporting the same' and in order 'the better to keep in and increase the current coins' of the kingdom.]

没有因为铸币中银的比价降低而下落。银块与黄金仍保持着适当比例;出于同样的原因,铜块与白银也保持着适当比例。①

在威廉三世时期的银币改革以后,银块的价格仍然略高于造币厂价格。洛克先生认为,这种高价应归因于允许银块的出口、禁止银币的出口。② 他认为,允许银块出口必然会使得国内对银块的需要大于对银币的需要。可是,国内需要银币的人大多是出于普通买卖,就必然比需要银块的人多得多,他们大多的目的都是为出口或为其他目的。现在也同样允许金块的出口、禁止金币的出口,而且金块价格却降低到了造币厂价格之下。那时铸币中的白银与黄金的比价,也跟现今一样,是估值太低了。如同现今一样,那时的金币(当时的金币也没被认为需要有什么改革)支配一切铸币的真实价值。既然以前的银币改革,不能使银块价格降低到造币厂的价格,现今任何类似的改革很可能做不到这一点。

<small>洛克对银块高价的解释是不对的。</small>

如果想要使银币能够和金币一样地接近标准重量,那么根据现今的比价,一几尼金币所能兑换的银币和它所能换回的银块相比就要多。如果把含有十足标准重量的银币熔成银块,然后再拿这些铸成的银块兑换成金币,然后用这些金币去换回银币,这样是有利可图的。防止这种弊病发生的唯一方法似乎就只有改变金银的比价。

<small>如果改革银币,它就会被熔化。</small>

---

① 足量的银币不会继续保持流通,因为相对于几尼和通常旧的已有损坏的银币,流通中的金块比其锻造的表面价值更多。
② 洛克:《提高货币价值的再思考》第 2 版(1695 年)第 58~60 页。国外硬币或金银块的输出在查理二世十五年的第七章的法案中被批准。由于根据经验发现货币和金块大量被运往可以自由输出同类物品的地方,就可以保持和增加目前英国的流通货币。

be the only method of preventing this inconveniency.

Silver ought to be rated higher and should not be legal tender for more than a guinea. The inconveniency perhaps would be less if silver was rated in the coin as much above its proper proportion to gold as it is at present rated below it; provided it was at the same time enacted that silver should not be a legal tender for more than the change of a guinea; in the same manner as copper is not a legal tender for more than the change of a shilling. No creditor could in this case be cheated in consequence of the high valuation of silver in coin; as no creditor can at present be cheated in consequence of the high valuation of copper. The bankers only would suffer by this regulation. When a run comes upon them they sometimes endeavour to gain time by paying in sixpences, and they would be precluded by this regulation from this discreditable method of evading immediate payment. They would be obliged in consequence to keep at all times in their coffers a greater quantity of cash than at present; and though this might no doubt be a considerable inconveniency to them, it would at the same time be a considerable security to their creditors. ①

If it were properly rated, silver bullion would fall below the mint price without any recoinage. Three pounds seventeen shillings and ten-pence halfpenny (the mint price of gold) certainly does not contain, even in our present excellent gold coin, more than an ounce of standard gold, and it may be thought, therefore, should not purchase more standard bullion. But gold in coin is more convenient than gold in bullion, and though, in England, the coinage is free, yet the gold which is carried in bullion to the mint, can seldom be returned in coin to the owner till after a delay of several weeks. In the present hurry of the mint, it could not be returned till after a delay of several months. This delay is equivalent to a small duty, and renders gold in coin somewhat more valuable than an equal quantity of gold in bullion. ② If in the English coin silver was rated according to its proper proportion to gold, the price of silver bullion would probably fall below the mint price even without

---

① [Harris, writing nearly twenty years earlier, had said, ' it would be a ridiculous and vain attempt to make a standard integer of gold, whose parts should be silver; or to make a motley standard, part gold and part silver. ' —*Money and Coins*, pt. I. , § 36.]

② [*I. e.* , an ounce of standard gold would not actually fetch £ 3 17s. 10 $\frac{1}{2}$d. if sold for cash down.]

要减少上述弊病的发生,可以尝试着这样做:调高现今铸币的黄金和白银的适当比例(调高现今低于这比值的银价比值),并且同时规定除了可以兑换一几尼的银币之外的零头不得充作法定货币,这种规定类似于铜币除了可以兑换先令外不得充作法定货币。正如现时对铜的高估不会使债权人吃亏一样,那么,高估银的价值绝不会使任何债权人吃亏。在这种规定下,只会使银行业者吃亏。当银行挤兑发生时,他们借以拖延时间的支付款项的方式往往是用最小的 6 便士银币。如果实行了这种规定,将会阻止他们再来使用这种市区信用的方法来避免立即支付。因此他们将不得不经常在金柜中保有更大数量的现金,这可以很大程度地保障债权人的利益,尽管这对银行业者来说是不利的。①

即使今日优良的金币,3 镑 17 先令 10 便士半(金的造币厂价格),肯定也不含有多于一盎司以上的标准黄金;因此,有人认为,这样多的金币不应当换回更多的标准金块。但是,相对于金块而言,金币在使用上更加便利;况且,英国虽然没有铸币费,但金块送往造币厂,往往须在好几个星期之后才能得到金币。现今的造币厂工作又很繁忙,要好几个月以后才能拿到金币。用这种方式拖延时间,也等于抽收小额的铸币税,使金币的价值略高于金块的价值。② 所以,英国铸币银如果可以与金保持适当的比例,那么,即使不实行银币改革也能使银块价格落到造币厂价格之下;

---

① 哈里斯先生早在 20 年前就这样说过:制定一个金块的整体统一的标准是一种可笑而又徒劳的尝试,它的组成部分应当是银;制定一个混合的标准,一部分是金,一部分是银。见《货币与硬币》第 1 部分第 36 节。

② 也就是说一盎司标准金实际上如果用现金支付,不能售出 3 镑 17 先令 10 便士半。

	any reformation of the silver coin; the value even of the present worn and defaced silver coin being regulated by the value of the excellent gold coin for which it can be changed.
A seignorage would prevent melting and discourage exportation.	A small seignorage or duty upon the coinage of both gold and silver would probably increase still more the superiority of those metals in coin above an equal quantity of either of them in bullion. The coinage would in this case increase the value of the metal coined in proportion to the extent of this small duty; for the same reason that the fashion increases the value of plate in proportion to the price of that fashion. The superiority of coin above bullion would prevent the melting down of the coin, and would discourage its exportation. If upon any public exigency it should become necessary to export the coin, the greater part of it would soon return again of its own accord. Abroad it could sell only for its weight in bullion. At home it would buy more than that weight. There would be a profit, therefore, in bringing it home again. In France a seignorage of about eight per cent. is imposed upon the coinage,① and the French coin, when exported, is said to return home again of its own accord. ②
Fluctuations in the market price of gold and silver are due to ordinary commercial causes, but steady divergence from mint price is due to the state of the coin.	The occasional fluctuations in the market price of gold and silver bullion arise from the same causes as the like fluctuations in that of all other commodities. The frequent loss of those metals from various accidents by sea and by land, the continual waste of them in gilding and plating, in lace and embroidery, in the wear and tear of coin, and in that of plate; require, in all countries which possess no mines of their own, a continual importation, in order to repair this loss and this waste. The merchant importers, like all other merchants, we may believe, endeavour, as well as they can, to suit their occasional importations to what, they judge, is likely to be the immediate demand. With all their attention, however, they sometimes over-do the business, and sometimes under-do it. When they import more bullion than is wanted, rather than incur the risk and trouble of exporting it again, they are sometimes willing to sell a part of it for something less

---

① [This erroneous statement is repeated below, p. 442, and also vol. ii., p. 53, where the calculations on which it is based are given. See the note on that passage.]

② [The question of seignorage is further discussed at some length in the chapter on Commercial Treaties, vol. ii., pp. 51-57.]

甚至现今磨损了的银币价值,也会受其所能够兑换的优良金币的价值的支配。

金银币小额铸币税的课征,会使得金银铸币的价值进一步高出等数量的条块金银价值。这时,铸币金属的价值中会加进来等比例的铸造税额,就如同金银器皿中包含了制造费用的大小一样。铸币价值高于金银块,一方面能够阻止铸币的熔解,另一方面能够阻止铸币的出口。出于当前某种急需而出口的货币中的大部分不久也会流回本国。在外国的本国铸币只能按照条块的重量来出售,但是在国内它的购买力价值却具有超过其重量价值的特点。所以带回已经出口到他国的货币是可以获利的。法国存在8%的铸币税,①因此据说,法国出口的货币都会自动回到本国来。②

<small>铸币税会阻止熔化和出口。</small>

金银条块市价偶然波动和一切其他商品市价偶然波动有着相同的原因。海陆运输途中的意外事件常会使金属遭受损失;在镀金、包金、镶边和装饰的过程中也会存在金属的消耗;铸币及器皿都会有自然磨损。所以,自己不拥有矿藏的国家,为了弥补这类损失和消耗,就需要不断进口金银。我相信,进口金银的商人也像其他商人一样,会尽力做出准确判断使金银的进口适合于当时的需要。可是,无论他们注意得多周到,还是时常会出现进口过多或过少的局面。倘若进口了多于需求的金银条块,他们情愿以低于一般价格或平均价格的售价出售一部分给国内需求者,而不愿冒着危险和困难重新出口返回国外;相反,倘若进口了少于

<small>金银市场价格的波动是普通商业原因,但是铸币厂定价偏离稳定市场价格是由于铸币的原因。</small>

---

① 这个错误的表述在下面第442页被重述,在第2卷第53页那里给出了计算的基础。参见该页的注解。

② 小额铸币税问题将进一步在《通商条约》第2卷第51~57页中被讨论。

than the ordinary or average price. When, on the other hand, they import less than is wanted, they get something more than this price. But when, under all those occasional fluctuations, the market price either of gold or silver bullion continues for several years together steadily and eonstantly, either more or less above, or more or less below the mint price: we may be assured that this steady and constant, either superiority or inferiority of price, is the effect of something in the state of the coin, which, at that time, renders a certain quantity of coin either of more value or of less value than the precise quantity of bullion which it ought to contain. The constancy and steadiness of the effect, supposes a proportionable constancy and steadiness in the cause.

<small>The price of goods is adjusted to the actual contents of the coinage.</small> The money of any particular country is, at any particular time and place. more or less an accurate measure of value according as the current coin is more or less exactly agreeable to its standard, or contains more or less exactly the precise quantity of pure gold or pure silver which it ought to contain. If in England, for example, forty-four guineas and a half contained exactly a pound weight of standard gold, or eleven ounces of fine gold and one ounce of alloy, the gold coin of England would be as accurate a measure of the actual value of goods at any particular time and place as the nature of the thing would admit. But if, by rubbing and wearing, forty-four guineas and a half generally contain less than a pound weight of standard gold; the diminution, however, being greater in some pieces than in others; the measure of value comes to be liable to the same sort of uncertainty to which all other weights and measures are commonly exposed. As it rarely happens that these are exactly agreeable to their standard, the merchant adjusts the price of his goods, as well as he can, not to what those weights and measures ought to be, but to what, upon an average, he finds by experience they actually are. In consequence of a like disorder in the coin, the price of goods comes, in the same manner, to be adjusted, not to the quantity of pure gold or silver which the coin ought to contain, but to that which, upon an average, it is found by experience it actually does contain.

By the money-price of goods, it is to be observed, I understand always the quantity of pure gold or silver for which they are sold, without any regard to the denomination of the coin. Six shillings and eight-pence, for example, in the time of Edward I., I consider as the same money-price with a pound sterling in the present times; because it contained, as nearly as we can judge, the same quantity of pure silver.

需求的金银条块,则他们可得到高于一般价格的市场价格。但是,即使就是在这种偶然变动下,金银条块的市价也在好几年内稳定地保持着持续的状态,或略高于造币厂价格或略低于造币厂价格的状态,我们可以这样说,这种状态的出现一定起因于铸币本身的某种情况,这种情况使得一定数量铸币的价值在这几年内高于或低于铸币中应含有的精确的金银。这种影响的稳定和持续,是与相应的原因的稳定和持续有关。

任何一个国家的货币,在某一特定时间和特定地方,可以通过看通用的铸币是怎样准确地符合于它的标准,来判断是否可以看作准确的价值尺度,也就是说,要看铸币所包合的纯金量或纯银量是否准确地符合标准。例如,英国的44个半几尼含金量刚好是一镑标准金,即11盎司纯金和一盎司合金,那么这种金币在任何时间和地方都可以成为商品实际价值的正确尺度。倘若这44个半几尼被磨损消耗成为所含合标准金重量不到一镑了,而且磨损的程度又各不相同,那这种价值尺度就会像其他各种度量衡一样可能会不准确。商人们尽量不按照应当有的度量衡标准,而按照他们凭一般经验觉得实际上是的那种度量衡标准来调整自己商品价格,是因为完全符合标准的度量衡很少见。如果铸币出现混乱的情况,货物的价格也不是按铸币应当含有的纯金量或纯银量来调整的,而是按商人凭借自己经验觉察到的铸币实际含量来调整的。

> 货物的价格按照铸币的实际价格来调整。

应当指出,所谓的商品货币价格,我觉得总是指这些货物能换回的纯金量或纯银量,与铸币名称毫无关系。例如,倘若爱德华一世时代6先令8便士的货币价格和今日一镑的货币价格被看作同一的货币价格,我们可以判断出,两者所含纯银数量相同。

CHAPTER VI

Of the Component Parts Of The Price Of Commodities

Quantity of labour is originally the only rule of value,

In that early and rude state of society which precedes both the accumulation of stock and the appropriation of land, the proportion between the quantities of labour necessary for acquiring different objects seems to be the only circumstance which can afford any rule for exchanging them for one another. If among a nation of hunters, for example, it usually costs twice the labour to kill a beaver which it does to kill a deer, one beaver should naturally exchange for or be worth two deer. It is natural that what is usually the produce of two days or two hours labour, should be worth double of what is usually the produce of one day's or one hour's labour.

allowance being made for superior hardship,

If the one species of labour should be more severe than the other, some allowance will naturally be made for this superior hardship; and the produce of one hour's labour in the one way may frequently exchange for that of two hours labour in the other.

and for uncommon dexterity and ingenuity.

Or if the one species of labour requires an uncommon degree of dexterity and ingenuity, the esteem which men have for such talents, will naturally give a value to their produce, superior to what would be due to the time employed about it. Such talents can seldom be acquired but in consequence of long application, and the superior value of their produce may frequently be no more than a reasonable compensation for the time and labour which must be spent in acquiring them. In the advanced state of society, allowances of this kind, for superior hardship and superior skill, are commonly made in the wages of labour; and something of the same kind must probably have taken place in its earliest and rudest period.

第六章 论商品价格的组成部分

在早期尚未开化的社会里,资本累积和土地私有都不存在,获取各种物品所需要花费的劳动量之间的比例好像成为了各种物品相互交换的唯一标准和依据。比如说,在狩猎民族之中,捕杀一头海狸需要花费的劳动是捕杀一头鹿需要花费劳动的两倍,那么一头海狸当然就和两头鹿相交换。所以,通常来说以下情况是很自然的:两天劳动的产物的价值相当于一天劳动的产物价值的两倍,两小时劳动产物的价值相当于一小时劳动产物的价值的两倍。

> 劳动数量最初是唯一的价格尺度。

如果一种劳动比另一种劳动更为艰苦,当然就要对这种更为艰苦的劳动适当考虑补贴。因而一小时艰苦程度较高的劳动的产物,就可以和两小时艰苦程度较低的劳动的产物相交换了。

> 考虑劳动的艰苦程度,

如果一种劳动需要超过平常水平很多的技巧和智能,那么为对具有这种技能的人表示尊重,对于他的劳动产物自然要给予超过他劳动时间所应得的价值。具有经过多年苦练才能获得的这种技能的人来说,他生产的劳动产品应当获得较高的价值,这样也只不过是对获得技能所需费去的劳动与时间,给以合理的报酬。在进步的社会里,在劳动工资方面对特别艰苦的工作和特别熟练的劳动通常都会加以考虑。在社会的最初尚未开化时期或

> 和超出平常的熟练与技巧。

> The whole produce then belongs to the labourer,

In this state of things, the whole produce of labour belongs to the labourer; and the quantity of labour commonly employed in acquiring or producing any commodity, is the only circumstance which can regulate the quantity of labour which it ought commonly to purchase, command, or exchange for.

> but when stock is used, something must be given for the profits of the undertaker, and the value of work resolves itself into wages and profits.

As soon as stock has accumulated in the hands of particular persons, some of them will naturally employ it in setting to work industrious people, whom they will supply with materials and subsistence, in order to make a profit by the sale of their work, or by what their labour adds to the value of the materials. In exchanging the complete manufacture either for money, for labour, or for other goods, over and above what may be sufficient to pay the price of the materials, and the wages of the workmen, something must be given for the profits of the undertaker of the work who hazards his stock in this adventure. The value which the workmen add to the materials, therefore, resolves itself in this case into two parts, of which the one pays their wages, the other the profits of their employer upon the whole stock of materials and wages which he advanced. He could have no interest to employ them, unless he expected from the sale of their work something more than what was sufficient to replace his stock to him; and he could have no interest to employ a great stock rather than a small one, unless his profits were to bear some proportion to the extent of his stock.

> Profits are not merely wages of inspection and direction.

The profits of stock, it may perhaps be thought, are only a different name for the wages of a particular sort of labour, the labour of inspection and direction. They are, however, altogether different, are regulated by quite different principles, and bear no proportion to the quantity, the hardship, or the ingenuity of this supposed labour of inspection and direction. They are regulated altogether by the value of the stock employed, and are greater or smaller in proportion to the extent of this stock. Let us suppose, for example, that in some particular place, where the common annual profits of manufacturing stock are ten per cent. there are two different manufactures, in each of which twenty workmen are employed at the rate of fifteen pounds a year each, or at the expence of three hundred a year in each manufactory. Let us suppose too, that the coarse materials annually wrought up in the one cost only seven hundred pounds, while the finer materials in

许可能也考虑过这种情况。

在这种状态下,劳动者拥有自己生产的全部产物。一种物品可换回或可支配的劳动量由获得或生产这种物品所花费的劳动量来决定。

> 当时的全部劳动产品属于劳动者。

一旦资本在某些人手中积聚起来以后,当然就有一些人,利用手中的资本来驱使勤劳的人劳动,给他们提供原材料与生活资料,以获得劳动产物的售卖或劳动使原材料加工增殖的一种利润。劳动产品与货币、劳动或其他货物的交换所得除了足够支付原材料的资本和劳动工资的剩余部分,属于企业家作为他把资本投在这企业而得的利润。在这种情况下,原材料增加的价值分为两个部分:一部分为劳动者工资的支付,另一部分是支付给雇主垫付原材料和工资的那全部资本的利润。只有在出售劳动产物以后的所得抵偿了他所垫付的资本还能让他有利可图的时候,他才有雇用工人的兴趣;而且,只有在他所得的利润能和他所垫付的资本额保持相当大的比例时,他才会有进行大投资而不是进行小投资的兴趣。

> 使资本必须提供一些东西作为家利因此工资和利润的价值分为工资和利润。

资本的利润被某些人认为只是监督指挥这种劳动的工资的别名。但利润与工资又完全不一样,它们受着两个完全不同的原则的支配,资本的利润而且跟监督指挥这种劳动的数量、强度与技巧并不成比例,而是与投资额的大小成比例,完全只是受所投资本的价值支配。假定某处年利为 10%,存在着两个不同的制造业。一处雇用了 20 个劳动者,工资每人每年 15 镑,那么这个制造业的雇主每年支付工资总额 300 镑。又假定另外一处每年所加工的粗糙原料只值 700 镑,但是所加工出来的精细原料值 7000

> 利润不仅仅是监督和指挥。

the other cost seven thousand. The capital annually employed① in the one will in this case amount only to one thousand pounds; whereas that employed in the other will amount to seven thousand three hundred pounds. At the rate of ten per cent. therefore, the undertaker of the one will expect an yearly profit of about one hundred pounds only while that of the other will expect about seven hundred and thirty pounds. But though their profits are so very different, their labour of inspection and direction may be either altogether or very nearly the same. In many great works, almost the whole labour of this kind is committed to some principal clerk. His wages properly express the value of this labour of inspection and direction. Though in settling them some regard is had commonly, not only to his labour and skill, but to the trust which is reposed in him, yet they never bear any regular proportion to the capital of which he oversees the management; and the owner of this capital, though he is thus discharged of almost all labour, still expects that his profits should bear a regular proportion to his capital. In the price of commodities, therefore, the profits of stock constitute a component part altogether different from the wages of labour, and regulated by quite different principles.

The labourer shares with the employer, and labour alonno longer regulates value.

In this state of things, the whole produce of labour does not always belong to the labourer. He must in most cases share it with the owner of the stock which employs him. Neither is the quantity of labour commonly employed in acquiring or producing any commodity, the only circumstance which can regulate the quantity which it ought commonly to purchase, command, or exchange for. An additional quantity, it is evident, must be due for the profits of the stock which advanced the wages and furnished the materials of that labour.

when land has all become private property, rent constitutes a third component part of the price of most commodities.

As soon as the land of any country has all become private property, the landlords, like all other men, love to reap where they never sowed,② and demand a rent even for its natural produce. The wood of the forest, the grass of the field, and all the natural fruits of the

① ['The capital annually employed' is the working expenses for twelve nonths, not the capital in the usual modern sense.]

② [. Buchanan, ed. *Wealth of Nations*, 1814, vol. i. , p. 80, says: They do so. But the question is why this apparently unreasonable demand is so generally complied with. Other men love also to reap where they never sowed, but the landlords alone, it would appear, succeed in so desirable an object. ']

镑。这样算来,第一处每年投下的资本不过1000镑;①而第二处却有7300镑。因此,按10%的年利计算,第一家企业每年预期可得100镑的利润;第二家企业每年却预期得到730镑的利润。虽然他们的利润额相差很大,但是他们的监督性劳动却几乎没有什么区别,或者完全相同。在许多大工厂里,这种监督性的劳动几乎都是由某些重要的职员来负责。他的工资恰好可以正确地表示监督指挥这种劳动的价值。虽然在决定这个职员的工资时,不仅仅考虑他的劳动和技巧,而且考虑他所负的责任;不过,他的工资所得和他管理监督的资本并不保持一定的比例。资本所有者就不同了,他们虽然几乎不劳动,却希望其利润与资本形成一定的比例。所以,在商品价格中,资本的利润成为一个组成部分,它完全不同于劳动工资,而且完全受不相同原则的支配。

这样看来,劳动的全部产物并不是完全属于劳动者,在更多的时候是要跟雇用他的资本所有者分享的。通常取得或生产任何一种商品的劳动量,不能单独决定这种商品一般所应具有的交换、支配或购买的劳动量。显然,还存在着另一个决定因素,也就是对劳动垫付工资并提供材料的资本的利润。

<small>劳动产物再不单独属于劳动者,雇主享有分配价值。</small>

在任何国家,土地一旦完全成为私有财产,地主会像其他一切资本所有者一样,想不劳而获,②甚至对土地上的自然产物都要求地租。森林中的林木,田野的草,土地上的自然果实,在土地共

<small>当土地全部都成为私有财产时,地租成为多数商品价格的第三个组成部分。</small>

---

① 每年投入的资本是指12个月的工作支出,而不是现代通常意义上的资本。

② 布坎南著《国民财富》(1814年)第1卷第80页说道:"他们是这样的。但问题是为什么这个明显很无理的要求一般都能被遵守。其他人也喜欢不劳而获,但惟有地主能够达到了这样的目的呢。"

— 115 —

earth, which, when land was in common, cost the labourer only the trouble of gathering them, come, even to him, to have an additional price fixed upon them. He must then pay for the licence to gather them; and must give up to the landlord a portion of what his labour either collects or produces. This portion, or, what comes to the same thing, the price of this portion, constitutes the rent of land, and in the price of the greater part of commodities makes a third component part.

<small>The real value of all three parts is measured by labour.</small>   The real value of all the different component parts of price, it must be observed, is measured by the quantity of labour which they can, each of them, purchase or command. Labour measures the value not only of that part of price which resolves itself into labour, but of that which resolves itself into rent, and of that which resolves itself into profit.

<small>In an improved society all three parts are generally present, for example, in corn,</small>   In every society the price of every commodity finally resolves itself into some one or other, or all of those three parts; and in every improved society, all the three enter more or less, as component parts, into the price of the far greater part of commodities.

In the price of corn, for example, one part pays the rent of the landlord, another pays the wages or maintenance of the labourers and labouring cattle① employed in producing it, and the third pays the profit of the farmer. These three parts seem either immediately or ultimately to make up the whole price of corn. A fourth part, it may perhaps be thought, is necessary for replacing the stock of the farmer, or for compensating the wear and tear of his labouring cattle, and other instruments of husbandry. But it must be considered that the price of any instrument of husbandry, such as a labouring horse, is itself made up of the same three parts; the rent of the land upon which he is reared, the labour of tending and rearing him, and the profits of the farmer who advances both the rent of this land, and the wages of this labour. Though the price of the corn, therefore, may pay the price as well as the maintenance of the horse, the whole price still resolves itself either immediately or ultimately into the same three parts of rent, labour,② and profit.

---

① [Smith overlooks the fact that his inclusion of the maintenance of labouring cattle here as a sort of wages requires him to include it in the national income or 'wealth of the nation,' and therefore to reckon the cattle themselves as part of the nation.]

② [The use of 'labour' instead of the more natural 'wages' here is more probably the result of its use five lines higher up than of any feeling of difficulty about the maintenance of cattle.]

有的时代只有人民付出劳动去采集,但土地私有以后不仅出力还要付出代价。劳动者必须把他所生产或所采集的产物的一部分交给地主,所交出这一部分的代价就是土地的地租,它便成为大多数商品价格中的第三个组成部分。

必须清楚的是,这些所有不同部分各自的真实价值由各自所能购买或所能支配的劳动量来衡量。不仅价格中分解成为劳动的那一部分的价值由劳动来衡量,而且分解成为地租和利润的那些部分的价值也由劳动衡量。所有三个部分的真实价值都由劳动量来衡量。

在每一个社会,商品价格归根到底都分解成为三部分或其三者之一。在每一个进步社会,这三者都或多或少地成为绝大部分商品价格的组成部分。每一个进步社会中,这三部分一般都存在。

就拿谷物价格来说。包括了这样三部分:一部分是地主的地租,另一部分是劳动者的工资及耕畜①的维持费,第三部分农场主所得的利润。谷物的全部价格直接或最终由这三部分构成。还有人认为应当有第四部分存在,即农场主资本的抵偿部分,也就是补充耕畜或农具的损耗。但应该看到耕畜或农具的价格本身就由这三部分构成。比如耕马的价格就已经包括了三部分:饲马土地的地租,饲马劳动者的工资,农场主垫付地租和饲马劳动工资的资本的利润。虽然支付耕马的代价及其维持费包含在谷物价格中,但归根到底其全部价格还是直接或最终由地租、劳动②和例如谷物。

---

① 斯密忽略了这样的事实,即在此他将耕畜的维持费作为一种工资成本包含在内,也要求他在国民收入或国民的财富中也包含它,因此将牲畜本身算作国民财富的一部分。

② 这里的表述使用"劳动"而不是更为自然的"工资",很有可能是由于文中提到了影响价格的五点,而用"工资"比较难以说明牲畜维持费。

In the price of flour or meal, we must add to the price of the corn, the profits of the miller, and the wages of his servants; in the price of bread, the profits of the baker, and the wages of his servants; and in the price of both, the labour of transporting the corn from the house of the farmer to that of the miller, and from that of the miller to that of the baker, together with the profits of those who advance the wages of that labour.

The price of flax resolves itself into the same three parts as that of corn. In the price of linen we must add to this price the wages of the flax-dresser, of the spinner, of the weaver, of the bleacher, &c. together with the profits of their respective employers.

As any particular commodity comes to be more manufactured, that part of the price which resolves itself into wages and profit, comes to be greater in proportion to that which resolves itself into rent. In the progress of the manufacture, not only the number of profits increase, but every subsequent profit is greater than the foregoing; because the capital from which it is derived must always be greater. The capital which employs the weavers, for example, must be greater than that which employs the spinners; because it not only replaces that capital with its profits, but pays, besides, the wages of the weavers; and the profits must always bear some proportion to the capital. ①

In the most improved societies, however, there are always a few commodities of which the price resolves itself into two parts only, the wages of labour, and the profits of stock; and a still smaller number, in which it consists altogether in the wages of labour. In the price of sea-fish, for example, one part pays the labour of the fishermen, and the other the profits of the capital employed in the fishery. Rent very seldom makes any part of it, though it does sometimes, as I shall shew hereafter. It is otherwise, at least through the greater part of

---

① [The fact that the later manufacturer has to replace what is here called the capital, i. e., the periodical expenditure of the earlier manufacturer, does not necessarily require him to have a greater capital to deal with the same produce. It need not be greater if he requires less machinery and buildings and a smaller stock of materials.]

利润这三部分组成。

就拿面粉价格来说,它应当包含谷物价格,面粉厂主的利润_{面粉或粗粉,}及其付给雇工的工资;而面包价格,还要加上面包师的利润及其付给雇工的工资。但将谷物从农场主那里运到面粉厂,将面粉从面粉厂运到面包房所需要的劳动垫付,也是需要若干资本的。那么这两种商品中还应包含运送谷物和面粉劳动的工资和垫付工资的资本的利润。

再如亚麻的价格,同样可分为三个组成部分,这跟谷物没有_{和亚麻。}什么不同。除了亚麻布的价格,它还包含亚麻清理工、纺工、织工、漂白工的劳动工资,这些工人各自雇主的利润。

物品越接近于制造的完成阶段,其价格中工资利润部分所占的比例就越发超出地租部分。制造阶段的程度越高,利润的项目越多,由于后一阶段的制造者比前者需要更多资本,相对于前一阶段制造者来说他能获得更多的利润。比如织工的雇用资本就大于纺工的雇用资本。因为,织工的雇用资本中包含了纺工的雇用资本、利润及织工的工资,利润和资本总保持着某种比例。_{在高度加工的商品中,地租的比重较小。}①

不过在最进步社会,也存在只包含劳动工资及资本利润两个部分价格的少数商品,只包含劳动工资的商品也有少量存在。例如,海产鱼类的价格就只由两个部分组成:渔夫劳动的支付,渔业资本利润的支付。有时,在此种价格中也会有地租,但极少见,我以后要说明这一点。欧洲大部分的河上渔业与海上渔业截然两_{在三种组成部分中,商品只有两种,甚至只有一种。}

---

① 事实是后来制造者不得不重置所谓的资本,即早期制造者的定期支出,不一定要求他拥有更多的资本来进行相同的生产。如果他需要更少的机器和建筑,更少的物资储备,那么就不一定需要更多资本了。

Europe; in river fisheries. A salmon fishery pays a rent, and rent, though it cannot well be called the rent of land, makes a part of the price of a salmon as well as wages and profit. In some parts of Scotland a few poor people make a trade of gathering, along the sea-shore, those little variegated stones commonly known by the name of Scotch Pebbles. The price which is paid to them by the stone-cutter is altogether the wages of their labour; neither rent nor profit make any part of it.

<small>But all must have at least one,</small> But the whole price of any commodity must still finally resolve itself into some one or other, or all of those three parts; as whatever part of it remains after paying the rent of the land, and the price of the whole labour employed in raising, manufacturing, and bringing it to market, must necessarily be profit to somebody. ①

<small>and the price of the whole annual produce resolves itself into wages, profits and rent,</small> As the price or exchangeable value of every particular commodity, taken separately, resolves itself into some one or other, or all of those three parts; so that of all the commodities which compose the whole annual produce of the labour of every country, taken complexly, must resolve itself into the same three parts, and be parcelled out among different inhabitants of the country, either as the wages of their labour, the profits of their stock, or the rent of their land. ② The whole of what is annually either collected or produced by the labour of every society, or what comes to the same thing, the whole price of it, is in this manner originally distributed among some of its different members. Wages, profit, and rent, are the three original sources of all revenue as well as of all exchangeable value. All other revenue③ is ultimately derived from some one or other of these.

<small>which are the only original kinds of revenue.</small> Whoever derives his revenue from a fund which is his own, must draw it either from his labour, from his stock, or from his land. The revenue derived from labour is called wages. That derived from stock, by the person who manages or employs it, is called profit. That derived from it by the person who does not employ it himself, but lends it to another, is called the interest or the use of money. It is the compensation which the borrower pays to the lender, for the profit which

---

① [Only true if 'commodity' be understood to include solely goods which constitute income.]

② [The 'whole annual produce' must be taken to mean the income and not the whole mass of goods produced, including those which perish or are used up in the creation of others.]

③ [Some parts of this 'other revenue', *viz.*, interest and taxes, are mentioned in the next paragraph. It is perhaps also intended to include the rent of houses.]

样。欧洲的鲑鱼大体上都要支付地租虽然不能严格地被称为土地地租,但和工资与利润一起成为鲑鱼价格的一部分。苏格兰某些地方的少数穷人在海岸拾集一种苏格兰玛瑙彩色小石子,石匠只是付给他们劳动的工资,其中既不含地租也不含利润。

但是任何一件商品的全部价格,最后仍然是由三个部分或其中之一构成的。总价格减去土地的地租、种植、制造乃至搬运所需要的全部劳动之后剩余的部分就是利润。① <small>所有价格都要包含一部分,但</small>

任何一件商品的价格或交换价值,分开来说,都由三个部分或其中部分构成;从总体上看来,构成一国劳动年产物的商品价格总额,必然由三个部分构成,而且作为劳动工资、土地地租②以及资本利润分配给在国内不同居民。一个社会每年劳动采集或生产的综合,或者说它的全部价格也就是按照这样的三部分在社会不同成员中的某些人中进行分配的。工资、利润和地租,是一切收入和一切可交换价值的三个源泉。所有其他收入③归根到底都是来自这三种收入中的某些部分。<small>全部物价分解为工资、利润、地租,而年产价格也分为工资、利润、地租。</small>

每个人从自己的资源所获得的收入都无非来自他的劳动、资本或土地。来自劳动的收入称为工资。来自管理或运用资本的收入称为利润。自有资本借让他人使用而获得的收入,称为货币的利息或利益。这是借入者付给贷出者的利息报酬,借入者利用借入资金赚取利润。运用借入资金所得的利润,一部分归借用人 <small>这三者是唯一的收入来源。</small>

---

① 只有当商品被理解为仅包含收入的商品时,才是正确的。
② "年产量"是指收入不是生产的所有商品,也包含了用于其他产品生产、消耗在其他产品中的物品。
③ 其他的利润的某些部分,利润和税收在下面一段将被提到。也很可能打算包含房租。

he has an opportunity of making by the use of the money. Part of that profit naturally belongs to the borrower, who runs the risk and takes the trouble of employing it; and part to the lender, who affords him the opportunity of making this profit. The interest of money is always a derivative revenue, which, if it is not paid from the profit which is made by the use of the money, must be paid from some other source of revenue, unless perhaps the borrower is a spendthrift, who contracts a second debt in order to pay the interest of the first. The revenue which proceeds altogether from land, is called rent, and belongs to the landlord. The revenue of the farmer is derived partly from his labour, and partly from his stock. To him, land is only the instrument which enables him to earn the wages of this labour, and to make the profits of this stock. All taxes, and all the revenue which is founded upon them, all salaries, pensions, and annuities of every kind, are ultimately derived from some one or other of those three original sources of revenue, and are paid either immediately or mediately from the wages of labour, the profits of stock, or the rent of land.

<small>They are sometimes confounded,</small>

When those three different sorts of revenue belong to different persons, they are readily distinguished; but when they belong to the same they are sometimes confounded with one another, at least in common language.

<small>for example, a gentleman farmer's rent is called profit,</small>

A gentleman who farms a part of his own estate, after paying the expence of cultivation, should gain both the rent of the landlord and the profit of the farmer. He is apt to denominate, however, his whole gain, profit, and thus confounds rent with profit, at least in common language. The greater part of our North American and West Indian planters are in this situation. They farm, the greater part of them, their own estates, and accordingly we seldom hear of the rent of a plantation, but frequently of its profit.

<small>a common farmer's wages are called profit,</small>

Common farmers seldom employ any overseer to direct the general operations of the farm. They generally too work a gaod deal with their own hands, as ploughmen, harrowers, &c. What remains of the crop after paying the rent, therefore, should not only replace to them their stock employed in cultivation, together with its ordinary profits, but pay them the wages which are due to them, both as labourers and overseers. Whatever remains, however, after paying the rent and keeping up the stock, is called profit. But wages evidently make a part of it. The farmer, by saving these wages, must necessarily gain them. Wages, therefore, are in this ease confounded with profit.

An independent manufacturer, who has stock enough both to purchase materials, and to maintain himself till he can carry his work

作为冒险经营的报酬,另一部分归贷出者,作为给借用人提供获利机会的报酬。利息从来都是一种派生的收入,只要借入者不是借债还债的浪子,那么他偿还利息所用的款项只能是经营借入资金所得的利润或是其他收入的所得。被称为地租的完全来自土地收入的部分属于地主。农场主的收入有来自劳动的一部分,也有来自资本的一部分。他认为土地不过是使他能够借以获得劳动工资和赚取资本利润的工具。一切赋税,一切以赋税,一切源于赋税的收入、养老金和各种年金,最后都是来自这三个部分,都直接间接以劳动工资、资本利润或土地地租的形式分配出去。

当三种不同的收入分属不同的个人时很容易被区分;倘若属于同一个人,就很容易混淆,至少按通常说法是这样的。_{它们有时会混淆,}

一个乡绅自己耕种自有土地时,在支付耕种费用以后,还应当以地主身份获得地租,并以农场主身份获得利润。可是,这两部分往往被他统称为利润,这样地租和利润就被混淆了,至少按通常说法是这样的。在北美和西印度的我国种植园主,很多时自己耕种自有土地,因此,种植园的利润要比种植园的地租被提及得少很多。_{例如,一个乡绅农场主的利润称为地租,}

农场主一般很少雇用人来监督指导农场的日常工作。通常他们自己也参加劳动,例如犁耕、耙土等。所以,他的全部收入在支付地租之后,还包含投入资本的偿还及其利润,以及自己作为劳动者和监工所应得的那部分工资。但是,收回资本和支付地租之后的剩余被统称为利润。很显然其中含有了工资。这样的场合又将工资和利润混淆了。_{一个普通的农场主的被工资称为利润,}

一个独立工作的制造业者所拥有的资本足够多到来购买原材料并维持生活直到其货物上市,那么他就应该获得以下两项收

<small>and so are an independent manufacturer's wages,</small> to market, should gain both the wages of a journeyman who works under a master, and the profit which that master makes by the sale of the journeyman's work. His whole gains, however, are commonly called profit, and wages are, in this case too, confounded with profit.

<small>while the rent and profit of a gardener cultivating his own land are considered earnings of labour.</small> A gardener who cultivates his own garden with his own hands, unites in his own person the three different characters, of landlord, farmer, and labourer. His produce, therefore, should pay him the rent of the first, the profit of the second, and the wages of the third. The whole, however, is commonly considered as the earnings of his labour. Both rent and profit are, in this case, confounded with wages.

<small>A great part of the annual produce goes to the idle; the proportion regulates the increase or diminution of the produce.</small> As in a civilized country there are but few commodities of which the exchangeable value arises from labour only, rent and profit contributing largely to that of the far greater part of them, so the annual produce of its labour will always be sufficient to purchase or command a much greater quantity of labour than what was employed in raising, preparing, and bringing that produce to market. If the society were annually to employ all the labour which it can annually purchase, as the quantity of labour would increase greatly every year, so the produce of every succeeding year would be of vastly greater value than that of the foregoing. But there is no country in which the whole annual produce is employed in maintaining the industrious. The idle every where consume a great part of it; and according to the different proportions in which it is annually divided between those two different orders of people, its ordinary or average value must either annually increase, or diminish, or continue the same from one year to another.

入：一是被老板雇佣的工人的工资；二是老板售卖工人产品后所获得的利润。这两项收益普通也被统称为利润。这样的场合也把工资和利润混淆了。

一个独立的制造业主的工资也是如此，

一个自营花园的园艺者，可以同时被称为地主、农场主或是劳动者。因此他所生产的产品应支付给他地租、农场主自有资金的利润和劳动者的工资。但是通常情况下却把他的全部收入看作他的劳动所得。这样的场合也把地租和利润被混淆了。

自营园艺地利被看作他的劳动所得。利用自己土地的园艺者，租润都是他所

在一个文明国家内，由于交换价值单纯来自劳动的商品极其罕见，绝大部分商品的交换价值都在很大程度地来源于利润和地租，因此社会全部劳动年产物所能购买或支配的劳动总量要比种植、加工和运输生产它们以及投入市场所花费的劳动量大大超出。如果社会每年都全部雇用所能购买的全部劳动量，又因为劳动量将每年都大幅增加，这样的话，次年将生产出比前一年具有更多价值的产物。但是没有这样一个国家，用全部年产物来维持勤劳人民地生活。每个国家都会有一部分游手好闲地阶层来消费勤劳人民地劳动成果。那么，每国年产物的平均价值是每年递增还是每年递减，或是保持不变，关键是要看该国年产物每年分配给这两个不同阶层人民的比例。

年产物的大部分归游手好闲者；这比例决定着产物的增加和减少。

— 125 —

CHAPTER VII
Of the Natural And Market Price Of Commodities[1]

<small>Ordinary or average rates of wages, profit,</small>   There is in every society or neighbourhood an ordinary or average rate both of wages and profit in every different employment of labour and stock. This rate is naturally regulated, as I shall show hereafter,[2] partly by the general circumstances of the society, their riches or poverty, their advancing, stationary, or declining condition; and partly by the particular nature of each employment.

<small>and rent</small>   There is likewise in every society or neighbourhood an ordinary or ayerage rate of rent, which is regulated too, as I shall show hereafter,[3] partly by the general circumstances of the society or neighbourhood in which the land is situated, and partly by the natural or improved fertility of the land.

<small>may be called natural rates,</small>   These ordinary or average rates may be called the natural rates of wages, profit, and rent, at the time and place in which they commonly prevail.

<small>to pay which a commodity is sold at its natural price,</small>   When the price of any commodity is neither more nor less than what is sufficient to pay the rent of the land, the wages of the labour, and the profits of the stock employed in raising, preparing, and bringing it to market, according to their natural rates, the commodity is then sold for what may be called its natural price.

---

   [1]   [The chapter follows *Lectures*, pp. 173-182, very closely.]
   [2]   [Below, chaps. viii. and ix.]
   [3]   [Below, chap. xi.]

第七章　商品的自然价格和市场价格[1]

在所有的社会和其邻近地区,每种用途的劳动和资本对应的工资和利润都有一个普通的或者平均的比率。正如我将在后面所要阐述的,[2]这个比率一部分要受到社会的一般情况,即社会的贫富、进步、停滞或者衰退状况的自然调控,一部分还要受到这些不同用途的具体性质的调控。

同样,正如我将在后面所要阐述的,[3]在所有社会和其邻近地区,也同样存在一个普通的或平均的地租率。这个比率也是一部分要受到土地所处的社会和其邻近地区的一般情况的自然调控,一部分还要受土地自然的肥沃或改良的程度调控。

这些普通的或者平均的比率,可以称作当时当地通行的工资率、利润或者地租自然率。

如果当一种商品所售出的价格恰好可以支付生产、制造这种商品和将商品运往市场所使用的按照其自然率支付的地租、工资和利润,这种商品就可以说是按其自然价格出售的。

---

① 这一章与《关于法律、警察、岁入及军备的演讲》第173~182页关系非常密切。

② 下面,第八章、第九章。

③ 下面,第十一章。

— 127 —

<small>or for what it really costs, which includes profit,</small>

The commodity is then sold precisely for what it is worth, or for what it really costs the person who brings it to market; for though in common language what is called the prime cost of any commodity does not comprehend the profit of the person who is to sell it again, yet if he sells it at a price which does not allow him the ordinary rate of profit in his neighbourhood, he is evidently a loser by the trade; since by employing his stock in some other way he might have made that profit. His profit, besides, is his revenue, the proper fund of his subsistence. As, while he is preparing and bringing the goods to market, he advances to his workmen their wages, or their subsistence; so he advances to himself, in the same manner, his own subsistence, which is generally suitable to the profit which he may reasonably expect from the sale of his goods. Unless they yield him this profit, therefore, they do not repay him what they may very properly be said to have really cost him.

<small>since no one will go on selling without profit.</small>

Though the price, therefore, which leaves him this profit, is not always the lowest at which a dealer may sometimes sell his goods, it is the lowest at which he is likely to sell them for any considerable time; at least where there is perfect liberty, or where he may change his trade as often as he pleases.

<small>Market price</small>

The actual price at which any commodity is commonly sold is called its market price. It may either be above, or below, or exactly the same with its natural price.

The market price of every particular commodity is regulated by the proportion between the quantity which is actually brought to market, <small>is regulated by the quantity brought to market and the effectual demand.</small> and the demand of those who are willing to pay the natural price of the commodity, or the whole value of the rent, labour, and profit, which must be paid in order to bring it thither. Such people may be called the effectual demanders, and their demand the effectual demand; since it may be sufficient to effectuate the bringing of the commodity to market. It is different from the absolute demand. A very poor man may be said in some sense to have a demand for a coach and six; he might like to have it; but his demand is not an effectual demand, as the commodity can never be brought to market in order to satisfy it.

商品这样售出的价格恰好与其价值相等,或者说恰好与出售这种商品实际上所花费的成本相等。尽管按照普通的说法,所谓商品的原始成本并没有包括再次出售这种商品时的利润,但如果他在再次出售时没有得到所在地区一般的利润率,那么他显然在这笔买卖中遭受了损失。原因在于如果他把资本投放在其他地方,就可能获得利润。何况,他的利润就是他的收入,也是他正当的生活资料来源。当制造商品并把它送往市场销售的过程中,他需要预先垫付劳动者的工资或生活资料,同样也要预先垫付他自己的生活费用,这个费用与他可以预期能从销售该商品获得的利润大体相当。所以说,如果没有能够从商品的销售中获得利润,他也就没有能够从这种商品的销售中收回他的实际费用。

按照实际销售这包含了利润,或者说实际销售中含有其成本。

虽然说能够为他提供利润的价格,并不总是一个商人出卖其货物时的最低价格,但长期中这却是他愿意出卖其货物的最低价格。至少在那些绝对自由或者可以随时随意转换行业的地方情况就是这样子的。

没有愿意有时续他商品,因为人没有意愿利润还继续销售的品。

通常商品卖出去的实际价格就叫做它的市场价格。它可能高于、低于或者恰好等于它的自然价格。

市场价格

每种商品的市场价格,都要受到该商品的实际市场供给量和愿意支付商品自然价格的人的需求量,即愿意支付商品进入市场销售必须支付的地租、劳动工资和利润的全部价值的人的需求量之间的比例的调控。其中愿意支付商品的自然价格的人可以称作有效需求者。他们的需求也可以称作有效需求。因为这种需求完全可以让商品的出售出去。这种需求不同于绝对需求。一个很穷的人可能在某种意义上而言有一辆马车和六匹马的需求,但这种需求并不是有效需求。因为不可能有人把这些商品运往

受市场上的商品数量和有效的需求调控。

国民财富的性质与原理

<small>When the quantity brought falls short of the effectual demand, the market price rises above the natural;</small>

When the quantity of any commodity which is brought to market falls short of the effectual demand, all those who are willing to pay the whole value of the rent, wages, and profit, which must be paid in order to bring it thither, cannot be supplied with the quantity which they want. Rather than want it altogether, some of them will be willing to give more. A competition will immediately begin among them, and the market price will rise more or less above the natural price, according as either the greatness of the deficiency, or the wealth and wanton luxury of the competitors, happen to animate more or less the eagerness of the competition. Among competitors of equal wealth and luxury the same deficiency will generally occasion a more or less eager competition, according as the acquisition of the commodity happens to be of more or less importance to them. Hence the exorbitant price of the necessaries of life during the blockade of a town or in a famine.

<small>when it exceeds the effectual demand the market price falls below the natural;</small>

When the quantity brought to market exceeds the effectual demand, it cannot be all sold to those who are willing to pay the whole value of the rent, wages and profit, which must be paid in order to bring it thither. Some part must be sold to those who are willing to pay less, and the low price which they give for it must reduce the price of the whole. The market price will sink more or less below the natural price, according as the greatness of the excess increases more or less the competition of the sellers, or according as it happens to be more or less important to them to get immediately rid of the commodity. The same excess in the importation of perishable, will occasion a much greater competition than in that of durable commodities; in the importation of oranges, for example, than in that of old iron.

<small>when It is just equal to the effectual demand the market and natural price coincide.</small>

When the quantity brought to market is just sufficient to supply the effectual demand and no more, the market price naturally comes to be either exactly, or as nearly as can be juaged of, the same with the natural price. The whole quantity upon hand can be disposed of for this price, and cannot be disposed of for more. The competition of the different dealers obliges them all to accept of this price, but does

市场来满足他的需求。

如果市场上一种商品的供给量少于对这种商品的有效需求，那么并非所有愿意支付将商品送到市场出售所必须支付的地租、劳动工资和利润的全部价值的人都能得到他们需要的数量的商品供给。其中有些人不愿就此罢休，宁愿支付更高的价格。于是就在需求者中间产生了竞争。这样市场价格就会或多或少地高于自然价格，价格高于的程度要视商品的缺乏程度和竞争者富有程度和奢侈程度所导致的竞争激烈程度的大小而定。但如果竞争者同样富有和同样奢侈，商品缺乏所导致的竞争激烈程度就要看商品对于竞争者的重要性大小了。所以，当城市遭到封锁或者发生饥荒时，生活必需品的价格都是特别的高。

而当市场上一种商品的供给量超过了这种商品的有效需求，这种商品就不是全部都能出售给那些愿意支付将商品送到市场出售所必须支付的地租、劳动工资和利润的全部价值的人。其中一部分商品不得不卖给出价较低的人，这个较低的价格必然也会使整个商品的价格降低。这样市场价格就会或多或少地降到低于自然价格，下降的程度要视超出需求的部分加剧卖方竞争的程度，或者说要视卖方急于将商品卖出的程度而定。如果超过需求的程度相同，那么那些比较容易腐败的商品就要比耐用性商品所引发的竞争激烈得多。例如，柑橘过多就要比旧铁过多引发更大的卖方竞争。

如果市场上这种商品的供给量恰好等于这种商品的有效需求时，市场价格就会自然而然地和自然价格相等，或者基本相等同。这样，手头的所有商品都可以以这个自然价格出售，但无法取得更高的价格。不同商人之间的竞争就使得他们都不得不接

not oblige them to accept of less.

<small>It naturally suits itself to the effectual demand.</small> The quantity of every commodity brought to market naturally suits itself to the effectual demand. It is the interest of all those who employ their land, labour, or stock, in bringing any commodity to market, that the quantity never should exceed the effectual demand; and it is the interest of all other people that it never should fall short of that demand.

<small>When it exceeds that demand, some of the component parts of its price are below their natural rate;</small> If at any time it exceeds the effectual demand, some of the component parts of its price must be paid below their natural rate. If it is rent, the interest of the landlords will immediately prompt them to withdraw a part of their land; and if it is wages or profit, the interest of the labourers in the one case, and of their employers in the other, will prompt them to withdraw a part of their labour or stock from this employment. The quantity brought to market will soon be no more than sufficient to supply the effectual demand. All the different parts of its price will rise to their natural rate, and the whole price to its natural price.

<small>when it falls short, some of the component parts are above their natural rate.</small> If, on the contrary, the quantity brought to market should at any time fall short of the effectual demand, some of the component parts of its price must rise above their natural rate. If it is rent, the interest of all other landlords will naturally prompt them to prepare more land for the raising of this commodity; if it is wages or profit, the interest of all other labourers and dealers will soon prompt them to employ more labour and stock in preparing and bringing it to market. The quantity brought thither will soon be sufficient to supply the effectual demand. All the different parts of its price will soon sink to their natural rate, and the whole price to its natural price.

<small>Natural price is the central price to which actual prices gravitate.</small> The natural price, therefore, is, as it were, the central price, to which the prices of all commodities are continually gravitating. Different accidents may sometimes keep them suspended a good deal above it, and sometimes force them down even somewhat below it. But whatever may be the obstacles which hinder them from settling in this center

受这个价格,但也使他们不能接受更低的价格。

每种商品进入市场的数量自然会使自己适应于有效需求。这是因为,市场商品数量不超过有效需求是所有将商品送到市场出售支付地租、劳动工资和利润的商人的共同利益;而市场商品数量不少于有效需求则是其他所有人的共同利益。

如果某个时候市场上商品数量超过了有效需求,那么它的价格的某些组成部分就必然会降到自然率以下。如果那部分为地租,地主的利益很快就会使得他们撤回一部分土地;如果下降部分为工资或利润,劳动者或者雇主的利益也会很快使得他们把劳动或资本从这种用途中撤回一部分劳动或资本。这样,市场上商品数量很快就会恰好等于商品的有效需求,价格中所有的组成部分也很快就会都升到它们各自的自然水平,而整个价格也又升回自然价格。

与之相反,如果某个时候市场上商品数量少于它的有效需求时,那么它的价格的某些组成部分就必然会上升到自然率以上。如果那部分为地租,地主的利益就会自然地促使他们准备更多土地来生产这种商品;如果那部分是工资或利润,那么与之有利益关系的劳动者或者商人也会很快就使用更多的劳动或资本来制造这种商品并将其送往市场销售。这样,市场上商品数量很快就足以供应它的有效需求了,价格中所有组成部分很快就下降到它们的自然水平,而整个价格也又回到了自然价格。

这样,自然价格就可以说是中心价格,所有商品的价格都不断地受其吸引。尽管各种偶然事件有时候会将商品价格抬高到中心价格以上,有时候会迫使商品价格降低到中心价格以下。所以,不管有什么样的障碍会阻碍商品价格固定在这个静止、持续

of repose and continuance, they are constantly tending towards it.

<small>Industry suits itself to the effectual demand.</small> The whole quantity of industry annually employed in order to bring any commodity to market, naturally suits itself in this manner to the effectual demand. It naturally aims at bringing always that precise quantity thither which may be sufficient to supply, and no more than supply, that demand.

<small>but the quantity produced by a given amount of industry sometimes fluctuates.</small> But in some employments the same quantity of industry will in different years produce very different quantities of commodities; while in others it will produce always the same, or very nearly the same. The same number of labourers in husbandry will, in different years, produce very different quantities of corn, wine, oil, hops, &c. But the same number of spinners and weavers will every year produce the same or very nearly the same quantity of linen and woollen cloth. It is only the average produce of the one species of industry which can be suited in any respect to the effectual demand; and as its actual produce is frequently much greater and frequently much less than its average produce, the quantity of the commodities brought to market will sometimes exceed a good deal, and sometimes fall short a good deal, of the effectual demand. Even though that demand therefore should continue always the same, their market price will be liable to great fluctuations, will sometimes fall a good deal below, and sometimes rise a good deal above, their natural price. In the other species of industry, the produce of equal quantities of labour being always the same, or very nearly the same, it can be more exactly suited to the effectual demand. While that demand continues the same, therefore, the market price of the commodities is likely to do so too, and to be either altogether, or as nearly as can be judged of, the same with the natural price. That the price of linen and woollen cloth is liable neither to such frequent nor to such great variations as the price of corn, every man's experience will inform him. The price of the one species of commodities varies only with the variations in the demand: That of the other varies not only with the variations in the demand, but with the much greater and more frequent variations in the quantity of what is brought to market in order to supply that demand.

The occasional and temporary fluctuations in the market price of any commodity fall chiefly upon those parts of its price which resolve themselves into wages and profit. That part which resolves itself into rent is less affected by them. A rent certain in money is not in the least

的中心价格,但商品价格却总是经常地趋向这个中心。

为了使一种商品上市,每年投入的全部劳动量自然也会按照这个方式自动适应于有效需求。其目的自然在于总是能为市场提供足够而又不过多的供给量,以满足有效需求。

<small>劳动自动适应于有效需求</small>

然而,同样的劳动量,在有些行业中在不同的年度中会生产出大不相同的商品量,而在有些行业中的生产量却常常相等或者几乎相等。例如在农业中,同样数量的劳动者在不同的年度中生产出来的谷物、葡萄酒、油、蛇麻花等商品数量非常不同;但同样数量的纺工和织工每年生产出来的麻布和呢绒数量就相等或者几乎相等。对于有的行业,只有它的平均产量才在各个方面适应有效需求。但实际产量比起平均产量却有时大得多、有时小得多,所以市场上商品供给量有时远远超过有效需求,有时又远远小于有效需求。所以即便有效需求能保持不变,商品的市场价格也仍然会发生变动,有时远远高于自然价格,有时又远远低于自然价格。而对于其他一些行业说,由于同样的劳动量的产量总是相等或者几乎相等,所以它的产量也更能准确地适应有效需求。在有效需求保持不变时,商品的市场价格也保持不变,和自然价格完全相等或者大致接近相等。每个人的经验都告诉我们,麻布和呢绒的价格不像谷物那样经常发生变动,价格变化幅度也没有谷物那样大。麻布和呢绒的价格只随需求的变动而变动,但谷物的价格不仅随着需求的变动而变动,还随着上市的商品供给量的多少而发生更大、更频繁的变动。

<small>但一定量的劳动的产量有时会发生变动</small>

商品市场价格的偶然的和暂时的变动,主要是影响价格中的工资和利润,而对地租则没有太大的影响。对于用货币来确定的地租,无论其比率还是价值,都不受变动的影响。对于以自然产

| 国民财富的性质与原理

The fluctuations fall on wages and profit more than on rent, affected by them either in its rate or in its value. A rent which consists either in a certain proportion or in a certain quantity of the rude produce, is no doubt affected in its yearly value by all the occasional and temporary fluctuations in the market price of that rude produce; but it is seldom affected by them in its yearly rate. In settling the terms of the lease, the landlord and farmer endeavour, according to their best judgment, to adjust that rate, not to the temporary and occasional, but to the average and ordinary price of the produce.

affecting them in different proportions according to the supply of commodities and labour. Such fluctuations affect both the value and the rate either of wages or of profit, according as the market happens to be either over-stocked or under-stocked with commodities or with labour; with work done, or with work to be done. A public mourning raises the price of black cloth (with which the market is almost always under-stocked upon such occasions), and augments the profits of the merchants who possess any considerable quantity of it. It has no effect upon the wages of the weavers. The market is under-stocked with commodities, not with labour; with work done, not with work to be done. It raises the wages of journeymen taylors. The market is here under-stocked with labour. There is an effectual demand for more labour, for more work to be done than can be had. It sinks the price of coloured silks and cloths, and thereby reduces the profits of the merchants who have any considerable quantity of them upon hand. It sinks too the wages of the workmen employed in preparing such commodities, for which all demand is stopped for six months, perhaps for a twelvemonth. The market is here over-stocked both with commodities and with labour.

But market price may be kept above natural for a long time, But though the market price of every particular commodity is in this manner continually gravitating, if one may say so, towards the natural price, yet sometimes particular accidents, sometimes natural causes, and sometimes particular regulations of police, may, in many commodities, keep up the market price, for a long time together, a good deal above the natural price.

in consequence of want of general knowledge of high profits, When by an increase in the effectual demand, the market price of some particular commodity happens to rise a good deal above the natural price, those who employ their stocks in supplying that market are generally careful to conceal this change. If it was commonly known, their great profit would tempt so many new rivals to employ their stocks in the same way, that, the effectual demand being fully

物的一定比例或者一定数量来确定的地租,其每年的价值会受到变动的影响,但比率却不受影响。在商量租佃条约时,地主和农夫都可能根据自己的判断,尽量使地租的比率适应生产物的平均价格或者普通价格,而不是去适应那些暂时的偶然的价格。

这些偶然和暂时的变动对于工资和利润价值与比率的影响,要根据市场上商品或劳动力的积存过多还是不足,现有制产品或尚待完成的产品过多还是不足的情况而定。在国丧时,由于黑布库存常常总是不足,所以黑布市场价格就会上涨,持有大量黑布的商人的利润也就增加了。但是,仅仅是商人的利润增加了,它对织布工人的工资却没有任何影响。原因在于此时市场上库存不足的是商品,而不是劳动。库存不足的是已有的制成品,而不是尚未完成的产品。不过国丧会提高裁缝的工资。因为此时这种劳动力不足,有对更多的劳动力、更多需要完成的工作的有效需求。国丧会降低彩色丝绸和棉布的价格,也会降低持有大量这些商品的商人的利润和生产这些商品的劳动者的工资。因为对于这些商品的需求会停止6个月或者12个月。于是,这类商品和这类劳动都过剩了。

尽管可以说所有商品的市场价格都会不断地趋向自然价格,但有时因为某些意外事件,有时因为自然的原因,有时因为特殊的政策法规,商品的市场价格可能会在很长时间内远远超出自然价格水平。

当由于某种商品的有效需求增加,商场价格高出自然价格很多时,拥有这种商品库存的供给者一般都会小心翼翼地隐瞒这种变化。因为如果被人知道的话,他们巨额的利润就会吸引许多新的竞争者涌向这边进行投资。如此一来有效需求就会得到充分

	supplied, the market price would soon be reduced to the natural price, and perhaps for some time even below it. If the market is at a great distance from the residence of those who supply it, they may sometimes be able to keep the secret for several years together, and may so long enjoy their extraordinary profits without any new rivals. Secrets of this kind, however, it must be acknowledged, can seldom be long kept; and the extraordinary profit can last very little longer than they are kept.
or in consequence of secrets in manufactures,	Secrets in manufactures are capable of being longer kept than secrets in trade. A dyer who has found the means of producing a particular colour with materials which cost only half the price of those commonly made use of, may, with good management, enjoy the advantage of his discovery as long as he lives, and even leave it as a legacy to his posterity. His extraordinary gains arise from the high price which is paid for his private labour. They properly consist in the high wages of that labour. But as they are repeated upon every part of his stock, and as their whole amount bears, upon that account. a regular proportion to it, they are commonly considered as extraordinary profits of stock. ①
which may operate for long periods,	Such enhancements of the market price are evidently the effects of particular accidents, of which, however, the operation may sometimes last for many years together.
or in consequence of scarcity of peculiar soils,	Some natural productions require such a singularity of soil and situation, that all the land in a great country, which is fit for producing them, may not be sufficient to supply the effectual demand. The whole quantity brought to market, therefore, may be disposed of to those who are willing to give more than what is sufficient to pay the rent of the land which produced them, together with the wages of the labour, and the profits of the stock which were employed in preparing and bringing them to market, according to their natural rates. Such commodities may continue for whole centuries together to be sold at

---

① [They are called profits simply because all the gains of the master-manufacturer are called profits. They can scarcely be said to have been 'considered' at all; if they had been they would doubtless have been pronounced to be, in the words of the next paragraph ' the effects of a particular accicent,' namely, the possession of peculiar knowledge on the part of the dyer.]

的满足,商品的市场价格很快就会降低到自然价格,甚至还可能会降低到自然价格以下。如果这些供给者离市场很远,他们有时就可以保守秘密好几年,在此期间他们就可以独享这种超额利润。然而,必须承认很少能长期保守这种秘密,而那些秘密一旦泄露,也就不能长期保守超额利润了。

制造业中的秘密比商业中的秘密能够保守得久一些。如果一个染匠发明了一种制造染料的方法,使他所用材料的费用仅仅是通常方法所用费用的一半,如果他处理得当,就可以终生享受这种发明的好处,甚至可以将其传给子孙后代。这种超额获利可以对他个人劳动支付的高价钱,所以可适当地说是他个人劳动的高工资,但同时因为他资本的每一部分都一再获得这种超额所得,且其超额所得总额与其资本保持一定比例,所以这种超额所得一般都被认为是资本的超额利润。①

或者是因为制造业秘密的原因,

显然是由于某些特殊意外的事件,抬高了市场价格,不过有时这种作用可能会持续很多年。

能长期起作用,它会

有些自然产物的生长需要特定的土壤和特定的地理位置,所以在一个大国中那些适于生产这些产物的全部土地利用起来都可能无法满足有效需求。故此,这种自然产物的全部上市产品量可能只能售给那些愿意支付超过生产所用的地租、制造和送往市场销售的劳动自然率工资和资本自然率利润价格的人。这种商品可能会连续好几个世纪都能按这样高的价格出售,其价格中

或者是因为土地稀有特殊性,

---

① 他们被称为是利润仅仅是因为主要制造者的所有收入都被称为利润。据说他们根本很少被考虑到;如果被考虑到的话,无疑他们将会在下面一段的文字("一个特定事件的影响")中谈及,即织工掌握的专用技能。

this high price; and that part of it which resolves itself into the rent of land is in this case the part which is generally paid above its natural rate. The rent of the land which affords such singular and esteemed productions, like the rent of some vineyards in France of a peculiarly happy soil and situation, bears no regular proportion to the rent of other equally fertile and equally well-cultivated land in its neighbourhood. The wages of the labour and the profits of the stock employed in bringing such commodities to market, on the contrary, are seldom out. of their natural proportion to those of the other employments of labour and stock in their neighbourhood.

<small>which may continue for ever.</small> Such enhancements of the market price are evidently the effect of natural causes which may hinder the effectual demand from ever being fully supplied, and which may continue, therefore, to operate for ever.

<small>A monopoly has the same effect as a trade secret,</small> A monopoly granted either to an individual or to a trading company has the same effect as a secret in trade or manufactures. The monopolists, by keeping the market constantly under-stocked, by never fully supplying the effectual demand, sell their commodities much above the natural price, and raise their emoluments, whether they consist in wages or profit, greatly above their natural rate.

<small>the price of monopoly being the highest which can be got.</small> The price of monopoly is upon every occasion the highest which can be got. The natural price, or the price of free competition, on the contrary, is the lowest which can be taken, not upon every occasion indeed, but for any considerable time together. The one is upon every occasion the highest which can be squeezed out of the buyers, or which, it is supposed, they will consent to give: The other is the lowest which the sellers can commonly afford to take, and at the same time continue their business.

The exclusive privileges of corporations, statutes of apprenticeship,① and all those laws which restrain, in particular employments,

---

① [Playfair in a note on this passage ed. *Wealth of Nations*, 1805, vol. i., p. 97 says: 'This observation about corporations and apprenticeships scarcely applies at all to the present day. In London, for example, the freemen only can carry on certain businesses within the city: there is not one of those businesses that may not be carried on elsewhere, and the produce sold in the city. If Mr. Smith's principle applied, goods would be dearer in Cheapside than in Bond Street, which is not the case.']

地租部分通常也会获得超过按自然率计算的地租。就像法国的某些具有优良土壤和地理位置的葡萄园的地租一样,生产这些独特珍贵产物的土地的地租与其周围同样肥沃和同样精耕细作的土地的地租并没有任何经常固定的比例。而与之相反,那些将商品运往市场予以销售的劳动工资和资本利润,却和周围地区的劳动工资和资本利润往往保持着一种自然的比例。

因为这种情况造成的市场价格提高,显然是因为自然的缘故。这种原因就造成有效需求无法得到充分的供给,它的作用也就因此而永远地保持下去。

> 它可能永远地保持下去。

让个人或者商业公司获得垄断权,它的效果就如商业或者制造业掌握了秘密一样。垄断者经常通过让市场存货不足,从而使有效需求永远无法满足。这样一来,他们就可以按照远远超过自然价格的市场价格出售他们的商品,这样无论是工资或是利润,他们都可以获得远远超过自然率的报酬。

> 垄断的效果就如商业秘密一样。

无论任何时候,垄断价格都是它所能获得的最高价格。而与之相反,自然价格或者自由竞争的价格,虽然未必每个时期都是如此,但在长期中却是有可能的最低价格。无论任何时候垄断价格都是向购买者所能索取到的最高价格,或者是设想中购买者所同意支付的最高价格,而自然价格或者自由竞争的价格,却通常是出售者所能接受的最低价格,也是他们愿意继续营业的最低价格。

> 垄断价格是所能获得的最高价格。

行业组织的排他特权、学徒法规[①]和所有其他那些限制某

---

① 普雷法尔在《国民财富》(1805)第1卷第97页该段的注解中这样说道:"对学徒和公司的观察很少在当今应用。例如在伦敦,自由人仅仅能在城市之内进行商业活动,其他商业活动不能在此之外进行,并且产品只能在市内销售。如果斯密的原则适用,吉普赛街(位于伦敦)的商品要比在邦德街的昂贵。"

| 国民财富的性质与原理

Corporation privileges, etc. are enlarged monopolies. the competition to a smaller number than might otherwise go into them, have the same tendency, though in a less degree. They are a sort of enlarged monopolies, and may frequently, for ages together, and in whole classes of employments, keep up the market price of particular commodities above the natural price, and maintain both the wages of the labour and the profits of the stock employed about them somewhat above their natural rate.

Such enhancements of the market price may last as long as the regulations of police which give occasion to them.

Market price is seldom long below natural price. The market price of any particular commodity, though it may continue long above, can seldom continue long below, its natural price. Whatever part of it was paid below the natural rate, the persons whose interest it affected would immediately feel the loss, and would immediately withdraw either so much land, or so much labour, or so much stock, from being employed about it, that the quantity brought to market would soon be no more than sufficient to supply the effectual demand. Its market price, therefore, would soon rise to the natural price. This at least would be the case where there was perfect liberty.

though apprenticeship and corporation laws sometimes reduce wages much below the natural rate for a certain period. The same statutes of apprenticeship and other corporation laws indeed, which, when a manufacture is in prosperity, enable the workman to raise his wages a good deal above their natural rate, sometimes oblige him, when it decays, to let them down a good deal below it. As in the one case they exclude many people from his employment, so in the other they exclude him from many employments. The effect of such regulations, however, is not near so durable in sinking the workman's wages below, as in raising them above, their natural rate. Their operation in the one way may endure for many centuries, but in the other it can last no longer than the lives of some of the workmen who were bred to the business in the time of its prosperity. When they are gone, the number of those who are afterwards educated to the trade will naturally suit itself to the effectual demand.

一行业竞争人数从而使有些愿意参与竞争的人无法参与竞争的各种法规,尽管在程度上稍差一点,但却与垄断有着相同的倾向。它们是一种扩大了的垄断,他们常常甚至数年可以使一些行业里的某些商品的市场价格保持在自然价格之上,使得行业的劳动工资和资本利润维持在略高于自然率的水平上。

只要造成这种情况的法规存在着,因此而造成的市场价格提高可能就会长期地持续下去。

任何一种商品的市场价格可能会长期地超过自然价格,但却不会长期地低于自然价格。原因在于如果价格中哪一组成部分低于了自然率,利益受到影响的人立即就会感觉到损失,他们就会立即从这上面投入的土地、劳动或者资本中撤回一部分,从而使得进入市场的商品量恰好仅够满足有效需求。因此这样很快使市场价格就又回升到自然价格。至少在那些有完全自由的地方情况就是如此。

尽管在制造业繁荣时,学徒法和其他各种法规可以将劳动者的工资抬高到自然率之上,但当制造业衰落时,却也会使得劳动者的工资降低到自然率之下。因为在前种情况下,这些法规会限制别人进入该行业,而在后种情况下,又会限制他们进入别的行业。不过,这些法规对于降低劳动者工资所起的作用却没有提高劳动者工资所起的作用那样持久。这些法规在前种情况下所起的作用可能会持续几百年,而后种情况下法规所起的作用仅限于那些在行业兴旺时接受培训的劳动者的有生之年。在他们过世以后,学习这个行业的劳动者人数就会自动地适应了有效需求。

The police must be as violent as that of Indostan or antient Egypt①(where every man was bound by a principle of religion to follow the occupation of his father, and was supposed to commit the most horrid sacrilege if he changed it for another), which can in any particular employment, and for several generations together, sink either the wages of labour or the profits of stock below their natural rate.

This is all that I think necessary to be observed at present concerning the deviations, whether occasional or permanent, of the market price of commodities from the natural price.

<small>Natural price varies with the natural rate of wages, profit and rent.</small> The natural price itself varies with the natural rate of each of its component parts, of wages, profit, and rent; and in every society this rate varies according to their circumstances, according to their riches or poverty, their advancing, stationary, or declining condition. I shall, in the four following chapters, endeavour to explain, as fully and distinctly as I can, the causes of those different variations.

<small>Wages will be dealt with in chapter viii., profit in chapter ix.,</small> First, I shall endeavour to explain what are the circumstances which naturally determine the rate of wages, and in what manner those circumstances are affected by the riches or poverty, by the advancing, stationary, or declining state of the society.

Secondly, I shall endeavour to show what are the circumstances which naturally determine the rate of profit, and in what manner too those circumstances are affected by the like variations in the state of the society.

<small>differences of wages and profit in chapter x.,</small> Though pecuniary wages and profit are very different in the different employments of labour and stock; yet a certain proportion seems commonly to take place between both the pecuniary wages in all the different employments of labour, and the pecuniary profits in all the different employments of stock. This proportion, it will appear hereafter, depends partly upon the nature of the different employments, and partly upon the different laws and policy of the society in which they are carried on. But though in many respects dependent upon the laws and policy, this proportion seems to be little affected by the riches or poverty of that society; by its advancing, stationary, or declining condition; but to remain the same or very nearly the same in all those different states. I shall, in the third place, endeavour to explain all the different circumstances which regulate this proportion.

<small>and rent in chapter xi.</small> In the fourth and last place, I shall endeavour to show what are the circumstances which regulate the rent of land, and which either raise or lower the real price of all the different substances which it produces.

---

① [In *Lectures*, p. 168, the Egyptian practice is attributed to 'a law of Sesostris'.]

只有在印度和古埃及,①根据教规那里的人们必须子承父业,如果他们变更职业的话就会被认为犯了最可怕的亵渎神灵之罪,只有这种情况下才可以使得长达几代之中一个行业的劳动工资和资本利润长期维持在自然率以下。

我想我所要说的关于商品的市场价格偶然的或者长期的偏离自然价格也就仅此而已了。

自然价格本身会随着其组成部分:工资、利润和地租的自然率的变动而变动。而在每一个社会中,这种自然率又会随着社会的状况即社会的贫富、进步、衰退或者停滞的变动而变动。我将在接下来的四章里尽我所能地阐述造成这些变动的原因。自然价格会随着工资、利润和地租的自然率的变动而变动,

第一,我想尽力说明的是,什么情况在自然地决定着工资率,而这些情况又是怎样地受社会的贫富、进步、衰退或停滞的影响。在第八章中讨论工资,

第二,我想尽力说明,什么情况在自然地决定着利润率,而这些情况又是如何地受社会中类似变动的影响。在第九章中讨论利润,

第三,尽管应用于不同用途的货币工资和货币利润会差异很大,但这些不同用途的劳动的货币工资和资本的货币利润却似乎存在着一定的比例。在后章中将会看到,这个比例部分取决于这些不同用途的性质,部分取决于所处社会的不同法律和政策。但这个比例似乎并不受所在社会贫富、进步、衰退或停滞等状况的影响,而在所有这些不同的社会状况中比例都保持不变或者几乎保持不变。我将尽力说明调节该比例的所有不同的情况。第十章讨论工资和利润的差别,

第四,我将尽力说明,什么情况支配着土地的地租,什么情况提高或者降低土地的不同生产物的实际价格。第十一章讨论地租。

---

① 在《关于法律、警察、岁入及军备的演讲》第 168 页中,埃及人如此要归因于他们国家的 Sesostris 法。

— 145 —

CHAPTER VIII
Of The Wages Of Labour

<small>Produce is the natural wages of labour. O-riginally the whole belonged to the labourer.</small>   The produce of labour constitutes the natural recompence or wages of labour.

In that original state of things, which precedes both the appropriation of land and the accumulation of stock, the whole produce of labour belongs to the labourer. He has neither landlord nor master to share with him.

<small>If this had continued, all things would have become cheaper,</small>   Had this state continued, the wages of labour would have augmented with all those improvements in its productive powers, to which the division of labour gives occasion. All things would gradually have become cheaper. ① They would have been produced by a smaller quantity of labour; and as the commodities produced by equal quantities of labour would naturally in this state of things be exchanged for one another, they would have been purchased likewise with the produce of a smaller quantity.

<small>though in appearance many things might have become dearer.</small>   But though all things would have become cheaper in reality, in appearance many things might have become dearer than before, or have been exchanged for a greater quantity of other goods. ② Let us suppose, for example, that in the greater part of employments the productive powers of labour had been improved to tenfold, or that a day's labour could produce ten times the quantity of work which it had done originally; but that in a particular employment they had been

---

① [The word 'cheaper' is defined by the next sentence as 'produced by a smaller quantity of labour'.]

② [It would be less confusing if the sentence ran: 'But though all things would have become cheaper in the sense just attributed to the word, yet in the sense in which the words cheaper and dearer are ordinarily used many things might have become dearer than before.']

— 146 —

第八章 劳动工资论

劳动的生产物构成劳动的自我回报或自然工资。

在土地私有和资本累积尚未发生的原始社会状态下,劳动的全部产物归属劳动者所有,没有地主和雇主来同他分享。

这种状态如果继续下去,劳动工资将会随着分工所引起的劳动生产力的改进而提高。而一切物品也将日渐低廉。① 用较小的劳动量就能将它们生产出来。由于等量劳动所生产的不同商品可以互相交换,因此,在这种状态下,要购买各种商品,都是只需较少劳动量的生产物。

不过一切物品,尽管实际上变得低廉些,但表面上却有一些物品变得比以前昂贵。即可以交换更多数量的其他物品。② 如果假定大多数产业的劳动生产力增加 10 倍,或者说现今一天劳动的生产量是以前一天的劳动量的 10 倍;而某一种产业的劳动生产力却只增加一倍,即该产业现今一天劳动的生产量只是两倍于以前一天的劳动生产量。在这场合,如果以这大多数产业一天的

---

① "低廉"即下文的"用较小的劳动量就能将它们生产出来"。

② 如果这句话换个说法的话,就能使人更清楚一些:"不过尽管所有物品因为字面上变得更便宜一些,然而在这些字面上更便宜和更昂贵但经常被用到的东西却可能比以前更昂贵一些。"

improved only to double, or that a day's labour could produce only twice the quantity of work which it had done before. In exchanging the produce of a day's labour in the greater part of employments, for that of a day's labour in this particular one, ten times the original quantity of work in them would purchase only twice the original quantity in it. Any particular quantity in it, therefore, a pound weight, for example, would appear to be five times dearer than before. ① In reality, ② however, it would be twice as cheap. Though it required five times the quantity of other goods to purchase it, it would require only half the quantity of labour either to purchase or to produce it. The acquisition, therefore, would be twice as easy③ as before.

<small>This state was ended by the appropriation of land and accumulation of stock,</small>

But this original state of things, in which the labourer enjoyed the whole produce of his own labour, could not last beyond the first introduction of the appropriation of land and the accumulation of stock. It was at an end, therefore, long before the most considerable improvements were made in the productive powers of labour, and it would be to no purpose to trace further what might have been its effects upon the recompense or wages of labour.

<small>rent being the first deduction,</small>

As soon as land becomes private property, the landlord demands a shale of almost all the produce which the labourer can either raise, or collect from it. His rent makes the first deduction from the produce of the labour which is employed upon land.

<small>and profit the second, both in agriculture, and other arts and manufactures.</small>

It seldom happens that the person who tills the ground has wherewithal to maintain himself till he reaps the harvest. His maintenance is generally advanced to him from the stock of a master, the farmer who employs him, and who would have no interest to employ him, unless he was to share in the produce of his labour, or unless his stock was to be replaced to him with a profit. This profit makes a second deduction from the produce of the labour which is employed upon land.

The produce of almost all other labour is liable to the like deduc-

---

① [I. e., 'would in the ordinary, sense of the word be five times dearer than before'.]

② [I. e., 'in the sense attributed to the word above'.]

③ [If the amount of labour necessary for the acquisition of a thing measures its value, 'twice as cheap' means simply, twice as easy to acquire.]

劳动生产物,与这一产业一天的劳动生产物相交换,那么前者以原工作量的 10 倍,仅能购入后者原工作量的 2 倍。因此,这样看上去,后者的任何数量,以一磅为例,就似乎要比以前贵 5 倍。①但事实上②却是比以前便宜了 1/2。因为尽管购买这一磅物品所需的其他物品量五倍于以前,但生产或购买这一磅货物所需的劳动量却仅等于以前的二分之一。所以,获得此物会比以前容易③了一半。

但这种原始状态,即劳动者独享全部劳动生产物的状态,只持续到有了土地私有和资本累积,就宣告结束了。所以,在劳动生产力有更大的改善之前,这种原始状态就已经不复存在了。要就此对劳动回报或劳动工资所可能有的影响作进一步的探讨,那将是毫无意义的。

原始状态,在私有土地和资本累积之后就终止了。

一旦土地成为了私有财产,地主就向劳动者从土地生产出来或采集到的几乎全部物品索取一份。因此,地主的地租便成了花在土地上的劳动的产物的第一次扣除。

首先应扣除地租,

一般的种田人大都没有能维持自己的生活到收获时的资料。他们的生活费用通常是由雇用他们的农场主从他的资本中垫付的。除非他能分享这些劳动者的劳动的产物,换言之,除非他在收回资本时能得到利润,否则他就不会去雇用劳动者。由此,利润便成为了要从花在土地上的劳动的产物的第二次扣除。

其次应扣除利润,在农业中如此,

其实,不仅是在农业生产物中,一切其他劳动的产物也都要

---

① 也就是说通常意义上比五倍更昂贵一些。
② 也就是说这个意义归因于上面的文字。
③ 如果获得一个物有所值的东西必然需要花费一定的劳动数量,则"便宜了一半"仅仅意味着获得此物比以前容易了一半。

— 149 —

tion of profit. In all arts and manufactures the greater part of the workmen stand in need of a master to advance them the materials of their work, and their wages and maintenance till it be compleated. ① He shares in the produce of their labour, or in the value which it adds to the materials upon which it is bestowed; and in this share consists his profit.

<small>The independent workman gets profits as well as wages,</small>

It sometimes happens, indeed, that a single independent workman has stock sufficient both to purchase the materials of his work, and to maintain himself till it be compleated. He is both master and workman, and enjoys the whole produce of his own labour, or the whole value which it adds to the materials upon which it is bestowed. It includes what are usually two distinct revenues, belonging to two distinct persons, the profits of stock, and the wages of labour.

<small>but this case is infrequent.</small>

Such cases, however, are not very frequent, and in every part of Europe, twenty workmen serve under a master for one that is independent; and the wages of labour are every where understood to be, what they usually are, when the labourer is one person, and the owner of the stock which employs him another.

<small>Wages depend on contract between masters and workmen.</small>

What are the common wages of labour, depends every where upon the contract usually made between those two parties, whose interests are by no means the same. The workmen desire to get as much, the masters to give as little as possible. The former are disposed to combine in order to raise, the latter in order to lower the wages of labour.

<small>The masters have the advantage,</small>

It is not, however, difficult to foresee which of the two parties must, upon all ordinary occasions, have the advantage in the dispute, and force the other into a compliance with their terms. The masters, being fewer in number, can combine much more easily; and the law, besides, authorises, or at least does not prohibit their combinations, while it prohibits those of the workmen. We have no acts of parliament against combining to lower the price of work; but many against combining to raise it. In all such disputes the masters can hold out much longer. A landlord, a farmer, a master manufacturer, or

---

① [The provision of tools to work with and buildings to work in is forgotten.]

扣除利润。在一切的工艺和制造业中,大部分的劳动者在工作完成以前都需要有一个雇主为他们垫付工资,提供原材料和支付生活费。① 而雇主则分享他们的劳动产物。也就是分享劳动使原材料所增加的那部分价值;这一分享的份额便构成雇主的利润。

当然,一个独立工作的工人有时候也有足够的资本,来自行购买原材料和维持自己的生活,一直到工作完成。他兼有劳动者和雇主的双重身份,享有自己全部劳动的产物。即享有自身劳动所附加在原材料上的全部价值。于是他的所得包含了通常归两种不同身份的人所有的两种不同的收入——资本利润与劳动工资。

不过这种情况也并不多见。在欧洲,这种比例是20∶1,也就是在雇主下面工作的工人有20个,独立工作的工人才有一个。而劳动工资一般被理解为:在劳动者为一方而雇用他的资本所有者为另一方情况下,劳动所获得的工资。

通常情况下所说的劳动工资,一般取决于劳资两方所订立的合同;而这两方的利益关系是不一致的。劳动者希望得到的尽可能多,雇主则希望给予的尽可能少。劳动者都想联合起来以提高工资,而雇主却想联合起来以减低工资。

然而,在一般的情况下,要预知两方谁占有利地位,谁能迫使对方接受自己的条件,并不困难。雇主的人数比较少,团结起来比较容易;并且,这种联合为法律所允许,至少不会被禁止。而相反,法律却禁止劳动者的联合。我们没有一个法令取缔为减低劳动价格而联合的组织,却有许多的法律取缔为提高劳动价格而联合的团体。另外,在所有这种争议当中雇主总比劳动者坚持得

---

① 为工作提供工具和建筑物,被忘记了。

— 151 —

merchant, though they did not employ a single workman, could generally live a year or two upon the stocks which they have already acquired. Many workmen could not subsist a week, few could subsist a month, and scarce any a year without employment. In the long-run the workman may be as necessary to his master as his master is to him, but the necessity is not so immediate.

though less is heard of masters, combinations than of workmen's.

We rarely hear, it has been said, of the combinations of masters, though frequently of those of workmen. But whoever imagines, upon this account, that masters rarely combine, is as ignorant of the world as of the subject. Masters are always and every where in a sort of tacit, but constant and uniform combination, not to raise the wages of labour above their actual rate. To violate this combination is every where a most unpopular action, and a sort of reproach to a master among his neighbours and equals. We seldom, indeed, hear of this combination, because it is the usual, and one may say, the natural state of things which nobody ever hears of. Masters too sometimes enter into particular combinations to sink the wages of labour even below this rate. These are always conducted with the utmost silence and secrecy, till the moment of execution, and when the workmen yield, as they sometimes do, without resistance, though severely felt by them, they are never heard of by other people. Such combinations, however, are frequently resisted by a contrary defensive combination of the workmen; who sometimes too, without any provocation of this kind, combine of their own accord to raise the price of their labour. Their usual pretences① are, sometimes the high price of provisions; sometimes the great profit which their masters make by their work. But whether their combinations be offensive or defensive, they are always abundantly heard of. In order to bring the point to a speedy decision, they have always recourse to the loudest clamour, and sometimes to the most shocking violence and outrage. They are desperate, and act with the folly and extravagance of desperate men, who must either

---

① [The word is used as elsewhere in Adam Smith without the implication of falsity now attached to it: a pretence is simply something put forward.]

久。地主、农场主、制造业主或商人就算不雇用一个劳动者,通常也能靠自身的资本维持一两年的生活。而劳动者如果失业,许多工人根本连维持一星期生活都成为困难,能支持一个月的很少,能维持一年的简直就没有。从长远来说,雇主需要劳动者的程度和劳动者需要雇主的程度基本相同,但前者的需要却没有那样迫切。

可以说,我们经常听说工人的联合,却很少听到雇主的联合。但如果有人因此认为雇主很少联合,那就太不明事故,不了解真相了。为使劳动工资不超过实际工资率,雇主们随时随地都保持着一种心照不宣的团结一致的联合。违反这种联合,无论在何地都是一种很不受欢迎的行为,会被近邻和同业者谴责。我们之所以很少听到这种结合,是因为那是一种很普通、自然的结合,很少被人提及。此外,雇主们也进行特殊的联合,把劳动工资减低到其实际工资率以下。此种结合总是进行得极其隐秘,直到达到目的。这时劳动者虽然沉痛地感受到了资方的这种联合,却往往无法抵抗而屈服,因此不被外人知晓。不过雇主的这种联合,也往往会引起工人们组织自卫性联合抵抗。有时即使没有雇主的这种结合,工人们也会为了提高劳动价格而自动联合起来。他们的理由,①有时是食品价格过高,有时是雇主从他们的劳动得到的利润过多。而他们的联合,无论是防御性的还是进攻性的,总是能被人们所听到。为了使问题尽快解决,他们总是声势大造,有时甚至诉诸于可怕的暴力。他们处于绝望之中,因此铤而走险。为

> 尽管我听到工人的联合往往比听到雇主的联合多。

---

① 斯密在此使用这个单词并不含有现代所含有的虚假的意思:一个理由仅仅是提出某件事物。

国民财富的性质与原理

starve, or frighten their masters into an immediate compliance with their demands. The masters upon these occasions are just as clamorous upon the other side, and never cease to call aloud for the assistance of the civil magistrate, and the rigorous execution of those laws which have been enacted with so much severity against the combinations of servants, labourers, and journeymen. The workmen, accordingly, very seldom derive any advantage from the violence of those tumultuous combinations, which, partly from the interposition of the civil magistrate, partly from the superior steadiness of the masters, partly from the necessity which the greater part of the workmen are under of submitting for the sake of present subsistence, generally end in nothing, but the punishment or ruin of the ringleaders.

<small>But masters cannot reduce wages below a certain rate,</small>

But though in disputes with their workmen, masters must generally have the advantage, there is however a certain rate below which it seems impossible to reduce, for any considerable time, the ordinary wages even of the lowest species of labour.

<small>namely, subsistence for a man and something over for a family.</small>

A man must always live by his work, and his wages must at least be sufficient to maintain him. They must even upon most occasions be somewhat more; otherwise it would be impossible for him to bring up a family, and the race of such workmen could not last beyond the first generation. Mr. Cantillon seems, upon this account, to suppose that the lowest species of common labourers must every where earn at least double their own maintenance, in order that one with another they may be enabled to bring up two children; the labour of the wife, on account of her necessary attendance on the children, being supposed no more than sufficient to provide for herself. ① But one-half the children born, it is computed, die before the age of manhood. ② The poorest labourers, therefore, according to this account, must, one with another, attempt to rear at least four children, in order that two may have an equal chance of living to that age. But the necessary maintenance of four children, it is supposed, may be nearly equal to that of one man. The labour of an able-bodied slave, the same author adds, is computed to be worth double his maintenance; and that of the meanest labourer, he thinks, cannot be worth less than that of an

---

① [*Essai sur la nature du commerce en généal*, 1755, pp. 42-47.]

② [*I. e.*, before completing their seventeenth year, as stated by Dr. Halley, quoted by Cantillon, *Essai*, pp. 42, 43.]

了使自己不致饿死,就威胁雇主立即答应他们的要求。这种情况下,雇主也同样高声呼喊,请求地方官援助,并要求严厉执行禁止工人联合的法律。因此,工人很少能从那些愤怒联合的暴动中得到什么利益。这部分是因为官员们的干涉,部分是因为雇主的不动摇,部分是因为大多数劳动者为了眼前生计而不得不屈服。所以这些联合常常以为首者受到惩罚或被处死而告终。

不过,尽管在争议中雇主常常处于有利地位,但仍然存在着一定的标准,使得在相当长的期间内,即使要把最低级劳动者的普通工资降到这一定标准之下似乎也是不可能的。

雇主们不能把工资降到一定标准之下,

一个人总是需要靠工作来维持生活,至少是他的基本生活。在大多数场合,工资还得多一点,或多或少超过足够维持他的基本生活的程度,否则劳动者就不能养家也不能传宗接代了。由此,肯提伦先生推测,即使是最下级普通劳动者,也至少要取得二倍于维持自身生存所需的生活费,以便供养两个儿女;而他的妻子,由于要照顾儿女,其劳动所得只要够维持自己的生存即可。① 不过,根据一般计算,有一半的儿童在未成年之前就夭折了。按照上述计算推测,最贫穷的劳动者一般都想至少生育四个孩子,以便能有两个活到成年。② 这样,四个孩子的必要的生活费也许只和一个成年男了的生活费相等。他还补充道,一个强壮奴隶劳动的价值是其生活费用的两倍,而一个最低级的劳动者劳动的价值不应低于一个健壮的奴隶劳动的价值。因此,有一点看

即一个人的工资必须能维持自身生活和略高一些来维持家庭生活,

---

① 具体论述见肯提伦的《论一般商业的性质》,1755 年版,第 42~47 页。

② 肯提伦在《论一般商业的性质》第 42、43 页中引用了哈雷博士的话,成年指年满 17 岁及以上。

able-bodied slave. Thus far at least seems certain, that, in order to bring up a family, the labour of the husband and wife together must, even in the lowest species of common labour, be able to earn something more than what is precisely necessary for their own maintenance; but in what proportion, whether in that above mentioned, or in any other, I shall not take upon me to determine.

<small>Wages may be considerably above this rate,</small>

There are certain circumstances, however, which sometimes give the labourers an advantage, and enable them to raise their wages considerably above this rate; evidently the lowest which is consistent with common humanity.

<small>when there is an increasing demand for labourers,</small>

When in any country the demand for those who live by wages; labourers, journeymen, servants of every kind, is continually increasing; when every year furnishes employment for a greater number than had been employed the year before, the workmen have no occasion to combine in order to raise their wages. The scarcity of hands occasions a competition among masters, who bid against one another, in order to get workmen, and thus voluntarily break through the natural combination of masters not to raise wages.

<small>which is caused by an increase of the funds destined for the payment of wages. The funds consist of</small>

The demand for those who live by wages, it is evident, cannot increase but in proportion to the increase of the funds which are destined for the payment of wages. These funds are of two kinds; first, the revenue which is over and above what is necessary for the maintenance;① and, secondly, the stock which is over and above what is necessary for the employment of their masters.

When the landlord, annuitant, or monied man, has a greater revenue than what he judges sufficient to maintain his own family, he employs either the whole or a part of the surplus in maintaining one or more menial servants.② Increase this surplus, and he will naturally increase the number of those servants.

<small>surplus revenue,</small>

When an independent workman, such as a weaver or shoe-maker,

---

① [There is no attempt to define 'maintenance,' and consequently the division of a man's revenue into what is necessary for his maintenance and what is over and above is left perfectly vague.]

② [It seems to be implied here that keeping a menial servant, even to perform the most necessary offices(e. g. , to nurse the infant child of a widower), is not 'maintaining' a family.]

来似乎是肯定的:为供养一个家庭,即使是最低等的普通劳动者,夫妇两人劳动所得,也须或多或少地超过维持他们自身生存所必需的费用。但是超过多少,是以什么比例,是按上述比例,还是按其他比例,我就不加以确定了。

但某些情况下,劳动者也处于有利地位,使他们能够将工资提到远远超过上述标准程度。上述工资明显只是符合普通人道标准的最低工资。

> 工资可能大大超过这个标准。

不论在哪个国家,如果对那些靠工资生活的人,如工人、散工、仆役等的需求不断地增加;也就是,如果每年提供的就业机会都比前一年多,劳动者就没有必要为提高工资而联合。劳动力的缺乏会导致雇主之间的竞争;为了获得工人,雇主们竞相抬价,从而自动打破了雇主们防止工资提高的自然联合。

> 当对工人需求增加时,工资上升。

显然,对靠工资生活的劳动者的需求必定会同计划用于支付劳动工资的资金的增加而成比例地增加。这种资金有两种:第一,超过必要的生活费的收入;①第二,超过雇主自己使用所需要的资本。

> 对工人的需求的增加,是由于用于支付劳动工资的资金的增加。

当地主、领年金的人、有钱人认为自己的收入除了维持自身生存和养家外还有剩余,他们就会把剩余的全部或一部分,用来雇用一个或几个仆人。② 所以,剩余额增加,他们所雇用的家仆自然也会增加。

独立工作的劳动者,如织工、鞋匠等所有的资本,如果除了购

> 超过必要生活费的收入。

---

① 由于没有企图去定义"维持生活费用",这样一个人收入所划分的必要生活费用和超出部分之间的界线就很模糊了。

② 这里的意思似乎是,维持一个仆人,即便是做最必要的工作(如抚养一个鳏夫的婴儿),也不含在一个家庭的"维持生活费用"之内。

and surplus stock. The demand for labourers has got more stock than what is sufficient to purchase the materials of his own work, and to maintain himself till he can dispose of it, he naturally employs one or more journeymen with the surplus, in order to make a profit by their work. Increase this surplus, and he will naturally increase the number of his journeymen.

therefore increases with the increase of national wealth.   The demand for those who live by wages, therefore, necessarily increases with the increase of the revenue and stock of every country, and cannot possibly increase without it. The increase of revenue and stock is the increase of national wealth. ① The demand for those who live by wages, therefore, naturally increases with the increase of national wealth, and cannot possibly increase without it.

High wages are occasioned by the increase, not by the actual greatness of national wealth.   It is not the actual greatness of national wealth, but its continual increase, which occasions a rise in the wages② of labour. It is not, accordingly, in the richest countries, but in the most thriving, or in those which are growing rich the fastest, that the wages of labour are highest. England is certainly, in the present times, a much richer③ country than any part of North America. The wages of labour, however, are much higher in North America than in any part of England. In the province of New York, common labourers earn④ three shillings and sixpence currency, equal to two shillings sterling, a day; ship carpenters, ten shillings and sixpence currency, with a pint of rum worth sixpence sterling, equal in all to six shillings and sixpence sterling; house carpenters and bricklayers, eight shillings currency, equal to four shillings and sixpence sterling; journeymen taylors, five shillings currency, equal to about two shillings and ten pence sterling.

---

① [Above, p. 1, the wealth of a nation was treated as synonymous with its annual produce, and there has been hitherto no suggestion that its stock must be considered.]

② [Apparently this is a slip for 'occasions high wages', At any rate the next sentences require this assertion and not that actually made.]

③ [The method of calculating wealth by the amount of annual produce per head adopted above, p. 1, is departed from here and below, p. 73, and frequently in later passages, in favour of the calculation by amount of capital wealth.]

④ This was written in 1773, before the commencement of the late disturbances.

买自己工作所需的原材料和维持自身在产品出售之前的生活外,还有剩余,那他自然会用这些剩余来雇用一个或几个工匠,以便从他们的劳动中获利。随着这种剩余的增加,他所雇工匠的人数也随之增加。

<small>雇主使用超过自己所需要的资本。</small>

因此,对工资劳动者的需求,必然随着一国的收入和资本的增加而增长。后者没有增加,对工资劳动者的需求也不会增加。收入和资本的增加就是国民财富的增长。① 因此,对工资劳动者的需求,自然会随国民财富的增加而增加。没有国民财富的增加,也就没有对工资劳动者的需求的增加。

<small>所以,对人民的需求随国民财富的增长而增长。</small>

然而使劳动工资②上升的,并不是巨大的现有国民财富,而是国民财富的不断增长。因此,最高的劳动工资不是出现在最富裕的国家,而是出现在最繁荣,也就是正在最迅速地变得富裕的国家。当前英格兰肯定比北美各地富裕,③然而北美的劳动工资却比英格兰的任何地方都高。纽约地区,一个普通劳动者一天的工资是 3 先令 6 便士,④相当于英币二先令;一个造船木匠一天的工资是 10 先令 6 便士,外加价值英币 6 便士的酒一品脱,共相当于英币 6 先令 6 便士;建房木匠和砌砖匠为 8 先令,相当于英币 4 先令 6 便士;裁缝工为 5 先令,相当于英币 2 先令 10 便士。这些价

<small>工资由国民财富增长的大小而不是由它的实际决定。</small>

---

① 上面在《绪论及全书设计》中,把国民财富当作是它每年的产物的同义词,一直没有提出过要考虑它的成本。

② 显然这是为"偶尔的高工资"作铺垫,无论如何接下来的句子需要这个论断,但事实并非如此。

③ 上面在《绪论及全书设计》中采用的按年度人均产出额计算财富的方法,从这里和下面的第 73 页被舍弃了,后面许多段落中,使用按资本量计算财富的方法。

④ 这是在 1773 年写的,是在上次动乱开始之前。

| 国民财富的性质与原理

North America is more thriving than England. These prices are all above the London price; and wages are said to be as high in the other colonies as in New York. The price of provisions is every where in North America much lower than in England. A dearth has never been known there. In the worst seasons, they have always had a sufficiency for themselves, though less for exportation. If the money price of labour, therefore, be higher than it is any where in the mother country, its real price, the real command of the necessaries and conveniencies of life which it conveys to the labourer, must be higher in a still greater proportion.

But though North America is not yet so rich as England, it is much more thriving, and advancing with much greater rapidity to the further acquisition of riches. The most decisive mark of the prosperity of any country is the increase of the number of its inhabitants. In Great Britain, and most other European countries, they are not supposed to double in less than five hundred years. In the British colonies in North America, it has been found, that they double in twenty or five-and-twenty years. ① Nor in the present times is this increase principally owing to the continual importation of new inhabitants, but to the great multiplication of the species. Those who live to old age, it is said, frequently see there from fifty to a hundred, and sometimes many more, descendants from their own body. Labour is there so well rewarded that a numerous family of children, instead of being a burthen is a source of opulence and prosperity to the parents. The labour of each child, before it can leave their house, is computed to be worth a hundred pounds clear gain to them. A young widow with four or five

---

① [Petty, *Political Arithmetic*, 1699, p. 18, made the period for England 360 years. Gregory King, quoted by Davenant, *Works*, ed. Whitworth, 1771, vol. ii. , p. 176, makes it 435 years in the past and probably 600 in the future. In 1703 the population of Virginia was 60,000, in 1755 it was 300,000, and in 1765 it was 500,000, 'by which they appear to have doubled their numbers every twenty years as nigh as may be'. —*The Present Stat of Great Britain and North America with regard to Agriculture, Population, Trade and Manufactures*, 1767, p. 22, note. 'The original number of persons who in 1643 had settled in New England was 21,200. Ever since, it is reckoned that more have left them than have gone to them. In the year 1760 they were increased to half a million. They have therefore all along doubled their own number in twenty-five years.' — Richard Price, *Observations on Reversionary Payments*, etc. , 1771, pp. 204, 205.]

格都高于伦敦的价格。据说在其他殖民地的工资也和纽约同样高。而食品的价格,北美各地却都比英格兰低很多。因此北美从来没有发生过饥荒现象。即使在最坏的年度,也不过是出口减少,他们同样足够维持自己的生活。因此,北美劳动的货币价格如果比母国任何地方都高,那么其真实价格,即它为劳动者提供的对生活必需品和便利品的实际支配能力,在比例上就必然更高。

　　目前北美虽然没有英格兰那么富裕,但却比英格兰更繁荣,并以更快的速度走向富裕。衡量一国繁荣与否的最明显的标志,就是居民人数的增长。在英国以及欧洲大多数其他国家,在大约500年内,居民人数据说增加不到一倍,而在北美的英属殖民地,人口在20年或25年内就翻了一番。① 就目前而言,这种迅速增加的主要原因,并不是新居民的不断涌入,而是本土人口的迅速繁衍。据说,那里的高龄老人往往能亲眼看到50到100甚至更多的嫡系子孙。由于那里劳动报酬优厚,多子女不但不是家庭的负担,反而成为家庭富裕和兴旺的源泉。据推算,在离开父母之前,每个儿女所创造的价值足有100镑。一个有四五个孩子的青年

---

　　① 配第著《政治算术》(1699年、第18页)研究了英格兰360年的期间。引述戴维南的话,格雷戈里·金、怀特·沃斯在Works(1771年,第2卷,第176页)中研究了过去的435年和将来的大致600年时间。在1703年,弗吉尼亚人口为6万,1765年为50万。"看来似乎人口数量以每20年近乎两倍的速度在增长"——《大不列颠和北美洲农业、人口、贸易和制造业的现状》(1767年,第22页注解)。"1643年定居于新英格兰的最初人口为2万1200人。从那以后,据估计越来越多的人来此定居。到1760年,这里的人口已经有了大致50万了。因此在25年的时期内,这里的人口一直以成倍的速度在增长。"——理查德·普里斯。Observations On Reversionary Payments, etc. (1771年,第204、205页)。

young children, who, among the middling or inferior ranks of people in Europe, would have so little chance for a second husband, is there frequently courted as a sort of fortune. The value of children is the greatest of all encouragements to marriage. We cannot, therefore, wonder that the people in North America should generally marry very young. Notwithstanding the great increase occasioned by such early marriages, there is a continual complaint of the scarcity of hands in North America. The demand for labourers, the funds destined for maintaining them, increase, it seems, still faster than they can find labourers to employ.

<small>Wages are not high in a stationary country however rich.</small>   Though the wealth of a country should be very great, yet if it has been long stationary, we must not expect to find the wages of labour very high in it. The funds destined for the payment of wages, the revenue and stock of its inhabitants, may be of the greatest extent; but if they have continued for several centuries of the same, or very nearly of the same extent, the number of labourers employed every year could easily supply, and even more than supply, the number wanted the following year. There could seldom be any scarcity of hands, nor could the masters be obliged to bid against one another in order to get them. The hands, on the contrary, would, in this case, naturally multiply beyond their employment. There would be a constant scarcity of employment, and the labourers would be obliged to bid against one another in order to get it. If in such a country the wages of labour had ever been more than sufficient to maintain the labourer, and to enable him to bring up a family, the competition of the labourers and the interest of the masters would soon reduce them to this lowest rate which is consistent with common humanity. China has been long one of the richest, that is, one of the most fertile, best cultivated, most industrious, and most populous countries in the world. ① It seems, however, to have been long stationary. Marco Polo, who visited it more than five hundred years ago,② describes its cultivation, industry, and populousness, almost in the same terms in which they are described by travellers in the present times. It had perhaps, even long before his time, acquired that full complement of riches which the nature

---

① [Here we have a third method of calculating the riches or wealth of a country, namely by the amount of produce per acre. For other references to this 'wealth' of China see the index, s. v. China.]

② [The date of his arrival was 1275.]

寡妇,在欧洲的中层及下层人民中,很少有机会能再找到丈夫;而在北美,这些儿女却成为一种财富,诱使男子向她求婚。儿女的价值对结婚是最大鼓励。因此,北美人的早婚就毫不奇怪。尽管早婚使人口大规模地增加,北美人民却仍然不断发出劳动力不足的抱怨。对劳动力需求的增加和维持劳动者生活的资金的增加,似乎仍比劳动力供给的增加要快得多。

即使一国非常富有,但若长久陷于停滞状态,我们就不能指望那里有很高的工资。计划用于支付工资的资金,即居民的收入和资本,可能到了最大的数目。但它如果数世纪都不变或者基本不变,那么每年所雇用的劳动者人数就很容易供应下一年的劳动者人数,甚至会有剩余。这样,就不会存在劳动力短缺的现象,雇主也不会为获得劳动者而相互抬价。而另一方面,劳动力的增加却会很自然地超过就业机会,导致就业机会不足。于是为获得工作,劳动者不得不互相竞争。如果一国劳动者的工资,本来足够养活他们自己和家庭,还有剩余,那么劳动者之间的竞争以及和雇主的利害关系,不久就会使工资降到合乎普通人道标准的最低工资。长期以来中国都是世界上最富的国家——土地最肥沃,耕种得最好,人口最多,人民最勤劳。① 然而,它似乎陷入了长期的停滞状态。五百年前②访问过中国的马可·波罗关于其耕种、产业和人口稠密状况的记述与当今旅行家关于它们报告,几乎没有什么区别。可能在马可·波罗时代以前好久,中国的财富就已达到

一国即
国富使
很有发
有,展
,如也
果很
停慢
滞,
,工
工资
资会
低
。

---

① 这里我们有了第三种计算一个国家国民财富的方法,即每亩地的产出量。

② 马可·波罗到达中国的时间为 1275 年。

of its laws and institutions permits it to acquire. The accounts of all travellers, inconsistent in many other respects, agree in the low wages of labour, and in the difficulty which a labourer finds in bringing up a family in China. If by digging the ground a whole day he can get what will purchase a small quantity of rice in the evening, he is contented. The condition of artificers is, if possible, still worse. Instead of waiting indolently in their work-houses, for the calls of their customers, as in Europe, they are continually running about the streets with the tools of their respective trades, offering their service, and as it were begging employment. The poverty of the lower ranks or people in China far surpasses that of the most beggarly nations in Europe. In the neighbourhood of Canton many hundred, it is commonly said, many thousand families have no habitation on the land, but live constantly in little fishing boats upon the rivers and canals. The subsistence which they find there is so scanty that they are eager to fish up the nastiest garbage thrown overboard from any European ship. Any carrion, the carcase of a dead dog or eat, for example, though half putrid and stinking, is as welcome to them as the most wholesome food to the people of other countries. Marriage is encouraged in China, not by the profitableness of children, but by the liberty of destroying them. In all great towns several are every night exposed in the street, or drowned like puppies in the water. The performance of this horrid office is even said to be the avowed business by which some people earn their subsistence.

China is not going backwards and labourers there keep up their numbers.

China, however, though it may perhaps stand still, does not seem to go backwards. Its towns are no-where deserted by their inhabitants. The lands which had once been cultivated are no-where neglected. The same or very nearly the same annual labour must therefore continue to be performed, and the funds destined for maintaining it must not, consequently, be sensibly diminished. The lowest class of labourers, therefore, notwithstanding their scanty subsistence, must some way or another make shift to continue their race so far as to keep up their usual numbers.

In a declining country this would not be the case.

But it would be otherwise in a country where the funds destined for the maintenance of labour were sensibly decaying. Every year the demand for servants and labourers would, in all the different classes of employments, be less than it had been the year before. Many who had been bred in the superior classes, not being able to find employment in their own business, would be glad to seek it in the lowest.

了其法律制度所允许的富裕程度。旅行家们的报告,虽然有很多相互矛盾的地方,但是关于中国劳动工资低廉和劳动者难于养活家人的记述,却是众口一词。中国的劳动者在田里耕种了一天,所得的报酬如果能够购买少量的米,他们就觉得满足了。工匠们的状况则更为恶劣。他们不像欧洲的工匠,总是悠闲地在自己的作坊内等候顾客,而是随身背着工具在大街上奔走,乞求工作。中国下层人民的贫困程度,远远超过欧洲最穷国家人民的贫困程度。据说,在广州附近地区,成百上千户人家,在陆地上没有房屋,而生活在河面的小渔船中。因为衣食缺乏,这些人往往连欧洲船舶上投弃的最污秽废物都渴望打捞。腐烂的动物尸体,如一只死猫或死狗,即使一半都已烂掉并发臭,他们得到它会非常高兴,就像别国居民得到卫生食品一样。结婚在中国是受到鼓励的,但这并不是由于生儿育女有利可图,而是由于他们有杀害儿童的自由。在大的城市里,每晚总会有若干婴儿被遗弃街头,或者像小狗一样被溺死。而这种可怕的工作,却据说是一部分人公认的谋生手段。

不过,中国尽管可能处于停滞状态,但似乎还没有退步。那里城市没有被居民遗弃;耕地也没有任其荒芜;每年仍有不变或几乎不变的劳动力被雇用。计划用来维持劳动的资金也没有明显减少。最下层劳动者的生活虽然很贫困,但还能勉强维持下去,使其种族能保持通常的人数。

而在计划用来维持劳动的资金显著减少的国家里,情况就完全不同了。对各种职业所需要的仆役和劳动者的需求,都会比前一年少。许多不能在上等职业中找到工作的在上等阶层长大的人,也会乐意在最下等的职业中寻找工作。这样最下等职业中,

没倒那能维持自己的人数。中国有退,里的劳动者

在一个衰退的国家里,情况就不是这样。

The lowest class being not only overstocked with its own workmen, but with the overflowings of all the other classes, the competition for employment would be so great in it, as to reduce the wages of labour to the most miserable and scanty subsistence of the labourer. Many would not be able to find employment even upon these hard terms, but would either starve, or be driven to seek a subsistence either by begging, or by the perpetration perhaps of the greatest enormities. Want, famine, and mortality would immediately prevail in that class, and from thence extend themselves to all the superior classes, till the number of inhabitants in the country was reduced to what could easily be maintained by the revenue and stock which remained in it, and which had escaped either the tyranny or calamity which had destroyed the rest. This perhaps is nearly the present state of Bengal, and of some other of the English settlements in the East Indies. In a fertile country which had before been much depopulated, where subsistence, consequently, should not be very difficult, and where, notwithstanding, three or four hundred thousand people die of hunger in one year, we may be assured that the funds destined for the maintenance of the labouring poor are fast decaying. The difference between the genius of the British constitution which protects and governs North America, and that of the mercantile company which oppresses and domineers in the East Indies, cannot perhaps be better illustrated than by the different state of those countries.

The liberal reward of labour, therefore, as it is the necessary effect, so it is the natural symptom of increasing national wealth. The scanty maintenance of the labouring poor, on the other hand, is the natural symptom that things are at a stand, and their starving condition that they are going fast backwards.

In Great Britain wages are above the lowest rate, In Great Britain the wages of labour seem, in the present times, to be evidently more than what is precisely necessary to enable the labourer to bring up a family. In order to satisfy ourselves upon this point it will not be necessary to enter into any tedious or doubtful calculation of what may be the lowest sum upon which it is possible to do this. There are many plain symptoms that the wages of labour are nowhere in this country regulated by this lowest rate which is consistent with common humanity.

First, in almost every part of Great Britain there is a distinction, even in the lowest species of labour, between summer and winter wages. Summer wages are always highest. But on account of the extraordinary

不但有了超过需要的本阶级的劳动者,而且还有从其他阶级涌入的人。结果导致就业竞争变得非常激烈,使劳动工资降低到了劳动者生活极其贫困的水平。即使接受这些苛刻条件,也还有许多人找不到工作。在这种情况下,他们要么挨饿,要么沦为乞丐,要么铤而走险搞罪恶的勾当。穷困、饥饿和死亡等灾祸在最下等的劳动者身上蔓延,并扩展到所有上层阶级,一直到国内居民人数减少到经过苛政和灾难而仅存的收入和资本所能维持的人数。孟加拉以及东印度的其他英属殖民地的现状,几乎就是如此。在一个土地肥沃而人口又大大减少的国家,维持生活应不是那么困难。而每年仍有三四十万人因饥饿而濒于死亡。由此,我们可以断言,该国计划用来维持贫困劳动者的生活费正在迅速减少。英国保护和治理北美的政治机构和压迫与统治东印度的商业公司的宪法是不同性质的。这两地的不同状况也许是再好不过的说明。

因此,优厚的劳动报酬,是国民财富不断增长的必然结果,同时又是国民财富增长的自然标志。相反,贫穷的劳动者生活资料贫乏,是社会停滞不前的征兆,而劳动者处于饥饿状态则是社会迅速退步的征兆。

在英国目前的劳动工资,显然已经超过了维持劳动者一家生活所必需的数额。为了证明这一点的正确性,我们无须作冗长烦琐或靠不住的计算,来推测劳动者至少需要多少工资,才能养家糊口。有许多明显的现象表明,不列颠各地的劳动工资并不是以符合人道标准的最低工资为准则的。

<small>在大不列颠,工资高于最低工资标准。</small>

第一,在不列颠,几乎每个地方,甚至最低级的劳动中也有夏季工资与冬季工资的明显区分。夏季工资总是最高。但冬季有

since (1) there is a difference between winter and summer wages,

expence of fewel, the maintenance of a family is most expensive in winter. Wages, therefore, being highest when this expence is lowest, it seems evident that they are not regulated by what is necessary for this expence; but by the quantity and supposed value of the work. A labourer, it may be said indeed, ought to save part of his summer wages in order to defray his winter expence; and that through the whole year they do not exceed what is necessary to maintain his family through the whole year. A slave, however, or one absolutely dependent on us for immediate subsistence, would not be treated in this manner. His daily subsistence would be proportioned to his daily necessities.

(2) wages do not fluctuate with the price of provisions,

Secondly, the wages of labour do not in Great Britain fluctuate with the price of provisions. These vary every-where from year to year, frequently from month to month. But in many places the money price of labour remains uniformly the same sometimes for half a century together. If in these places, therefore, the labouring poor can maintain their families in dear years, they must be at their ease in times of moderate plenty, and in affluence in those of extraordinary cheapness. The high price of provisions during these ten years past has not in many parts of the kingdom been accompanied with any sensible rise in the money price of labour. It has, indeed, in some; owing probably more to the increase of the demand for labour than to that of the price of provisions.

(3) wages vary more from place to place than the price of provisions,

Thirdly, as the price of provisions varies more from year to year than the wages of labour, so, on the other hand, the wages of labour vary more from place to place than the price of provisions. The prices of bread and butcher's meat are generally the same or very nearly the same through the greater part of the united kingdom. These and most other things which are sold by retail, the way in which the labouring poor buy all things, are generally fully as cheap or cheaper in great towns than in the remoter parts of the country, for reasons which I shall have occasion to explain hereafter. But the wages of labour in a great town and its neighbourhood are frequently a fourth or a fifth part, twenty or five-and-twenty per cent. higher than at a few miles distance. Eighteen pence a day may be reckoned the common price of labour in London and its neighbourhood. At a few miles distance it

薪炭的临时开支,故冬季一个家庭的生活费用最大。生活费支出最低时工资反而最高,表明劳动工资是不受最低生活所需要的费用支配的,而受劳动的数量和假定的价值的支配。可以说,劳动者应从夏季工资中节约一部分进行储存,以支付冬季费用,这样实际上他全年的工资并没有超过他一年中维持家庭生活所需要的数额。但一个奴隶或绝对依赖他人过日子的人所得到的待遇,就不是这样了。他的日常的生活资料都和他每天的需要相对应。

第二,在不列颠,劳动工资不随食品价格的变动而波动。食品价格各地年年变动,甚至经常一月一变。但许多地方劳动的货币价格,有时经过半世纪还保持不变。因此,这些地方的贫穷劳动者,如果在食品最昂贵的年份,能够维持他的家庭,那么,在食品价格中等而供给又很充足的年份,则必然能过上舒适的生活;而在食品非常低廉的年份,就能过上比较优裕生活。在近十年中,不列颠有许多地方食物昂贵,而劳动的货币价格并没有随之显著提高。诚然,在有些地方的劳动的货币价格确实提高了一些,但原因与其说是食物的昂贵,倒不如说是因为劳动需求的增加。

第三,就不同年份来说,食品价格的变动大于劳动工资的变动;而就不同地方来说,劳动工资的变动却大于食品价格的变动。在不列颠几乎所有的地方面包和家畜肉的价格一般相同或基本相同。这些商品以及大多数其他零售商品(贫穷劳动者通过零售购买的一切商品),在大城市与在僻远地方价格是同样便宜的,甚至在大城市还更加便宜,其原因我将在下文中说明。但大城市和其附近的劳动工资,却往往比数里之外的劳动工资高1/5或1/4,即高20%或25%。伦敦及其附近地区普通劳动的价格,大约是每

falls to fourteen and fifteen pence. Ten pence may be reckoned its price in Edinburgh and its neighbourhood. At a few miles distance it falls to eight pence, the usual price of common labour through the greater part of the low country of Scotland, where it varies a good deal less than in England. ① Such a difference of prices, which it seems is not always sufficient to transport a man from one parish to another, would necessarily occasion so great a transportation of the most bulky commodities, not only from one parish to another, but from one end of the kingdom, almost from one end of the world to the other, as would soon reduce them more nearly to a level. After all that has been said of the levity and inconstancy of human nature, it appears evidently from experience that a man is of all sorts of luggage the most difficult to be transported. If the labouring poor, therefore, can maintain their families in those parts of the kingdom where the price of labour is lowest, they must be in affluence where it is highest.

and (4) frequently wages and the price of provisions vary in opposite directions, as grain is cheaper and wages are higher in England than in Scotland;

Fourthly, the variations in the price of labour not only do not correspond either in place or time with those in the price of provisions, but they are frequently quite opposite.

Grain, the food of the common people, is dearer in Scotland than in England, whence Scotland receives almost every year very large supplies. But English corn must be sold dearer in Scotland, the country to which it is brought, than in England, the country from which it comes; and in proportion to its quality it cannot be sold dearer in Scotland than the Scotch corn that comes to the same market in competition with it. The quality of grain depends chiefly upon the quantity of flour or meal which it yields at the mill, and in this respect English grain is so much superior to the Scotch, that, though often dearer in appearance, or in proportion to the measure of its bulk, it is generally cheaper in reality, or in proportion to its quality, or even to the measure of its weight. The price of labour, on the contrary,

---

① [The difference between England and Scotland in this respect is attributed to the English law of settlement below, p. 142.]

日18便士。几英里之外,即降到14便士或15便士。爱丁堡及其附近地区普通劳动的价格,大约是每日10便士。几英里以外,就降到了8便士。而8便士是苏格兰低地大部分地方的普通劳动的通常价格。在这里劳动价格的变动要比在英格兰小得多。① 这种价格上的差异,虽然并不足以驱使一个人由一教区移到另一教区,但商品价格上的差异,却必然导致许多容积巨大的货物从一教区运到另一教区,从国内的一个地方运到另一个地方,甚至是从世界的一端运到另一端,这样不久就使它们价格降到一个接近的水平。人性的善变,虽早有定论,但根据经验,人类却显然又是安土重迁的。因此,贫穷的劳动者,在不列颠劳动力价格最低廉的地方,要是能够维持家庭生活,那在不列颠工资最高的地方就一定能过上比较富足的生活。

第四,劳动价格的变动不仅就时间说或就地方说,不与食品价格的变动相一致,而且还常常相反。

（4）工资和价格的变化相反,如英格兰相较苏格兰,工资高,谷物的常反,英格兰比,工资较高而价格低;

谷物作为老百姓的食物,其价格在苏格兰比在英格兰高,前者几乎每年都从后者进口大量的谷物。英格兰供应谷物,而苏格兰进口谷物,因此同样的谷物在苏格兰售卖的价格必然高于在英格兰售卖的价格。但英格兰谷物在苏格兰市场上售卖的价格,也不能高于和它同质量苏格兰本地谷物的价格。谷物的品质,主要取决于它可磨得的面粉量。在这一方面,英格兰谷物胜过苏格兰谷物。所以,虽然从表面上看,或从其体积甚至重量大小来看,英格兰谷物的价格高于苏格兰谷物的价格,但就其实质(品质或重

---

① 英格兰与苏格兰的差别在这方面的不同,要归因于英格兰的《和解法》。

is dearer in England than in Scotland. If the labouring poor, therefore, can maintain their families in the one part of the united kingdom, they must be in affluence in the other. Oatmeal indeed supplies the common people in Scotland with the greatest and the best part of their food, which is in general much inferior to that of their neighbours of the same rank in England. This difference, however, in the mode of their subsistence is not the cause, but the effect, of the difference in their wages; though, by a strange misapprehension, I have frequently heard it represented as the cause. It is not because one man keeps a coach while his neighbour walks a-foot, that the one is rich and the other poor; but because the one is rich he keeps a coach, and because the other is poor he walks a-foot.

During the course of the last century, taking one year with another, grain was dearer in both parts of the united kingdom than during that of the present. This is a matter of fact which cannot now admit of any reasonable doubt; and the proof of it is, if possible, still more decisive with regard to Scotland than with regard to England. It is in Scotland supported by the evidence of the public fiars, annual valuations made upon oath, according to the actual state of the markets, of all the different sorts of grain in every different county of Scotland. If such direct proof could require any collateral evidence to confirm it, I would observe that this has likewise been the case in France, and probably in most other parts of Europe. With regard to France there is the clearest proof. [1] But though it is certain that in both parts of the united kingdom grain was somewhat dearer in the last century than in the present, it is equally certain that labour was much cheaper. If the labouring poor, therefore, could bring up their families then, they must be much more at their ease now. In the last century, the most usual day-wages of common labour through the greater part of Scotland were sixpence in summer and five-pence in winter. Three shillings a week, the same price very nearly, still continues to be paid in some parts of the Highlands and Western Islands. Through the greater part of the low country the most usual wages of common labour are now eight-pence a day; ten-pence, sometimes a shilling about Edinburgh, in the counties which border upon England, probably on account of that neighbourhood, and in a few other places where there has lately been a considerable rise in the demand for labour, about Glasgow,

---

[1] [Hume, *History*, ed. of 1773, vol. vi., p. 178, quoting Rymer's *Foedera*, tom. xvi., p. 717. This was for service in Germany.]

量)来说,通常却比苏格兰便宜一些。而劳动的价格,在苏格兰却比在英格兰低。因此,贫苦劳动者如果在联合王国的一部分即苏格兰,能维持其家庭生活,那么在联合王国的另一部分即英格兰,就一定能过上富裕的生活。现在,燕麦片是苏格兰普通人民最常食用的最好食物,这和英格兰同阶级人民最常食用的食物比较,就差得多了。不过这种生活方式的差异,不是两地人民工资差异的原因,而是他们工资差异的结果。可是我却常常听见许多人倒果为因。一个人富有而另一个人贫穷,并不是因为前者有马,而后者却步行,而恰恰是因为前者富裕有能力备马车,而后者贫穷不得不步行。

　　上个世纪,按各年度计算,英格兰、苏格兰两地谷物的价格,都比本世纪高。目前来看,这是个毋庸置疑的事实。而在苏格兰证据比在英格兰更为清晰。在这一点上,苏格兰每年的公定谷价就可作证明。在苏格兰每年要按市场的实际状况,对所属各地不同谷物的价格进行宣誓评估。如果这种直接证据还需要其他旁证来证明的话,我可以说,法国甚至欧洲大多数地方的情况也是如此。在法国,我们有最明确的证据。① 不过尽管上个世纪英格兰、苏格兰两地谷物价格略高于本世纪,但上世纪两地劳动价格,却比本世纪低得多,这也是同样无可置疑的。因此,假使贫穷的劳动者,在上个世纪能够养家糊口,那么,他现在必定能过上舒适得多的日子。上个世纪,在苏格兰的大多数地方,普通劳动的日工资,一般夏天为6便士,冬天为5便士,一个星期3先令或大约3先令。在苏格兰高地及西部各岛若干地方,这个价格持续至今。而在苏格兰低地,现在普通劳动的一般工资,为一天8便士。在爱丁堡附近,在邻近英格兰而可能受英格兰影响的各县市,以及

<small>上个世纪谷物价格比本世纪高,劳动价格低;</small>

---

① 休谟《英格兰史》,1773年,第6卷,第178页。

Carron, Ayr-shire, &c. In England the improvements of agriculture, manufactures and commerce began much earlier than in Scotland. The demand for labour, and consequently its price, must necessarily have increased with those improvements. In the last century, accordingly, as well as in the present, the wages of labour were higher in England than in Scotland. They have risen too considerably since that time, though, on account of the greater variety of wages paid there in different places, it is more difficult to ascertain how much. In 1614, the pay of a foot soldier was the same as in the present times, eight pence a day. When it was first established it would naturally be regulated by the usual wages of common labourers, the rank of people from which foot soldiers are commonly drawn. Lord Chief Justice Hales,① who wrote in the time of Charles II. computes the necessary expence of a labourer's family, consisting of six persons, the father and mother, two children able to do something, and two not able, at ten shillings a week, or twenty-six pounds a year. If they cannot earn this by their labour, they must make it up, he supposes, either by begging or stealing. He appears to have enquired very carefully into this subject.② In 1688, Mr. Gregory King, whose skill in political arithmetic is so much extolled by Doctor Davenant,③ computed the ordinary income of labourers and out-servants to be fifteen pounds a year to a family, which he supposed to consist, one with another, of three and a half persons. ④ His calculation, therefore, though different in appearance, corresponds very nearly at bottom with that of judge Hales. Both suppose the weekly expence of such families to be about twenty pence a head. Both the pecuniary income and expence

---

① [Sir Matthew Hales.]

② See his scheme for the maintenance of the Poor, in Burn's History of the Poor-laws.

③ [Davenant, *Essay upon the probable Methods of Making a People Gainers in the Balance of Trade*, 1699. pp. 15, 16; in *Works*, ed. Whitworth, vol. ii., p. 175.]

④ [Scheme D in Davenant, *Balance of Trade*, in *Works* Scheme B, vol. ii., p. 184.]

在劳动需求最近正大大增加的格拉斯哥、卡隆和爱州等附近,普通劳动的一般工资为一天10便士,有时甚至一先令。英格兰的农业、工业、商业的改进,比苏格兰早得多。劳动的需求和劳动的价格,也必然随它们的改良而增加。因此,在上个世纪和本世纪,英格兰的劳动工资始终高于苏格兰。而且从那时起,英格兰的劳动工资大大提高。但由于英格兰不同地方支付的工资变化较大,所以,要确定英格兰工资的增加率比较困难。1614年,一名步兵一天的饷银,与现在一样同为8便士。最初规定这种饷额时,必然是以普通劳动者的一般工资为标准的,因为步兵普遍来自这个阶层。查理二世时,高等法院院长黑尔斯,①曾推算六口之家的劳动者(父亲、母亲,略能工作的子女二人,全不能工作子女二人)的费用,为一星期10先令,即一年26镑。他认为,如果他们不能靠自己的劳动赚到这个数目,他们就得靠乞讨或盗窃来凑数。黑尔斯对这问题好像下了一番工夫研究。② 曾被戴维南③博士极力称赞的擅长政治和数学的格雷戈里·金,也曾于1688年推算了一般劳动者及外仆的普通收入。假定平均由三个半人组合成的家庭,一年需要费用15镑。④ 从表面上看,金的计算,好像与黑尔斯的计算有出入,但实际上是大体一致的。他们都认为,这种家庭一星期的费用,大约是每人20便士。从那时起,在联合王国的多

---

① 即马修·黑尔斯爵士。
② 参阅他所订的济贫计划,见波恩的《济贫法史》。
③ 戴维南:《论使人民成为贸易差额中获利者的办法》,1699年,第15、16页。《Works》怀特沃斯编著,第2卷,第175页。
④ 《论使人民成为贸易差额中获利者的办法》,第2卷,第184页,计划D。

of such families have increased considerably since that time through the greater part of the kingdom; in some places more, and in some less; though perhaps scarce any where so much as some exaggerated accounts of the present wages of labour have lately represented them to the public. The price of labour, it must be observed, cannot be ascertained very accurately any where, different prices being often paid at the same place and for the same sort of labour, not only according to the different abilities of the workmen, but according to the easiness or hardness of the masters. Where wages are not regulated by law, all that we can pretend to determine is what are the most usual; and experience seems to show that law can never regulate them properly, though it has often pretended to do so.

while other necessaries and conveniencies have also become cheaper. The real recompence of labour, the real quantity of the necessaries and conveniencies of life which it can procure to the labourer, has, during the course of the present century, increased perhaps in a still greater proportion than its money price. Not only grain has become somewhat cheaper, but many other things, from which the industrious poor derive an agreeable and wholesome variety of food, have become a great deal cheaper. Potatoes, for example, do not at present, through the greater part of the kingdom, cost half the price which they used to do thirty or forty years ago. The same thing may be said of turnips, carrots, cabbages; things which were formerly never raised but by the spade, but which are now commonly raised by the plough. All sort of garden stuff too has become cheaper. The greater part of the apples and even of the onions consumed in Great Britain were in the last century imported from Flanders. The great improvements in the coarser manufactures of both linen and woollen cloth furnish the labourers with cheaper and better cloathing; and those in the manufactures of the coarser metals, with cheaper and better instruments of trade, as well as with many agreeable and convenient pieces of houshold furniture. Soap, salt, candles, leather, and fermented liquors, have, indeed, become a good deal dearer; chiefly from the taxes which have been laid upon them. The quantity of these, however, which the labouring poor are under any necessity of consuming, is so very small, that the increase in their price does not compensate the diminution in that of so many other things. The common complaint that luxury extends itself even to the lowest ranks of the people, and that the labouring poor will not now be contented with the same food, cloathing and lodging which satisfied them in former times, may convince us that it is not the money price of labour only, but its real recompence,

数地方,这种家庭的货币收入与费用都大大增加了,不过有的地方增加得多些,有的地方增加得少些。而且没有像最近向公众披露的现今劳动工资增加的幅度那么多。当然,必须指出,任何地方的劳动价格,都不能精确地确定。因为,就算是同一地方同一种类的劳动,工资的高低也往往取决于劳动者的巧拙及雇主的宽吝。在工资没有法律规定的地方,我们能确定的只是最一般的工资。而且,经验似乎表明,法律虽然多次企图规定工资,却从来没有做出过适当的规定。

本世纪,劳动的真实报酬,即劳动使劳动者所能得到的生活必需品和便利品的真实数量的增加,可能在比例上大于其货币价格的增长。不仅谷物的价格变得更加便宜,而且那些被贫穷劳动者当作可口和卫生食品的许多其他东西的价格,也下降了许多。比如,现今联合王国大多数地方马铃薯的价格,只有三四十年前的一半。萝卜、胡萝卜、卷心菜等从前用锹栽种而今普通用犁种植的蔬菜的价格,也同样低廉。几乎所有的蔬菜水果都变得比以前低廉。上个世纪英国消费的大部分苹果和洋葱,都是由佛兰德进口的。粗麻布和粗呢绒制造工艺上的大改良,给劳动者提供了质量更好价格更低的衣服。粗金属加工的大改良,不仅给劳动者提供了质优价廉的劳动工具,而且提供了许多适用和便利的家具。当然,肥皂、食盐、蜡烛、皮革及发酵酒,由于对它们的税收加重而提高了价格。但对贫穷劳动者所必须消费的那部分产品税收来说却少了。因此,这小部分商品价格的上涨,并不会抵消其他大部分物品价格的下落。现在人们往往抱怨奢侈之风,蔓延到下层阶级。现今,连贫穷的劳动者也对以前感到满足的衣食住条件感到不满了。这使我们可以确信,劳动的货币价格和其真实价

which has augmented.

High earnings of labour are an advantage to the society.

Is this improvement in the circumstances of the lower ranks of the people to be regarded as an advantage or as an inconveniency to the society?① The answer seems at first sight abundantly plain. Servants, labourers and workmen of different kinds, make up the far greater part of every great political society. But what improves the circumstances of the greater part can never be regarded as an inconveniency to the whole. No society can surely be flourishing and happy, of which the far greater part of the members are poor and miserable. It is but equity, besides, that they who feed, cloath and lodge the whole body of the people, should have such a share of the produce of their own labour as to be themselves tolerably well fed, cloathed and lodged.

Poverty does not prevent births,

Poverty, though it no doubt discourages, does not always prevent marriage. It seems even to be favourable to generation. A halfstarved Highland woman frequently bears more than twenty children, while a pampered fine lady is often incapable of bearing any, and is generally exhausted by two or three. Barrenness, so frequent among women of fashion, is very rare among those of inferior station. Luxury in the fair sex, while it inflames perhaps the passion for enjoyment, seems always to weaken, and frequently to destroy altogether, the powers of generation.

but is unfavourable to the rearing of children,

But poverty, though it does not prevent the generation, is extremely unfavourable to the rearing of children. The tender plant is produced, but in so cold a soil, and so severe a climate, soon withers and dies. It is not uncommon, I have been frequently told, in the Highlands of Scotland for a mother who has borne twenty children not to have two alive. Several officers of great experience have assured me, that so far from recruiting their regiment, they have never been

---

① [Berkeley, *Querist*, 5th ed., 1752, qu. 2, asks 'whether a people can be called poor where the common sort are well fed, clothed and lodged'. Hume, 'On Commerce,' says: 'The greatness of a state and the happiness of its subjects, however independent they may be supposed in some respects, are commonly allowed to be inseparable with regard to commerce.'—*Political Discourses*, 1752, p. 4.]

格都上升了。

　　下层阶级生活状况的这种改善,是对社会有利还是不利呢?[①] 这问题的答案一看就十分明显。仆人、劳动者和各种工人占了任何巨大政治社会人口的多数。任何社会最大部分成员境遇的改善,都不能视为对社会全体不利。如果一个社会有大部分成员陷于贫困悲惨的状态,那么这个社会绝不能被说是繁荣幸福的。而且,供给社会全体以衣服、食物、住所的人,只有在自身劳动生产物中能够分享一部分,使自己能得到过得去的衣食住条件,才算是真正的公平。

> 劳动的高收益对社会有利。

　　贫困无疑不会使人想结婚,但并不会阻止人们结婚。贫穷似乎还有利于生育。苏格兰高地处于半饥饿状态的妇女,常常会生20个以上的子女;而生活富足的上等社会妇女,却往往不生育,或只生两三个。上等社会常患怀孕症,而在下等社会却极其少有。女性的奢靡,虽然能燃起享乐的热情,却似乎会削弱甚至常常破坏生育能力。

> 贫穷不会阻止生育,

　　不过贫困虽然不能阻止生育,但极其不利于子女的抚养。一棵幼嫩的植物长出来了,但却生长在寒冷的土壤和恶劣的气候中,不久就会枯萎、死亡。我常听人们说起,苏格兰高地一位母亲生育二十多个子女而养不活两个的事,是很平常的。几个经验丰富的军官告诉我说,在部队内出生的全部士兵们的子女,远远不

> 但贫穷不利于儿童的抚养,

[①] 乔治·贝克莱在《质问者》(第5版,1752年)问题2中问道:"一个居住于大部分人都得到很好的衣食住行保障的国家的人可以被称为穷人吗?"休谟:"商业的情况下。"他的意思即:尽管某些方面一个国家的伟大和人民的幸福可能是独立的,但就商业而言通常是不可分割的。见休谟《政治演说》(1752年,第4页)。

able to supply it with drums and fifes from all the soldiers children that were born in it. A greater number of fine children, however, is seldom seen any where than about a barrack of soldiers. Very few of them, it seems, arrive at the age of thirteen or fourteen. In some places one half the children born die before they are four years of age; in many places before they are seven; and in almost all places before they are nine or ten. This great mortality, however, will every where be found chiefly among the children of the common people, who cannot afford to tend them with the same care as those of better station. Though their marriages are generally more fruitful than those of people of fashion, a smaller proportion of their children arrive at maturity. In foundling hospitals, and among the children brought up by parish charities, the mortality is still greater than among those of the common people.

<small>and so restrains multiplication, while the liberal reward of labour encourages it,</small> Every species of animals naturally multiplies in proportion to the means of their subsistence, and no species can ever multiply beyond it. But in civilized society it is only among the inferior ranks of people that the scantiness of subsistence can set limits to the further multiplication of the human species; and it can do so in no other way than by destroying a great part of the children which their fruitful marriages produce.

The liberal reward of labour, by enabling them to provide better for their children, and consequently to bring up a greater number, naturally tends to widen and extend those limits. It deserves to be remarked too, that it necessarily does this as nearly as possible in the proportion which the demand for labour requires. If this demand is continually increasing, the reward of labour must necessarily encourage in such a manner the marriage and multiplication of labourers, as may enable them to supply that continually increasing demand by a continually increasing population. If the reward should at any time be less than what was requisite for this purpose, the deficiency of hands would soon raise it; and if it should at any time be more, their excessive multiplication would soon lower it to this necessary rate. The market would be so much under-stocked with labour in the one case, and so much over-stocked in the other, as would soon force back its price to that proper rate which the circumstances of the society required.

够补充部队的兵力,即使只用来充当部队的吹鼓手都不够。不过,在兵营附近看到的可爱的儿童,却比其他地方都多。然而这些孩子却很少能长到十三四岁。有些地方出生的儿童,在四岁前,就死去一半;有许多地方,则是不到七岁;在几乎所有的地方,九、十岁前都会死去一半。这么大的死亡率,在任何地方的下层人民中都可以看到。他们没有能力像上层人民那样较好地抚养子女。虽然他们的婚姻,比上流社会的人结合能生出更多的子女,但他们的子女能达到成年的却比较少。育婴堂和教区慈善会内所收养的儿童,与普通人家的儿童相比,死亡率更大。

各种动物的繁衍和他们的生活资料成自然的比例。没有一种动物的繁殖能超出这个比例。但在人类文明社会,只有在下层人民中,生活资料的缺乏才限制人类的进一步繁殖。而要改变这一点,除了杀死他们多产的婚姻所生的大多数子女以外,没有其他办法。

<small>贫穷限制繁衍的报酬,因此贫穷了,丰厚的劳动报酬却鼓励繁殖。</small>

丰厚的劳动报酬,能使劳动者改善他们儿女的生活,使他们能够养大较多的儿女,自然就会放宽和扩大上述限度。不过应当指出,上述限度扩大的程度必然尽可能和对劳动的需求相称。如果该需求持续增加,丰厚的劳动报酬必然会鼓励劳动者结婚和繁殖,使他们能够通过不断增加人口,来满足不断增加的劳动需求。如果什么时候劳动的报酬不够鼓励人口的增殖,那么劳动者的缺乏立刻就会提高劳动的报酬。而如果什么时候劳动的报酬过分鼓励人口的增殖,劳动者的过剩立刻就会使劳动的报酬下降,减到其应有的标准。在前一种情况下,市场上的劳动供给严重不足,在后一种情形下,市场上的劳动供给又严重过剩。这两种结果都会迫使劳动价格很快回到社会所需要的适当程度。就像

It is in this manner that the demand for men, like that for any other commodity, necessarily regulates the production of men; quickens it when it goes on too slowly, and stops it when it advances too fast. It is this demand which regulates and determines the state of propagation in all the different countries of the world, in North America, in Europe, and in China; which renders it rapidly progressive in the first, slow and gradual in the second, and altogether stationary in the last. ①

as the wear and tear of the free man must be paid for just like that of the slave, though not so extravagantly.

The wear and tear of a slave, it has been said, is at the expence of his master; but that of a free servant is at his own expence. The wear and tear of the latter, however, is, in reality, as much at the expence of his master as that of the former. The wages paid to journeymen and servants of every kind must be such as may enable them, one with another, to continue the race of journeymen and servants, according as the increasing, diminishing, or stationary demand of the society may happen to require. But though the wear and tear of a free servant be equally at the expence of his master, it generally costs him much less than that of a slave. The fund destined for replacing or repairing, if I may say so, the wear and tear of the slave, is commonly managed by a negligent master or careless overseer. That destined for performing the same office with regard to the free man, is managed by the free man himself. The disorders which generally prevail in the Economy of the rich, naturally introduce themselves into the management of the former: The strict frugality and parsimonious attention of the poor as naturally establish themselves in that of the latter. Under such different management, the same purpose must require very different degrees of expence to execute it. It appears, accordingly, from the experience of all ages and nations, I believe, that the work done by freemen comes cheaper in the end than that performed by slaves. It is found to do so even at Boston, New York, and Philadelphia, where the wages of common labour are so very high.

High wages increase population.

The liberal reward of labour, therefore, as it is the effect of increasing wealth, so it is the cause of increasing population. To complain

---

① [Berkeley, *Querist*, qu. 62, asks 'whether a country inhabited by people well fed, clothed and lodged would not become every day more populous ? And whether a numerous stock of people in such circumstances would not constitute a flourishing nation?']

对其他商品的需求必然支配其他商品的生产一样,对人口的需求也必然会支配人口的生产。当人口增长过慢,则加速其增长;增长过快,则抑制其增长。正是这一需求在世界各地——不论在北美、欧洲,还是在中国,支配和调节着人口的繁殖。它在北美,成为促进人口迅速增加的原因;在欧洲,成为人口缓慢增加的原因;在中国,就成为人口增长停滞的原因。①

据说,奴隶的损耗导致其雇主的损失,而自由佣工的损耗,则是其自身的损失。事实上,后者的损耗与前者的损耗一样都是其雇主的损失。支付给各种短工和佣工的工资,都必须能使他们按照社会对他们的需求,增加、减少或保持不变,来维持其种族。不过,自由佣工的损耗虽然同样是雇主的损失,但比起奴隶的损耗来说,雇主所受损失又要小得多。如果我可这样说,用作替换和充补奴隶所耗费的资金,通常都是由疏忽大意的主人或粗心的监工管理。而充补自由佣工所耗费的资金却由自由佣工自己管理。富人在钱财管理上常陷入混乱,自然会体现到对上述资金的管理中;而穷人的处处节省和精打细算也必然在上述的管理中得到体现。在两种不同的管理之下,完成相同的目的所需要的花费就大不相同。所以,根据过去多年和不同国家的经验,我相信,由自由人完成工作,最终会比由奴隶完成工作成本更低廉。即使是在普通劳动工资很高的波士顿、纽约和费城等地方,情况也是这样。自由佣工的损耗和奴隶的损耗一样要得到补偿,尽管不是那么昂贵。

因此,丰厚的劳动报酬,既是财富增长的结果又是人口增加高工资会增加人口。

---

① 贝克莱《质问者》(第 5 版,1752 年)问题 62 问道:是否一个人民衣食住行都得到很好保障的国家就不会变得人口越来越多? 在这种情况下是否大量的人口将不会组成一个繁荣昌盛的国家?

of it, is to lament over the necessary effect and cause of the greatest public prosperity.

<small>The progressive state is the best for the labouring poor.</small>　　It deserves to be remarked, perhaps, that it is in the progressive state, while the society is advancing to the further acquisition, rather than when it has acquired its full complement of riches, that the condition of the labouring poor, of the great body of the people, seems to be the happiest and the most comfortable. It is hard in the stationary, and miserable in the declining state. The progressive state is in reality the cheerful and the hearty state to all the different orders of the society. The stationary is dull; the declining melancholy.

<small>High wages encourage industry.</small>　　The liberal reward of labour, as it encourages the propagation, so it increases the industry of the common people. The wages of labour are the encouragement of industry, which, like every other human quality, improves in proportion to the encouragement it receives. A plentiful subsistence increases the bodily strength of the labourer, and the comfortable hope of bettering his condition, and of ending his days perhaps in ease and plenty, animates him to exert that strength to the utmost. Where wages are high, accordingly, we shall always find the workmen more active, diligent, and expeditious, than where they are low; in England, for example, than in Scotland; in the neighbourhood of great towns, than in remote country places. Some workmen, indeed, when they can earn in four days what will maintain them through the week, will be idle the other three. This, however, is by no means the case with the greater part. ① Workmen, on the contrary, when they are liberally paid by the piece, are very apt to over-work themselves, and to ruin their health and constitution in a few years. A carpenter in London, and in some other places, is not supposed to last in his utmost vigour above eight years. Something of the same kind happens in many other trades, in which the workmen are paid by the piece; as they generally are in manufactures, and even in country labour, wherever wages are higher than ordinary. Almost every

---

　　①　[This is a more favourable view than that taken in *Lectures*, p. 257.]

的原因。对丰富的劳动报酬进行抱怨,也就是对社会最大繁荣的必然结果与原因发出悲叹。

也许应当指出,不是在社会获得最大财富的时候,而是在社会处于进步状态并日益富裕的过程中,贫穷劳动者,即人民的大多数,其生活状况似乎最幸福、最安适。在社会停滞状态下,生活是艰难的;在倒退的状态下,是悲惨的。进步状态,实际上是社会各阶层快乐和满足的状态;停滞状态是无味呆滞的状态;而倒退状态则是悲惨的状态。

<small>进步状态对贫穷劳动者来说是最佳状态</small>

丰厚的劳动报酬,鼓励人口的增长,也鼓励普通人民的勤勉。劳动工资是对勤勉的奖励。勤勉就像人类其他任何品质一样,越受奖励越会表现出来。富足的生活资料,增进了劳动者的体力,而改善生活的美好希望和对晚年优裕生活的憧憬,则使他们更加努力。因此,高工资地方的劳动者,总是比低工资地方的劳动者活跃、勤劳和效率更高。例如,英格兰劳动者与苏格兰劳动者相比,大城市附近的劳动者和僻远农村的劳动者相比,前者都强于后者。诚然有些工人如果能在四天中挣得足以维持一星期生活的生活费用,可能将无所事事地度过其余三天;但就大多数劳动者来说,并非如此。① 相反,在工人的工资按件计算能得到丰厚报酬时,许多劳动者往往没几年就把身体累垮了。据说,伦敦及其他一些地方的木匠最精壮的时期不超过八年。在工资按件计算的许多其他行业,也常有此种现象发生。制造业通常是计件工资,就连农村劳动在工资较高的地方,也是按件计算工资。几乎

<small>高工资鼓励勤勉。</small>

---

① 相比于《关于法律、警察、岁入及军备的演讲》中第257页中的观点,这是个更加可取的观点。

class of artificers is subject to some peculiar infirmity occasioned by excessive application to their peculiar species of work. Ramuzzini, an eminent Italian physician, has written a particular book concerning such diseases. ① We do not reckon our soldiers the most industrious set of people among us. Yet when soldiers have been employed in some particular sorts of work, and liberally paid by the piece, their officers have frequently been obliged to stipulate with the undertaker, that they should not be allowed to earn above a certain sum every day, according to the rate at which they were paid. Till this stipulation was made, mutual emulation and the desire of greater gain, frequently prompted them to over-work themselves, and to hurt their health by excessive labour. Excessive application during four days of the week, is frequently the real cause of the idleness of the other three, so much and so loudly complained of. Great labour, either of mind or body, continued for several days together, is in most men naturally followed by a great desire of relaxation, which, if not restrained by force or by some strong necessity, is almost irresistible. It is the call of nature, which requires to be relieved by some indulgence, sometimes of ease only, but sometimes too of dissipation and diversion. If it is not complied with, the consequences are often dangerous, and sometimes fatal, and such as almost always, sooner or later, bring on the peculiar infirmity of the trade. If masters would always listen to the dictates of reason and humanity, they have frequently occasion rather to moderate, than to animate the application of many of their workmen. It will be found, I believe, in every sort of trade, that the man who works so moderately, as to be able to work constantly, not only preserves his health the longest, but, in the course of the year, executes the greatest quantity of work.

_{The opinion that cheap years encourage idleness is erroneous.}   In cheap years, it is pretended, workmen are generally more idle, and in dear ones more industrious than ordinary. A plentiful subsistence therefore, it has been concluded, relaxes, and a scanty one quickens their industry. That a little more plenty than ordinary may render some workmen idle, cannot well be doubted; but that it should have this effect upon the greater part, or that men in general should

---

① [*De morbis artificum diatriba*, 1700, translated into English (*A Treatise on the Diseases of Tradesmen*) by R. James, 1746.]

每一种技工，由于从事特殊的职业，往往因操劳过度而患上特殊的疾病。意大利著名医生拉穆齐尼，曾著有专书来探讨这类疾病。① 我们并不把我们的士兵看作勤劳人民的一部分，但在当他们从事某种特殊工程而按件领受丰厚工资时，军官常须与参加工程的人约定他们每日的报酬，不得超过一定数额。在这种约定订立之前，士兵常因希望得到较大报酬而相互竞争，操劳过度，损害健康。一星期中四天的过度劳动，乃是其余三天懒散的真正原因，而其他人对了这三天的懒散，却大发牢骚。大多数人在连续几天的紧张脑力或体力劳动之后，都自然会有一种想要休息的强烈愿望。这愿望除非受到暴力或某种强烈需求的压制，否则几乎是压制不住的。这是本性的要求——在紧张劳动之后，有一定的放纵和快乐：有时只是悠闲一会儿，有时却是消遣和娱乐。如果不满足这种需求，其结果常常是很危险的，有时甚至是致命的，迟早会得某种职业上的疾病。如果雇主能听从理性及人道主义的要求，就不应经常鼓励劳动者尽量工作，而应提醒他们适量工作。我相信，这样在各个行业，一个每天适度工作的人能够持续不断地长期工作，不仅可以长期保持健康，而且在一年中也能完成更多的工作。

有人认为，在物价较低的年度，劳动者大多比平时懒惰；在物价较高的年度，则比平时勤奋。由此得到结论：生活资料丰富会使劳动者放松、懒散起来；而生活资料不足则会使劳动者更加勤奋。说生活资料比平常丰富，可能会使一部分劳动者懒散，这是毋庸置疑的。但如果说大多数劳动者都会因此懒于工作，或者

_{物价低会鼓励懒惰的观点是错误的。}

---

① 见 R. 詹姆士的英译本《论行业工人的疾病》，1746 年版。

work better when they are ill fed than when they are well fed, when they are disheartened than when they are in good spirits, when they are frequently sick than when they are generally in good health, seems not very probable. Years of dearth, it is to be observed, are generally among the common people years of sickness and mortality, which cannot fail to diminish the produce of their industry.

<small>Wages are high in cheap years,</small>
In years of plenty, servants frequently leave their masters, and trust their subsistence to what they can make by their own industry. But the same cheapness of provisions, by increasing the fund which is destined for the maintenance of servants, encourages masters, farmers especially, to employ a greater number. Farmers upon such occasions expect more profit from their corn by maintaining a few more labouring servants, than by selling it at a low price in the market. The demand for servants increases, while the number of those who offer to supply that demand diminishes. The price of labour, therefore, frequently rises in cheap years.

In years of scarcity, the difficulty and uncertainty of subsistence make all such people eager to return to service. But the high price of provisions, by diminishing the funds destined for the maintenance of servants, disposes masters rather to diminish than to increase the number of those they have. In dear years too, poor independent workmen frequently consume the little stocks with which they had used to supply themselves with the materials of their work, and are obliged to become journeymen for subsistence. More people want employment than can easily get it; many are willing to take it upon lower terms than ordinary, and the wages of both servants and journeymen frequently sink in dear years.

<small>and low in dear years, so that masters commend dear years.</small>
Masters of all sorts, therefore, frequently make better bargains with their servants in dear than in cheap years, and find them more humble and dependent in the former than in the latter. They naturally, therefore, commend the former as more favourable to industry. Landlords and farmers, besides, two of the largest classes of masters, have another reason for being pleased with dear years. The rents of the

说,人们在吃得不好时比吃得好的时候工作得更好,在精神不振时比兴致勃勃时工作更好,在生病时比在健康时工作更好,那这种说法好像是不太可靠。应指出,对普通劳动者来说,饥荒的年份往往是其疾病或死亡的年份,而这势必会减少他们的劳动产出。

在物资丰厚的年份,佣工常常会离开主人而靠自己的勤奋劳动创造的价值生活。但食品价格的低廉也会用来维持佣工的资金增加,从而鼓励雇主尤其是农业家,雇用更多的佣工。因为在这种情形下,农场主与其以低廉的市价出卖谷物,倒不如以此雇用更多佣工,以期从中获得更大的利润。对佣工的需求增加,而其相应的供给人数却减少,这样,劳动价格就往往在物价低廉时上涨。物价低的年份中工资却较高。

在物资短缺的年份,维持生计的困难与生活的不安定,使这些佣工又希望回到原有的工作岗位。但由于食品的价格较高减少了用来维持劳动的资金,使雇主倾向于减少现有的佣工,而不是增加。并且,在物价高涨的年度,贫穷的独立劳动者往往将以前用来购买生产材料的少数资本全部提出来用于消费,于是不得不沦为雇工。想要得到工作的人数多,而就业机会少,许多人不得不接受比通常低的条件,以获取工作。所以,在物价高涨的年份,佣工和帮工的工资往往较低。

因此,各种雇主在物价高的年份和劳动者订立合同,比在物价低的年份订立更为有利。而且他们会发现,劳动者在前一种场合比在后一种场合,更加恭顺,更听话。所以,很自然地,雇主们认为物价高涨的年份对他们的事业更为有利。此外,地主和农场主喜欢物价高涨的年份,还有另一个理由。那就是,地主的地租因此雇主喜欢物价高的年份。

one and the profits of the other depend very much upon the price of provisions. Nothing can be more absurd, however, than to imagine that men in general should work less when they work for themselves, than when they work for other people. A poor independent workman will generally be more industrious than even a journeyman who works by the piece. The one enjoys the whole produce of his own industry; the other shares it with his master. The one, in his separate independent state, is less liable to the temptations of bad company, which in large manufactories so frequently ruin the morals of the other. The superiority of the independent workman over those servants who are hired by the month or by the year, and whose wages and maintenance are the same whether they do much or do little, is likely to be still greater. Cheap years tend to increase the proportion of independent workmen to journeymen and servants of all kinds, and dear years to diminish it.

<small>Messance shows that in some French manufactures more is produced in cheap years.</small> A French author of great knowledge and ingenuity, Mr. Messance, receiver of the tailles in the election of St. Etienne, endeavours to show that the poor do more work in cheap than in dear years, by comparing the quantity and value of the goods made upon those different occasions in three different manufactures; one of coarse woollens carried on at Elbeuf; one of linen, and another of silk, both which extend through the whole generality of Rouen. It appears from his account, which is copied from the registers of the public offices, that the quantity and value of the goods made in all those three manufactures has generally been greater in cheap than in dear years; and that it has always been greatest in the cheapest, and least in the dearest years. All the three seem to be stationary manufactures, or which, though their produce may vary somewhat from year to year,

<small>No connexion is visible between dearness or cheapness of the years and the variations in Scotch linen and Yorkshire woollen manufactures.</small> are upon the whole neither going backwards nor forwards.

The manufacture of linen in Scotland, and that of coarse woollens in the west riding of Yorkshire, are growing manufactures, of which the produce is generally, though with some variations, increasing both in quantity and value. Upon examining, however, the accounts which have been published of their annual produce, I have not been able to observe that its variations have had any sensible connection with the dearness or cheapness of the seasons. In 1740, a year of great scarcity, both manufactures, indeed, appear to have declined very considerably. But in 1756, another year of great scarcity, the

和农场主的利润在很大程度上取决于粮食的价格。不过,如果认为一般人在为自己工作时工作得较少,而在为别人工作时工作得较多,那是再荒谬不过的了。一个贫穷的独立劳动者,往往比拿计件工资的工人干活卖力。那是因为前者享有自己劳动的全部产物,而后者则要与雇主分享。大制造厂中的雇工容易受坏的朋友的诱惑,导致堕落;而独立劳动者却由于处于分散的独立状态,不易受此影响。独立劳动者的工作效率比工资以年或月计的雇工可能大得多,因为后者不论工作多少,都得到同样的工资和津贴。物价较低的年月,会降低独立劳动者对各种帮工和佣工的比例而物价高涨的年月,则会增高这个比例。

麦桑斯先生是法国一位博学多才的作家,在圣·艾蒂安被选为收税官。为了说明贫民在物价低廉时所做的工作比物价高涨时多,他曾把三种制造品(埃尔伯夫的粗毛料和卢昂到处都是的麻织品与丝织品)在物价低时和物价高时的产量及价值,进行比较。据他从官厅登记簿上抄下的统计报告显示,这三种制造品在物价较低的年份的产量及价值,一般都比物价较高年份的大;物价最低的年份,产量与价值往往最大,而物价最高的年份,产量与产值却最小。而这三种制造业却似乎都处于停滞状态,其产量每年虽略有出入,但总的说来,却是不增不减。

苏格兰的麻织业和约克郡西区的粗毛织品制造业,同是成长中的制造业。其产量与价值总的来说,虽然时有变动,但大体上都是一直在增加。不过,查阅这些制造品年产额公布的记录,我却没有发现年产量和产值的变动与不同时期的物价高低有什么明显的关系。的确,在物资极其匮乏的1740年,这两种制造业都有较大的衰退,但在物资仍是非常不足的1756年,苏格兰麻织业

麦桑斯表明,法国一些制造业的产量反而在物价年份中低的产却高。

从苏格兰的麻织业和约克郡西区的粗毛织品制造业,没有发现产量和产值的变动与不同时期物价高低有什么明显关系。

Scotch manufacture made more than ordinary advances. The Yorkshire manufacture, indeed, declined, and its produce did not rise to what it had been in 1755 till 1766, after the repeal of the American stamp act. In that and the following year it greatly exceeded what it had ever been before, and it has continued to advance ever since.

<small>The produce depends on other circumstances, and more of it escapes being reckoned in cheap years.</small>　The produce of all great manufactures for distant sale must necessarily depend, not so much upon the dearness or cheapness of the seasons in the countries where they are carried on, as upon the circumstances which affect the demand in the countries where they are consumed; upon peace or war, upon the prosperity or declension of other rival manufactures, and upon the good or bad humour of their principal customers. A great part of the extraordinary work, besides, which is probably done in cheap years, never enters the public registers of manufactures. The men servants who leave their masters become independent labourers. The women return to their parents, and commonly spin in order to make cloaths for themselves and their families. Even the independent workmen do not always work for public sale, but are employed by some of their neighbours in manufactures for family use. The produce of their labour, therefore, frequently makes no figure in those public registers of which the records are sometimes published with so much parade, and from which our merchants and manufacturers would often vainly pretend to announce the prosperity or declension of the greatest empires.

<small>There is, however, a connexion between the price of labour and that of provisions.</small>　Though the variations in the price of labour, not only do not always correspond with those in the price of provisions, but are frequently quite opposite, we must not, upon this account, imagine that the price of provisions has no influence upon that of labour. The money price of labour is necessarily regulated by two circumstances; the demand for labour, and the price of the necessaries and conveniencies of life. The demand for labour, according as it happens to be increasing, stationary, or declining, or to require an increasing, stationary, or declining population, determines the quantity of the necessaries and conveniencies of life which must be given to the labourer; and the money price of labour is determined by what is requisite for purchasing this quantity. Though the money price of labour, therefore, is sometimes high where the price of provisions is low, it would be still higher, the demand continuing the same, if the price of provisions was high.

却有超过常年的进展。而同年约克郡粗毛织品制造业却发生了衰退。其生产额直至 1766 年,即直到美洲印花税法废止,才恢复到 1755 年的产量。在 1766 年和其后的 1767 年,约克郡制造品生产额才超过了以往任何一年,并从此持续增长。

以出口到远地为目的的一切大制造业的产量,与其说它必然取决于产地旺季价格的高低,倒不如说其必然取决于消费国中影响商品需求的环境,取决于和平还是战争,取决于其他竞争厂商的繁荣还是衰落,取决于那些商品的购买者是乐意买还是不乐意买。此外,还有部分可能在物价低廉时制造的额外产品,大部分没有登记在制造业公开记录上。男佣工离开雇主,成为独立劳动者;女佣人回到父母家中从事纺织,为自己及家庭制造衣服。甚至连独立劳动者也未必制造商品售给大众,而是受雇于邻居,制造一些家庭用品。因此,他们的劳动产品,经常没有登记在公开的记录上。这些记录有时是十分夸张的,而我们商人和制造业者却常常根据这种记录,妄断最大帝国的盛衰。

劳动价格的变动,虽然不一定总与食品价格的变动相一致,甚至常常完全相反。但我们不能因此就认为,食品价格对劳动的价格完全没有影响。劳动的货币价格,必然受两种条件的支配:第一,是对劳动的需求量;第二,是生活必需品和便利品的价格。对劳动的需求,根据它是在增加、减少或保持不变,或按照它所需要的劳动人口数量是增加的、减少的还是保持不变的,决定必须给予劳动者的生活必需品和便利品的数量。而劳动的货币价格,则取决于购买这一数量所需要的金额。所以,在食物价格低廉的地方,劳动的货币价格有时却很高,而在食物昂贵、劳动需求持续不变的地方,劳动的货币价格还会更高。

It is because the demand for labour increases in years of sudden and extraordinary plenty, and diminishes in those of sudden and extraordinary scarcity, that the money price of labour sometimes rises in the one, and sinks in the other.

<small>In years of plenty there is a greater demand for labour,</small>

In a year of sudden and extraordinary plenty, there are funds in the hands of many of the employers of industry, sufficient to maintain and employ a greater number of industrious people than had been employed the year before; and this extraordinary number cannot always be had. Those masters, therefore, who want more workmen, bid against one another, in order to get them, which sometimes raises both the real and the money price of their labour.

<small>and in years of scarcity a less demand,</small>

The contrary of this happens in a year of sudden and extraordinary scarcity. The funds destined for employing industry are less than they had been the year before. A considerable number of people are thrown out of employment, who bid against one another, in order to get it, which sometimes lowers both the real and the money price of labour. In 1740, a year of extraordinary scarcity, many people were willing to work for bare subsistence. In the succeeding years of plenty, it was more difficult to get labourers and servants.

<small>and the effect of variations in the price of provisions is thus counterbalanced.</small>

The scarcity of a dear year, by diminishing the demand for labour, tends to lower its price, as the high price of provisions tends to raise it. The plenty of a cheap year, on the contrary, by increasing the demand, tends to raise the price of labour, as the cheapness of provisions tends to lower it. In the ordinary variations of the price of provisions, those two opposite causes seem to counterbalance one another; which is probably in part the reason why the wages of labour are everywhere so much more steady and permanent than the price of provisions.

<small>Increase of wages increases prices, but the cause of increased wages tends to diminish prices.</small>

The increase in the wages of labour necessarily increases the price of many commodities, by increasing that part of it which resolves itself into wages, and so far tends to diminish their consumption both at home and abroad. The same cause, however, which raises the wages of labour, the increase of stock, tends to increase its productive powers, and to make a smaller quantity of labour produce a greater quantity of work. The owner of the stock which employs a great number of labourers, necessarily endeavours, for his own advantage, to make such a proper division and distribution of employment, that they may be enabled to produce the greatest quantity of work possible. For

第一篇　第八章

　　劳动的货币价格，在突然非常富足的年份会上升，而在突然非常匮乏的年份会下落。这是因为在前一情形下，劳动的需求增加，而在后一种情形下，劳动的需求减少。

　　在突然非常富足的年份，许多雇主手中的资金足够维持和雇用比前一年更多的劳动者，而这些超过平常需要的劳动者，却未必能雇到。于是，需要雇用更多工人的雇主，便相互竞争、抬价。这就使得劳动的货币价格及真实价格提高。丰年中对劳动者的需求更大。

　　在突然非常匮乏的年份，情形正好相反。用来雇用劳动者的资金，比前一年度更少，导致许多人失业，于是为获得职业他们相互竞争，使得劳动的真实价格与货币的价格都下降。譬如在1740年这个大的荒年里，有许多人只要有饭吃就愿意工作。而在此后的几个大丰年里，雇用劳动者和佣工就比较困难了。荒年中对劳动的需求减少。

　　在物价昂贵的年份，由于食品价格昂贵减少了劳动需求，因而会降低劳动的价格；而食品价格的上涨，会提高劳动的价格。反之，物价低廉的年份，由于食品价格的低廉增加了劳动需求，因而会抬高劳动的价格；而食品跌价，又会降低劳动的价格。在食品价格的一般变动中，这两种对立原因似乎会互相抵消。这也许就是劳动工资之所以到处都比食物价格稳定得多、持久得多的部分原因。食品价格变动对劳动工资的影响就这样被抵消了。

　　劳动工资的增加，必然抬高许多商品的价格（按价格中工资增高的那一部分比例），并由此减少了国内外这些商品的消费。但是，同样是这个使劳动工资增加的原因，即资本的增加，却会促进劳动生产力的增长，使较少的劳动能够生产较多的产品。雇用大量劳动者的资本家，为增进自身利益，势必会妥当地分配他们的工作，使他们能够生产尽可能多的产品。基于同一原因，雇主工资加会提高商品价格，但工资加这一原因又会降低商品价格。

the same reason, he endeavours to supply them with the best machinery which either he or they can think of. What takes place among the labourers in a particular workhouse, takes place, for the same reason, among those of a great society. The greater their number, the more they naturally divide themselves into different classes and subdivisions of employment. More heads are occupied in inventing the most proper machinery for executing the work of each, and it is, therefore, more likely to be invented. There are many commodities, therefore, which, in consequence of these improvements, come to be produced by so much less labour than before, that the increase of its price is more than compensated by the diminution of its quantity.

还会力图把他和他的工人所能想到的最好机械配备给他们。在某一特定工厂劳动者间发生的事,由于同一理由,也会在整个社会的劳动者之间发生。劳动者的人数越多,他们的分工当然就越细。就会有更多的人能够从事于发明各人完成每种工作的最适用的机械。因此更多的机器就能更容易地发明出来。由于这些机器的改进,许多物品就能用比以前少得多的劳动生产出来。这样,劳动量的减少就不仅抵偿了劳动价格的增加而且还会有剩余。

CHAPTER IX

Of The Profits Of Stock

<small>Profits depend on increase and decrease of wealth, falling with the increase of wealth.</small> The rise and fall in the profits of stock depend upon the same causes with the rise and fall in the wages of labour, the increasing or declining state of the wealth of the society; but those causes affect the one and the other very differently.

The increase of stock, which raises wages, tends to lower profit. When the stocks of many rich merchants are turned into the same trade, their mutual competition naturally tends to lower its profit; and when there is a like increase of stock in all the different trades carried on in the same society, the same competition must produce the same effect in them all. ①

<small>The rate is difficult to ascertain.</small> It is not easy, it has already been observed, to ascertain what are the average wages of labour even in a particular place, and at a particular time. We can, even in this ease, seldom determine more than what are the most usual wages. But even this can seldom be done with regard to the profits of stock. Profit is so very fluctuating, that the person who carries on a particular trade cannot always tell you himself what is the average of his annual profit. It is affected, not only by every variation of price in the commodities which he deals in, but by the good or bad fortune both of his rivals and of his customers, and by a thousand other accidents to which goods when carried either by sea or by land, or even when stored in a warehouse, are liable. It varies, therefore, not only from year to year, but from day to day, and almost from hour to hour. To ascertain what is the average profit of all the different trades carried on in a great kingdom, must be

---

① [This statement is somewhat amplified below, where the increasing intensity of the competition between the owners of capital is attributed to the gradually increasing difficulty of finding ' a profitable method of employing any new capital '.]

第九章 论资本利润

资本利润的增减与劳动工资的增减一样,都同样取决于社会财富。但社会财富对二者的影响却截然不同。利润依赖于财富的增减,

尽管资本的增加会提高工资,但也会降低利润。如果在同一行业中有许多富商都投入资本,他们之间的竞争必然会导致该行业利润的降低;而如果同一社会中所有不同行业的资本都同样增加了,那么同样的竞争也必然会导致所有行业产生同样的结果即利润都会降低①。利润随着财富的增加而下降。

前文已经指出,即使要确定某一特定地方和特定时间的劳动的平均工资都非常不容易。而且,我们所能确定的也仅仅是最普通的工资而已。但就资本的利润而言,想确定这一点也是很难达到的。利润极其容易变动,经营某一特定行业的人也未必都能够说出他每年的平均利润是多少。因为利润不但受到他所经营的那些商品价格变动的影响,而且要受到其竞争对手和顾客运气的好坏、商品在海陆运输中甚至在仓库里所可能遭遇的许多意外事故的影响。因此,利润不仅年年变动,日日变动,甚至每时每刻都

---

① 这种说法在随后略有扩展,那里将资本所有人之间的竞争的加剧归因于找到"使用任何新资本的有利方法"逐渐变得越来越困难。

much more difficult; and to judge of what it may have been formerly, or in remote periods of time, with any degree of precision, must be altogether impossible.

<small>but may be inferred from the rate of interest,</small> But though it may be impossible to determine with any degree of precision, what are or were the average profits of stock, either in the present, or in ancient times, some notion may be formed of them from the interest of money. ① It may be laid down as a maxim, that wherever a great deal can be made by the use of money, a great deal will commonly be given for the use of it; and that wherever little can be made by it, less will commonly be given for it. ② According, therefore, as the usual market rate of interest varies in any country, we may be assured that the ordinary profits of stock must vary with it, must sink as it sinks, and rise as it rises. The progress of interest, therefore, may lead us to form some notion of the progress of profit.

<small>which has fallen in England,</small> By the 37th of Henry VIII. all interest above ten per cent. was declared unlawful. More, ③ it seems, had sometimes been taken before that. In the reign of Edward VI. religious zeal prohibited all interest. This prohibition, however, like all others of the same kind, is said to have produced no effect, and probably rather increased than diminished the evil of usury. The statute of Henry VIII. was revived by the 13th of Elizabeth, cap. 8. and ten per cent. continued to be the legal rate of interest till the 21st of James I. when it was restricted to eight per cent.

---

① [But that interest will not always bear the same proportion to profit is recognised]

② [C. 9, 'an act against usury'. On the ground that previous Acts and laws had been obscure it repeals them all, and prohibits the repurchase of goods sold within three months before, and the obtaining by any device more than 10 per cent. per annum for forbearing payment of money. Its real effect was to legalise interest up to 10 per cent.]

③ [5 & 6 Ed. VI. , c. 20, forbade all interest, and repealed 37 Hen. VIII. , c. 9, alleging in its preamble that that Act was not intended to allow usury, as 'divers persons blinded with inordinate love of themselves' imagined, but was intended against all usury, 'and yet nevertheless the same was by the said act permitted for the avoiding of a more ill and inconvenience that before that time was used'.]

在变动。要确定在一个大国里各种行业的平均利润,就必然会更加困难;而要相当准确地确定以前或一段时间内的平均利润,那肯定是完全不可能的。

不过,我们虽然不可能相当准确地确定以前或现在资本的平均利润,但我们可以从货币的利息上得到一些相关的概念。可以确定这样一个原则:在使用货币获利较多的地方,通常对货币的使用会支付较多的报酬;在使用货币获利较少的地方,通常对货币的使用只会支付较少的报酬①。我们由此可以确定,资本的平均利润必然会随着一国市场的平均利息率的变动而变动。利息率下落,利润必随之下降;利息率上升,利润必随之上升。因此,利息的变动情况,可使我们知道一些利润变动情况的概念。

亨利八世三十七年,法令宣布一切利息均不得超过10%,否则为非法②。可见在此之前的利息有时是在10%以上的。其后的爱德华六世,由于对宗教的狂热而禁止了一切利息③。但这种禁令,据说和其他同性质的各种禁令一样,没有产生效果。高利贷的危害不但没有减少,反而增加了。于是,伊丽莎白女王十三年的法令第八条的规定,又使原亨利八世的法令产生效力了。此

---

① 但事实上利息并不总是与利润保持同一比例。
② "反高利贷法"。基于以前的法令模糊不清就把以前的法令都废除了,并且禁止回购前3个月内售出的商品和禁止通过任何放高利贷手段获得的每年超过10%的收入。它实际的作用就在于将利率合法化地升至10%。
③ 爱德华六世五年和爱德华六世六年的第20号法令,禁止所有的利率和废除亨利八世上述的法令。在它的导言中宣称该法令无意于允许高利贷,而是为了反对所有的高利贷。"但是情况都是一样的,上述法律是为了排除以前所用法律带来的不好和不便之处。"

— 201 —

It was reduced to six per cent. soon after the restoration, and by the 12th of Queen Anne, to five per cent. All these different statutory regulations seem to have been made with great propriety. They seem to have followed and not to have gone before the market rate of interest, or the rate at which people of good credit usually borrowed. Since the time of Queen Anne, five per cent. seems to have been rather above than below the market rate. Before the late war, ① the government borrowed at three per cent. ; and people of good credit in the capital, and in many other parts of the kingdom, at three and a half, four, and four and a half per cent.

while wealth has been increasing.

Since the time of Henry VIII. the wealth and revenue of the country have been continually advancing, and, in the course of their progress, their pace seems rather to have been gradually accelerated than retarded. They seem, not only to have been going on, but to have been going on faster and faster. The wages of labour have been continually increasing during the same period, and in the greater part of the different branches of trade and manufactures the profits of stock have been diminishing.

Profits are lower in towns, where there is much stock, than in the country, where there is little.

It generally requires a greater stock to carry on any sort of trade in a great town than in a country village. The great stocks employed in every branch of trade, and the number of rich competitors, generally reduce the rate of profit in the former below what it is in the latter. But the wages of labour are generally higher in a great town than in a country village. In a thriving town the people who have great stocks to employ, frequently cannot get the number of workmen they want, and therefore bid against one another in order to get as many as they can, which raises the wages of labour, and lowers the profits of stock. In the remote parts of the country there is frequently not stock sufficient to employ all the people, who therefore bid against one another in order to get employment, which lowers the wages of labour, and raises the profits of stock.

Interest is higher in Scotland, a poor country, than in England.

In Scotland, though the legal rate of interest is the same as in England, the market rate is rather higher. People of the best credit there seldom borrow under five per cent. Even private bankers in Edinburgh give four per cent. upon their promissory notes, of which payment either in whole or in part may be demanded at pleasure.

---

① [That of 1756 – 1763.]

后,10%继续作为法定利息率,直到詹姆士一世二十一年,才把它定为8%。复辟后不久它又降低到6%。安妮女王十二年,又降到了5%。这一切的法规,看来都极其适当。它们都是跟在市场利息率或有良好信用的人的经常借款利息率变动之后制定出的,而不是走在前头。自从安妮女王时代以来,5%的利息率似乎是高于市场利息率,而非低于市场利息率。在最近一次战争①以前,政府曾以3%的利息率借款,而王国首都及国内的其他许多地方,有良好信用的人则以3.5%、4%、4.5%等的利息率借款。

我们国家自亨利八世以来,财富和收入都在不断增加,而且在这种增长的过程中,其速度似乎是逐渐加快的,而不是减慢的。财富不仅在增长,而且增长得愈来愈快。这一时期的劳动工资在不断增加,而大部分商业和制造业的资本利润却在不断减少。

> 财富一直在增加。

在大城市经营一种行业,往往需要比在乡村更多的资本。各商业部门所投入资本的庞大和富裕竞争者人数的众多,使得城市的资本利润率一般低于农村的利润率。而城市的劳动工资,却一般比农村高。在繁荣的城市,拥有大量生产资本的雇主却往往不能按他们所需要的人数雇到工人,于是互相竞争,从而抬高了劳动工资而减低了资本利润。在没有充足的资本来雇用所有劳动者的农村,普通劳动者为了获得工作而相互竞争,于是劳动工资下降,而资本利润上升。

> 由于城市资本充足,因此在城市的比农村低。

苏格兰的法定利息率虽然和英格兰相同,但市场利息率却比英格兰高许多。该地信用良好的人,很少能以低于5%的利息率借到款。就连爱丁堡的私有银行,对于随时能兑现全部或部分的

> 穷的苏格兰的利息率比英格兰高。

---

① 指的1756~1763年的战争。

Private bankers in London give no interest for the money which is deposited with them. There are few trades which cannot be carried on with a smaller stock in Scotland than in England. The common rate of profit, therefore, must be somewhat greater. The wages of labour, it has already been observed, are lower in Scotland than in England. ①
The country too is not only much poorer, but the steps by which it advances to a better condition, for it is evidently advancing, seem to be much slower and more tardy.

So too in France, a country probably less rich than England, The legal rate of interest in France has not, during the course of the present century, been always regulated by the market rate. In 1720 interest was reduced from the twentieth to the fiftieth penny, or from five to two per cent. In 1724 it was raised to the thirtieth penny, or to $3\frac{1}{3}$ per cent. In 1725 it was again raised to the twentieth penny, or to five per cent. In 1766, during the administration of Mr. Laverdy, it was reduced to the twenty-fifth penny, or to four per cent. The Abbe Terray raised it afterwards to the old rate of five per cent. The supposed purpose of many of those violent reductions of interest was to prepare the way for reducing that of the public debts; a purpose which has sometimes been executed. France is perhaps in the present times not so rich a country as England; and though the legal rate of interest has in France frequently been lower than in England, the market rate has generally been higher; for there, as in other countries, they have several very safe and easy methods of evading the law. The profits of trade, I have been assured by British merchants who had traded in both countries, are higher in France than in England; and it is no doubt upon this account that many British subjects chuse rather to employ their capitals in a country where trade is in disgrace, than in one where it is highly respected. The wages of labour are lower in France than in England. When you go from Scotland to England, the difference which you may remark between the dress and countenance of the common people in the one country and in the other, sufficiently indicates the difference in their condition. The contrast is still greater when you return from France. France, though no doubt a richer country than Scotland, seems not to be going forward so fast.

---

① See Denisart, Article Taux des Interest, tom, iii, p. 18. (J. B. Denisart, *Collection de decisions nouvelles et de notions relatives a la jurisprudence actulle*, 7th ed., 1771. s. v.)

期票也给予了4%的利息。伦敦的私人银行,对于储蓄的资金不给利息。在苏格兰,几乎经营所有的行业,所需的资本都比在英格兰要少。因此,苏格兰普通的利润率必定比英格兰要高。前面已经说过,苏格兰的劳动工资比英格兰的低。还有,苏格兰不仅比英格兰穷,而且其发展的速度也慢得多,尽管它确实是在前进。

在本世纪,法国的法定利息率并不总是受市场利息率的支配①。在1720年,它从1/20跌落到1/50,即由5%跌落到2%。在1724年,它涨到1/30,或者说涨到3.3%。在1725年,它又涨到1/20,即涨到了5%。1766年,在拉维迪执政期间,它又减到了1/25,即4%。之后,神父特雷执政期间,它又恢复到了原来的5%。据推测,这样多次强行降低法定利息率的目的是为降低公债利息率做准备。这个目的有时确实达到了。目前,法国也许没有英国那样富裕。尽管法国的法定利息率一般比英国低,而市场利息率却一般高于英国。这是因为法国和其他国家一样,人们有很安全和很容易的绕开法律的方法。有位在英法两国经商的英国商人告诉我,法国的商业利润比英国的高。正基于这个原因,许多英国人愿意把资本投在轻商的法国而不愿把资本投在重商的英国。在法国,劳动工资比英国低。如果你由苏格兰到英格兰,可以看到这两地普通人民服装和面色的差异,它能允分地表明这两地社会状况的差异。而如果你从法国回到英格兰来,这种对比就更为鲜明。法国的确比苏格兰富裕,但其进步的速度却似乎不及苏格兰。国内对于苏格兰的一般或者说普遍的看法是,它

---

① 见 J. B. 丹尼森的《关于利息率》第7版,1771年,第3卷,第18页。

国民财富的性质与原理

It is a common and even a popular opinion in the country, that it is going backwards; an opinion which, I apprehend, is ill-founded even with regard to France, but which nobody can possibly entertain with regard to Scotland, who sees the country now, and who saw it twenty or thirty years ago.

<small>but lower in Holland, which is richer than England.</small> The province of Holland, on the other hand, in proportion to the extent of its territory and the number of its people, is a richer country than England. The government there borrow at two per cent., and private people of good credit at three. The wages of labour are said to be higher in Holland than in England, and the Dutch, it is well known, trade upon lower profits than any people in Europe. The trade of Holland, it has been pretended by some people, is decaying, and it may perhaps be true that some particular branches of it are so. But these symptoms seem to indicate sufficiently that there is no general decay. When profit diminishes, merchants are very apt to complain that trade decays; though the diminution of profit is the natural effect of its prosperity, or of a greater stock being employed in it than before. During the late war the Dutch gained the whole carrying trade of France, of which they still retain a very large share. The great property which they possess both in the French and English funds, about forty millions, it is said, in the latter (in which I suspect, however, there is a considerable exaggeration);①the great sums which they lend to private people in countries

---

① [Postlethwayt, *Dictionary of Commerce*, 2nd ed., 1757, vol. i., p. 877, 5. v. Funds, says that the amount of British funds held by foreigners has been estimated by some at one-fifth and by others at one-fourth of the whole debt. But Magens, *Universal Merchant* (ed. Horsley), 1753, p. 13, thought it 'more than probable that foreigners are not concerned in anything like one-fourth'. He had been informed 'that most of the money which the Dutch have here is in Bank, East India and South Sea stocks, and that their interest in them might amount to one-third of the whole'. Fairman, *Account of the Public Funds*, 7th ed., 1824, p. 229, quotes an account drawn up in the year 1762, showing how much of the several funds transferable at the Bank of England then stood in the names of foreigners, 'which is also in Sinclair, *History of the Public Revenue*, pt. iii., 1790, p. 366. From this it appears that foreigners held £4,627,858 of Bank stock and £10,328,537 in the other funds, which did not include South Sea and East India stock. Fairman had reason to believe that the South Sea holding amounted to £2,500,000 and the East Indian to more than £500,000, which would make in all about £18,000,000. In 1806, he says, the total claiming exemption from income tax (foreigners were exempt) was £18,500,000, but this did not include Bank stock.]

正在倒退；但这种见解，即使对法国来说，也是没有任何依据的；一个在二三十年前曾到过苏格兰看到过那边情况而现在又去那边的人，就绝不会有这种看法。

相反，就领土面积和人口的比例来说，荷兰比英格兰更富裕。荷兰政府以2%的利息率借款，而有良好信用的私人则以3%的利息率借款。据说，荷兰的劳动工资比英格兰的高。大家都知道，荷兰人经商所获的利润比欧洲其他国家的都低。于是有人说，荷兰的商业正在衰退。就某些商业部门来说，也许确实如此。但上面所说的事实也可表明，该国商业似乎并没有普遍衰退。当利润减少时，商人们往往会抱怨商业衰落了；但事实上利润减少，是商业繁盛的自然结果，或者说是所投资本比以前更多的自然结果。在上次英法战争期间，荷兰人乘机获得了法国的全部运输业务。而且直到现今，还有一大部分运输业操纵在荷兰人的手中。荷兰人拥有英法的大宗国债。据说，单在英国，就有大约 4000 万英镑（但我认为这种说法有点夸大）①。此外，荷兰人还把巨额资

比荷兰更富裕但是英格兰的利息却低。

----

① 波斯尔斯威特：《商业词典》（第2版，1757年，第1卷，第877页）。"资金"一词是说，有人估计外国人拥有的不列颠资金总额应该是全部债务的五分之一，而其他人估计为四分之一。但根据马根斯《环球商人》（霍斯利主编，1753年，第13页）说"外国人持有量极可能不到四分之一"。他了解到"荷兰在这里持有的钱，视'银行、东印度和南海'股票，其利息可能会占到总额的三分之一"。法尔曼，《公共资产账户》（第7版，1824年，第229页）引述道："1762年账户上提取的资金显示了这几种资金在英格兰银行的流动性，然后停留在国外账户名目上。"这点从辛克莱《公共收入的历史》（第3部分，1790年，第366页）中也可以看到。从这些可以看到，外国人持有4621858镑的银行股票和10328537镑的其他资产，这还不包括南海和东印度股票。明眼人有理由相信南海公司持有总量为2500000镑的资产，东印度公司持有500000镑的资产，总计18000000镑。1806年，他说扣除税收（外国人是免税的）总计18500000镑，但不包括银行股票。

where the rate of interest is higher than in their own, are circumstances which no doubt demonstrate the redundancy of their stock, or that it has increased beyond what they can employ with tolerable profit in the proper business of their own country: but they do not demonstrate that that business has decreased. As the capital of a private man, though acquired by a particular trade, may increase beyond what he can employ in it, and yet that trade continue to increase too; so may likewise the capital of a great nation.

In the peculiar case of new colonies high wages and high profits go together, but profits gradually diminish.

In our North American and West Indian colonies, not only the wages of labour, but the interest of money, and consequently the profits of stock, are higher than in England. In the different colonies both the legal and the market rate of interest run from six to eight per cent. High wages of labour and high profits of stock, however, are things, perhaps, which scarce ever go together, except in the peculiar circumstances of new colonies. A new colony must always for some time be more under-stocked in proportion to the extent of its territory, and more under-peopled in proportion to the extent of its stock, than the greater part of other countries. They have more land than they have stock to cultivate. What they have, therefore, is applied to the cultivation only of what is most fertile and most favourably situated, the land near the sea shore, and along the banks of navigable rivers. Such land too is frequently purchased at a price below the value even of its natural produce. Stock employed in the purchase and improvement of such lands must yield a very large profit, and consequently afford to pay a very large interest. Its rapid accumulation in so profitable an employment enables the planter to increase the number of his hands faster than he can find them in a new settlement. Those whom he can find, therefore, are very liberally rewarded. As the colony increases, the profits of stock gradually diminish. When the most fertile and best situated lands have been all occupied, less profit can be made by the cultivation of what is inferior both in soil and situation, and less interest can be afforded for the stock which is so employed. In the greater part of our colonies, accordingly, both the legal and the market rate of interest have been considerably reduced during the course of the present century. As riches, improvement, and population have increased,

金贷给比本国利息率高的国外私人。这些情况,无疑表明了他们资本的过剩,或者说他们的资本已经增加到了投在本国适当行业上却不能得到相应利润的程度,但这并不表示商业在衰退。就好像在某一行业经营获得的私人资本,已经增加到不能再全部投入到这一行业上的程度,然而这一行业仍在继续增长;大国的资本也同样可能这样。

在我们的北美和西印度的殖民地,不仅劳动工资而且货币利息和资本利润都比英格兰高。在各个殖民地,法定利息率和市场利息率在6%—8%之间。然而,劳动的高工资和资本的高利润同时存在,在其他地方这是很少见的,这是存在于新殖民地特殊情况下的特有现象。一块新的殖民地,与其他大多数国家不同,其资本的数量与领土面积相比较以及人口数与资本数相比较,在一定时期必定相对不足。他们所拥有的土地,多于他们的资本所能耕种的土地,所以,他们只把资本投在土壤最肥沃、位置最便利的土地上,即在那些靠近海滨和可以航行的河流沿岸土地。而购买这些土地的价格往往会低于其自然生产物的价值。为购买并改良这些土地而投入的资本,必然会产生极大的利润,因而足够支付较高的利息。投在这种利润丰厚的土地上的资本的迅速积累,使种植园所有者需要雇用的工人数,很快增加到新殖民地不能供应的程度。这样,他们能在新殖民地找到的劳动者的报酬就十分丰厚。然而,随着殖民地的扩展,资本利润会逐渐减少。在土质最肥沃和位置最好的土地被全部占有之后,耕种土壤和位置较差的土地就使所能取得的利润减少了,只能为投入在土地上的资本提供较低的利息。在本世纪,英国大部分殖民地法定利息率和市场利息率都大大降低了。随着财富的增加、工作的改良及人

特殊情况下新殖民地同时出现高工资和高利润的情况,但随之资本利润会逐渐减少。

interest has declined. The wages of labour do not sink with the profits of stock. The demand for labour increases with the increase of stock whatever be its profits; and after these are diminished, stock may not only continue to increase, but to increase much faster than before. It is with industrious nations who are advancing in the acquisition of riches, as with industrious individuals. A great stock, though with small profits, generally increases faster than a small stock with great profits. Money, says the proverb, makes money. When you have got a little, it is often easy to get more. The great difficulty is to get that little. The connection between the increase of stock and that of industry, or of the demand for useful labour, has partly been explained already, but will be explained more fully hereafter in treating of the accumulation of stock.

New territories and trades may raise profits even in a country advancing in riches.

The acquisition of new territory, or of new branches of trade, may sometimes raise the profits of stock, and with them the interest of money, even in a country which is fast advancing in the acquisition of riches. The stock of the country not being sufficient for the whole accession of business, which such acquisitions present to the different people among whom it is divided, is applied to those particular branches only which afford the greatest profit. Part of what had before been employed in other trades, is necessarily withdrawn from them, and turned into some of the new and more profitable ones. In all those old trades, therefore, the competition comes to be less than before. The market comes to be less fully supplied with many different sorts of goods. Their price necessarily rises more or less, and yields a greater profit to those who deal in them, who can, therefore, afford to borrow at a higher interest. For some time after the conclusion of the late war, not only private people of the best credit, but some of the greatest companies in London, commonly borrowed at five per cent. who before that had not been used to pay more than four, and four and a half per cent. The great accession both of territory and trade, by our acquisitions in North America and the West Indies, will sufficiently account for this, without supposing any diminution in the capital stock of the society. So great an accession of new business to be carried on by the old stock, must necessarily have diminished the quantity employed in a great number of particular branches, in which the competition being less, the profits must have been greater.

口的增长,利息降低了。但劳动工资却不与资本利润一起下降。不论资本利润如何,对劳动的需求都随着资本的增长而增加。尽管利润减少,但资本却继续增加,而且还要比以前增加得更为迅速。就这一点来说,勤劳的国家和勤劳的个人一样,都在获取财富。一般来说,大的资本虽然利润较低,但比高利润的小资本,却增加得更为迅速。俗语说,钱生钱。当已经取得了一点,要取得更多就会比较容易。最困难的是取得这一点。在前面,我已经对资本的增加和劳动的增长(对有用劳动需求的增长)之间的关系,作了部分的说明。在以后关于资本积累的讨论中,我会做出更加详细的说明。

获得新领土或开拓新行业,即使是在财富正迅速增长的国家,也可能会提高资本利润以及增加与此有关的货币利息。由于国家的资本,不足以满足这种新获得或新发展所带来的全部行业的资金需求,所以只把它投在能提供最大利润的那些部门上。以前投在其他行业上的资本也有一部分肯定会被撤回来,转而投入利润更大的新行业。所以,那些旧行业竞争就没有以前那么激烈了,市场上各种商品的供给也相应减少。商品减少,其价格必然或多或少地上升,这就为经营者提供了更大的利润,而他们也有能力以比从前高的利息率借入资金。在最近一次战争结束后不久,有良好信用的个人,乃至伦敦一些最大的公司,一般都以5%的利息率借款。在此之前,他们几乎没有借过4%或4.5%以上利息的借款。这一点可以从英国占领北美和西印度曾经增加英国领土与商业得到充分说明,不用设想社会财富会有任何减少。旧资本所要经营的行业增加得那么多,必然会减少许多特定行业的资本量。结果在这些行业中,由于竞争的缓和,利润必然增加。

<small>新获得新领土或开拓新行业即会提高利润,在日益富裕的国家也是如此。</small>

| 国民财富的性质与原理

I shall hereafter have occasion to mention the reasons which dispose me to believe that the capital stock of Great Britain was not diminished even by the enormous expence of the late war.

<small>Diminution of capital stock raises profits.</small>   The diminution of the capital stock of the society, or of the funds destined for the maintenance of industry, however, as it lowers the wages of labour, so it raises the profits of stock, and consequently the interest of money. By the wages of labour being lowered, the owners of what stock remains in the society can bring their goods at less expence to market than before, and less stock being employed in supplying the market than before, they can sell them dearer. Their goods cost them less, and they get more for them. Their profits, therefore, being augmented at both ends, can well afford a large interest. The great fortunes so suddenly and so easily acquired in Bengal and the other British settlements in the East Indies, may satisfy us that, as the wages of labour are very low, so the profits of stock are very high in those ruined countries. The interest of money is proportionably so. In Bengal, money is frequently lent to the farmers at forty, fifty, and sixty per cent. and the succeeding crop is mortgaged for the payment. As the profits which can afford such an interest must eat up almost the whole rent of the landlord, so such enormous usury must in its turn eat up the greater part of those profits. Before the fall of the Roman republic, a usury of the same kind seems to have been common in the provinces, under the ruinous administration of their proconsuls. The virtuous Brutus lent money in Cyprus at eight – and – forty per cent. as we learn from the letters of Cicero. ①

In a country which had acquired that full complement of riches which the nature of its soil and climate, and its situation with respect to other countries, allowed it to acquire; which could, therefore, advance no further, and which was not going backwards,

---

① [Ad Atticum, VI., i., 5, 6. Cicero had arranged that a six – year – old debt should be repaid with interest at the rate of 12 per cent. per annum, the principal being increased by that amount for each of the six years. This would have very nearly doubled the principal, but Brutus, through his agent, kept asking for 48 per cent., which would have multiplied it by more than fifteen. However, Cicero asserted that the 12 per cent. would have satisfied the cruellest usurers.]

我相信,最近一次战争的巨大开支,并没有使不列颠的财富减少,其原因我将在以后章节加以说明。

然而,社会财富即维持产业的资金的减少,必然使劳动工资降低,进而提高资本利润和货币利息。由于劳动工资降低,社会上剩余资本的所有者,就能够用比以前少的费用将商品提供给市场;由于供应市场的资本比以前少,他们能够以比从前高的价格出售货物。商品的成本低了,而所得多了,其利润从两方面增加,因此能够支付较高的利息。在孟加拉和东印度其他英属殖民地,获得巨额财产是如此之快、如此之易。这一事实,充分说明这些贫穷地区的劳动工资非常低而资本利润非常高。其货币利息也相应的非常高。在孟加拉资金往往以40%、50%或60%的利息贷给农场主,并将下一时期的收获物作为抵押。要能够支付这种高利息的利润,必然会侵吞地主的几乎所有地租;而这样庞大的高利贷,必然侵占利润的大部分。罗马共和国衰亡以前,各地方在总督涸泽而渔的暴政下,这样高的利息非常普遍。从西塞罗[1]的书中,我们可以知道,连道德高尚的布鲁塔斯也曾在塞浦路斯岛以48%的利息放贷①。

一国的财富如果已达到它的土壤、气候以及相对于其他国家的位置所允许获得的限度,因而没有可能再进一步增加,但却也

---

① 见《致庞培的信》(Ad Atticum),第6卷第一章第5、6节。西塞罗认为一个6年期的债务利率应该是每年12%,本金在这6年中逐年增长。这样下来本金几乎会翻一番,但布鲁塔斯通过他的代理人却要求48%的利率,这样几乎增加15倍了。然而西塞罗说12%的利率已经让最贪婪的放贷者满意了。

[1] 西塞罗(Cicero),公元前106~前43年,古罗马政治家、雄辩家、著作家。

国民财富的性质与原理

both the wages of labour and the profits of stock would probably be very low. In a country fully peopled in proportion to what either its territory could maintain or its stock employ, the competition for employment would necessarily be so great as to reduce the wages of labour to what was barely sufficient to keep up the number of labourers, and, the country being already fully peopled, that number could never be augmented. In a country fully stocked in proportion to all the business it had to transact, as great a quantity of stock would be employed in every particular branch as the nature and extent of the trade would admit. The competition, therefore, would every - where be as great, and consequently the ordinary profit as low as possible.

In a country as rich as it possibly could be, profits as well as wages would be very low,

But perhaps no country has ever yet arrived at this degree of opulence. China seems to have been long stationary, and had probably long ago acquired that full complement of riches which is consistent with the nature of its laws and institutions. But this complement may be much inferior to what, with other laws and institutions, the nature of its soil, climate, and situation might admit of. A country which neglects or despises foreign commerce, and which admits the vessels of foreign nations into one or two of its ports only, cannot transact the same quantity of business which it might do with different laws and institutions. In a country too, where, though the rich or the owners of large capitals enjoy a good deal of security, the poor or the owners of small capitals enjoy scarce any, but are liable, under the pretence of justice, to be pillaged and plundered at any time by the inferior man-

but there has never yet been any such country, Interest is raised by defective enforcement of contracts,

darines, the quantity of stock employed in all the different branches of business transacted within it, can never be equal to what the nature and extent of that business might admit. In every different branch, the oppression of the poor must establish the monopoly of the rich, who, by engrossing the whole trade to themselves, will be able to make very large profits. Twelve per cent. accordingly is said to be the common interest of money in China, and the ordinary profits of stock must be sufficient to afford this large interest.

A defect in the law may sometimes raise the rate of interest considerably above what the condition of the country, as to wealth or poverty, would require. When the law does not enforce the performance of contracts, it puts all borrowers nearly upon the same footing with bankrupts or people of doubtful credit in better regulated countries. The uncertainty of recovering his money

没有发生衰退。那么,此时它的劳动工资和资本利润也许都很低。当一国人口的数量,已完全达到其领土可以维持或其资本可以雇用的限度,在此状态下,就业竞争必将十分激烈,使劳动工资降低到只够维持现有劳动者人数的地步。并且这时人口已经饱和,不可能再有增加。一国的资本,如果与国内必须经营的各行业所需要的资本相比,还有剩余。那么各行业所使用的资本,就达到了各行业的性质和范围所能容纳的限度。由此,各地方的竞争就激烈到极点,而普通利润也降到最低。

但是,也许还没有一个国家已经达到这种富裕程度。中国似乎长期处于停滞状态,其财富也许在很久以前就已经完全达到了该国法律制度所允许的限度,但如果改变他的法律制度,那么该国的土壤、气候和地理位置所可允许的限度,可能比上述限度要大得多。一个忽视或鄙夷对外贸易、只允许外国船舶驶入其中一两个港口的国家,是无法经营在不同法制体制下所可能经营的那么多交易。另外,在富人或大资本家享有很大安全,而穷人或小资本家不但不能享有安全,而且随时都有可能被下级官吏以执法为借口而强加掠夺的国家,国内所经营的各种行业,都是不可能投入足够多的资本来达到按照各种行业的性质和范围所能容纳的程度。在各行业中,压迫穷人,就必然要使富人的垄断成为制度。富人通过垄断就能获取极大的利润。所以,中国一般的利息率据说是12%,而资本的普通利润必须能够支付这么高的利息。

法律上的缺陷,有时会使一国利息率升高到远远超过它的实际状况(如贫富状况)所能承受的程度。当法律不能强制人们履行契约时,那一切借款人所处的地位都和法制健全的国家中的破产者或信用不好者的地位几乎相当。放贷人收回借款的把握

makes the lender exact the same usurious interest which is usually required from bankrupts. Among the barbarous nations who over – run the western provinces of the Roman empire, the performance of contracts was left for many ages to the faith of the contracting parties. ① The courts of justice of their kings seldom intermeddled in it. The high rate of interest which took place in those ancient times may perhaps be partly accounted for from this cause.

and by prohibition.　　When the law prohibits interest altogether, it does not prevent it. Many people must borrow, and nobody will lend without such a consideration for the use of their money as is suitable, not only to what can be made by the use of it, but to the difficulty and danger of evading the law. The high rate of interest among all Mahometan nations is accounted for by Mr. Montesquieu, not from their poverty, but partly from this, ②and partly from the difficulty of recovering the money, ③

The lowest rate of profit must be more than enough to compensate losses,　　The lowest ordinary rate of profit must always be something more than what is sufficient to compensate the occasional losses to which every employment of stock is exposed. It is this surplus only which is neat or clear profit. What is called gross profit comprehends frequently, not only this surplus, but what is retained for compensating such extraordinary losses. The interest which the borrower can afford to pay is in proportion to the clear profit only.

and so must the lowest rate of interest.　　The lowest ordinary rate of interest must, in the same manner, be something more than sufficient to compensate the occasional losses to which lending, even with tolerable prudence, is exposed. Were it not more, charity or friendship could be the only motives for lending.

In a country as rich as it possibly could be interest would be so low that only the wealthiest people could live on it.　　In a country which had acquired its full complement of riches, where in every particular branch of business there was the greatest quantity of stock that could be employed in it, as the ordinary rate of clear profit would be very small, so the usual market rate of interest which could be afforded out of it, would be so low as to render it impossible for any but the very wealthiest people to live upon the interest of their money.

---

① [*Lectures*, pp. 130 – 134.]

② [*l. e.*, the danger of evading the law.]

③ [*Esprit des lois*, liv. xxii., ch 19,]

不大,就使他向其他借款人索取的利息和向破产者在借款时索取的利息一样高。在横行于罗马帝国西部各地的未开化民族中,很长时间以来契约是否履行只凭当事者的信用①,他们王国的法院很少过问此事。当时的高利息率,恐怕部分也是由此引起的。

如果法规要完全禁止利息,也不可能收到效果。许多人必须借入资金;而出借人,不仅要考虑这笔资金的用法,也就是使用它时的报酬,而且还会要求补偿规避法律的风险。孟德斯鸠说,一切伊斯兰教国家利息率之所以高,并不是因为他们贫穷,而是部分因为法律禁止利息②,部分因为贷款难以收回③。禁止利息也会导致高利率。

最低的普通利润率,除了要能够补偿投资可能遭遇的意外损失以外,还必须有盈余。只有这一剩余才能算是纯利润或净利润。通常所说的总利润,除了包含这种剩余以外,还包含了为补偿意外损失而留下的部分。借款人所能够支付的利息,只与纯利润成比例。最低利润率,必须足以补偿投资的意外损失。

出借资金,就算相当谨慎,也有受意外损失的可能。所以,最低的普通利息率就和最低的普通利润率一样,除了补偿借贷可能遇到的意外损失外,还必须有盈余。如果没有盈余,那么出借资金的动机就只能是出于善心或友情了。最低利息率也如此。

在达到极度富裕,并且用于各行业的资本已达到最大限度的国家,一般纯利润率很低。因而这种利润所能支付的平均市场利息率也很低。因此除了大富商外,任何人都没办法靠货币利息生活。小资产者和中等有产者,都必须监督自己资本的用途。几乎所有人都在一个极度富裕的国家,只有富人才能靠利息生活。

---

① 《关于法律、警察、岁入及军备的演讲》,第 130~134 页。
② 即触犯法律的危险。
③ 《论法的精神》,liv. xxii,第 19 章。

All people of small or middling fortunes would be obliged to superintend themselves the employment of their own stocks. It would be necessary that almost every man should be a man of business, or engage in some sort of trade. The province of Holland seems to be approaching near to this state. It is there unfashionable not to be a man of business. ① Necessity makes it usual for almost every man to be so, and custom every where regulates fashion. As it is ridiculous not to dress, so is it, in some measure, not to be employed, like other people. As a man of a civil profession seems awkward in a camp or a garrison, and is even in some danger of being despised there, so does an idle man among men of business.

<small>The highest rate of profit would eat up all rent and leave only wages.</small>
The highest ordinary rate of profit may be such as, in the price of the greater part of commodities, eats up the whole of what should go to the rent of the land, and leaves only what is sufficient to pay the labour of preparing and bringing them to market, according to the lowest rate at which labour can any – where be paid, the bare subsistence of the labourer. The workman must always have been fed in some way or other while he was about the work; but the landlord may not always have been paid. The profits of the trade which the servants of the East India Company carry on in Bengal may not perhaps be very far from this rate.

<small>The proportion of interest to profit rises and falls with the rate of profit.</small>
The proportion which the usual market rate of interest ought to bear to the ordinary rate of clear profit, necessarily varies as profit rises or falls. Double interest is in Great Britain reckoned, what the merchants call, a good, moderate, reasonable profit; terms which I apprehend mean no more than a common and usual profit. In a country where the ordinary rate of clear profit is eight or ten per cent., it may be reasonable that one half of it should go to interest, wherever business is carried on with borrowed money. The stock is at the risk of the borrower, who, as it were, insures it to the lender; and four or five per cent. may, in the greater part of trades, be both a sufficient profit upon the risk of this insurance, and a sufficient recompence for the trouble of employing the stock. But the proportion between interest and clear profit might not be the same in countries where the ordinary rate of profit was either a good deal lower, or a good deal higher. If it were a good deal

---

① [Joshua Gee, *Trade and Navigation of Great Britain Considered*, 1729, p. 128, notices the fact of the Dutch being all engaged in trade and ascribes it to the deficiency of valuable land.]

得成为商人,或者从事某种产业。荷兰的现状,似乎正变得与此相似。在那里,商人算是时髦人物①。现实需要使得几乎所有的人都习以为常地去这样做。同时习俗又处处支配着时尚。好像如若不和别人穿上同样的服装,便会成为笑柄;不和别人同样从事商业,也不免成为笑柄。一个游手好闲的人,置身于商人中间,就好像一个文官置身于军队中一样,就会感到一种尴尬,甚至是被轻视。

最高的平均利润率也许是这样一种利润率——它在大部分商品价格中完全占去本应归作地租的那一部分,只剩下足够支付商品生产及运到市场所需劳动的最低工资,即按照所有地方仅足以维持生存的工资。在工人们从事工作时,总得设法养活他们;但地主却不一定这样做。东印度公司职员在孟加拉经营所取得的商业利润,恐怕和这个最高比率相差不远。

<small>高的利润率会占去所有的地租,而只留下工资。</small>

平常市场利息率对平均纯利润率的比例,必随利润升降而变化。在英国,商人把相当于两倍利息的利润,看作合理的利润。我认为,这所谓的合理的利润,就是平均利润。在一个平均纯利润率为8%或10%的国家,用借来的资金经营商业的人,用所得利润的一半作为利息应该是合理的。资本由借用人承担风险,他似乎是给出借人保险;在大部分行业中,4%或5%,既可作为这种所冒风险的足够补偿,也可作为不辞辛苦运用这笔资本的足够补偿。不过,在普通利润率低得多或高得多的国家,利息和纯利润的比例就可能不会像上述那样了。如果利润率低得多,就不能以

<small>利息与利润率之间的比例,随着利润率的变化而变化。</small>

---

① 乔舒亚·吉:《大不列颠贸易与航海研究》(1729年,第128页),注意到荷兰人全民皆商的事实,把这个现象归因于荷兰土地贫乏。

国民财富的性质与原理

lower, one half of it perhaps could not be afforded for interest; and more might be afforded if it were a good deal higher.

<small>Countries with low profits can sell as cheap as those with low wages; and in reality high profits tend to raise prices more than high wages.</small>

In countries which are fast advancing to riches, the low rate of profit may, in the price of many commodities, compensate the high wages of labour, and enable those countries to sell as cheap as their less thriving neighbours, among whom the wages of labour may be lower.

In reality high profits tend much more to raise the price of work than high wages. If in the linen manufacture, for example, the wages of the different working people, the flax – dressers, the spinners, the weavers, &c. should, all of them, be advanced two pence a day; it would be necessary to heighten the price of a piece of linen only by a number of two pences equal to the number of people that had been employed about it, multiplied by the number of days during which they had been so employed. That part of the price of the commodity which resolved itself into wages would, through all the different stages of the manufacture, rise only in arithmetical proportion to this rise of wages. But if the profits of all the different employers of those working people should be raised five per cent. that part of the price of the commodity which resolved itself into profit, would, through all the different stages of the manufacture, rise in geometrical proportion to this rise of profit. The employer of the flax – dressers would in selling his flax require an additional five per cent. upon the whole value of the materials and wages which he advanced to his workmen. The employer of the spinners would require an additional five per cent. both upon the advanced price of the flax and upon the wages of the spinners. And the employer of the weavers would require a like five per cent. both upon the advanced price of the linen yarn and upon the wages of the weavers. In raising the price of commodities the rise of wages operates in the same manner as simple interest does in the accumulation of debt. The rise of profit operates like compound interest. ① Our merchants and master – manufacturers complain much of the bad

---

① [According to the view of the subject here set forth, if the three employers each spend £100 in wages and materials, and profits are at first 5 per cent. and then rise to 10 per cent. , the finished commodity must rise from £331 0s. 3d. to £364 2s. , while if, on the other hand. the wages rise from £100 to £105, the commodity will only rise to £347 11s. 3d. It is assumed either that profits mean profits on turn – over and not on capital per annum, or else that the employers each have their capital turned over once a year. But even when one or other of these assumptions is granted, it is clear that the 'simple interest' may easily be greater than the 'compound'. In the examples just given we doubled profits, but only added one – twentieth to wages. If we double wages and leave profits at 5 per cent , the commodity should rise from £331 0s. 3d. to £662 0s. 6d.]

一半作为利息;如果利润率高得多,就可能以一半以上作为利息。

在财富迅速增长的国家,许多商品价格的低利润可以弥补高的劳动工资。这样它们的商品,就能与繁荣程度较低并且劳动工资可能也较低的邻国的商品以同样低廉的价格出售。

事实上,高利润抬高产品价格的倾向比高工资大得多。例如,在麻布制造厂不同工种的工人,如梳麻工、纺工、织工等的工资,如果每天均提高两便士。那么一匹麻布所需提高的价格,仅仅等于生产这一匹麻布所雇的工人人数,乘以他们生产这一匹麻布的工作日数,再乘以两便士。商品价格中属于工资的那一部分,在生产的一切不同阶段,按算术级数递次增加。但如果雇用这些工人的所有雇主的利润,都提高5%,那么商品价格中归于利润的那一部分,在一切生产阶段,就会按照几何级数递次增加。也就是说,梳麻工的雇主在卖麻时,除了要求他所垫付的材料和工人工资的全部价值,还另加上5%的资金。纺工的雇主,也要求在他所垫付的麻价和工人工资的全部价值上,另外加上5%。同理,织工的雇主,也同样要求另外加上5%。因此,工资增高对商品价格升高的作用,就好像单利对债额累积的作用。而利润增高对它的作用,却好像复利一样①。我国的商人和制造者只对高

---

① 根据这里提出的有关这个问题的观点,如果三个雇主对原料和工资各支付100镑,那么利率起初为5%,随后升至10%,制成品价格肯定由331镑3便士升至364镑2先令;与之相反,如果工资由100镑升到105镑,商品价格则将升到347镑11先令3便士。这是假定,要么利润意味着周转资本的利润而不是每年资本的利润,要么每个雇主只能使其资本每年周转一次。但是,不论是哪种假定,显然"单利"很容易比"复利"多。在刚才提到的例子中,我们使利润加倍,工资只增加1/20。如果是工资翻倍,利润仍然为50%,而商品价格却由331镑3便士升至662镑6便士。

effects of high wages in raising the price, and thereby lessening the sale of their goods both at home and abroad. They say nothing concerning the bad effects of high profits. They are silent with regard to the pernicious effects of their own gains. They complain only of those of other people. ①

---

① [This paragraph is not in ed. 1; the epigram at the end, however, did not make its appearance here for the first time in ed. 2, since it occurs in a slightly less polished form in vol. i.]

工资在提高物价、从而减少国内外销售的作用,大发牢骚;却对高利润的恶果,只字不提。对自己得利而产生的恶果,他们保持沉默;却对他人得利而产生的后果,大加抱怨①。

---

① 本段在第 1 版中没有,这里结尾讽刺的话只有在第 2 版中才首次出现,因为它在随后的第 2 卷中以略浅修饰的形式出现了。

CHAPTER X

Of Wages And Profit In The Different Employments Of Labour And Stock[1]

<small>Advantages and disadvantages tend to equality where there is perfect liberty.</small>   The whole of the advantages and disadvantages of the different employments of labour and stock must, in the same neighbourhood, be either perfectly equal or continually tending to equality. If in the same neighbourhood, there was any employment evidently either more or less advantageous than the rest, so many people would crowd into it in the one case, and so many would desert it in the other, that its advantages would soon return to the level of other employments. This at <small>Actual differences of pecuniary wages and profits are due partly to counterbalancing circumstances and partly to want of perfect liberty.</small> least would be the case in a society where things were left to follow their natural course, where there was perfect liberty,[2] and where every man was perfectly free both to chuse what occupation he thought proper, and to change it as often as he thought proper. Every man's interest would prompt him to seek the advantageous, and to shun the disadvantageous employment.

Pecuniary wages and profit, indeed, are every-where in Europe extremely different according to the different employments of labour and stock. But this difference arises partly from certain circumstances in the employments themselves, which, either really, or at least in the imaginations of men, make up for a small pecuniary gain in some, and counter-balance a great one in others; and partly from the policy

---

[1] [The general design of this chapter, as well as many of its details, was doubtless suggested by Cantillon Essai, pt. 1, chaps. vii. and viii.]

[2] [Above, pp. 58, 64.]

— 224 —

第十章　工资、利润随劳动与
资本用途的不同而不同①

不同用途的劳动和资本的利弊,总的说来,在同一地区内,必然完全相同或不断趋于相同。若在同一地方内,某一用途明显地比其他用途更好或更差。那么,就会有许多人放弃比较不好的用途,转而投入比较好的用途。这样,这种用途的利益,不久便回到和其他各种用途相等水平。至少,在一切事物都听任其自然发展的社会,即在一切都任其完全自由②的社会,每个人都能自由地选择自己认为最适当的职业,并且能随时自由改变自己职业的社会,情形的确会如此。每个人的利益关系必然会促使他寻找好的用途,避开不好的用途。

的确,欧洲各地的货币工资和货币利润,随着劳动和资本用途的不同而有所不同。但这种不同,部分源于各种用途本身的情况。这些情况,或者真有其事,或者至少存在于一般人的想像中,要对某些行业的微薄的收益有所补偿,而对另一些行业的丰厚的

在完全自由的地区,不同用途的劳动的利弊必然趋同。

工资和货币利润的实际差别,部分地因此彼此抵消,部分地源于完全缺乏自由。

---

① 本章的大体设计和其中的许多细节,毫无疑问来源于肯提伦的启示,《论一般商业的性质》,第1部分,第7、8章。
② 见上面的第58、64页。

of Europe, which no-where leaves things at perfect liberty.

The particular consideration of those circumstances and of that policy will divide this chapter into two parts.

PART I *Inequalities Arising From The Nature Of The Employments Themselves*①

<small>There are five counterbalancing circumstances:</small>

The five following are the principal circumstances which, so far as I have been able to observe, make up for a small pecuniary gain in some employments, and counter-balance a great one in others: first, the agreeableness or disagreeableness of the employments themselves; secondly, the easiness and cheapness, or the difficulty and expence of learning them; thirdly, the constancy or inconstancy of employment in them; fourthly, the small or great trust which must be reposed in those who exercise them; and fifthly, the probability or improbability of success in them.

<small>(1) Wages vary with the agreeableness of the employment.</small>

First, The wages of labour vary with the ease or hardship, the cleanliness or dirtiness, the honourableness or dishonourableness of the employment. Thus in most places, take the year round, a journeyman taylor earns less than a journeyman weaver. His work is much easier. A journeyman weaver earns less than a journeyman smith. His work is not always easier, but it is much cleanlier. A journeyman blacksmith, though an artificer, seldom earns so much in twelve hours as a collier, who is only a labourer, does in eight. His work is not quite so dirty, is less dangerous, and is carried on in day-light,

---

① [The foregoing introductory paragraphs would lead a logical reader to expect part I of the chapter to be entitled: ' Inequalities of pecuniary wages and profit which merely counterbalance inequalities of other advantages and disadvantages. ' The rather obscure title actually chosen is due to ' the fact that nearly a quarter of the part is occupied by a discussion of three further conditions which must be present in addition to ' perfect freedom ' in order to bring about the equality of total advantages and disadvantages. The chapter would have been clearer if this discussion had been placed at the beginning, but it was probably an afterthought.]

收益有所抵消。还有一部分是因为欧洲各国的政策不让事物完全自由发展。

本章将分两节,来讨论这些情况及相应政策。

第一部分 起因于职业自身性质的不均等①

就我所能观察到的情况来说,主要有以下五种。它们一方面对某些职业的微薄的报酬给予补偿,另一方面又对另一些职业的丰厚的报酬加以抵消:第一,职业本身的愉快性或不愉快性;第二,职业学习的难易和学费的多少;第三,职业的稳定性或不稳定性;第四,职业所须担负的责任的轻重;第五,职业成功的可能或不可能。〔有五种互相抵消的情况:〕

第一,劳动工资因为业务困难或容易、清洁或肮脏、有尊贵或卑贱而有所不相同。由此,在大多数地方,就整年来计算,缝纫工的收入比织工少,这是因为缝纫工的工作比较容易。织工的收入比铁匠为少,这是因为织工的工作虽然并不总是比铁匠容易但却清洁得多。铁匠虽然是一种技工,但工作12小时所得,却往往不及一个普通煤矿工人工作八小时所得,这是因为铁匠的工作,不像煤矿工那么危险那么脏,而且他是在白天在地面上工作。对于〔(1)工资随职业本身令本人愉悦与否而有所不同。〕

---

① 前面引言中的段落,将会让一个逻辑清晰的读者认为本章第一部分的标题应该是"货币工资和货币利润的不平等仅仅抵消其他利弊的不平等"。事实上之所以采取本文中这样模糊的标题,是因为这一部分有大概1/4的篇幅是在讨论"完全自由"之外的另外三种必须讨论的情况,以引出总的利弊的平等。本来这种讨论应该放在开头的地方,那样本章就会简洁一些,但这恐怕是事后才这么想罢了。

and above ground. Honour makes a great part of the reward of all honourable professions. In point of pecuniary gain, all things considered, they are generally under-recompensed, as I shall endeavour to show by and by. Disgrace has the contrary effect. The trade of a butcher is a brutal and an odious business; but it is in most places more profitable than the greater part of common trades. The most detestable of all employments, that of public executioner, is, in proportion to the quantity of work done, better paid than any common trade whatever.

<small>Some very agreeable employments are exceedingly ill paid.</small> Hunting and fishing, the most important employments of mankind in the rude state of society, become in its advanced state their most agreeable amusements, and they pursue for pleasure what they once followed from necessity. In the advanced state of society, therefore, they are all very poor people who follow as a trade, what other people pursue as a pastime. Fishermen have been so since the time of① Theocritus. A poacher is every-where a very poor man in Great Britain. In countries where the rigour of the law suffers no poachers, the licensed hunter is not in a much better condition. The natural taste for those employments makes more people follow them than can live comfortably by them, and the produce of their labour, in proportion to its quantity, comes always too cheap to market to afford anything but the most scanty subsistence to the labourers.

<small>The same thing is true of profits.</small> Disagreeableness and disgrace affect the profits of stock in the same manner as the wages of labour. The keeper of an inn or tavern, who is never master of his own house, and who is exposed to the brutality of every drunkard, exercises neither a very agreeable nor a very creditable business. But there is scarce any common trade in which a small stock yields so great a profit.

Secondly, The wages of labour vary with the easiness and cheapness, or the difficulty and expence of learning the business.

---

① See Idyllium xxi. [This merely describes the life of two poor fishermen The note appears first in ed. 2.]

一切体面的职业，荣誉可以说构成了报酬的大部分。就金钱的收入来说，考虑到各方面因素，从事这些职业的报酬一般都是偏低的，这将在本文后面加以论述。而在不体面的职业上，情形正好相反。屠夫的职业是粗蛮又讨厌的，但在大部分地方，他们得到的比其他大部分普通职业多。其中刽子手这种职业，是最可嫌恶的了。然而，就工作量而言，他的报酬比任何普通职业都要多。

在未开化社会最为重要的两种职业被认为是打鱼和狩猎，而在进步社会，却成为了最令人愉快的娱乐。以前为生活需要而渔猎，今日却为消遣而渔猎。因此在进步社会，把别人用作消遣的事当作职业的人，生活都是极贫穷的。自西奥克里塔斯时代以来，渔民一直都极其贫困。① 在英国各地私猎者都是一些极贫穷的人。在严禁偷猎的国家，即使有特许证的狩猎者，他们的状况也不见得好多少。大多数人操此职业是因为他们对这种职业有天然的兴趣，而不是因为这一职业能给他们提供优裕生活。他们劳动生产物的售价与相应的劳动量相比，总是过于廉价，只能维持劳动者最贫困的生活。

一些非常令人愉快的职业报酬却很低。

不愉快和不体面对资本利润的影响和对劳动工资的影响相同。一个小旅馆或小酒店的老板绝不是自己店铺的真正主人，随时可能有醉客们蛮横无理。他们所从事的职业是不体面和不让人愉快的职业。但在普通营业中，很少有像这样以小额资本得到大额利润。

利润也是如此。

第二，劳动工资因职业本身学习的难易、学费的多少而不同。

---

① 见《田园诗》第 21 节，仅仅是描写了两个贫穷的渔夫的生活。这个注解第一次出现在第 2 版中。

(2) Wages vary with the cost of learning the business.

When any expensive machine is erected, the extraordinary work to be performed by it before it is worn out, it must be expected, will replace the capital laid out upon it, with at least the ordinary profits. A man educated at the expence of much labour and time to any of those employments which require extraordinary dexterity and skill, may be compared to one of those expensive machines. The work which he learns to perform, it must be expected, over and above the usual wages of common labour, will replace to him the whole expence of his education, with at least the ordinary profits of an equally valuable capital. It must do this too in a reasonable time, regard being had to the very uncertain duration of human life, in the same manner as to the more certain duration of the machine.

The difference between the wages of skilled labour and those of common labour, is founded upon this principle.

The cost or apprenticeship accounts for the wages of manufacturers being higher than those of country labourers.

The policy of Europe considers the labour of all mechanics, artificers, and manufacturers, as skilled labour; and that of all country labourers as common labour. It seems to suppose that of the former to be of a more nice and delicate nature than that of the latter. It is so perhaps in some cases; but in the greater part it is quite otherwise, as I shall endeavour to shew by and by. The laws and customs of Europe, therefore, in order to qualify any person for exercising the one species of labour, impose the necessity of an apprenticeship, though with different degrees of rigour in different places. They leave the other free and open to every body. During the continuance of the apprenticeship, the whole labour of the apprentice belongs to his master. In the mean time he must, in many cases, be maintained by his parents or relations, and in almost all cases must be cloathed by them. Some money too is commonly given to the master for teaching him his trade. They who cannot give money, give time, or become bound for more than the usual number of years; a consideration which, though it is not always advantageous to the master, on account of the usual idleness of apprentices, is always disadvantageous to the apprentice. In country labour, on the contrary, the labourer, while he is employed about the easier, learns the more difficult parts of his business, and his own labour maintains him through all the different stages of his

安装任何高价机器,必然希望机器在报废以前所完成的特定工作可以收回所投入的资本,并至少获得普通利润。一种花费了许多劳动和时间才学会的需要特殊技艺和灵巧的职业,类似于一台高价机器。这种职业的人在从事工作时,必然期望,获得高于普通劳动的工资,以收回全部学费,并至少取得普通利润。并且考虑到人的寿命长短极不确定,所以还必须在适当的时间内做到这一点,就像机器在比较确定的寿命之内,必须在适当时期内收回成本和取得利润一样。

> (2)工资随着职业学习的成本高低而不同。

技术工人劳动工资和一般工人劳动工资之间的差异,就是建立在这个原则之上。

欧洲的政策是把机械师、技工和制造师的劳动看作熟练的技术性的劳动,而把一切农村劳动者的劳动看作普通劳动。这种政策似乎认为,前者的劳动比后者的劳动在性质上更精细更巧妙。在一些场合或许是这样,但在大多数情况下却完全不是这样,对此我将在下面加以说明。因此,欧洲各国的法律习俗,为了使某人有从事某种劳动的资格,都要求他先当学徒,尽管在各地规定的严格程度有所不同。而对于另一种劳动,则全凭个人自由。学徒期内,其全部劳动都归师傅所有。同时,在许多情况下,学徒的生活费还要由父母或亲戚负担;至于衣物,几乎都是由父母或亲戚负担。通常学徒还要给师傅一些钱作为学费。出不起金钱的学徒就给付时间,也就是说,要做得比一般学徒年限长。不过,这种情况对师傅未必有利,因为学徒一般很懒惰;但这对学徒来说就不利了。反之,就农村劳动来说,劳动者在被雇从事简易工作的时候却能学会比较复杂的工作。在受雇期中的任何阶段,他都能以自己的劳动养活自己。因此,欧洲各国的机械师、技工和制

> 学徒的说明了导致了制造业的工资比农村劳动者工资高。

employment. It is reasonable, therefore, that in Europe the wages of mechanics, artificers, and manufacturers, should be somewhat higher than those of common labourers. ① They are so accordingly, and their superior gains make them in most places be considered as a superior rank of people. This superiority, however, is generally very small; the daily or weekly earnings of journeymen in the more common sorts of manufactures, such as those of plain linen and woollen cloth, computed at an average, are, in most places, very little more than the day wages of common labourers. Their employment, indeed, is more steady and uniform, and the superiority of their earnings, taking the whole year together, may be somewhat greater. It seems evidently, however, to be no greater than what is sufficient to compensate the superior expence of their education.

Education for liberal professions is more costly and the pecuniary recompense consequently higher.

Education in the ingenious arts and in the liberal professions, is still more tedious and expensive. The pecuniary recompence, therefore, of painters and sculptors, of lawyers and physicians, ought② to be much more liberal: and it is so accordingly.

Profits are not much affected by this circumstance.

The profits of stock seem to be very little affected by the easiness or difficulty of learning the trade in which it is employed. All the different ways in which stock is commonly employed in great towns seem, in reality, to be almost equally easy and equally difficult to learn. One branch either of foreign or domestic trade, cannot well be a much more intricate business than another.

Thirdly, The wages of labour in different occupations vary with

---

① [This argument seems to be modelled closely on Cantillon, *Essai*, pp. 23, 24, but probably also owes something to Mandeville, *Fable of the Bees*, pt. ii. , dialogue vi. , vol. ii. , p. 423. Cp. *Lectures*, pp. 173-175.]

② [The 'ought' is equivalent to it is reasonable they should be' in the previous paragraph, and to 'must' in 'must not only maintain him while he is idle' on p. 105. Cp. 'doivent' in Cantillon, *Essai*, p. 24: 'Ceux donc qui emploient des artisans ou gens de métier, doivent nécessairement payer leur travail plus haut que celui d'un laboureur ou man œuvre.' The meaning need not be that it is ethically right that a person on whose education much has been spent should receive a large reward, but only that it is economically desirable, since otherwise there would be a deficiency of such persons.]

造师的工资略高于普通劳动者的工资,是合理的。① 也正是由于这一点,他们在很多地方成为了高人一等的人。但一般来说,他们这种优越性也是很有限的。在普通制造业中,像单色亚麻和呢绒这类的制造工人一天或一星期的工资,平均算来,和普通劳动者一天或一星期的工资相差无几。可能是由于他们的工作,比较稳定而且单一,但按全年来计算,也许这种优越性略大些。但很明显,这些似乎不足以补偿他们受教育时更多费用的花费。

精巧艺术和自由职业的学习所需的时间更长、费用更大。所以,画师和雕刻师、律师和医生的货币报酬当然应当②更加丰厚,而事实上也是如此。<small>自由职业者的教育费用较高,因此其货币报酬也更高。</small>

但资本利润,却好像很少受资本所投入的那一行业学习难易的影响。大城市里通常运用资本的各种方法,就学习难易的程度来说,似乎完全相等。国外或国内贸易的部门业务,基本不会比另一部门业务繁难多少。<small>利润不受上述情况的影响。</small>

第三,不同职业的劳动工资随职业的稳定性或不稳定性而

---

① 这段论证似乎完全受肯提伦《论一般商业的性质》(第 23、24 页)的影响,但是也部分受孟德维尔《蜜蜂的寓言》(第 2 部分,对话 6,第 2 卷,第 423 页。《关于法律、警察、岁入及军备的演讲》第 6 章,第 173~175 页)的影响。

② "应当" 词的含义,就等于上段提到的"是合理的"和第 105 页提到的"不仅要足以维持他们没有工作时的生活"中的"要"。这个意思并非是说伦理上一个人教育支出很多的话就应该获得丰厚回报是正确的,而仅仅是说这在经济上是可取的,否则就会缺乏这样的人。

国民财富的性质与原理

(3) Wages vary with constancy of employment.

the constancy or inconstancy of employment. ① Employment is much more constant in some trades than in others. In the greater part of manufactures, a journeyman may be pretty sure of employment almost every day in the year that he is able to work. A mason or bricklayer, on the contrary, can work neither in hard frost nor in foul weather, and his employment at all other times depends upon the occasional calls of his customers. He is liable, in consequence, to be frequently without any. What he earns, therefore, while he is employed, must not only maintain him while he is idle, but make him some compensation for those anxious and desponding moments which the thought of so precarious a situation must sometimes occasion. Where the computed earnings of the greater part of manufacturers, accordingly, are nearly upon a level with the day wages of common labourers, those of masons and bricklayers are generally from one half more to double those wages. Where common labourers earn four and five shillings a week, masons and bricklayers frequently earn seven and eight; where the former earn six, the latter often earn nine and ten, and where the former earn nine and ten, as in London, the latter commonly earn fifteen and eighteen. No species of skilled labour, however, seems more easy to learn than that of masons and bricklayers. Chairmen in London, during the summer season, are said sometimes to be employed as bricklayers. The high wages of those workmen, therefore, are not so much the recompence of their skill, as the compensation for the inconstancy of their employment.

A house carpenter seems to exercise rather a nicer and more ingenious trade than a mason. In most places, however, for it is not universally so, his day-wages are somewhat lower. His employment, though it depends much, does not depend so entirely upon the occasional

---

① [The treatment of this head would have been clearer if it had begun with a distinction between 'day-wages' (mentioned lower down on the page) and annual earnings. The first paragraph of the argument claims that annual earnings as well as day-wages will be higher in the inconstant employment so as to counterbalance the disadvantage or repulsive force of having 'anxious and desponding moments'. In the subsequent paragraphs, however, this claim is lost sight of, and the discussion proceeds as if the thesis was that annual earnings are equal though day-wages may be unequal.]

不同。① 有些行业中的职业比其他行业种的职业稳定得多。大部分制造业工匠,只要他能够工作,一年中几乎每天都会有工作做。而相反,泥水匠或砌砖匠在霜冻或恶劣的天气中便完全不能工作。即使在天气好的时候,他们有无工作仍须取决于顾客的偶然召唤。因此,他们可能常常没有工作。这样,他们在被雇佣时的收入,不仅要足以维持他们没有工作时的生活,而且对于他在不安定环境中不时感到的焦虑和沮丧也应该给予一些补偿。所以,大部分制造业工人的收入,计算起来和普通劳动者日工资基本相同,而泥水匠和砌砖匠所得一般却有普通劳动工资的一倍半到两倍。一个地方,如果普通劳动者一星期可挣得4、5先令,泥水匠和砌砖匠则往往可挣得7、8先令。而前者如果为6先令,则后者常为9、10先令。像伦敦这种地方,如果前者为9、10先令,则后者常为15到18先令。不过,在各种熟练劳动中,像泥水匠和砌砖匠这种劳动似乎是最容易学的。据说,伦敦轿夫在夏天有时就被雇为砌砖匠。因此,这类劳动者的高工资,与其说是对他们技术的报酬,倒不如说是对他们工作不稳定的报酬。

(3) 工资随着职业稳定与否而发生变化

建房子的木匠所从事的职业,比起泥水匠的工作来似乎更精细、更有技巧。但在许多地方,并不是说在一切地方,建筑木匠每天的工资却比泥水匠低一些。这是因为他们的工作,虽然也在一

---

① 如果刚开始就区分"日工资(本页下文中提到)"和年收益,对这个标题的处理就会更加清晰一些。论证的第一段认为,在个固定的职业的年收益和日工资应该高一些,以便抵消在"焦虑和消沉时候"的不利和压力。但在后来的段落中,这个主张就不见了踪迹,讨论的主题似乎成了尽管日工资不相等,但年收益还是相等。

calls of his customers; and it is not liable to be interrupted by the weather.

When the trades which generally afford constant employment, happen in a particular place not to do so, the wages of the workmen always rise a good deal above their ordinary proportion to those of common labour. In London almost all journeymen artificers are liable to be called upon and dismissed by their masters from day to day, and from week to week, in the same manner as day-labourers in other places. The lowest order of artificers, journeymen taylors, accordingly, earn there half a crown a day, though eighteen pence may be reckoned the wages of common labour. In small towns and country villages, the wages of journeymen taylors frequently scarce equal those of common labour; but in London they are often many weeks without employment, particularly during the summer.

When the inconstancy of employment is combined with the hardship, disagreeableness, and dirtiness of the work, it sometimes raises the wages of the most common labour above those of the most skilful artificers. A collier working by the piece is supposed, at Newcastle, to earn commonly about double, and in many parts of Scotland about three times the wages of common labour. His high wages arise altogether from the hardship, disagreeableness, and dirtiness of his work. His employment may, upon most occasions, be as constant as he pleases. The coal-heavers in London exercise a trade which in hardship, dirtiness, and disagreeableness, almost equals that of colliers; and from the unavoidable irregularity in the arrivals of coal-ships, the employment of the greater part of them is necessarily very inconstant. If colliers, therefore, commonly earn double and triple the wages of common labour, it ought not to seem unreasonable that coal-heavers should sometimes earn four and five times those wages. In the enquiry made into their condition a few years ago, it was found that at the rate at which they were then paid, they could earn from six to ten shillings a day.

定程度上取决于顾客的临时召唤,但却不像泥水匠那样完全取决于顾客的偶然召唤;而且还不像泥水匠那样那么容易受天气的影响。

如果一般的经常提供稳定工作的职业,在某个地方不提供稳定工作,那么这些职业的工人的工资就会上升,远远超过该职业工人的工资和普通劳动工资的通常比例。伦敦所有的下层技工,就像其他地方的打日工的佣人一样,每天、每星期都有可能被雇主雇佣或解雇。因此,伦敦最下层的技工,如裁缝工,一天能挣得半克朗,尽管普通劳动者的工资是每天18便士。在小城市和乡村地方,裁缝工的工资常常还不及普通劳动者的工资。而在伦敦,尤其是在夏天,裁缝工有时几个星期都找不到工作。

如果除了工作不稳定外,再加上艰苦、让人不愉快和肮脏的话,这种即使是最普通的劳动,有时也可能使其工资超过最熟练的技工。计件工资的煤矿工,在纽卡斯一般可得到比普通劳动人约多一倍的工资。在苏格兰许多地方,可得到的大约比普通劳动高两倍。他们得到高的工资,完全是由于他们工作的艰苦、令人不愉快和不清洁。在大多数情况下,他们要工作多久都可以,只要他们愿意。就艰苦、令人不愉快和不清洁来说,伦敦运煤工人的职业几乎和他们相同,但由于运炭船到达的时间不定期,所以大部分运煤工人的工作必然是很不固定的。因此,通常煤矿工如果能得到两倍或三倍于普通劳动的工资;那么,运煤工人有时可能得到四倍、五倍于普通劳动的工资,这似乎不应该被认为不合理。根据几年前对运煤工人的调查,按当时工资率,每天能赚到6

国民财富的性质与原理

Six shillings are about four times the wages of common labour in London, and in every particular trade, the lowest common earnings may always be considered as those of the far greater number. How extravagant soever those earnings may appear, if they were more than sufficient to compensate all the disagreeable circumstances of the business, there would soon be so great a number of competitors as, in a trade which has no exclusive privilege, would quickly reduce them to a lower rate.

The constancy or inconstancy of employment cannot affect① the ordinary profits of stock in any particular trade. Whether the stock is or is not constantly employed depends, not upon the trade, but the trader.

Constancy does not affect profits.

Fourthly, The wages of labour vary according to the small or great trust which must be reposed in the workmen. ②

(4) Wages vary with the trust to be reposed.

The wages of goldsmiths and jewellers are every-where superior to those of many other workmen, not only of equal, but of much superior ingenuity; on account of the precious materials with which they are intrusted.

We trust our health to the physician; our fortune and sometimes our life and reputation to the lawyer and attorney. Such confidence

---

① [That 'stock' consists of actual objects seems to be overlooked here. The constancy with which such objects can be employed is various: the constancy with which the hearse of a village is employed depends on the number of deaths, which may be said to be the trade,' and is certainly not the trader'. There is no difference of profits corresponding to differences of day-wages due to unequal constancy of employment, for the simple reason that 'profits' are calculated by their amount per-annum, but the rural undertaker, liable to long interruption of business in healthy seasons, may just as well as the bricklayer be supposed to receive 'some compensation for those anxious and desponding moments which the thought of so precarious a situation must sometimes occasion'.]

② [The argument foreshadowed in the introductory paragraphs of the chapter requires an allegation that it is a disadvantage to a person to have trust reposed in him, but no such allegation is made. Cantillon, *Essai*, p. 27, says: lorsqu'il faut de la *capacité* et de la confiance, on paie encore le travail plus cher, comme aux jouailliers, teneurs de compte, caissiers, et autres. Hume, *History*, ed. of 1773, vol. viii., p. 323, says: 'It is a familiar rule in all business that every man should be pad in proportion to the trust reposed in him and the power which he enjoys.']

先令至 10 先令。而据说 6 先令,大约是伦敦普通劳动工资的 4 倍。不论什么职业,最低的普通工资往往可认为是从事这一职业的绝大多数人所得的报酬。他们的所得无论是否过高,如果除补偿职业上一切不适意的情况外还有剩余,那么在一个没有垄断特权的行业里,不久就一定会有许多竞争者出现,很快就会把工资率降下来。

而任一行业资本的普通利润,都不可能受资本所在行业的稳定或不稳定的影响。资本是否稳定地使用并不取决于行业,而取决于经营该行业的人。① 资本固定与否并不影响利润。

第四,劳动的工资,随劳动者所须承担的责任大小的不同而不相同。②

各地金匠和宝石匠的工资,不仅比其他具有相当技巧的许多劳动者高,而且比其他具有更大技巧的许多劳动者高。这是因为托付给他们的是贵重的材料。(4)工资的高低与所承担的责任相关。

我们把自己的身体健康托付给医生;把财产,有时甚至把自己的生命和名誉托付给律师或辩护士。这样重大的信任我们绝

---

① 由实物构成的"资本"在这里似乎被忽略了。采用什么样的实物资本其稳定性也是不同的:一个村庄棺材的稳定数目取决于死亡人数,这可以说是"交易"而当然不能说是"交易者"。由于工作稳定性的不均等导致的不同的日工资的利润是没有差别的,原因很简单,就在于这里的"利润"是基于他们的年产量,而对于农村业主来说,经常在好的时节中断他们的工作。这样很可能像砖瓦匠那样,考虑到有时肯定会存在这样那样焦虑和消沉的时刻从而给收入带来不稳定,而要求获得一定补偿。

② 这段论证已经在本章序言中预示了,它要求一个将责任置身于一人身上是不利的论断,但这个论断并未得到。肯提伦,《论一般商业的性质》第 27 页提到"这是个众所周知的规则即在所有的商业中一个人的收益要与他所承受的责任和他拥有的权力成比例"。

could not safely be reposed in people of a very mean or low condition. Their reward must be such, therefore, as may give them that rank in the society which so important a trust requires. The long time and the great expence which must be laid out in their education, when combined with this circumstance, necessarily enhance still further the price of their labour.

<small>Profits are unaffected by trust.</small>
When a person employs only his own stock in trade, there is no trust; and the credit which he may get from other people, depends, not upon the nature of his trade, but upon their opinion of his fortune, probity, and prudence. The different rates of profit, therefore, in the different branches of trade, cannot arise from the different degrees of trust reposed in the traders. ①

Fifthly, The wages of labour in different employments vary according to the probability or improbability of success in them. ②

<small>(5) Wages vary with the probability of success.</small>
The probability that any particular person shall ever be qualified for the employment to which he is educated, is very different in different occupations. In the greater part of mechanic trades, success is almost certain; but very uncertain in the liberal professions. Put your son apprentice to a shoemaker, there is little doubt of his learning to make a pair of shoes: But send him to study the law, it is at least twenty to one if ever he makes such proficiency as will enable him to live by the business. In a perfectly fair lottery, those who draw the prizes ought to gain all that is lost by those who draw the blanks. In a profession where twenty fail for one that succeeds, that one ought to gain all that should have been gained by the unsuccessful twenty. The counsellor at law who, perhaps, at near forty years of age, begins to

---

① [But some trades, e. g. , that of a banker, may be necessarily confined to persons of more than average trustworthiness, and this may raise the rate of profit above the ordinary level if such persons are not sufficiently plentiful.]

② [The argument under this head, which is often misunderstood, is that pecuniary wages are (on the average, setting great gains against small ones) less in trades where there are high prizes and many blanks. The remote possibility of obtaining one of the high prizes is one of the circumstances which in the imaginations of men make up for a small pecuniary gain Cantillon, *Essai*, p. 24, is not so subtle, merely making remuneration proportionate to risk.]

不能放心地委托给平庸或低微的人。所以他们得到的报酬必须使其能够保持接受这一重大委托所需的社会地位。这样再加上他们接受教育所花费的漫长时间与巨额费用,使他们的劳动价格更加提高。

如果一个人只是用自己的资本经营生意,就无所谓受到什么委托。而他能否从他人那里取得信用,并不取决于他所经营的行业的性质,而取决于别人对他的财产、诚实和谨慎的评价。因此,不同行业的不同利润率,不可能是由于经营各行业的人所承担的责任的不同而造成的。①

〔利润率受责任大小影响不大〕

第五,各种职业的劳动工资,因取得成功的可能性的大小的不同而不同。②

〔(5)工资随着成功可能性大小不同而不同〕

每个经过职业学习的人能否胜任将来的职业,此可能性的大小在不同的职业而大不相同。大部分的机械业中,成功基本都是有把握的;而就自由职业来说,却很没有把握。例如,把孩子送去学作鞋匠,无疑他能学会制鞋;但如果送孩子去学法律,那么它能精通法律并以此为生的可能性最多是 20:1。在完全公正的彩票中,中奖者应得到未中奖者所失去的全部。因而在这种成功者一人而不成功者就有 20 人的职业中,成功的这一个人,应享有不成功的那 20 个人本应得到而没有得到的全部。一个律师大概要到

---

① 一些行业,诸如银行业,可能就必须授予高于平均水平的责任。如果这些行业的职员不是充分的多的话,他们的利润率就会提高到高于平均水平。

② 这个论证的标题经常会让人误解,认为货币工资在具有较高价格和许多空缺的行业会较低。一种很难获得高价格的情况是"人们只创造了很小的货币收入"的情况。肯提伦(《论一般商业的性质》,第 24 页)认为事情并非这么微妙,实际上仅仅是报酬与风险成正比。

— 241 —

make something by his profession, ought to receive the retribution, not only of his own so tedious and expensive education, but of that of more than twenty others who are never likely to make any thing by it. How extravagant soever the fees of counsellors at law may sometimes appear, their real retribution is never equal to this.① Compute in any particular place, what is likely to be annually gained, and what is likely to be annually spent, by all the different workmen in any common trade, such as that of shoemakers or weavers, and you will find that the former sum will generally exceed the latter. But make the same computation with regard to all the counsellors and students of law, in all the different inns of court, and you will find that their annual gains bear but a very small proportion to their annual expence, even though you rate the former as high, and the latter as low, as can well be done. The lottery of the law, therefore, is very far from being a perfectly fair lottery; and that, as well as many other liberal and honourable professions, is, in point of pecuniary gain, evidently under-recompenced.

<small>Law and similar professions are nevertheless crowded.</small> Those professions keep their level, however, with other occupations, and, notwithstanding these discouragements, all the most generous and liberal spirits are eager to crowd into them. Two different causes contribute to recommend them. First, the desire of the reputation which attends upon superior excellence in any of them; and, secondly, the natural confidence which every man has more or less, not only in his own abilities, but in his own good fortune.

<small>Public admiration makes a part of the reward of superior abilities,</small> To excel in any profession, in which but few arrive at mediocrity, is the most decisive mark of what is called genius or superior talents. The public admiration which attends upon such distinguished abilities, makes always a part of their reward; a greater or smaller in proportion as it is higher or lower in degree. It makes a considerable part of that reward in the profession of physic; a still greater perhaps in that of law; in poetry and philosophy it makes almost the whole.

---

① [Lectures, p. 175.]

将近 40 岁时才能从职业取得一些收益,其所得的报酬应不仅应补偿他自己为受教育所花的时间和巨大费用,而且应补偿那些完全没有收益的 20 多个人的教育所花费的时间与费用。就算律师所收的费用有时显得过高,他的真正报酬却从未达到这么多。①算一下在某一地方任一行业的普通工人,如鞋匠或织工此类,一年间可能收入的总额和其一年间可能支出的总额,就会发现他们的收入一般多于支出。但是如果你用同样的方法对所有的律师和各法律协会的实习律师的支出与收入进行统计,你就会发现他们的年收入(即使你在估计时尽量提高他们年收入,并尽量减低他们年支出),只占年支出的很小的一部分。所以法律业这个彩票,绝不是一种完全公平的彩票。法律业与其他许多自由、体面的职业,所得到的报酬,在金钱方面,显然都是很不足的。

尽管这一职业有一些令人沮丧的地方,但它却仍能与其他职业一起发展,所有慷慨豁达的人都争先恐后地向这一行业挤来。这是由于有两个原因鼓舞他们:第一,希望在这些行业取得卓越成就的名利心;第二,这些人对于自己的才能和幸运的或多或少地天生的自信心。

可是法律和类似行业确实人员拥挤。

一个人如果在一种做到中等水平也不容易的职业里能表现出众,就最明确地表示出他具有所谓天才或卓越的才干。由这一卓越才干所博得的人们的赞赏,常常也构成了他的报酬的一部分。这一报酬是大还是小,就要看赞赏的程度的大小。对医生来说,这构成了全部报酬中的相当可观的部分;对律师来说,所占的部分也许更大;在诗歌或哲学界,它几乎占了全部。

公众的赞赏是能力报酬的一部分,卓越被赞赏。

---

① 《关于法律、警察、岁入及军备的演讲》,第 175 页。

> except in the peculiar case of players, operasingers, &c.

There are some very agreeable and beautiful talents of which the possession commands a certain sort of admiration; but of which the exercise for the sake of gain is considered, whether from reason or prejudice, as a sort of public prostitution. The pecuniary recompence, therefore, of those who exercise them in this manner, must be sufficient, not only to pay for the time, labour, and expence of acquiring the talents, but for the discredit which attends the employment of them as the means of subsistence. The exorbitant rewards of players, opera-singers, operadancers, &c. are founded upon those two principles; the rarity and beauty of the talents, and the discredit of employing them in this manner. It seems absurd at first sight that we should despise their persons, and yet reward their talents with the most profuse liberality. While we do the one, however, we must of necessity do the other. Should the public opinion or prejudice ever alter with regard to such occupations, their pecuniary recompence would quickly diminish. More people would apply to them, and the competition would quickly reduce the price of their labour. Such talents, though far from being common, are by no means so rare as is imagined. Many people possess them in great perfection, who disdain to make this use of them; and many more are capable of acquiring them, if any thing could be made honourably by them.

The over-weening conceit which the greater part of men have of their own abilities, is an ancient evil remarked by the philosophers and moralists of all ages. Their absurd presumption in their own good fortune, has been less taken notice of. It is, however, if possible, still more universal. There is no man living who, when in tolerable health and spirits, has not some share of it. The chance of gain is by

> The greater part of men have an over-weening conceit of their abilities;

every man more or less over-valued, and the chance of loss is by most men undervalued, and by scarce any man, who is in tolerable health and spirits, valued more than it is worth.

That the chance of gain is naturally over-valued, we may learn from the universal success of lotteries. The world neither ever saw,

有些才能是非常令人愉快和赞美的,能取得这种才能的人一定能博得某种赞赏;但如果用这些才能来谋取利益,世人就会出于理性或偏见认为是公开出卖灵魂。因此,运用此种才能牟利的人,所得报酬,不仅要补偿他学习这种技能所花费的时间、劳动和费用,而且要弥补他以此谋生而招致的名誉上的损失。演员、歌剧唱角、歌剧舞蹈者等所得的丰厚的报酬,就是由于这两个原则:一、才能的稀缺和美好;二、由于以这种方式运用才能而蒙受的声名上的损失。我们在一方面鄙视其人格,而在另一方面却又对其才能给予十分丰厚的回报,这乍一看,似乎很不合理。但事实上,正是因为我们鄙视他们的人格,所以要用丰厚的报酬来酬劳他们的才能。如果世人对这些职业的意见或偏见改变,他们的金钱报酬就会很快减少。因为更多的人会从事这些职业,竞争必然会使他们劳动的价格很快降低。这种才能虽然远不是一般的,但绝不是像世人所想像的那么稀有。许多具有这种才能几近完美的人,却不屑用它来图利谋生,这种人不算少。而且更多人也是能学到这种才能的,如果运用这种才能来谋生不会损害名誉的话。

> 除了特场演出的合员、歌唱家、剧歌剧等。

大多数人对于自己的才能过于自负。这是历代哲学家和道德家所说的一种由来已久的恶行。对于自己将幸运的不合理猜测,不大被人们所重视。而且要是可以这样说的话,对自己的幸运妄加猜测,恐怕比前者还更普遍。任何一个身体和精神都还不错的人,总免不了对自己的幸运抱有几分自信。每一个人,对成功的机会,都会或多或少地高估;而大多数人,对失败的机会,会作过低的估计。任何一个身体和精神都相当不错的人,都会对自己做出过高的估计。

> 大多数人对于自己的才能过于自负:

我们从购买彩票的人都认为自己能中这一事实可以看出,

— 245 —

lotteries show that the chance of gain is overvalued. nor ever will see, a perfectly fair lottery; or one in which the whole gain compensated the whole loss; because the undertaker could make nothing by it. In the state lotteries the tickets are really not worth the price which is paid by the original subscribers, and yet commonly sell in the market for twenty, thirty, and sometimes forty per cent. advance. The vain hope of gaining some of the great prizes is the sole cause of this demand. The soberest people scarce look upon it as a folly to pay a small sum for the chance of gaining ten or twenty thousand pounds; though they know that even that small sum is perhaps twenty or thirty per cent. more than the chance is worth. In a lottery in which no prize exceeded twenty pounds, though in other respects it approached much nearer to a perfectly fair one than the common state lotteries, there would not be the same demand for tickets. In order to have a better chance for some of the great prizes, some people purchase several tickets, and others, small shares in a still greater number. There is not, however, a more certain proposition in mathematics, than that the more tickets you adventure upon, the more likely you are to be a loser. Adventure upon all the tickets in the lottery, and you lose for certain; and the greater the number of your tickets the nearer you approach to this certainty.

and the moderate profit of insurers shows that the chance of loss is undervalued. That the chance of loss is frequently undervalued, and scarce ever valued more than it is worth, we may learn from the very moderate profit of insurers. In order to make insurance, either from fire or searisk, a trade at all, the common premium must be sufficient to compensate the common losses, to pay the expence of management, and to afford such a profit as might have been drawn from an equal capital employed in any common trade. The person who pays no more than this, evidently pays no more than the real value of the risk, or the lowest price at which he can reasonably expect to insure it. But though many people have made a little money by insurance, very few have made a great fortune; and from this consideration alone, it seems evident enough, that the ordinary balance of profit and loss is not more advantageous in this, than in other common trades by which so many people make fortunes. Moderate, however, as the premium

成功的机会自然而然地被人们估计得过高。完全公平的彩票,即以全部所得能抵偿全部损失的彩票,不仅从来没有过,就连以后也永远不会有。因为要是这样,经营者便会从中一无所得。就国营彩票来说,彩票实际上并不等于购买者所给付的价格的价值,市场上通常按超过实际价值的20%、30%乃至40%的价格出售。产生彩票这种需求的唯一原因,就是大家想中大奖的妄想。一个清醒稳重的人,也不会认为,以小额资金得到取得一万镑乃至两万镑的中奖机会是愚蠢的,虽然他们明知用以购买彩票的小额资金的实际价值比中奖机会的实际价值也许要高20%或30%。如果一种彩票奖金不超过20镑,即使在其他方面比普通国营彩票还更接近于完全公平,要购这种彩票的人恐怕也会少得多。为了增加中大奖的机会,有的人同时购买彩票几张奖券,有的人则多买几种彩票。但是,你冒险购买的彩票越多,你损失的可能性就越大,这是数学上再确定不过的原则。如果你冒险购买全部彩票,那么你肯定会亏。你购买彩票的数量越多,你就越接近于上述损失。

对彩票的购买表明了人们对成功机会的高估。

我们从保险业者微薄的利润可以看出,损失的机会常常是被低估了,很少估得比它的价值高。将火险或海上险当作一种事业来经营,普通保险费必须足以补偿普通的损失,支付管理的费用,并提供资本要是投入其他一般行业所能取得的利润。一个只给付了不多保险费的被保险人,显然只给付了风险的真实价值,即只给付了可指望的保险的最低价格。虽然许多人经营保险获得了一点利润,但几乎没有人出此发大财。单从这一点就可见,保险业中得利与损失相抵,不像对许多其他行业那么有利可图而使得许多人发财。不过,尽管保险费一般都很低廉,许多人却轻视

从保险业者微薄的利润可以看出人们对风险估计的过低。

— 247 —

of insurance commonly is, many people despise the risk too much to care to pay it. Taking the whole kingdom at an average, nineteen houses in twenty, or rather, perhaps, ninety-nine in a hundred, are not insured from fire. Sea risk is more alarming to the greater part of people, and the proportion of ships insured to those not insured is much greater. Many sail, however, at all seasons, and even in time of war, without any insurance. This may sometimes perhaps be done without any imprudence. When a great company, or even a great merchant, has twenty or thirty ships at sea, they may, as it were, insure one another. The premium saved upon them all, may more than compensate such losses as they are likely to meet with in the common course of chances. The neglect of insurance upon shipping, however, in the same manner as upon houses, is, in most cases, the effect of no such nice calculation, but of mere thoughtless rashness and presumptuous contempt of the risk.

<small>Young people are particularly prone to overvalue the chance of gain and under-value the risk of loss.</small>

The contempt of risk and the presumptuous hope of success, are in no period of life more active than at the age at which young people chuse their professions. How little the fear of misfortune is then capable of balancing the hope of good luck, appears still more evidently in the readiness of the common people to enlist as soldiers, or to go to sea, than in the eagerness of those of better fashion to enter into what are called the liberal professions.

<small>For this reason soldiers ar poorly paid, and sailors not much better.</small>

What a common soldier may lose is obvious enough. Without regarding the danger, however, young volunteers never enlist so readily as at the beginning of a new war; and though they have scarce any chance of preferment, they figure to themselves, in their youthful fancies, a thousand occasions of acquiring honour and distinction which never occur. These romantic hopes make the whole price of their blood. Their pay is less than that of common labourers, and in actual service their fatigues are much greater

The lottery of the sea is not altogether so disadvantageous as that of the army. The son of a creditable labourer or artificer may frequently go to sea with his father's consent; but if he enlists as a soldier, it is always without it. Other people see some chance of his making something by the one trade: nobody but himself sees any of his making any thing by the other. The great admiral is less the object

危险而不愿支付保险费。就拿全英国平均推算,每 20 户中就有 19 户,甚至每 100 户中有 99 户,没有投火险。海上风险,在许多人看来更为可怕,因此,保险船只对未保险船只的比例比上述比例大得多。但无论在什么季节,甚至在战争期间,都还是会有许多船只没有投保。像这样做有时并不是由于不小心。一家大公司或者一位大商人,如果有二三十只船同时在海面航行,它们似乎可以说是相互保险的。而由此节约下来的保险费,也许已足够补偿在一般情况下所可能遭受的损失。然而,在大多数情况下,船只不保海险、房屋不保火险,并不是这种精密计算的结果,而是由于轻率大意和蔑视风险。

轻视危险和奢望成功,在一生中选择自己职业的青年时期最为活跃。在这一时期,对不幸的恐惧抵不住对幸运的希望。这从普通青年踊跃地应征参军或出海航行,比从上流社会青年热衷于从事所谓自由职业看得更加明显。

青年人特别容易估高功的机会,估低损失的危险。

普通士兵可能遭受的损失是很明显的。然而,青年志愿者不顾危险,在新战争开始时十分踊跃地应征。尽管升迁的机会十分渺茫,但他们在青年的幻想中设想有许多可以获得荣誉和表现自己的机会,但事实上这种机会几乎没有。这些空虚的希望,就成为他们流血的全部价值。他们的报酬比普通劳动者低,而在服役期间,他们的辛苦比普通劳动者却大得多。

因此士兵的报酬低微,海军的处境比陆军好不了多少。

总的说来,海军的不可预测事件,并不像陆军那样不利。一个有声誉的工人或技工的儿子往往可以得到父亲的允许而去航海。可是,如果他去作陆军士兵,他的父亲就一般不会同意。因为就航海来说,人们也认为有几分成功的机会,而当陆军,除了他自己,谁都不认为有成功的机会。这就是为什么伟大的海军将

of public admiration than the great general, and the highest success in the sea service promises a less brilliant fortune and reputation than equal success in the land. The same difference runs through all the inferior degrees of preferment in both. By the rules of precedency a captain in the navy ranks with a colonel in the army; but he does not rank with him in the common estimation. As the great prizes in the lottery are less, the smaller ones must be more numerous. Common sailors, therefore, more frequently get some fortune and preferment than common soldiers; and the hope of those prizes is what principally recommends the trade. Though their skill and dexterity are much superior to that of almost any artificers, and though their whole life is one continual scene of hardship and danger, yet for all this dexterity and skill, for all those hardships and dangers, while they remain in the condition of common sailors, they receive scarce any other recompence but the pleasure of exercising the one and of surmounting the other. Their wages are not greater than those of common labourers at the port which regulates the rate of seamen's wages. As they are continually going from port to port, the monthly pay of those who sail from all the different ports of Great Britain, is more nearly upon a level than that of any other workmen in those different places; and the rate of the port to and from which the greatest number sail, that is the port of London, regulates that of all the rest. At London the wages of the greater part of the different classes of workmen are about double those of the same classes at Edinburgh. But the sailors who sail from the port of London seldom earn above three or four shillings a month more than those who sail from the port of Leith, and the difference is frequently not so great. In time of peace, and in the merchant service, the London price is from a guinea to about seven-and-twenty shillings the calendar month. A common labourer in London, at the rate of nine or ten shillings a week, may earn in the calendar month from forty to five-and-forty shillings. The sailor, indeed, over and above his pay, is supplied with provisions. Their value, however, may not perhaps always exceed the difference between his pay and that of the common labourer; and though it sometimes should, the excess will not be clear gain to the sailor, because he cannot share it with his

领，不像伟大的陆军将领那么受到广大民众崇拜的原因了。在海军中服务最大成功所可得到的名誉和利益，也不像陆军中同等的成功的人所得到的名利那么大。在海陆军中所有下级的军官中，都存在这样的差别。依据军阶规定，海军上校和陆军上校属于同一级别。但在公众的眼中，却并不把这两者同等看待。就好像在彩票中，大奖比较少，而小奖就比较多。因此，普通水兵，比起普通陆军士兵来说，就更常得到一定的好处和升迁的机会。而获得这种奖励的希望，就成为一般人愿意应征水兵的主要原因。普通水兵熟练的技能、技巧，虽然比几乎任何技工的技能和技巧都强得多，而且他们一生必须不断地与困难危险作搏斗。但在他们继续充当普通水兵的时候，就算他们有那么大的技能技巧，面临那么多的困难与危险，他们除了在运用技能与技巧克服困难与危险时的快感以外，并没有任何其他报酬。他们的工资并不会多于港口普通劳动者的工资，而他们的工资起着决定海员工资率的作用。由于他们不断地往返于各港口之间，因此不列颠各港口的海员，每月的工资，比各地任何其他劳动者的工资更趋于一致。而且，海员出入最多的伦敦港的工资率便决定了其他各港口的海员的工资率。伦敦大部分工人的工资大约为爱丁堡同等工人工资的两倍。但由伦敦出航的水手每月的工资，很少有比由利斯港出航的水手高出三四先令的。就和平时期商船上工作的海员来说，在伦敦的价格，按月计算，是大约21先令到27先令。而伦敦普通劳动者以一星期9或10先令计算，每月可赚到40乃至45先令。当然，水手除工资外，还免费供有食宿。但其总价值，却未必会超过他的工资与普通劳动者工资的差额。即使有时超过了，这超过额也不能算是水手的个人所得，因为他不能和家庭分享这些食

wife and family, whom he must maintain out of his wages at home.

<small>Dangers which can be surmounted attract, though mere unwholesomeness repels.</small>

The dangers and hair-breadth escapes of a life of adventures, instead of disheartening young people, seem frequently to recommend a trade to them. A tender mother, among the inferior ranks of people, is often afraid to send her son to school at a sea-port town, lest the sight of the ships and the conversation and adventures of the sailors should entice him to go to sea. The distant prospect of hazards, from which we can hope to extricate ourselves by courage and address, is not disagreeable to us, and does not raise the wages of labour in any employment. It is otherwise with those in which courage and address can be of no avail. In trades which are known to be very unwholesome, the wages of labour are always remarkably high. Unwholesomeness is a species of disagreeableness, and its effects upon the wages of labour are to be ranked under that general head.

<small>Profits vary with certainty of return.</small>

In all the different employments of stock, the ordinary rate of profit varies more or less with the certainty or uncertainty of the returns. These are in general less uncertain in the inland than in the foreign trade, and in some branches of foreign trade than in others; in the trade to North America, for example, than in that to Jamaica. The ordinary rate of profit always rises more or less with the risk. It does not, however, seem to rise in proportion to it, or so as to compensate it completely. Bankruptcies are most frequent in the most hazardous trades. The most hazardous of all trades, that of a smuggler, though when the adventure succeeds it is likewise the most profitable, is the infallible road to bankruptcy. The presumptuous hope of success seems to act here as upon all other occasions, and to entice so many adventurers into those hazardous trades, that their competition reduces the profit below what is sufficient to compensate the risk. To compensate it completely, the common returns ought, over and above the ordinary profits of stock, not only to make up for all occasional losses, but to afford a surplus profit to the adventurers of the same nature with the profit of insurers. But if the common returns were sufficient for

粮,而是必须用他的工资来维持他的家庭。

工作的危险和九死一生的冒险,并没有使青年人的勇气受到挫折,有时似乎反而会更鼓励他们去从事这类职业。下层人民,慈母们往往不愿把儿子送往海港城市的学校读书,因为害怕儿子看到海船,听到水手的谈话和冒险事迹,这些会引诱他们去当水手。正是在遥远的将来可能发生的危险,使他们渴望凭自己的勇敢和机智来摆脱危险,并没有使他们有所畏惧。尽管危险并不会提高这类职业的工资。至于一些不需要勇敢与机智的职业的情形就不同了。在一些很不卫生的行业,劳动工资总是特别丰厚。不卫生是一种令人不愉快的事情,它对劳动工资的影响应归入不愉快那个总项目。

> 不令人讨厌,但克服危险对年轻人有一种吸引力。尽管卫生条件可以服的危险

资本不同用途的普通利润率,多少随收益的确定与不确定而有所不同。一般地说,国内贸易的收益比对外贸易的收益确定。而对外贸易的一些部门,又比另一些部门确定。例如,对北美贸易的收益,就比对牙买加贸易的收益确定。平均利润率总是随风险程度的增加而增高,但增高的程度和风险大小似乎并不成比例。也就是说,增高的利润不一定能完全抵偿风险。破产在最危险行业中是最常见的。在所有行业中,最危险的要算走私了。在成功的场合,固然可以得到丰厚利润,但这种冒险也无可避免地会导致破产。成功的奢望在这场合所起的作用,和在其他场合一样,诱使了许多冒险者去参与这种危险的行业。他们的竞争,使利润降低到了不够补偿其风险的程度。要使风险得到完全弥补,其普通回报,就应在高于资本普通利润以外,不仅要弥补一切临时损失,还对冒险者提供一种与投保人利润性质相同的额外利润。但是,如果普通收益足够补偿这一切,那么这些行业的破产

> 随着收益确定不确定的程度而不同。利润

— 253 —

all this, bankruptcies would not be more frequent in these than in other trades. ①

Profits are less unequal than wages, and their inequality is often only due to the inclusion of wages,

Of the five circumstances, therefore, which vary the wages of labour, two only affect the profits of stock; the agreeableness or disagreeableness of the business, and the risk or security with which it is attended. In point of agreeableness or disagreeableness, there is little or no difference in the far greater part of the different employments of stock; but a great deal in those of labour; and the ordinary profit of stock, though it rises with the risk, does not always seem to rise in proportion to it. It should follow from all this, that, in the same society or neighbourhood, the average and ordinary rates of profit in the different employments of stock should be more nearly upon a level than the pecuniary wages of the different sorts of labour. They are so accordingly. The difference between the earnings of a common labourer and those of a well employed lawyer or physician, is evidently much greater than that between the ordinary profits in any two different branches of trade. The apparent difference, besides, in the profits of different trades, is generally a deception arising from our not always distinguishing what ought to be considered as wages, from what ought to be considered as profit.

as in the case of the profit of an apothecary,

Apothecaries profit is become a bye-word, denoting something uncommonly extravagant. This great apparent profit, however, is frequently no more than the reasonable wages of labour. The skill of an apothecary is a much nicer and more delicate matter than that of any artificer whatever; and the trust which is reposed in him is of much greater importance. He is the physician of the poor in all cases, and of the rich when the distress or danger is not very great. His reward, therefore, ought to be suitable to his skill and his trust, and it arises generally from the price at which he sells his drugs. But the whole drugs which the best employed apothecary, in a large market town, will sell in a year, may not perhaps cost him above thirty or forty pounds. Though he should sell them, therefore, for three or four hundred, or at a thousand per cent. profit, this may frequently be no more than the reasonable wages of his labour charged, in the only way

---

① [The fact is overlooked that the numerous bankruptcies may be counterbalanced by the instances of great gain. Below, on p. 127, the converse mistake is made of comparing great successes and leaving out of account great failures.]

就不会比其他行业更为常见。①

因此,使劳动工资存在差异的五种情况中,只有两种影响资本利润,即工作令人愉快还是让人不愉快,是安全还是存在风险。就让人愉快或不愉快而言,绝大多数不同资本的用途,都差不多或完全无差别;但在各种不同的劳动中却有着很大的区别。而且,资本的普通利润,虽然随风险的增大而增高,但增高程度却不一定和风险大小都成比。由此可见,在同一社会或其附近地区,用于不同用途资本的平均或一般利润率,应该比不同劳动的货币工资更接近于同一水平。事实上,也正如此。一个普通劳动者的收入和一个生意好的律师或医生收入的差异,明显比任何两种行业的普通利润的差异大得多。同时,行业间利润的表面差异往往给人造成错觉,这是因为我们没有把什么应当算作工资和什么应当算作利润的区别开来。

药剂师的利润这句话,已经成为过多获取利益的代名词。但是这种表面上很大的利润,往往只不过是劳动的合理报酬。药剂师的技能比其他一切技工的要精巧得多,并且他所受负担的责任也重得多。他是穷人的医生,而在病痛或危险比较轻微的时候,也是富人的医生。所以,他的报酬应当和他的技能与他所承担的责任相称,一般是包含在所出售的药品价格中。然而,在人的商业城市中,一个生意最兴隆的药剂师每年出卖的全部药品成本也许不过三四十镑。而他所卖的价格却是三四百镑,也就是以十倍的利润出售,但这些利润,可能也只不过是他的合理工资;他的合

---

① 无数的破产可能会被巨大的收益所抵消的事实被忽视了。下文中,就犯了相反的错误,即只考虑巨大的成功而不考虑巨大的失败。

in which he can charge them, upon the price of his drugs. The greater part of the apparent profit is real wages disguised in the garb of profit.

<small>or country grocer.</small>

In a small sea-port town,① a little grocer will make forty or fifty per cent. upon a stock of a single hundred pounds, while a considerable wholesale merchant in the same place will scarce make eight or ten per cent. upon a stock of ten thousand. The trade of the grocer may be necessary for the conveniency of the inhabitants, and the narrowness of the market may not admit the employment of a larger capital in the business. The man, however, must not only live by his trade, but live by it suitably to the qualifications which it requires. Besides possessing a little capital, he must be able to read, write, and account, and must be a tolerable judge too of, perhaps, fifty or sixty different sorts of goods, their prices, qualities, and the markets where they are to be had cheapest. He must have all the knowledge, in short, that is necessary for a great merchant, which nothing hinders him from becoming but the want of a sufficient capital. Thirty or forty pounds a year cannot be considered as too great a recompence for the labour of a person so accomplished. Deduct this from the seemingly great profits of his capital, and little more will remain, perhaps, than the ordinary profits of stock. The greater part of the apparent profit is, in this case too, real wages.

<small>The greater difference between retail and wholesale profits in town than country is due to the same cause.</small>

The difference between the apparent profit of the retail and that of the wholesale trade, is much less in the capital than in small towns and country villages. Where ten thousand pounds can be employed in the grocery trade, the wages of the grocer's labour make but a very trifling addition to the real profits of so great a stock. The apparent profits of the wealthy retailer, therefore, are there more nearly upon a level with those of the wholesale merchant. It is upon this account that goods sold by retail are generally as cheap and frequently much cheaper in the capital than in small towns and country villages. Grocery goods, for example, are generally much cheaper; bread and butcher's meat frequently as cheap. It costs no more to bring grocery

---

① [Doubtless Kirkcaldy was in Smith's mind.]

理工资除了加在药品价格上以外,可能没有第二种取得方法。因此,他的表面利润的绝大部分,是穿上了利润外衣的真实工资。

在一个海滨的小城市,①一个小杂货商人投入一百镑的资本,能获得40%或50%的利润;而同一地方资本万镑的大批发商人,却很难获得8%或10%的利润。他所经营的杂货业,对方便该地居民来说,也许是必要的,但狭小的市场可能不需要更大的资本投在这上面。但是,一个小杂货商人,不仅要靠自己的生意过活,而且还要过得和经营这一业务所必须有的各种资格相称。除拥有小额资本以外,他不仅要能读、能写、能算,还要能相当准确地判断五六十种不同商品的价格与质量,并能以最低的价格在市场上购买这些商品。简而言之,它必须具备一个大商人所需具备的一切知识。他之所以没有成为大商人,是因为他没有充足的资本。具有这样才能的人,每年获取三四十镑作为报酬,绝不能被认为过分。从他似乎很大的资本利润中,除去上述报酬,剩下的部分恐怕不会比普通利润多。所以,在此情况下,表面利润的大部分,实际上也是真实工资。

以小城镇杂货商的利润为例。

零售商的表面利润与批发商的表面利润之间的差异,在大城市比在小市镇和农村小得多。在杂货业能投资一万镑的地方,杂货商人的劳动工资,不过是相对于这么大资本的真实利润的一个很小的附加。因此,在那个地方富裕零售商表面利润比批发商表面利润更趋向一致。正由于这个原因,城市里的商品零售价格一般和小市镇及农村一样便宜,而且往往比后者更加便宜。举例来说,杂货一般就便宜得多;面包和肉往往是同样便宜。把杂货运

零售商与批发商之差别,在比小城镇要小。

---

① 毫无疑问,斯密心中的这个城市即柯卡尔迪。

goods to the great town than to the country village; but it costs a great deal more to bring corn and cattle, as the greater part of them must be brought from a much greater distance. The prime cost of grocery goods, therefore, being the same in both places, they are cheapest where the least profit is charged upon them. The prime cost of bread and butcher's meat is greater in the great town than in the country village; and though the profit is less, therefore they are not always cheaper there, but often equally cheap. In such articles as bread and butcher's meat, the same cause, which diminishes apparent profit, increases prime cost. The extent of the market, by giving employment to greater stocks, diminishes apparent profit; but by requiring supplies from a greater distance, it increases prime cost. This diminution of the one and increase of the other seem, in most cases, nearly to counter-balance one another; which is probably the reason that, though the prices of corn and cattle are commonly very different in different parts of the kingdom, those of bread and butcher's meat are generally very nearly the same through the greater part of it.

The lesser rate of profit in towns yields larger fortunes, but these mostly arise from speculation.

Though the profits of stock both in the wholesale and retail trade are generally less in the capital than in small towns and country villages, yet great fortunes are frequently acquired from small beginnings in the former, and scarce ever in the latter. In small towns and country villages, on account of the narrowness of the market, trade cannot always be extended as stock extends. In such places, therefore, though the rate of a particular person's profits may be very high, the sum or amount of them can never be very great, nor consequently that of his annual accumulation. In great towns, on the contrary, trade can be extended as stock increases, and the credit of a frugal and thriving man increases much faster than his stock. His trade is extended in proportion to the amount of both, and the sum or amount of his profits is in proportion to the extent of his trade, and his annual accumulation in proportion to the amount of his profits. It seldom happens, however, that great fortunes are made even in great towns by any one regular, established, and well-known branch of business, but in consequence of a long life of industry, frugality, and attention. Sudden fortunes, indeed, are sometimes made in such places by what is called the trade of speculation. The speculative merchant exercises no one regular, established, or well known branch of business.

往城市的费用并不会比运往小城市或农村多,但把谷物和牲畜运往城市的费用就大得多,因为它们大部分要从很远的地方运来。杂货的成本在城市和在农村一样多,因此,什么地方在货物价格中附加利润最少,价格就最便宜。而面包和肉的成本,在大城市高于农村,所以,虽然大城市的利润较低,这些货物的售价却未必总是更低,而往往是同样低廉。就面包和肉这类商品来说,这一原因减少了其表面利润,而增加了原始成本。市场的扩大,一方面会由于所用资本增多而减少其表面利润,另一方面又会由于需要从较远的地方得到供给而增加其原价。这种对表面利润的减少和增加的作用,在很多场合看来几乎可以互相抵消。谷物和牲畜的价格,虽然在王国各地很不相同;但面包和肉的价格,在王国的大多数地方一般基本相同,其原因也许就在这里。

虽然零售商与批发商的资本利润,在大城市一般比在小城市和农村要小,但从小资本开始经营而发大财的人,在城市常常可以看到,而在小城市和农村却几乎没有。在小城市和农村,由于市场狭隘,营业额常常不会随资本的扩大而增加。因此,在这些地方个别商人的利润率也许很高,但利润的总额却不是很大,他的年储蓄额也有很限。反之,在大城市商业营业额能随资本的增加而扩大,而勤俭商人的信用比其资本的增加还要快。这样,他的营业额随他的信用和资本的扩张而增大;他的利润总额则随他的营业的增大而增加;他每年积累的资金也相应地随利润总额的增大而增加。不过,即使是在大城市,也很少有人由于一种正常的、固定的和人所共知的行业而发大财。发大财主要是长时期的勤俭和小心经营的结果。当然,在这些地方,从事投机生意而突然致富的人也是有的;这些投机商并不是经营正常的、固定的

He is a corn merchant this year, and a wine merchant the next, and a sugar, tobacco, or tea merchant the year after. He enters into every trade when he foresees that it is likely to be more than commonly profitable, and he quits it when he foresees that its profits are likely to return to the level of other trades. His profits and losses, therefore, can bear no regular proportion to those of any one established and well-known branch of business. A bold adventurer may sometimes acquire a considerable fortune by two or three successful speculations; but is just as likely to lose one by two or three unsuccessful ones. This trade can be carried on no where but in great towns. It is only in places of the most extensive commerce and correspondence that the intelligence requisite for it can be had.

<small>The five circumstances thus counterbalance differences of pecuniary gains,</small>

The five circumstances above mentioned, though they occasion considerable inequalities in the wages of labour and profits of stock, occasion none in the whole of the advantages and disadvantages, real or imaginary, of the different employments of either. The nature of those circumstances is such, that they make up for a small pecuniary gain in some, and counter-balance a great one in others.

<small>but three things are necessary as well as perfect freedom:</small>

In order, however, that this equality may take place in the whole of their advantages or disadvantages, three things are requisite even where there is the most perfect freedom. First, the employments must be well known and long established in the neighbourhood; secondly, they must be in their ordinary, or what may be called their natural state; and, thirdly, they must be the sole or principal employments of those who occupy them.

<small>(1) the employments must be well known and long established,</small>

First, this equality can take place only in those employments which are well known, and have been long established in the neighbourhood.

Where all other circumstances are equal, wages are generally higher in new than in old trades. When a projector attempts to establish a new manufacture, he must at first entice his workmen from other employments by higher wages than they can either earn in their own trades, or than the nature of his work would otherwise require,

和人所共知的业务。他可能今年是谷物商,明年是酒商,后年又是糖商、烟草商或茶商。不论是哪种行业,只要他预见到这一行业有超过普通利润的可能,他就立刻进入该行业;一旦预见到该行业的利润将要降低到和其他行业相等,他就立刻离开。因此,他的利润和损失与其他任何正常的、固定的和人所共知的行业的利润与损失都不能相提并论。大胆的冒险者,有时也许由于两三次投机的成功就能获得大量财产,有时也许会因为两三次投机的失败而损失惨重。这种投机,除了大城市以外,在其他任何地方,都无法进行。因为从事这种经营所需要的情报,只在商业最繁荣、交易最频繁的地方才能获得。

如上所述的五种情况,虽然在很大程度上使得劳动工资与资本利润不相等,但却没有造成劳动或资本在不同用途上的实际上的或想像上的利害不均等。这些情况的实质就是使在一些收益小的行业中的投资得到补偿,并使另一些收益大的投资的利得有所抵消。

然而,要使不同用途的所有利得能有这样的平衡,即使是在最自由的地方,也必须具备三个条件:第一,那些投资用途,必须在当地及其附近为人所共知,而且已牢固确立。第二,那些投资必须处在一般状态,即所谓自然状态。第三,那些投资,必须是使用者唯一的或主要的投资。

第一,只有那些投资,在当地及其附近,为人所共知而且已牢固确立,才会有这样的平衡。

在所有其他情况都相同的地方,新行业的工资一般都高于旧的行业。当计划者打算建立一项新制造业时,最初他必须以高于其他行业或本行业所应有的工资,从其他行业中引诱招聘工人过

since new trades yield higher wages, and a considerable time must pass away before he can venture to reduce them to the common level. Manufactures for which the demand arises altogether from fashion and fancy, are continually changing, and seldom last long enough to be considered as old established manufactures. Those, on the contrary, for which the demand arises chiefly from use or necessity, are less liable to change, and the same form or fabric may continue in demand for whole centuries together. The wages of labour, therefore, are likely to be higher in manufactures of the former, than in those of the latter kind. Birmingham deals chiefly in manufactures of the former kind; Sheffield in those of the latter; and the wages of labour in those two different places, are said to be suitable to this difference in the nature of their manufactures.

and hrgher p- rofits: The establishment of any new manufacture, of any new branch of commerce, or of any new practice in agriculture, is always a speculation, from which the projector promises himself extraordinary profits. These profits sometimes are very great, and sometimes, more frequently, perhaps, they are quite otherwise; but in general they bear no regular proportion to those of other old trades in the neighbourhood. If the project succeeds, they are commonly at first very high. When the trade or practice becomes thoroughly established and well known, the competition reduces them to the level of other trades.

(2) the employments must be in their natural state, Secondly, this equality in the whole of the advantages and disadvantages of the different employments of labour and stock, can take place only in the ordinary, or what may be called the natural state of those employments.

since the demand for labour in each employment varies from time to time The demand for almost every different species of labour is sometimes greater and sometimes less than usual. In the one case the advantages of the employment rise above, in the other they fall below the common level. The demand for country labour is greater at haytime and harvest, than during the greater part of the year; and wages rise with the demand. In time of war, when forty or fifty thousand sailors are forced from the merchant service into that of the king, the demand for sailors to merchant ships necessarily rises with their scarcity, and their wages upon such occasions commonly rise from a guinea and seven-and-twenty shillings, to forty shillings and three

来，而且他将需要很长的时间才能把工资降到一般水平。而有些制造品，其需求完全是出于时尚和一时的爱好，这些制造品总是会不断变化的，而且很少能持久，因而不能看成是确立已久的产品。反之，对另一些制造品，其需要主要是由于使用和必要性而产生，它们不像上述制造品那么容易变化，同样的形式和构造，可能经历几个世纪。因此，劳动工资在前一类制造业比在后一类制造业中可能会高一些。伯明翰的制造业多为前一类；而雪菲尔德则主要经营后一类。据说，这两个不同地方的劳动工资就是与它们不同性质的制造品相适应的。

建立一种新的制造业、经营一种新的商业或实践一项新的农业措施，都是一种投机。而计划者则期望以此获得较大的利润。这种利润有时是很大的，但有时，也许只是很小的。但一般说来，它们的利润和当地及附近其他旧行业的利润，不会保持正常的比例。如果计划成功了，最初的利润通常是很高的。但当这行业或生产一经确立并且为人所共知的时候，竞争就会使其利润降到和其他行业相等的水平。

第二，只有在劳动和资本的不同用途处在一般状态，即所谓自然状态时，这些用途的利得从总体上说才会有这样的均衡。

对各种劳动的需求，有时比平常大，有时却比平常小。在前一种情况下，劳动收益增加到普通水平之上；而在后一种情况下，劳动收益降低到普通水平以下。对农村劳动力的需求，在割制甘草的时期和收获期比一年中大部分时期都大，其工资也随着需求的增加而升高；在战争期间，四五万原本为商船服务的海员被迫为国王服务，这样商船海员的需要，必然由于海员的稀缺而相对增加。而此时海员的工资，常由原来每月 21 先令至 27 先令上升

pounds a month. In a decaying manufacture, on the contrary, many workmen, rather than quit their old trade, are contented with smaller wages than would otherwise be suitable to the nature of their employment.

and profits fluctuate with the price of the commodity produced: The profits of stock vary with the price of the commodities in which it is employed. As the price of any commodity rises above the ordinary or average rate, the profits of at least some part of the stock that is employed in bringing it to market, rise above their proper level, and as it falls they sink below it. All commodities are more or less liable to variations of price, but some are much more so than others. In all commodities which are produced by human industry, the quantity of industry annually employed is necessarily regulated by the annual demand, in such a manner that the average annual produce may, as nearly as possible, be equal to the average annual consumption. In some employments, it has already been observed, the same quantity of industry will always produce the same, or very nearly the same quantity of commodities. In the linen or woollen manufactures, for example, the same number of hands will annually work up very nearly the same quantity of linen and woollen cloth. The variations in the market price of such commodities, therefore, can arise only from some accidental variation in the demand. A public mourning raises the price of black cloth. But as the demand for most sorts of plain linen and woollen cloth is pretty uniform, so is likewise the price. But there are other employments in which the same quantity of industry will not always produce the same quantity of commodities. The same quantity of industry, for example, will, in different years, produce very different quantities of corn, wine, hops, sugar, tobacco, &c. The price of such commodities, therefore, varies not only with the variations of demand, but with the much greater and more frequent variations of quantity, and is consequently extremely fluctuating. But the profit of some of the dealers must necessarily fluctuate with the price of the commodities. The operations of the speculative merchant are principally employed about such commodities. He endeavours to buy them up when he foresees that their price is likely to rise, and to sell them when it is likely to fall.

到 40 先令至 60 先令。但是,在日趋凋落的制造业中情形却正好相反。许多劳动者,不愿意离开原有的行业,而宁愿接受低于按其工作性质所应得的工资。

资本的利润,随着该资本所生产的商品的价格的变动而变动。当任何一种商品的价格上升到普通或平均价格之上的时候,为将这一商品运往市场而使用的资本,至少有一部分利润会上升到高于正常利润的水平;当价格下降时,利润也降到正常水平之下。一切商品的价格,都会或多或少地变动,但有些商品的价格变动得比其他商品大得多。在由人类劳动所生产的商品中,每年所投入的劳动量必然会受该年需求的支配,使每年的平均产量都尽可能地接近于该年的平均消费量。上面说过,在有些行业,相同量的劳动总是会生产出同量或几乎同量的商品。如在麻织业或呢绒制造业中,同一数量的劳动者,几乎年年都制造出同等数量的麻布或呢绒。因此,这类商品的市场价格变化就只能是由于需求的偶然变动。国丧会使黑布的价格上涨,但是由于对素麻布及粗呢的需求比较固定,所以,其价格也基本没有变动。但也有些行业,使用同等数量的劳动,未必能生产同等数量的商品。如在不同年份,同等劳动生产出的谷物、葡萄酒、啤酒花、糖、烟草等产品的数量,就很不一样。因此,这类商品的价格,不仅随需求的变动而变动,而且随商品数量更大和更频繁地变动而变动,因此这类商品价格的变动常常很大。但是,一些经营这类商品的商人的利润,必然随此类商品价格的变动而一起变动。投机商人的活动,主要就是对这类商品进行买卖。当他们预见到这种商品价格将会上升,就立即买入;预见到这种商品的价格将要下跌,就立即卖出。

> 资本利润随着商品价格的变动而变动;

and (3) the employments must be the principal employment of those who occupy them, since people maintained by one employment will work cheap at another,

Thirdly, this equality in the whole of the advantages and disadvantages of the different employments of labour and stock, can take place only in such as are the sole or principal employments of those who occupy them.

When a person derives his subsistence from one employment, which does not occupy the greater part of his time; in the intervals of his leisure he is often willing to work at another for less wages than would otherwise suit the nature of the employment.

like the Scotch cotters,

There still subsists in many parts of Scotland a set of people called Cotters or Cottagers, though they were more frequent some years ago than they are now. They are a sort of out-servants of the landlords and farmers. The usual reward which they receive from their masters is a house, a small garden for pot herbs, as much grass as will feed a cow, and, perhaps, an acre or two of bad arable land. When their master has occasion for their labour, he gives them, besides, two pecks of oatmeal a week, worth about sixteen pence sterling. During a great part of the year he has little or no occasion for their labour, and the cultivation of their own little possession is not sufficient to occupy the time which is left at their own disposal. When such occupiers were more numerous than they are at present, they are said to have been willing to give their spare time for a very small recompence to any body, and to have wrought for less wages than other labourers. In ancient times they seem to have been common all over Europe. In countries ill cultivated and worse inhabited, the greater part of landlords and farmers could not otherwise provide themselves with the extraordinary number of hands, which country labour requires at certain seasons. The daily or weekly recompence which such labourers occasionally received from their masters, was evidently not the whole price of their labour. Their small tenement made a considerable part of it. This daily or weekly recompence, however, seems to have been considered as the whole of it, by many writers who have collected the prices of labour and provisions in ancient times, and who have taken pleasure in representing both as wonderfully low.

Shetland knitters,

The produce of such labour comes frequently cheaper to market than would otherwise be suitable to its nature. Stockings in many parts of Scotland are knit much cheaper than they can any-where be wrought upon the loom. They are the work of servants and labourers,

第三,只有当劳动和资本的用途作为使用者的唯一或主要用途时,才能实现这些不同用途总体上的有利和不利的平等。

当某一个人以某一种职业为生,而该职业并不会占去他的大部分时间时,他往往就愿意在闲暇时间从事另一种职业,并且愿意接受低于按该工作性质所应有的工资。

在苏格兰许多地方,目前仍有一种被称作农场雇工的人。只不过这种人现在比前几年减少了。他们是地主和农场主的一种外佣工。他们从雇主那里取得的报酬通常是一间住宅,一坎莱园,一块足够饲养一头母牛的草场,也许还会有一两亩不太好的耕地。当雇主需要他们劳动时,也许每星期还会给他们两配克燕麦片,大约值16便士。在一年的大部分时间,雇主只需要他们的少量或是不需要他们的劳动,而他们自己那一点土地的耕种,也不会占去他们能由自己支配的全部时间。据说当以前这种雇工比现在多的时候,他们在闲暇时,都愿意以极小的报酬为任何人工作,愿意接受低于其他劳动者的工资。在古代,这种劳动者几乎遍布于欧洲各地。在土地种得很差并且人口稀少的国家,大部分地主和农场主,就是使用这种办法来解决某些季节需要特别多劳动者的问题。这些劳动者偶然得到的日报酬或周报酬,显然并不是他们劳动的全部价格。他们的小块租用地,在他们劳动的全部价格中应占很大一部分。不过,那些收集古代劳动及食品价格的作家,喜欢把这两者的价格说得非常低,并且似乎已经把这种劳动者偶然得到的日报酬或星期报酬看作其劳动的全部价格。

这类劳动的产物,在市场出售往往比应有的价格低。苏格兰许多地方编织的袜子就比其他任何地方用织机织成的袜子的价格还要便宜得多。这就是因为编织这些袜子的劳动者都是依靠

who derive the principal part of their subsistence from some other employment. More than a thousand pair of Shetland stockings are annually imported into Leith, of which the price is from five pence to seven pence a pair. At Learwick, the small capital of the Shetland islands, ten pence a day, I have been assured, is a common price of common labour. In the same islands they knit worsted stockings to the value of a guinea a pair and upwards.

<small>Scotch linen s-pinners,</small> The spinning of linen yarn is carried on in Scotland nearly in the same way as the knitting of stockings, by servants who are chiefly hired for other purposes. They earn but a very scanty subsistence, who endeavour to get their whole livelihood by either of those trades. In most parts of Scotland she is a good spinner who can earn twenty pence a week

<small>and London lodging house keepers.</small> In opulent countries the market is generally so extensive, that any one trade is sufficient to employ the whole labour and stock of those who occupy it. Instances of people's living by one employment, and at the same time deriving some little advantage from another, occur chiefly in poor countries. The following instance, however, of something of the same kind is to be found in the capital of a very rich one. There is no city in Europe, I believe, in which house-rent is dearer than in London, and yet I know no capital in which a furnished apartment can be hired so cheap. Lodging is not only much cheaper in London than in Paris; it is much cheaper than in Edinburgh of the same degree of goodness; and what may seem extraordinary, the dearness of house-rent is the cause of the cheapness of lodging. The dearness of house-rent in London arises, not only from those causes which render it dear in all great capitals, the dearness of labour, the dearness of all the materials of building, which must generally be brought from a great distance, and above all the dearness of groundrent, every landlord acting the part of a monopolist, and frequently exacting a higher rent for a single acre of bad land in a town, than can be had for a hundred of the best in the country; but it arises in part from the peculiar manners and customs of the people which oblige every master of a family to hire a whole house from top to bottom. A dwelling-house in England means every thing that is contained under the same roof. In France, Scotland, and many other parts of Europe, it frequently means no more than a single story. A tradesman

其他职业来获取他们主要的生活资料。每年都有1000双以上的袜子从设得兰进口到利斯,价格大约在每双5便士到7便士之间。据说,在设得兰群岛小小的首都勒韦克,普通劳动的一般价格为每天10便士。但是,在设得兰群岛他们所织成的绒线袜的价格却在每双一几尼以上。

在苏格兰,亚麻线的纺织主要是由受雇于其他工作的雇工来完成的,就像袜子的编织一样。这些人企图从这两份工作来得到他们的全部生活费用,但事实上得到的生活费极其微薄。在苏格兰,一个星期能赚20便士的女纺工就算是很好的纺工了。苏格兰的纺麻工,

在富裕国家,市场一般都十分广阔,以致任何一个行业都容纳投入这一行业的全部劳动和资本。以一种职业为生,同时又以另一种职业来谋取少许利益的情况,主要出现在穷国。不过,和上述情况有些相似的下列情况,却也出现在一个十分富裕的国家的首都。我相信,全欧洲没有一个城市房租比伦敦更高。但租用一套附有家具设施齐全的公寓的租金没有一个城市的比伦敦低。就同等质量的多余房屋来说,在伦敦租赁,不仅比巴黎便宜很多,而且比爱丁堡也便宜得多。也许让人惊奇的是,全房租的价格的高昂正是余屋租金低廉的原因。所有大城市房租的高昂都有很多原因:劳动价格昂贵;由于一般建筑材料必须由较远的地方供给,所以建筑材料昂贵;由于占垄断地位的各个地主,往往对于一亩街市上的不太好的地皮,要求的比最好的农田上百亩的土地更高的地租,由此导致地皮地租昂贵。伦敦房租高昂的原因,除上述三个以外,还有一个,就是伦敦人民所特有的风俗和习惯:各家主人都要租赁整个屋子。住宅,在法兰西和苏格兰以及欧洲其他地方,常常只意味着建筑物的一层;而在英格兰,却意味着同一屋

in London is obliged to hire a whole house in that part of the town where his customers live. His shop is upon the ground-floor, and he and his family sleep in the garret; and he endeavours to pay a part of his house-rent by letting the two middle stories to lodgers. He expects to maintain his family by his trade, and not by his lodgers. Whereas, at Paris and Edinburgh, the people who let lodgings have commonly no other means of subsistence; and the price of the lodging must pay, not only the rent of the house, but the whole expence of the family.

PART II *Inequalities Occasioned By The Policy Of Europe*

<small>The policy of Europe occasions more important inequalities</small> Such are the inequalities in the whole of the advantages and disadvantages of the different employments of labour and stock, which the defect of any of the three requisites above-mentioned must occasion, even where there is the most perfect liberty. But the policy of Europe, by not leaving things at perfect liberty, occasions other inequalities of much greater importance.

<small>in three ways:</small> It does this chiefly in the three following ways. First, by restraining the competition in some employments to a smaller number than would otherwise be disposed to enter into them; secondly, by increasing it in others beyond what it naturally would be; and, thirdly, by obstructing the free circulation of labour and stock, both from employment to employment and from place to place.

<small>(1) It restricts competition in some employments,</small> First, the policy of Europe occasions a very important inequality in the whole of the advantages and disadvantages of the different employments of labour and stock, by restraining the competition in some employments to a smaller number than might otherwise be disposed to enter into them.

The exclusive privileges of corporations are the principal means it makes use of for this purpose.

顶下的全部建筑物。伦敦商人必须在他的顾客所在的城市的地段租一整栋房子。他把第一层作为自己的店铺,顶楼作为他自己和家属的住所。而把中间两层,分租给房客以收回一部分房租。他主要靠他的生意来维持其家庭的生活,而并不指望以分租房屋的租金来维持家庭。但在巴黎和爱丁堡,分租部分房屋的人,往往专靠它来维持生活。因此,分租的租金,就不仅需要足够支付整个房屋的全部租金,并且还要足以维持其家庭生活的全部费用。

第二部分 因欧洲政策而引起的不均等

由上所述,即便是在最完全自由的地方,如果缺乏了上述三个条件的任何一个,就会产生劳动与资本在不同用途中的利害在总体上的不平等。但是,由于欧洲的政策不让事物有完全自由的发展,于此又产生了其他更为严重的不平等。_{欧洲政策引起了更为严重的不平等。}

欧洲的政策主要通过下面三种方式造成了这样的不平等:第一,限制某些行业中的竞争人数,使从业人数少于本来愿意加入这个行业的人数;第二,在别的行业增加从业人数使其增加到超过自然限度;第三,限制劳动和资本的自由流通,使它们不能从一个行业转移到其他行业,不能由一个地点转移到其他地点。_{欧洲政策造成不平等的三种方式:}

第一,由于限制某些行业中的竞争人数,使愿意加入该行业者不能加入。这样欧洲政策就在劳动和资本的不同用途的所有利害中产生了非常巨大的不平等。_{(1) 欧洲政策限制了某些行业中的竞争,}

行业组织的排他特权,是欧洲政策达到限制行业竞争人数的主要手段。

The exclusive privilege of an incorporated trade necessarily restrains the competition, in the town where it is established, to those who are free of the trade. To have served an apprenticeship in the town, under a master properly qualified, is commonly the necessary requisite for obtaining this freedom. The bye-laws of the corporation regulate sometimes the number of apprentices which any master is allowed to have, and almost always the number of years which each apprentice is obliged to serve. The intention of both regulations is to restrain the competition to a much smaller number than might otherwise be disposed to enter into the trade. The limitation of the number of apprentices restrains it directly. A long term of apprenticeship restrains it more indirectly, but as effectually, by increasing the expence of education.

In Sheffield no master cutler can have more than one apprentice at a time, by a bye-law of the corporation. In Norfolk and Norwich no master weaver can have more than two apprentices, under pain of forfeiting five pounds a month to the king. ① No master hatter can have more than two apprentices any-where in England, or in the English plantations, under pain of forfeiting five pounds a month, half to the king, and half to him who shall sue in any court of record. ② Both these regulations, though they have been confirmed by a public law of the kingdom, are evidently dictated by the same corporation spirit which enacted the bye-law of Sheffield. The silk weavers in London had scarce been incorporated a year when they enacted a bye-law, restraining any master from having more than two apprentices at a time. It required a particular act of parliament to rescind this bye-law.

---

① [Under 13 and 14 Car. Ⅱ., c. 5, § 18.]

② [8 Eliz., c. 11, § 8; 1 Jac. Ⅰ., c., 17, § 3; 5 Geo. Ⅱ., c. 22.]

一个行业组织的垄断必然在其所在的城市中限制竞争,只有那些享受本行业自由的人才能参与竞争。获得这种自由竞争机会的必要条件,通常是在当地一个有资格的师傅门下当过学徒。这种组织有时还规定了限制一个师傅所允许带的学徒的人数,通常还规定每个学徒所必须学习的年限。这两种规定的目的,就在于限制竞争人数,使愿意加入该行业者并不能都加入。学徒人数的规定,是直接限制竞争,而规定学徒学习期限又使得学习费用增加,同样间接地限制了行业竞争。

〔竞争人数通过赋予行业组织排他特权〕
〔限制竞争主要〕

在谢菲尔德[1]行业组织规定一个刀匠师傅同期所带学徒人数不得超过一人以上。在诺福克[2]和诺维奇,一个织工师傅同期所带学徒不得超过两人以上,违者每月必须向国王缴纳罚金五镑。① 在英格兰以及英格兰领属殖民地的帽匠师傅,同期所带学徒数也不得超过两个,违者每月的五镑罚金,一半上交国王,另一半要归向记录法庭控告的人。② 这两项规定虽然都是经王国公法确认,但显然是因雪菲尔德规定的这种行业组织精神所导致的。伦敦的丝织业行业组织成立不到一年,就规定每个师傅不得同期带学徒两人以上。后来通过议会的一道特别法令这个规则才得以废

〔排他特权规定了很长的学习期限和学徒人数。〕

---

① 查理二世十三、十四年第 5 号法令第 18 条。
② 伊丽莎白八年第 2 号法令第 8 条;詹姆斯一世一年第 17 号法令第 3 条;乔治二世五年第 22 号法令。
〔1〕 谢菲尔德(Sheffield):英格兰中北部一自治城市,位于曼彻斯特以东。它是个高度工业化的城镇,长期致力于刀剑物品和钢材生产。
〔2〕 诺福克:英国东部北海之滨的历史地区,建于史前年代,为东安哥里尔盎格鲁·撒克逊王国的一部分。它名字意为"北部人",与索福克"南部人"相对。

| 国民财富的性质与原理

Seven years is the usual period of apprenticeship.
  Seven years seem anciently to have been, all over Europe, the usual term established for the duration of apprenticeships in the greater part of incorporated trades. All such incorporations were anciently called universities; which indeed is the proper Latin name for any incorporation whatever. The university of smiths, the university of taylors, &c. are expressions which we commonly meet with in the old charters of ancient towns. ① When those particular incorporations which are now peculiarly called universities were first established, the term of years which it was necessary to study, in order to obtain the degree of master of arts, appears evidently to have been copied from the term of apprenticeship in common trades, of which the incorporations were much more ancient. As to have wrought seven years under a master properly qualified, was necessary, in order to entitle any person to become a master, and to have himself apprentices in a common trade; so to have studied seven years under a master properly qualified, was necessary to entitle him to become a master, teacher, or doctor (words anciently synonymous) in the liberal arts, and to have scholars or apprentices (words likewise originally synonymous) to study under him.

The Statute of Apprenticeship, which required it everywhere in England, has been confined to market towns,
  By the 5th of Elizabeth, commonly called the Statute of Apprenticeship. ② it was enacted, that no person should for the future exercise any trade, craft, or mystery at that time exercised in England, unless he had previously served to it an apprenticeship of seven years at least; and what before had been the bye-law of many particular corporations, became in England the general and public law of all trades carried on in market towns. For though the words of the statute are very general, and seem plainly to include the whole kingdom, by interpretation its operation has been limited to market towns, it having been held that in country villages a person may exercise several different trades, though he has not served a seven years apprenticeship to each, they being necessary for the conveniency of the inhabitants,

---

  ① [Madox, Firma Burg, , 1726, p. 32.]
  ② [C. 4, . § 31.]

除。

　　过去在整个欧洲,似乎大部分有同业组织的行业都把学徒学习期限定为七年。所有这样的组织在过去统称为 university,这的确对于一个同业组织来说是一个恰当的拉丁文名字。诸如铁匠 university,裁缝 university 等,在古代城市的特许状中随处可见。①在当今我们专门指代的大学(university)的这个特殊组织创建之初,其关于获得文学硕士学位所必需的学习期限的规定,显然就是源自于往昔行业组织关于学徒学习期限的规定。就好比一个人要想在普通行业成为师傅并能够带学徒,就必须在具有一定资格的师傅门下做学徒七年。同样地,一个人如果想在文学上成为硕士、教师或者博士(这三者在过去是同义语),并取得收带学生或学徒(此二者在过去也是同义语)的资格,也得在具有一定资格的师傅门下学习七年。

<small>一般的学徒学习期限都为七年。</small>

　　在伊丽莎白五年所颁布的通常称之为《学徒法》中规定,②此后任何人要想从事当时英格兰任何的手艺、工艺或技艺,都必须至少做七年学徒。于是以前英格兰各地许多行业组织自己的规则,都变成了城市各行业的公法。《学徒法》所用文字极为笼统,似乎包括了整个王国,但在解释上,其效力仅限于各城市。而在农村的一个劳动者,则可以同时从事几种不同的行业,尽管他对于每一种行业的技能都没有学习七年。但为便利农村居民,而且考虑到农村人口往往也不足以为每个行业提供足够人口,因此

<small>《学徒法》规定在英格兰学徒必须习艺七年,但该法律仅限于城市。</small>

---

　　① 见马多克斯:《自治城市》,1726 年,第 32 页。
　　② 第 4 号法令第 31 条。

| 国民财富的性质与原理

and the number of people frequently not being sufficient to supply each with a particular set of hands, ①

<small>and to trades existing when it was passed.</small>   By a strict interpretation of the words too the operation of this statute has been limited to those trades which were established in England before the 5th of Elizabeth, and has never been extended to such as have been introduced since that time. ② This limitation has given occasion to several distinctions which, considered as rules of police, appear as foolish as can well be imagined. It has been adjudged, for example, that a coach-maker can neither himself make nor employ journeymen to make his coach-wheels; but must buy them of a master wheel-wright; this latter trade having been exercised in England before the 5th of Elizabeth. ③ But a wheel-wright, though he has never served an apprenticeship to a coach-maker, may either himself make or employ journeymen to make coaches; the trade of a coach-maker not being within the statute, because not exercised in England at the time when it was made. ④ The manufactures of Manchester, Birmingham, and Wolverhampton, are many of them, upon this account, not within the statute; not having been exercised in England before the 5th of Elizabeth.

<small>The term varies in France,</small>   In France, the duration of apprenticeships is different in different towns and in different trades. In Paris, five years is the term required in a great number; but before any person can be qualified to exercise the trade as a master, he must, in many of them, serve five years more as a journeyman. During this latter term he is called the companion of his master, and the term itself is called his companionship.

---

① ['It hath been held that this statute doth not restrain a man from using several trades, so as he had been an apprentice to all; wherefore it indemnifies all petty chapmen in little towns and villages because their masters kept the same mixed trades before.' —Matthew Bacon, New 4 bridgement of the Law, 3rd ed., 1768, vol. iii, p. 553, s. v. Master and servant.]

② [Ibid., VoL iii., p.552.]

③ [Ibid., VoL i., p.553.]

④ [bacon cibid., iii., 5537, however, says distinctly: A coachmaker is within this statute on the authority of Ventris pepores, p.346.]

一个人同时从事几个行业也是必要的。①

另外，按照这个法令严格的解释，其适用范围也只限于伊丽莎白五年以前在英格兰已经兴起来的行业，而没有涉及此后新建立的行业。② 这种限制就因此引起了几个区别。作为政策法规，这些区别似乎是愚蠢至极。例如根据规定一个马车的制造人他自己是不能制造车轮的，而且他也不得自行雇人制造，他必须向车轮匠专门购买马车车轮。因为车轮制造业在伊丽莎白五年以前就已经在英格兰存在了。③ 但一个车轮匠即使从来都没有在马车制造人那里当过学徒，却也可以自己制造马车或者雇人制造。因为马车制造业是《学徒法》颁布以后才在英格兰出现的行业，所以这个行业就不受这项法令的限制。④ 在曼彻斯特、伯明翰和沃弗尔汉普顿等地的许多制造业，情况都和这个例子类似，他们是伊丽莎白五年以后在英格兰建立的，因此不在这个法令的规定之内而不受其约束。

在法国，学徒的学习期限，因城市不同、行业不同而各不相同。例如在巴黎，大多数的行业都是要求五年的学徒期，但许多行业中一个人取得该行业的师傅资格以前，他还必须作师傅五年的帮手。在此五年期间，他被称为师傅的帮工，而把这个时期称

---

① 该法案被认为并没有限制一个人从事几种行业，只要他是这几个行业的学徒就行。因此该法案算是对那些小村庄城镇小商小贩的补偿，因为以前他们的主人就是从事几种混合的行业。马修·培根《最新法律删节本》第3版，1768年，第3卷，第553页，"主人和奴仆"。
② 《最新法律删节本》第3版，第3卷，第552页。
③ 《最新法律删节本》，第1卷，第553页。
④ 但根据权威的凡提斯《报告集》第346页，培根（同上，第3卷，第553页）的说法却大相径庭："马车制造业属于此范围。"

| 国民财富的性质与原理

and Scotland, where the regulations are less oppressive.
  In Scotland there is no general law which regulates universally the duration of apprenticeships. The term is different in different corporations. Where it is long, a part of it may generally be redeemed by paying a small fine. In most towns too a very small fine is sufficient to purchase the freedom of any corporation. The weavers of linen and hempen cloth, the principal manufactures of the country, as well as all other artificers subservient to them, wheel-makers, reel-makers, &c. may exercise their trades in any town corporate without paying any fine. In all towns corporate all persons are free to sell butcher's meat upon any lawful day of the week. Three years is in Scotland a common term of apprenticeship, even in some very nice trades; and in general I know of no country in Europe in which corporation laws are so little oppressive.

All such regulations are as impertinent as oppressive.
  The property which every man has in his own labour, as it is the original foundation of all other property, ① so it is the most sacred and inviolable. The patrimony of a poor man lies in the strength and dexterity of his hands; and to hinder him from employing this strength and dexterity in what manner he thinks proper without injury to his neighbour, is a plain violation of this most sacred property. It is a manifest encroachment upon the just liberty both of the workman, and of those who might be disposed to employ him. As it hinders the one from working at what he thinks proper, so it hinders the others from employing whom they think proper. To judge whether he is fit to be employed, may surely be trusted to the discretion of the employers whose interest it so much concerns. The affected anxiety of the lawgiver lest they should employ an improper person, is evidently as

---

  ① [Contrast with this the account of the origin of property in the *Lectures*, pp. 107-127.]

— 278 —

为帮工期。

在苏格兰,对学徒的学习期限没有一个普遍约定的法规。不同的行业组织都有自己不同的期限规定。在那些期限较长的行业,通常可以通过交纳小额款项的方式来缩短学习期限。而且在大多数城市中,还可以通过支付极少的款项来买得任何行业组织的会员资格。苏格兰主要制造业——亚麻布和大麻布制造业的织工们,以及附属于他们的其他所有工匠,如车轮制造者、纺车制造者等,可以不支付任何款项而在任一自治城市操业。在所有的自治城市中,任何市民在一个星期内的法定日期内,都可以自由地贩卖肉类。在苏格兰,各个行业中学徒的学习期限普通都是三年,即便是一些非常精细的行业也是如此。一般而言,我还不知道还有哪个国家的行业组织的规定犹如苏格兰那么宽松。

一个人的劳动所有权是一切其他所有权的原始基础,①因此它是最神圣不可侵犯的。一个穷人所有的世袭财产,就是他的体力与技巧。在不侵害他人的前提下,不让他以他认为正当的方式使用他们的体力与技巧,就是对他这种神圣所有权的赤裸裸的侵犯。这不仅是对该劳动者的正当自由的侵犯,也是对对劳动雇用者的正当自由的侵犯。一方面妨碍一个人使其不能在自己认为适合的方式上劳动,另一方面也妨碍其他人按照自己认为合适的方式去雇佣他。一个人是否适合被雇用,毋庸置疑应该由那些与之有重大利害关系的雇主去定夺。立法当局假惺惺地担忧雇主们会雇佣不适当的劳动者,显然既是粗暴的,而且也是僭越的。

---

① 与《关于法律、警察、岁入及军备的演讲》(第107~127页)的初始产权的纪录形成对比。

impertinent as it is oppressive.

<small>Long apprenticeships are no security against bad work,</small>

The institution of long apprenticeships can give no security that insufficient workmanship shall not frequently be exposed to public sale. When this is done it is generally the effect of fraud, and not of inability; and the longest apprenticeship can give no security against fraud. Quite different regulations are necessary to prevent this abuse. The sterling mark upon plate, and the stamps upon linen① and woollen cloth,② give the purchaser much greater security than any statute of apprenticeship. He generally looks at these, but never thinks it worth while to enquire whether the workmen had served a seven years apprenticeship.

<small>and do not form young people to industry.</small>

The institution of long apprenticeships has no tendency to form young people to industry. A journeyman who works by the piece is likely to be industrious, because he derives a benefit from every exertion of his industry. An apprentice is likely to be idle, and almost always is so, because he has no immediate interest to be otherwise. In the inferior employments, the sweets of labour consist altogether in the recompence of labour. They who are soonest in a condition to enjoy the sweets of it, are likely soonest to conceive a relish for it, and to acquire the early habit of industry. A young man naturally conceives an aversion to labour, when for a long time he receives no benefit from it. The boys who are put out apprentices from public charities are generally bound for more than the usual number of years, and they generally turn out very idle and worthless.

Apprenticeships were altogether unknown to the ancients. The

---

① [Of Scotch manufacture, 10 Ann., c. 21; 13 Geo. I., c. 26.]
② [39 Eliz., c, 20; 43 Eliz., c. 10, § 7.]

长期学徒制，并不能保证在市场上不会经常出现不合格的制造品。如果一个市场上经常有不合格制造品出现，一般而言这不是无能的结果，而是因为市场上存在欺诈的结果。即便是最长的学徒年限，也不能保证不会出现欺诈。因此为防止这种流弊，就需要有一种完全不相同的规章制度。金属器皿上的纯度标志，麻布①和呢绒②上的检验标记，对他们所能给予购买者的保证，就要比任何学徒法所给予的保证大得多。通常购买者在判别货物时只要看到这些标志，绝不会去想这些制造品的工人到底做过七年学徒吗。

长期学徒制并不能保证不出现伪劣产品，

长期学徒制，也无助于培养年轻人的勤劳习惯。按件计酬的劳动者由于可以从劳动中获得利益，因此也更为可能勤勉。而一个学徒，由于利不关己，很可能变得懒惰，而且实际上的确如此。在那些低等之业中，劳动乐趣完全在于获得劳动报酬。谁能够最早享受到劳动的乐趣，谁就可能最早对劳动产生兴趣，也就最早养成勤勉的习惯。一个年轻人如果在长时间内从劳动中得不到丝毫利益，自然就会对劳动产生厌恶感。由公共慈善团体送去当学徒的儿童，他们年限一般都比较长，他们也成为了非常怠惰和无用的人。

长期学徒制也不能培养年轻人的勤勉习惯。

在古代是根本没有学徒制度的。在现代的任一法典中，师傅

---

① 苏格兰制造业，安妮女王十年第 21 号法令；乔治一世十三年第 26 号法令。

② 伊丽莎白三十九年第 20 号法令；伊丽莎白四十三年第 10 号法令第 7 条。

Apprenticeships were unknown to the ancients.

reciprocal duties of master and apprentice make a considerable article in every modern code. ① The Roman law is perfectly silent with regard to them. I know no Greek or Latin word (I might venture, I believe, to assert that there is none) which expresses the idea we now annex to the word Apprentice, a servant bound to work at a particular trade for the benefit of a master, during a term of years, upon condition that the master shall teach him that trade.

Long apprenticeships are altogether unnecessary.

Long apprenticeships are altogether unnecessary. The arts, which are much superior to common trades, such as those of making clocks and watches, contain no such mystery as to require a long course of instruction. The first invention of such beautiful machines, indeed, and even that of some of the instruments employed in making them, must, no doubt, have been the work of deep thought and long time, and may justly be considered as among the happiest efforts of human ingenuity. But when both have been fairly invented and are well understood, to explain to any young man, in the completest manner, how to apply the instruments and how to construct the machines, cannot well require more than the lessons of a few weeks: perhaps those of a few days might be sufficient. In the common mechanic trades, those of a few days might certainly be sufficient. The dexterity of hand indeed, even in common trades, cannot be acquired without much practice and experience. But a young man would practise with much more diligence and attention, if from the beginning he wrought as a journeyman, being paid in proportion to the little work which he could execute, and paying in his turn for the materials which he might sometimes spoil through awkwardness and inexperience. His education would generally in this way be more effectual, and always less tedious and expensive. The master, indeed, would be a loser. He would

---

① [The article on apprentices occupies twenty-four pages in Richard Burn's *Justice of the Peace*, 1764.]

和学徒之间的各种相互义务都是重要的内容,①但罗马法典却对此类义务只字未提。我们现在所谓学徒的概念,即在某一行业中,一个徒工必须为师傅的利益而工作一定的工作年限,这样师傅才教他该行业的手艺。我不知道在希腊文或拉丁语著作中存在一个类似的字眼来表述这个概念(但我相信在这两种文字中肯定没有这种字眼)。

很长的学徒学习期限是完全没有必要的。即便是比一般手艺都要高深很多的手艺,比如钟表制造手艺,都没有什么神秘的技术非要长期去传授。当然,这些奇妙机器的最初发明,甚至于连制造这些机器的一些工具的最初发明,无疑都是经过长期深刻思索的结果,它们的的确确是人类聪明才智的最可喜的成果之一。然而,一旦这些机器和工具得以发明,并为世人所理解后,要详尽地给年轻人讲解如何使用这些工具和如何制造钟表,大概也就几星期或者仅仅需要几天的讲授时间就够了。对于那些一般的机械工艺说,数天的讲授时间肯定是足够了。当然,即便是普通的手艺不经过大量的实践和历练也学得手的灵巧也是很难达到。但一个年轻人,刚开始就让他以帮工的身份进行劳动,根据其工作量来给以报酬,并且如果他因为笨拙和没有经验而损害材料的话也处以一定得赔偿,那他在操作过程中也肯定要勤勉得多细心得多。这样他的学习一般而言,更为有效,也可不用花那么

---

① 查理·波恩的《治安法官》(1764 年)用了 24 页的篇幅介绍关于学徒的情况。治安法官:某些国家的法院系统中最低一层的执法官,有权处理轻微的犯法行为,把案件呈交较高层的法院审理,主持婚礼,以及主持宣誓仪式。

lose all the wages of the apprentice, which he now saves, for seven years together. In the end, perhaps, the apprentice himself would be a loser. In a trade so easily learnt he would have more competitors, and his wages, when he came to be a complete workman, would be much less than at present. The same increase of competition would reduce the profits of the masters as well as the wages of the workmen. The trades, the crafts, the mysteries, ① I would all be losers. But the public would be a gainer, the work of all artificers coming in this way much cheaper to market.

<small>Corporations were established to keep up prices and consequently wages and profit;</small> It is to prevent this reduction of price, and consequently of wages and profit, by restraining that free competition which would most certainly occasion it, that all corporations, and the greater part of corporation laws, have been established. In order to erect a corporation, no other authority in ancient times was requisite in many parts of Europe, but that of the town corporate in which it was established. In England, indeed, a charter from the king was likewise necessary. But this prerogative of the crown seems to have been reserved rather for extorting money from the subject, than for the defence of the common liberty against such oppressive monopolies. Upon paying a fine to the king, the charter seems generally to have been readily granted; and when any particular class of artificers or traders thought proper to act as a corporation without a charter, such adulterine guilds, as they were called, were not always disfranchised upon that account, but obliged to fine annually to the king for permission to exercise their usurped privileges. ② The immediate inspection of all corporations, and of the bye-laws which they might think proper to enact for their own government, belonged to the town corporate in which they were established; and whatever discipline was exercised over them, proceeded

---

① [The last two terms seem to be used rather contemptuously. Probably Smith had fresh in his recollection the passage in which Madox ridicules as a 'piece of puerility' the use of the English word 'misterie.' derived from the Gallick word mestera, mistera and misteria,' as if it 'signified something μνστηριωδες, mysterious.'—*Firma Burgi*. 1726, pp. 33-35.]

② See Madox Firma Burgi, p. 26, &c. [This note appears first in ed. 2.]

多时间和那么多费用来进行学习。当然了,师傅这里就受损了。他将损失学徒在七年学习期限的所有工资,这些工资他本来是可以节省的。而且或许最终,学徒本人也将遭受损失。在一个非常容易学会的行业,他必将遭遇更多的竞争者。所以当他成为一个独立的劳动者时,他的工资也会比现在少得多。竞争的加剧,不仅会减低工人的工资,也会降低师傅的利润。从事那些行业、手艺和秘诀的劳动者都将成为受损者,①但整个社会的公众将成为获益者,他们可以在市场上以比现在低廉得多的价格买到各种工匠的制造品。

行业组织和大部分行业组织法规的制定,就是为了防止自己竞争所必然带来的价格下跌、工资下降和利润减少。在过去欧洲的很多地方,要想设立行业组织的话只需他所在的自治城市当局的许可即可。而在英格兰还须取得国王的特许状。不过,国王的这种特权似乎不是为了捍卫一般的自有,防止这些垄断事业的危害,而是为了向臣民榨取钱财。一般情况下,只要向国王缴纳一定的金额,这个特许状似乎很容易就得到。假如有工匠或者商人不经特许就设立了行业组织的话,这种所谓的非法行业组织未必就会被取消,它只需要每年向国王缴纳一定金额的罚金,就可以取得其继续行使其盗用的特权。② 一切这样的行业组织以及该组织认为适合自己组织管理的规则,都由行业组织所在地的自治

> 行业组织设立的目的就是为了维持价格,进而维持工资和利润;

---

① 后面两个用词似乎相当的轻蔑。这可能是因为斯密在使用搜集的关于马多克斯的文章时有点冒失吧。马多克斯在《自治城市》(1726 年,第33~35 页)里讽刺了不合适地使用英文单词"秘诀"(这个词源于高卢语的'神秘')的行为。

② 马多克斯:《自治城市》(Frima Burgi),第 26 页及以下。

commonly, not from the king, but from that greater incorporation of which those subordinate ones were only parts or members.

<small>by means of which the towns gained at the expense of the country,</small> The government of towns corporate was altogether in the hands of traders and artificers; and it was the manifest interest of every particular class of them, to prevent the market from being over-stocked, as they commonly express it, with their own particular species of industry; which is in reality to keep it always under-stocked. Each class was eager to establish regulations proper for this purpose, and, provided it was allowed to do so, was willing to consent that every other class should do the same. In consequence of such regulations, indeed, each class was obliged to buy the goods they had occasion for from every other within the town, somewhat dearer than they otherwise might have done. But in recompence, they were enabled to sell their own just as much dearer; so that so far it was as broad as long, as they say; and in the dealings of the different classes within the town with one another, none of them were losers by these regulations. But in their dealings with the country they were all great gainers; and in these latter dealings consists the whole trade which supports and enriches every town.

<small>being enabled to get the produce of a larger quantity of country labour in exchange for the produce of a smaller quantity of their own,</small> Every town draws its whole subsistence, and all the materials of its industry, from the country. It pays for these chiefly in two ways: first, by sending back to the country a part of those materials wrought up and manufactured; in which case their price is augmented by the wages of the workmen, and the profits of their masters or immediate employers: secondly, by sending to it a part both of the rude and manufactured produce, either of other countries, or of distant parts of the same country, imported into the town; in which case too the original price of those goods is augmented by the wages of the carriers or sailors, and by the profits of the merchants who employ them. In what is gained upon the first of those two branches of commerce, consists the advantage which the town makes by its manufactures; in what is gained upon the second, the advantage of its inland and foreign trade. The wages of the workmen, and the profits of their different employers, make up the whole of what is gained upon both. Whatever regulations,

城市来直接监督。所以对行业组织的管制,通常不是来自国王,而是来自于自治城市这个更大的同业组织,对于这个大组织来说,那些附属的行业组织只是其构成部分罢了。

自治城市的统治权完全控制在商人和工匠的手中,而这个政府就代表着他们这些阶层的利益。正如他们自己常说的,要使市场上总是呈现存货不足的状态,防止各自的产品在市场上存货过多,这样做显然是符合于他们各自利益的。各阶级都希望能制定合适的法规以达到此目的,而且在自己被允许制定法规的条件下,它也乐意同意其他一切阶级也都制定这样的法规。这样,各阶级都要以比这些法规制定以前稍高的价格,向市上的其他阶级购买他们所需要的货物。作为回报,他们自己的货物,也能同样以较高的价格卖出。正如他们说的,损益对抵了。在同一城市内各阶级都没有因为这个规则而蒙受损失。但在他们与乡村的交易中,他们都获得了巨大的收益。这种交易就这样支持着每个城市并使这些城市得以富裕繁荣。

<small>市富方城法使繁是乡裕牲村</small>

所有城市的全部生活资料与工业所需原料都来自于农村。城市支付这些生活资料与工业原料方法主要有两种:第一,把这些原料中的一部分经过加工制成后返回农村,这样由于物品的价格附加了工人的工资以及师傅或直接雇主的利润而提高了。第二,把由其他国家进口或由国内遥远地区输入本市的粗制品或制成品的一部分运往农村。这样,这些物品的价格就因为附加了水陆运输的工人工资以及雇用这些工人的商人的利润而提高了。城市从其第一种商业中获得的利益,就是城市制造业得到的利益;从第二种商业中获得的利益,就是通过对内对外贸易获得的利益。工人的工资和各个雇主的利润,就构成了这两种商业利益

<small>法能使少量农产品换取较多劳动产品 这些规使市以较少劳动的产品换取农村较多劳动的产品</small>

therefore, tend to increase those wages and profits beyond what they otherwise would be, tend to enable the town to purchase, with a smaller quantity of its labour, the produce of a greater quantity of the labour of the country. They give the traders and artificers in the town an advantage over the landlords, farmers, and labourers in the country, and break down that natural equality which would otherwise take place in the commerce which is carried on between them. The whole annual produce of the labour of the society is annually divided between those two different sets of people. By means of those regulations a greater share of it is given to the inhabitants of the town than would otherwise fall to them; and a less to those of the country.

<small>as the exports of a town are the real price of its imports.</small> The price which the town really pays for the provisions and materials annually imported into it, is the quantity of manufactures and other goods annually exported from it. The dearer the latter are sold, the cheaper the former are bought. The industry of the town becomes more, and that of the country less advantageous.

<small>That town industry is better paid is shown by the large fortunes made in it.</small> That the industry which is carried on in towns is, every-where in Europe, more advantageous than that which is carried on in the country, without entering into any very nice computations, we may satisfy ourselves by one very simple and obvious observation. In every country of Europe we find, at least, a hundred people who have acquired great fortunes from small beginnings by trade and manufactures, the industry which properly belongs to towns, for one who has done so by that which properly belongs to the country, the raising of rude produce by the improvement and cultivation of land. Industry, therefore, must be better rewarded, the wages of labour and the profits of stock must evidently be greater in the one situation than in the other. ① But stock and labour naturally seek the most advantageous employment. They naturally, therefore, resort as much as they can to the town, and desert the country.

The inhabitants of a town, being collected into one place, can easily combine together. The most insignificant trades carried on in towns have accordingly, in some place or other, been incorporated;

---

① [The argument is unsound in the absence of any proof that the more numerous successes are not counterbalanced by equally numerous failures.]

的全部。因此,不管何种法规,只要会使工资和利润超出一般水平,就会使城市能以较少的劳动量的产品购买到农村较多的劳动量的产品。这些法规由于使城市的商人和工匠们获得的利益大于乡村的地主、农场主及农业劳动者获得的利益,就破坏了城乡贸易上应有的自然平等。社会劳动的全部年产品,每年都是在城市和农村居民之间进行分的。由于有了类似的法规,这些年产品较大份额就分给了城市居民,而农村居民却只分了较少的份额。

城市对每年由农村输入的食品和原料的实际支付,就是它每年输往农村的全部制造品和其他货物。这些出口品的售价越高,输入品的购买价便越低。城市产业就获利更多,而农村产业则获利更少。

> 城市的出口是它对输入产品的真实支付。

我们无需作精确的计算,仅仅只需要通过一个非常简单而又明显的观察,就可以明白欧洲各地城市产业要比农村产业更为有利。在欧洲各国我们均可以看到,在城市中由小本经营商业和制造业这些城市固有行业最后发大财的,与农村经营改良和耕种土地这些农村固有行业以提高农产品产量而最后发大财的人数之比要超过100∶1。因此,城市产业的报酬必然比农村产业的报酬要高。劳动工资和资本利润城市也明显地要比农村大。① 而资本与劳动又自然会寻找利益最大化的用途。所以它们自然就会离开农村,流往城市。

> 城市产业比农村产业更为有利,这点可由城市发财比例比农村来看到。

城市居民聚集于一地,这样非常容易就联合起来。所以,城市里即便是最细微的行业在有些地方也有行业组织。而且即便

---

① 这种论证是无力的,因为并没有提供成功次数较多而不被失败次数也较多所抵消的任何证据。

国民财富的性质与原理

<small>Combination is easy to the inhabitants of a town,</small> and even where they have never been incorporated, yet the corporation spirit, the jealousy of strangers, the aversion to take apprentices, or to communicate the secret of their trade, generally prevail in them, and often teach them, by voluntary associations and agreements, to prevent that free competition which they cannot prohibit by bye-laws. The trades which employ but a small number of hands, run most easily into such combinations. Half a dozen wool-combers, perhaps, are necessary to keep a thousand spinners and weavers at work. By combining not to take apprentices they can not only engross the employment, but reduce the whole manufacture into a sort of slavery to themselves, and raise the price of their labour much above what is due to the nature of their work.

<small>and difficult to those of the country, who are dispersed and not governed by the corporation spirit No apprenticeship is prescribed for farming, though a difficult art,</small> The inhabitants of the country, dispersed in distant places, cannot easily combine together. They have not only never been incorporated, but the corporation spirit never has prevailed among them. No apprenticeship has ever been thought necessary to qualify for husbandry, the great trade of the country. After what are called the fine arts, and the liberal professions, however, there is perhaps no trade which requires so great a variety of knowledge and experience. The innumerable volumes which have been written upon it in all languages, may satisfy us, that among the wisest and most learned nations, it has never been regarded as a matter very easily understood. And from all those volumes we shall in vain attempt to collect that knowledge of its various and complicated operations, which is commonly possessed even by the common farmer; how contemptuously soever the very contemptible authors of some of them may sometimes affect to speak of him. There is scarce any common mechanic trade, on the contrary, of which all the operations may not be as completely and distinctly explained in a pamphlet of a very few pages, as it is possible for words illustrated by figures to explain them. In the history of the arts, now publishing by the French academy of sciences, several of them are actually explained in this manner. The direction of operations, besides, which must be varied with every change of the weather, as well as with many other accidents, requires much more judgment and discretion, than that of those which are always the same or very nearly the same.

这个地方完全没有行业组织的存在,行业组织那种嫉妒外乡人、不愿意收学徒、不愿把行业内的秘密传授外人的精神也会在当地居民中广为流传。这种组织精神,常常会引导他们通过自愿结盟或协议约定的方式,来防止那些不能靠法规来禁止的自由竞争。尤其是劳动者人数的行业,更容易形成这样的组织。举个例子,1000个纺工和织工维持生产所需要的梳毛工人,也许只需要六个人罢了。那么这些梳毛工人通过联合起来不收学徒,就不仅能够垄断这个行业,在整个毛纺织行业为所欲为,而且会将他们劳动的价格,抬高到远远超出他们这种工作性质所应有的工资。在城市比较容易形成联合组织。

而农村的居民却因为居住距离相隔很远,不容易联合起来。他们不但从来没有过同业组织,而且在他们中间也没有这种同业组织的精神。他们从不认为,耕种这个农村中最大的行业还必须经过当学徒才能拥有资格从事。然而,事实上除了所谓美术及自由职业以外,恐怕没有哪种职业会像农业那样需要那么多种类繁多的知识和经验了。看看那些用各中各样文字写的关于农业的浩如烟海的书籍吧,恐怕连最聪明睿智、最学识渊博的国民,也不会把农业当作是非常容易懂的事情吧。而且,在那些书籍中也很难找到一个普通农场主通常所需要掌握的农业的各种不同的复杂的操作的知识。一些无聊的作家在谈到农场主时有时还抱着轻蔑的态度,他们是何其无聊啊! 而与此相反,对任何一个普通的机械行业来说,几乎所有的操作都可以在寥寥数页的通过附加插图的小册子里予以详尽明了地说明。如今法国科学院所刊行的工艺史中,关于某些工艺的描述,实际上就是采用这种方法。另外,农村的操作还必须因天气变化和意外事件的发生而采取不同的方法,这就要比那些永远不变或者几乎完全不变的操作方法

or for the inferior branches of country labour, which require more skill than most mechanic trades.

Not only the art of the farmer, the general direction of the operations of husbandry, but many inferior branches of country labour, require much more skill and experience than the greater part of mechanic trades. The man who works upon brass and iron, works with instruments and upon materials of which the temper is always the same, or very nearly the same. But the man who ploughs the ground with a team of horses or oxen, works with instruments of which the health, strength, and temper, are very different upon different occasions. The condition of the materials which he works upon too is as variable as that of the instruments which he works with, and both require to be managed with much judgment and discretion. The common ploughman, though generally regarded as the pattern of stupidity and ignorance, is seldom defective in this judgment and discretion. He is less accustomed, indeed, to social intercourse than the mechanic who lives in a town. His voice and language are more uncouth and more difficult to be understood by those who are not used to them. His understanding, however, being accustomed to consider a greater variety of objects, is generally much superior to that of the other, whose whole attention from morning till night is commonly occupied in performing one or two very simple operations. How much the lower ranks of people in the country are really superior to those of the town, is well known to every man whom either business or curiosity has led to converse much with both. ① In China and Indostan accordingly both the rank and the wages of country labourers are said to be superior to those of the greater part of artificers and manufacturers. They would probably be so every-where, if corporation laws and the corporation spirit did not prevent it.

The superiority which the industry of the towns has every-where in Europe over that of the country, is not altogether owing to corporations and corporation laws. It is supported by many other regulations. The high duties upon foreign manufactures and upon all goods imported by alien merchants, all tend to the same purpose. Corporation laws enable the inhabitants of towns to raise their prices, without fea-

---

① [*Lectures*, p. 255.]

所需要的判断和思考要多得多。

不仅仅是农场主关于农业的一般操作方法的技术,甚至连农村中许多低级劳动所需要的技能与经验,也比大部分机械行业所需要的多得多。加工铜铁的工人,他们使用性质完全相同或者性质几乎相同工具与材料进行工作。但用一队马或者牛来耕土的农场主,却因不同的健康状态、体力和性情在不同的场合要采用不同的劳动工具去工作。他所加工的材料和他所使用的工具一样都是易变的,都需要他运用更多的判断力和思辨力来处理。被看作是愚蠢无知典型的普通庄稼汉,却几乎都有此种判断力与思辨力。当然了,他不像城市里的机械工那样善于社会交际,而且他的声音和语言,也会让那些没有听惯的人觉得粗俗和不易理解。但他习惯于思考各种不同的事物,因此他的理解力通常也要比那些整天只做一两种非常简单的操作的人强得多。那些因为业务关系或者好奇心而和农村的下层人民及城市下层人民打过很多交道的人都会观察到,前者要比后者聪明得多。① 据说在中国和印度,农村劳动者的地位与工资都比大多数工匠和制造业劳动工人要高。或许如果没有行业组织法规和组织精神作怪,世界各地都会和中国、印度一样。

不过城市的产业在欧洲各地要比农村产业优越,并不完全是由行业组织和同业组织法规导致的。还有其他许多法规也加剧了这种差别。通过对外国制造品和对外国商人进口的一切货物都征收高额进口税,都是有意增长这种城市的优越性。行业组织法规使城市居民可以抬高自己产品的价格,他们不必担心会因为

---

① 《关于法律、警察、岁入及军备的演讲》,第 255 页。

The superiority has declined in Great Britain. ring to be under-sold by the free competition of their own countrymen. Those other regulations secure them equally against that of foreigners. The enhancement of price occasioned by both is every-where finally paid by the landlords, farmers, and labourers of the country, who have seldom opposed the establishment of such monopolies. They have commonly neither inclination nor fitness to enter into combinations; and the clamour and sophistry of merchants and manufacturers easily persuade them that the private interest of a part, and of a subordinate part of the society, is the general interest of the whole.

In Great Britain the superiority of the industry of the towns over that of the country, seems to have been greater formerly than in the present times. The wages of country labour approach nearer to those of manufacturing labour, and the profits of stock employed in agriculture to those of trading and manufacturing stock, than they are said to have done in the last century, or in the beginning of the present. This change may be regarded as the necessary, though very late consequence of the extraordinary encouragement given to the industry of the towns. The stock accumulated in them comes in time to be so great, that it can no longer be employed with the ancient profit in that species of industry which is peculiar to them. That industry has its limits like every other; and the increase of stock, by increasing the competition, necessarily reduces the profit. The lowering of profit in the town forces out stock to the country, where, by creating a new demand for country labour, it necessarily raises its wages. It then spreads itself, if I may say so, over the face of the land, and by being employed in agriculture is in part restored to the country, at the expence of which, in a great measure, it had originally been accumulated in the town. That every-where in Europe the greatest improvements of the country have been owing to such over-flowings of the stock originally accumulated in the towns, I shall endeavour to show hereafter; and at the same time to demonstrate, that though some countries have by this course attained to a considerable degree of opulence, it is in itself necessarily slow, uncertain, liable to be disturbed and interrupted by innumerable accidents, and in every respect contrary to the order of nature and of reason. The interests, prejudices, laws and customs which have given occasion to it, I shall endeavour to explain as fully

本国同胞的自由竞争而降低价格。高额关税又同样使城市居民不担心外国商人的自由竞争。由这两种法规而引起的价格上涨，到最后都是由农村的地主、农场主和劳动者来买单。他们很少反对这种垄断的建立。通常他们既不想结成组织，也不适合进行联合。同时商人和制造者的叫嚣和诡辩又很容易地说服他们使他们相信，社会中的一部分而且是不重要的一部分的人的私利，就是整个社会的共同利益。

> 在不列颠，这种城市产业的优越地位已经下降。

过去的不列颠城市产业相对于农村产业的优越性似乎比现在更甚。与上个世纪或本世纪初叶相比，如今农村的劳动工资更加接近于制造业的劳动工资，如今的农业资本的利润也更加接近于商业和制造业的资本利润。这种迟来的结果，应该说是以前过分鼓励城市产业发展的必然结果。随着城市中资本量的积累，资本数额积累如此巨大，以至于再也不能通过把资本投资在城市特有产业上获得像以往那样丰厚的利润。就像其他的产业一样，城市特有的产业同样也有自己的限度，资本的积累导致竞争的加剧，最后必定会降低资本的利润。城市利润降低，就必然会让资本流向农村，在农村就产生了新的劳动需求，这样农村的劳动工资必然提高。原本大部分资本都是通过牺牲农村利益在城市中积累起来的，要是我可以这样说的话，这些资本通过自行在地面上扩散，而且通过在农村投资，最后部分资本回到了农村。我将在后面章节中详细阐述欧洲各地农村最大的改良，都是通过在城市积累的资本流回农村而实现的。另外我还将同时说明，虽然有些国家通过这个过程达到相当富裕的程度，但这个过程本身却是缓慢的、不确定的、易遭到无数的意外事件的干扰和阻挠的，而且无论从哪方面来说，都是违反自然和违反理性的。我将在本书的

and distinctly as I can in the third and fourth books of this inquiry.

Meetings of people in the same trade ought not to be facilitated,
People of the same trade seldom meet together, even for merriment and diversion, but the conversation ends in a conspiracy against the public, or in some contrivance to raise prices. It is impossible indeed to prevent such meetings, by any law which either could be executed, or would be consistent with liberty and justice. But though the law cannot hinder people of the same trade from sometimes assembling together, it ought to do nothing to facilitate such assemblies; much less to render them necessary.

as by registration of traders,
A regulation which obliges all those of the same trade in a particular town to enter their names and places of abode in a public register, facilitates such assemblies. It connects individuals who might never otherwise be known to one another, and gives every man of the trade a direction where to find every other man of it.

by the establishment of funds for the sick, widows and orphans,
A regulation which enables those of the same trade to tax themselves in order to provide for their poor, their sick, their widows and orphans, by giving them a common interest to manage, renders such assemblies necessary.

or by incorporation.
An incorporation not only renders them necessary, but makes the act of the majority binding upon the whole. In a free trade an effectual combination cannot be established but by the unanimous consent of every single trader, and it cannot last longer than every single trader continues of the same mind. The majority of a corporation can enact a bye-law with proper penalties, which will limit the competition more effectually and more durably than any voluntary combination whatever.

Corporations are un necessary, and corrupt the workmen.
The pretence that corporations are necessary for the better government of the trade, is without any foundation. The real and effectual discipline which is exercised over a workman, is not that of his corporation, but that of his customers. It is the fear of losing their employment which restrains his frauds and corrects his negligence. An

第三篇、第四篇中对产生此过程的各种利益、偏见、法律和习俗作尽可能详尽而明了的说明。

即使同行业的人是为了娱乐或消遣而聚集在一起时,他们的谈话也往往是阴谋对付公众或者图谋抬高价格。当然了,通过法律来阻止这类的集会是不可能办到的,这种法律要不就是难以实施,要不就是会违反自由和正义。虽然法律不能阻止同行业的人聚集在一起,但它不应该让这种集会便于举行,更不应该让这种集会非举行不可。

法律不应便于同行业人的集会,

规定在同一个城市的同一行业的人必须在公共登记簿上登记姓名住址的规则,就会让这种集会易于举行。这样就使原本可能根本无法彼此结识的同行业人联系起来,同行业的人可以通过这种途径联系到所有的其他人。

比如登记从业人员,

规定同行业的人捐钱以救助他们中的贫困者、患病者、寡妇和孤儿的规则,这样他们就有了共同利益需要管理,因此这项法律也使得集会成为必须。

给患病者、寡妇和孤儿捐钱建立基金,

行业组织不仅仅使得这种集会成为必须,而且大多数通过的决议对全体同业人员都有拘束力。而在一个自由行业里,除非同行业所有的人都同意,不然是不可能建立一个有效的联合的,而且这种联合只有在同行业所有人的意见都一致时才能得以保持存在。在行业组织中,大多数人通过的话就可以制定附带有适当惩罚条款的法规,这种法规要比任何自由联合起来的组织更能持久有效地限制自由竞争。

或者建立行业组织。

有种毫无根据的托词说,为着更好地管理行业,是有必要成立同业组织的。对工人真正有效的监督是来自于他们的顾客,而不是他们所属的同业组织。对于失业的恐惧才能使工人不敢欺

行业组织是没有必要的,它会腐蚀工人。

exclusive corporation necessarily weakens the force of this discipline. A particular set of workmen must then be employed, let them behave well or ill. It is upon this account, that in many large incorporated towns no tolerable workmen are to be found, even in some of the most necessary trades. If you would have your work tolerably executed, it must be done in the suburbs, where the workmen, having no exclusive privilege, have nothing but their character to depend upon, and you must then smuggle it into the town as well as you can.

It is in this manner that the policy of Europe, by restraining the competition in some employments to a smaller number than would otherwise be disposed to enter into them, occasions a very important inequality in the whole of the advantages and disadvantages of the different employments of labour and stock.

Secondly, the policy of Europe, by increasing the competition in some employments beyond what it naturally would be, occasions another inequality of an opposite kind in the whole of the advantages and disadvantages of the different employments of labour and stock.

(2) The policy of Europe increases competition in some trades.

It has been considered as of so much importance that a proper number of young people should be educated for certain professions, that, sometimes the public, and sometimes the piety of private founders have established many pensions, scholarships, exhibitions, bursaries, &c. for this purpose, which draw many more people into those trades than could otherwise pretend to follow them. In all christian countries, I believe, the education of the greater part of churchmen is paid for in this manner. Very few of them are educated altogether at their own expence. The long, tedious, and expensive education, therefore, of those who are, will not always procure them a suitable reward, the church being crowded with people who, in order to get employment, are willing to accept of a much smaller recompence than what such an education would otherwise have entitled them to; and in this manner the competition of the poor takes away the reward of the rich. It would be indecent, no doubt, to compare either a curate or a chaplain with a journeyman in any common trade. The pay of a curate or chaplain, however, may very properly be considered as of the same nature with the wages of a journeyman. They are, all three, paid for their work according to the contract which they may happen to make with their respective superiors. Till after the middle of the fourteenth

It cheapens the education of the clergy and thereby reduces their earnings:

第一篇　第十章

诈懈怠。排外的组织必然会削弱这种监督力量。于是一批特定的工人,不论他们行为好坏都必须得雇用他们。所以在许多有同业工会的城市里,往往找不到还算合格的工人,即便是在某些最为必需的行业也是如此。你如果想让你的产品稍微像样的话,那就必须到郊外来做,那里的劳动者没有特权只能凭自己的本事。然后你还得尽量把这些制成品秘密地运回城市。

欧洲政策正是通过这些方式限制了某些行业的竞争,使从业人数少于原本有意进入行业的人数,总体上就在劳动和资本不同用途导致的利害中造成了极大的不平等。

第二,欧洲政策又通过增加某些行业的竞争,使从业人数超过原本应有的人数,进而在劳动和资本的不同用途导致的利害中产生了与前面所述相反的另一种极大不平等。

很多人都认为让一定数量的年轻人受到某些行业的教育非常重要,因此许多诸如儿童寄宿教育费、奖学金、英格兰大学奖学金、苏格兰大学奖学金等名目各不相同的奖学金应运而生,他们有的源于公众捐助,有的是源于虔诚的私人捐助。产生的后果就是使很多原本无意进入该行业的人也进入了该行业。我相信,在所有基督教国家里大部分牧师的教育费用都是源于这个途径,很少有人愿意自己出钱来接受教育。因为教会中挤满了那些为了得到工作而宁愿接受比他们受的教育本应有的待遇低得多的报酬,他们花了很多的时间和高额的费用,却没有获得相应的报酬。这样富人应得的报酬,就被穷人的竞争夺去了。当然,我们把助理牧师或牧师同一个普通行业的帮工相比较肯定是有失体统的,但把助理牧师或牧师的薪酬与帮工的工资看作是同性质的却是未尝不可的。这三种人的工资报酬都是通过与他们上司签订工

(2) 欧洲政策增加了某些行业的竞争。它降低了牧师教育费用,也降低了他们的收入;但因此降低了教师教育费,但

— 299 —

century, five merks, containing about as much silver as ten pounds of our present money, was in England the usual pay of a curate or stipendiary parish priest, as we find it regulated by the decrees of several different national councils. ①At the same period four pence a day, containing the same quantity of silver as a shilling of our present money, was declared to be the pay of a master mason, and three pence a day, equal to nine pence of our present money, that of a journeyman mason.② The wages of both these labourers, therefore, supposing them to have been constantly employed, were much superior to those of the curate. The wages of the master mason, supposing him to have been without employment one third of the year, would have fully equalled them. By the 12th of Queen Anne, c. 1 2, it is declared, "That where" as for want of sufficient maintenance and encouragement to curates, "the cures have in several places been meanly supplied, the bishop is,"therefore, empowered to appoint by writing under his hand and seal "a sufficient certain stipend or allowance, not exceeding fifty and not" less than twenty pounds a year."③ Forty pounds a year is reckoned at present very good pay for a curate, and notwithstanding this act of parliament, there are many curacies under twenty pounds a year. There are journeymen shoemakers in London who earn forty pounds a year, and there is scarce an industrious workman of any kind in that metropolis who does not earn more than twenty. This last sum indeed does not exceed what is frequently earned by common labourers in many country parishes. Whenever the law has attempted to regulate the wages of workmen, it has always been rather to lower them than to raise them. But the law has upon many occasions attempted to raise the wages of curates, and for the dignity of the church, to oblige the rectors of parishes to give them more than the wretched maintenance which they themselves might be willing to accept of. And in both cases the law seems to have been equally in-

---

① 〔According to Richard Burn's *Ecclesiastical Law*, 1763, *s. v.* Curates, six marks was the pay ordered by a constitution of Archbishop Islip till 1378, when it was raised to eight.〕

② See the Statute of labourers, 25 Ed. Ⅲ.

③ 〔The quotation is not intended to be *verbatim*, in spite of the inverted commas.〕

作合同来获得的。我们发现,在 14 世纪中叶以前的几次不同的全国宗教会议所颁布的规定中,英格兰助理牧师或者领薪水的牧师的薪酬是 5 马克,大概相当于我们现在的 10 镑货币所含的白银量。① 而在同时期,一个泥瓦匠师傅的薪酬为一天 4 便士,其含银量大约与现在的 1 先令相当;一个泥瓦匠帮工的薪酬为一天 3 便士,大约相当于现在的 9 便士。② 所以如果这两种劳动者经常能被雇用的话,他们就要比助理牧师待遇优厚。如果一个泥瓦匠师傅每年有 2/3 时间在工作,他所得的工资就和一个助理牧师得到的薪酬相当了。安妮女王十二年第十二号法令规定:"由于没有对助理牧师提供充足的给养与鼓励,因此在有些地方助理牧师待遇非常差。兹特授权各地主教签字盖章,为助理牧师发放足够维持生活的俸禄或津贴。每年不超过 50 镑,不少于 20 镑。"③ 如今,一个助理牧师每年能拿到 40 镑就看作待遇非常优厚了。尽管法令规定了年薪不得少于 20 镑,但还有许多助理牧师的年薪不足 20 镑。在伦敦,有的制鞋帮工每年都可以得到 40 镑,而且几乎所有工作勤奋的劳动者其每年所获报酬都在 20 镑以上。当然 20 镑并没有超过许多农村教区的普通劳动者通常所得的收入。无论何时当法律试图规定工人工资时,它总是去降低工资,而不是提高工人工资。但法律却已经多次试图提高助理牧师的工资待遇了。而且为了保持教会的尊严,法律还规定教区长必须给助理牧师提供超过他们可能愿意接受的微薄的生活费用的报酬。

---

① 根据查理·波恩的《教会法》(1763 年),大教主伊斯利浦规定副牧师的待遇为 6 马克,直到 1378 年待遇才提高到 8 马克。
② 参见爱德华三世二十五年的《劳工法》。
③ 这里的引用尽管出现了逗号倒置,但并非是要蓄意地逐字照搬。

effectual, and has never either been able to raise the wages of curates, or to sink those of labourers to the degree that was intended; because it has never been able to hinder either the one from being willing to accept of less than the legal allowance, on account of the indigence of their situation and the multitude of their competitors; or the other from receiving more, on account of the contrary competition of those who expected to derive either profit or pleasure from employing them.

<small>so that it is only the great benefices, etc, which support the honour of the English and Roman Catholic Churches.</small>

The great benefices and other ecclesiastical dignities support the honour of the church, notwithstanding the mean circumstances of some of its inferior members. The respect paid to the profession too makes some compensation even to them for the meanness of their pecuniary recompence. In England, and in all Roman Catholic countries, the lottery of the church is in reality much more advantageous than is necessary. The example of the churches of Scotland, of Geneva, and of several other protestant churches, may satisfy us, that in so creditable a profession, in which education is so easily procured, the hopes of much more moderate benefices will draw a sufficient number of learned, decent, and respectable men into holy orders.

<small>The same cause, if present, would lower the reward of lawyers and physicians,</small>

In professions in which there are no benefices, such as law and physic, if an equal proportion of people were educated at the public expence, the competition would soon be so great, as to sink very much their pecuniary reward. It might then not be worth any man's while to educate his son to either of those professions at his own expence. They would be entirely abandoned to such as had been educated by those public charities, whose numbers and necessities would oblige them in general to content themselves with a very miserable recompence, to the entire degradation of the now respectable professions of law and physic.

<small>as it has done that of men of letters,</small>

That unprosperous race of men commonly called men of letters, are pretty much in the situation which lawyers and physicians probably would be in upon the foregoing supposition. In every part of Europe the greater part of them have been educated for the church, but

然而法律在这两方面的努力似乎都无济于事。一方面法律既没有能够提高助理牧师的工资到应有的水平,也没有能够把劳动者的工资降低到应该降低的程度。这是因为法律没法阻止前者因为处境贫困和竞争者众多而自愿接受比法定给养少的报酬;也不能阻止由于雇主们为了得到利润或者快乐而竞聘后者导致后者获得超过法定给养的报酬。

尽管教会中有些下级人员处境非常窘困,但巨额的圣职薪俸和教会的尊严依然能够维持教会的崇高地位。人们对于这种职业的尊敬,也可以补偿他们金钱报酬的微薄。在英格兰和所有的罗马天主教国家,教会实际上所能给予的奖赏比所需要的多得多。苏格兰、日内瓦的教会和一些其他新教教会的实例可以让我们确信,对于一个有这么大声誉,而且又非常容易得到受教育机会的职业来说,仅仅获得适当的圣职薪俸的希望就可以诱使很多有学问、品行正派和值得尊敬的人去充当圣职。

因此,仅仅只是巨额的圣职薪俸等维持着英格兰和罗马教会的荣耀。

而对于那些没有常年俸禄的律师和医师这类职业来说,如果也有那么多的人可以获得公费教育机会的话,那么不久这些职业上竞争就会变得非常激烈,从而大大降低他们金钱上的报酬。如此一来,通过自费方式来教育后代以使他们从事这些职业就变得很不划算了。届时这些行业的职位将完全由靠公共慈善机构培养出的人员担任。由于人数众多而且生活贫穷,通常人们就不得不满足于那微薄的报酬。律师和医师这些职业也因此就不会像现在那样受尊敬了。

如果律师和医生的职业也存在同样的原因的话,他们的报酬就会降低。

通常我们称之为文人的那些落魄之人,他们正是处于我们上述关于律师和医师的假设中发生的境况。在欧洲各地,他们中大部分接受教育就是为了供职于教会。但因为种种原因他们没有

文人的境遇就是如此。

have been hindered by different reasons from entering into holy orders. They have generally, therefore, been educated at the public expence, and their numbers are every-where so great as commonly to reduce the price of their labour to a very paultry recompence.

<small>and that of teachers,</small> Before the invention of the art of printing, the only employment by which a man of letters could make any thing by his talents, was that of a public or private teacher, or by communicating to other people the curious and useful knowledge which he had acquired himself: And this is still surely a more honourable, a more useful, and in general even a more profitable employment than that other of writing for a bookseller, to which the art of printing has given occasion. The time and study, the genius, knowledge, and application requisite to qualify an eminent teacher of the sciences, are at least equal to what is necessary for the greatest practitioners in law and physic. But the usual reward of the eminent teacher bears no proportion to that of the lawyer or physician; because the trade of the one is crowded with indigent people who have been brought up to it at the public expence; whereas those of the other two are incumbered with very few who have not been educated at their own. The usual recompence, however, of public and private teachers, small as it may appear, would undoubtedly be less than it is, if the competition of those yet more indigent men of letters who write for bread was not taken out of the market. Before the invention of the art of printing, a scholar and a beggar seem to have been terms very nearly synonymous. The different governors of the universities before that time appear to have often granted licences to their scholars to beg. ①

<small>who were much better paid in ancient times.</small> In ancient times, before any charities of this kind had been established for the education of indigent people to the learned professions, the rewards of eminent teachers appear to have been much more considerable. Isocrates, in what is called his discourse against the sophists, reproaches the teachers of his own times with inconsistency. "They make the most magnificent promises to their scholars, says he, and undertake to teach them to be wise, to be happy, and

---

① [Hume, *History*, ed. of 1773, vol. iii., p. 403, quotes Ⅱ Hen. Ⅶ., c. 22, which forbids students to beg without permission from the chancellor.]

能够取得圣职。他们通常都是受的公费教育,而且他们的人数到处都是如此众多,因此他们劳动的价格,普遍都低得非常可怜。

在印刷术发明以前,文人通过其才能获取报酬的唯一职业就是充当公立教师或者私立教师,换言之就是把自己学得的新奇而又有用的知识传授给别人。比起印刷术发明之后那种为书商写作的职业来说,这种职业肯定更加光荣,更加有用,而且一般来说收入也更加丰厚。要成为一个优秀的自然科学的教师所必需的时间、研究、天资、知识和勤奋,至少与成为一个伟大的律师和医师所需要的相同。但是,一般来说一个出色教师的报酬却无法与律师和医师所得到的报酬相提并论,因为担任前者职业的人员,都是那些靠公费来进行教育的穷人,而担当后者职业的人员,则基本上都是由受自费教育培养的。然而,尽管这些公立或者私立教师的薪酬非常微薄,要不是因为那些为了过活而写作的更加穷困的文人被赶出市场不与之竞争,这些教师待遇肯定比现在还要更低。在印刷术发明之前,学者和乞丐似乎差不多就是同义词。当时各个大学的校长,似乎经常在给他们的学生颁发乞讨特许证。①

在古代,当那些资助穷苦子弟接受教育的慈善机构没有成立之前,一个优秀教师的报酬似乎要比上面所说的高得多。苏格拉底在他所谓的反对诡辩学派的演说中,就曾谴责当时的教师言行不一。他说:"他们对他们自己的学生许下最冠冕堂皇的诺言,说要把学生教育成睿智、幸福和公正的人,做出这么大的贡献他们

---

① 休谟:《英格兰史》(1773 年,第 3 卷,第 403 页)引用了亨利八世二年第 22 号法令,没有官员的允许学生不得行乞。

to be just, and in return for so important a service they stipulate the paultry reward of four or five minæ. They who teach wisdom, continues he, ought certainly to be wise themselves; but if any man were to sell such a bargain for such a price, he would be convicted of the most evident folly."① He certainly does not mean here to exaggerate the reward, and we may be assured that it was not less than he represents it. Four minæ were equal to thirteen pounds six shillings and eight pence: five minæ to sixteen pounds thirteen shillings and four pence. Something not less than the largest of those two sums, therefore, must at that time have been usually paid to the most eminent teachers at Athens. Isocrates himself demanded ten minæ,② or thirty-three pounds six shillings and eight pence, from each scholar. When he taught at Athens, he is said to have had an hundred scholars. I understand this to be the number whom he taught at one time, or who attended what we would call one course of lectures, a number which will not appear extraordinary from so great a city to so famous a teacher, who taught too what was at that time the most fashionable of all sciences, rhetoric. He must have made, therefore, by each course of lectures, a thousand minæ, or 3, 333*l*. 6*s*. 8*d*. A thousand minæ,

---

① [§ § 3, 4. A very free but not incorrect translation. Arbuthnot, *Tables of Ancient Coins, Weights and Measures*, 2nd ed., 1754, P. 198, refers to but does not quote the passage as his authority for stating the reward of a sophist at four or five minæ. He treats the mina as equal to £ 3 4s. 7d., which at the rate of 62s. to the pound troy is considerably too low.]

② [Plutarch, *Demosthenes*, c. v., § 3; *Isocrates*, § 30.]

只要求四五迈纳[1]那么微薄的酬劳。"他接着说:"传授别人智慧的人,他自己本身肯定也应该是有智慧的。但如果一个人以这样的价格来做这笔买卖,他必会被判定为最愚蠢的蠢材。"①苏格拉底在这里肯定无意夸大当时教师的报酬。我们可以相信当时教师的报酬,正如他所说的那样多。4 迈纳,等于现在货币的 13 镑 6 先令 8 便士;5 迈纳,等于现在的 16 镑 13 先令 4 便士。所以当时雅典最优秀教师的报酬,通常都会大于这两个数目中最大的一个。苏格拉底本人向学生每人收取的是 10 迈纳,②等于现今的 33 镑 6 先令 8 便士。据说,他在雅典讲学时有 100 个学生。我认为这是他在一个时期讲学时的学生数,也就是我们所说的上一门课程的人数。而且像雅典这样大的城市,苏格拉底这样出众的老师,他所教授的又是当时非常盛行的修辞学,100 个学生的人数根本就不算太多。因此每讲授一门课程,苏格拉底肯定都能得到 1000 迈纳的报酬,即 3333 镑 6 先令 8 便士。在普鲁塔克在另一处提

---

① 第 3、4 节。这是非常随意但也算正确的翻译。阿布诺(Arbutnot)在《古代的货币和度量衡》(第 2 版,1754 年,第 198 页)中提到了这段话,但并没有被引来论证诡辩家的报酬是四五迈纳。他认为 1 迈纳等于 3 镑 4 先令 7 便士,按 62 先令等于 1 镑的比例来计算,的确是非常低啊。

② 普鲁塔克(Plutarch):《德摩斯梯尼》,第 5 章第 3 节,《苏格拉底》第 30 节。

[1] 迈纳(mina),古代希腊的金额单位,古代希腊的重量单位。

accordingly, is said by Plutarch in another place, to have been his Didactron, or usual price of teaching. ① Many other eminent teachers in those times appear to have acquired great fortunes. Gorgias made a present to the temple of Delphi of his own statue in solid gold. We must not, I presume, suppose that it was as large as the life. His way of living, as well as that of Hippias and Protagoras, two other eminent teachers of those times, is represented by Plato as splendid even to ostentation. ② Plato himself is said to have lived with a good deal of magnificence. Aristotle, after having been tutor to Alexander, and most munificently rewarded, as it is universally agreed, both by him and his father Philip, ③ thought it worth while, notwithstanding, to return to Athens, in order to resume the teaching of his school. Teachers of the sciences were probably in those times less common than they came to be in an age or two afterwards, when the competition had probably somewhat reduced both the price of their labour and the admiration for their persons. The most eminent of them, however, appear always to have enjoyed a degree of consideration much superior to any of the like profession in the present times. The Athenians sent Carneades the academic, and Diogenes the stoic, upon a solemn embassy to Rome; and though their city had then declined from its former

---

① [Arbuthnot, *Tables of Ancient Coins*, p. 198, says, 'Isocrates had from his disciples a didactron or reward of 1,000 minæ, £ 3, 229 3s. 4d. ,' and quotes 'Plut. in Isocrate,' which says nothing about a 'didactron,' but only that Isocrates charged ten minæ and had 100 pupils. — § § 9, 12, 30.]

② [It is difficult to discover on what passage this statement is based.]

③ [Plutarch, *Alexander*.]

到,苏格拉底通常的讲课薪酬是1000迈纳。① 那个时期的其他许多优秀的教师似乎都得到了数量不菲的财富。乔治阿斯(Gorgias)曾把纯金铸造的自己的金像赠送给特尔斐[1]寺院。我想我们当然不会认为他的金像会与他本人身体是同比例的。根据柏拉图的描述,当时另外两个著名的教师希匹阿斯(Hippias)和普罗塔哥拉(Protagors)的生活,和乔治阿斯的生活一样都很豪华,甚至都快到了奢华的程度。② 而且据说柏拉图他本人的生活也是非常阔绰。亚里士多德作为亚历山大王子的老师,众所周知他受到了亚历山大和他父亲菲力普的优厚待遇,③但亚里士多德自己却认为,回雅典学园去讲课是更为合算的。当时这些讲课老师的数量,或许比数十年后的老师数量要少。数十年后,也许是因为竞争的缘故,老师劳动的报酬和世人对他们的尊敬都有略微下降。不过他们当中最杰出的教师所享受到报酬和尊敬,或许比起今天从事该职业的人享受到的仍要多得多。雅典曾经派遣学院派大师卡尼阿得斯(Carneades)和斯多葛派大师第欧根尼(Diogenes)[2]作为庄严的使者出使罗马。虽然在当时雅典已经失去了

---

① 阿布诺(Arbuthnot)在《古代货币表》第198页说,"苏格拉底给学生上课的讲课费或者薪酬为1000迈纳,即3333镑6先令8便士",并引用普鲁塔克《苏格拉底》书中的话说,苏格拉底一个课程有100个学生,每人收取10迈纳。第9、12、30节。
② 很难找到这个陈述基于哪篇文章。
③ 普鲁塔克:《亚历山大》。
[1] 特尔斐(Delphi),古希腊城市,因有阿波罗神殿而出名,它位于希腊中部靠近帕拿苏斯山的一座古城,其年代至少可追溯到公元前17世纪。它曾是著名的阿波罗先知所在地。
[2] 第欧根尼:古希腊哲学家,哲学犬儒学派奠基人,强调自我控制和推崇善行。说他曾提着灯在雅典大街漫步寻找诚实的人。

grandeur, it was still an independent and considerable republic. Carneades too was a Babylonian by birth,① and as there never was a people more jealous of admitting foreigners to public offices than the Athenians, their consideration for him must have been very great.

<small>Perhaps this cheapness of teaching is no disadvantage to the public.</small>   This inequality is upon the whole, perhaps, rather advantageous than hurtful to the public. It may somewhat degrade the profession of a public teacher; but the cheapness of literary education is surely an advantage which greatly over-balances this trifling inconveniency. The public too might derive still greater benefit from it, if the constitution of those schools and colleges, in which education is carried on, was more reasonable than it is at present through the greater part of Europe.

<small>(3) The policy of Europe obstructs the free circulation of labour.</small>   Thirdly, the policy of Europe, by obstructing the free circulation of labour and stock both from employment to employment, and from place to place, occasions in some cases a very inconvenient inequality in the whole of the advantages and disadvantages of their different employments.

<small>Apprenticeship and corporation privileges obstruct circulation from employment to employment and from place to place. So that the changes of employment necessary to equalise wages are prevented.</small>   The statute of apprenticeship obstructs the free circulation of labour from one employment to another, even in the same place. The exclusive privileges of corporations obstruct it from one place to another, even in the same employment.

It frequently happens that while high wages are given to the workmen in one manufacture, those in another are obliged to content themselves with bare subsistence. The one is in an advancing state, and has, therefore, a continual demand for new hands: The other is in a declining state, and the super-abundance of hands is continually increasing. Those two manufactures may sometimes be in the same town, and sometimes in the same neighbourhood, without being able to

---

① [This is a slip. Carneades was a native of Cyrene, and it was his colleague Diogenes who was a Babylonian by birth.]

往日的辉煌,但仍然是一个独立的重要的共和国。另外,卡尼阿得斯是巴比伦人,①众所周知雅典人最嫉妒外人担任公职了,但他们居然在这种场合会派遣卡尼阿得斯作为使者,足见他们对这位大师是何其尊敬啊。

但从社会整体上看,前面所提到的不均等对于社会大众而言,或许是利大于弊的。虽然公立教师的地位会因此而略为下降,但文学教育费用的低廉带来的收益,肯定会大大抵消公立教师地位下降带来的利益损失。如果欧洲大部分地区的教育学校和学院的组织比现在更为合理,则社会由此而享受到的益处会更大。

这种教育费用的低廉对大众来说或许是有利的。

第三,由于欧洲政策妨碍劳动和资本的自由流动,使它们不能从一个行业转移到其他行业,不能由一个地点转移到其他地点,这样有时候就会因劳动和资本不同用途导致的利害在整体上产生非常不便的不平等。

(3)欧洲政策妨碍劳动的自由流动。

学徒法令限制劳动从一种职业到另一种职业的自由流动,甚至在同一地方也是如此;行业组织的排外特权又限制劳动从一个地方到另一个地方的自由流动,即便是同一职业也是如此。

学徒制度和行业组织的特权限制了劳动在各个行业和各个地方之间的流动。

我们会经常看到这样的现象,在一个制造业中他们的工人工资待遇很高,而另一个制造业的工人却不得不满足于仅仅维系基本的生活费。原因前者的行业是处于上升行业,因此不断对劳动力需求旺盛;而后者的行业处于衰退行业,劳动力过剩。这两种制造业有时可能在同一个城市,有时在同一城市中都相邻很近,

---

① 这是一个错误,卡尼阿得斯是一个塞里尼人,他的同事第欧根尼是巴比伦人。

lend the least assistance to one another. The statute of apprenticeship may oppose it in the one case, and both that and an exclusive corporation in the other. In many different manufactures, however, the operations are so much alike, that the workmen could easily change trades with one another, if those absurd laws did not hinder them. The arts of weaving plain linen and plain silk, for example, are almost entirely the same. That of weaving plain woollen is somewhat different; but the difference is so insignificant, that either a linen or a silk weaver might become a tolerable workman in a very few days. If any of those three capital manufactures, therefore, were decaying, the workmen might find a resource in one of the other two which was in a more prosperous condition; and their wages would neither rise too high in the thriving, nor sink too low in the decaying manufacture. The linen manufacture indeed is, in England, by a particular statute,① open to every body; but as it is not much cultivated through the greater part of the country, it can afford no general resource to the workmen of other decaying manufactures, who, wherever the statute of apprenticeship takes place, have no other choice but either to come upon the parish, or to work as common labourers, for which, by their habits, they are much worse qualified than for any sort of manufacture that bears any resemblance to their own. They generally, therefore, chuse to come upon the parish.

_{What obstructs the circulation of labour also obstructs that of stock.}   Whatever obstructs the free circulation of labour from one employment to another, obstructs that of stock likewise; the quantity of stock which can be employed n any branch of business depending very much upon that of the labour which can be employed in it. Corporation laws, however, give less obstruction to the free circulation of stock from one place to another than to that of labour. It is everywhere

---

① [15 Car. Ⅱ., c. 15.]

但它们之间却没有丝毫的互助。因为在前一个场合,学徒法令限制了他们相互协助。而在后一个场合中,学徒法令和垄断的行业组织都会限制它们之间的相互协助。其实,有许多不同种类的制造业它们的操作都非常相似,假若没有这些荒谬的法律的话,劳动很容易就可以从一个职业流动到另一职业。例如,织粗麻布的技术和织粗丝绸的技术基本上是完全相同的。而织粗呢绒的技术虽稍有差别,但差别并不大。一个麻织工或丝织工只需短短几天之内就可以基本掌握织粗呢绒的技术。因此,当这三种主要制造业中有一个行业陷入困境时,这个行业的劳动者就可以转入另外两种比较繁荣的制造业中。这样工人的工资在繁荣的行业中不会太高,而在衰退的行业中也不会太低。当然了,如今英格兰的麻布制造业已经因为特别法令①的通过而对全民开放。但由于整个行业在英格兰大部分地区还没有得到大力开发,所以麻布业并不能为其他的衰退行业的劳动者提供太多的就业机会。在学徒法实施的地方,那些衰退行业的劳动者别无出路,只有求助于教区救济或者充当普通的劳动者。但按照他们的习惯,他们本来更加适合于从事与自己行业类似的行业,而不适应做普通的劳动者。所以,通常情况下他们都选择了请助于教区救济。

凡是限制了劳动者在不同行业间的自由流动,也就同样限制了资本的自由流动。原因在于一种行业中吸纳的资本数量在很大程度上取决于该行业所能吸纳的劳动力的数量。不过,行业组织的法规对于资本从一个地方向另一个地方自由流动的限制要小于它对劳动自由流动的限制。无论在哪,一个富商在一个自制

劳动流动必限制,也必然制约资本流动,限制资本流动。

---

① 查理二世十五年第 15 号法令。

much easier for a wealthy merchant to obtain the privilege of trading in a town corporate, than for a poor artificer to obtain that of working in it.

<small>In England the circulation of labour is further obstructed by the poor law</small>

The obstruction which corporation laws give to the free circulation of labour is common, I believe, to every part of Europe. That which is given to it by the poor laws is, so far as I know, peculiar to England. It consists in the difficulty which a poor man finds in obtaining a settlement, or even in being allowed to exercise his industry in any parish but that to which he belongs. It is the labour of artificers and manufacturers only of which the free circulation is obstructed by corporation laws. The difficulty of obtaining settlements obstructs even that of common labour. It may be worth while to give some account of the rise, progress, and present state of this disorder, the greatest perhaps of any in the police of England.

<small>Each parish was to support its own poor under 43 Eliz., c. 2;</small>

When by the destruction of monasteries the poor had been deprived of the charity of those religious houses, after some other ineffectual attempts for their relief, it was enacted by the 43d of Elizabeth, c. 2. that every parish should be bound to provide for its own poor; and that overseers of the poor should be annually appointed, who, with the churchwardens, should raise, by a parish rate, competent sums for this purpose.

<small>these were determined by 13 and 14 Car. II. to be such as had resided forty days, within which time, however, a new inhabitant might be removed.</small>

By this statute the necessity of providing for their own poor was indispensably imposed upon every parish. Who were to be considered as the poor of each parish, became, therefore, a question of some importance. This question, after some variation, was at last determined by the 13th and 14th of Charles II.[1] when it was enacted, that forty days undisturbed residence should gain any person a settlement in any parish; but that within that time it should be lawful for two justices of the peace, upon complaint made by the churchwardens or overseers of

---

[1] [C. 12.]

城市中获得经商权就要比一个贫穷的技工获得劳作权容易得多。

我认为在欧洲各地都普遍存在着行业组织限制劳动的自由流动的现象。但济贫法对于劳动自由流动的限制的现象，据我所知却是英格兰所特有的。济贫法使得穷人在其所属的教区以外的其他地方很难获得居住权，要想找到工作就更为不易了。行业组织的法规还只是限制了技工和制造业劳动者的自由流动。而获得居住权的困难则甚至限制了普通劳动者的自由流动。这恐怕是英格兰最大的混乱政策了，我想可能有必要对它的起源、发展和现状略加阐述。

> 格劳动自由流动受到法律限制，英格兰劳动的自由流动还受济贫法限制。

如果修道院一旦被毁，贫民就失去了这些宗教组织的施舍庇护。政府也几次试图去救济这些贫民，但均无效果。伊丽莎白女王四十三年颁布了第二号法令，规定每一教区都有救助本区贫民的义务，每年都指定贫民管理员，他们会同教区委员通过征收教区税来筹集足额的贫民救济金。

> 伊丽莎白四十三年第二号法令，每个教区都须救助本区贫民；

根据这项法令每个教区都必须供养本区的贫民。但重要的问题是什么样的人才算是本区贫民呢？解决这个问题的方案几经修改，最终到查理二世十三年、十四年①，法令才得以确定下来。法令规定无论任何人，只要连续在一个郊区连续居住40天就可以获得该教区的户籍。但是在这40天的时间内，如果该贫民受到教区委员或者贫民管理员控诉的话，两个治安法官有权依

> 查理二世十三年、十四年法令规定了居住40天的贫民获得户籍，但此期令可离开其本区。

---

① 第12号法令。

the poor, to remove any new inhabitant to the parish where he was last legally settled;① unless he either rented a tenement of ten pounds a year, or could give such security for the discharge of the parish where he was then living, as those justices should judge sufficient.

Notice in writing was required from the new inhabitant by I James II.

Some frauds, it is said, were committed in consequence of this statute; parish officers sometimes bribing their own poor to go clandestinely to another parish and by keeping themselves concealed for forty days to gain a settlement there, to the discharge of that to which they properly belonged. It was enacted, therefore, by the 1st of James II.② that the forty days undisturbed residence of any person necessary to gain a settlement, should be accounted only from the time of his delivering notice in writing, of the place of his abode and the number of his family, to one of the churchwardens or overseers of the parish where he came to dwell.

Such notice was to be published in church under 3 W III.

But parish officers, it seems, were not always more honest with regard to their own, than they had been with regard to other parishes, and sometimes connived at such intrusions, receiving the notice, and taking no proper steps in consequence of it. As every person in a parish, therefore, was supposed to have an interest to prevent as much as possible their being burdened by such intruders, it was further enacted by the 3d of William III.③ that the forty days residence should be accounted only from the publication of such notice in writing on Sunday in the church, immediately after divine service.

---

① [This account of the provisions of the Acts regarding settlement, though not incorrect, inverts the order of the ideas which prompted them. The preamble complains that owing to defects in the law 'poor people are not restrained from going from one parish to another and therefore do endeavour to settle themselves in those parishes where there is the best stock,' and so forth, and the Act therefore gives the justices power, within forty days after any such person or persons coming so to settle as aforesaid,' to remove them 'to such parish where he or they were last legally settled either as a native, householder, sojourner, apprentice or servant for the space of forty days at the least'. The use of the term 'settlement' seems to have originated with this Act.]

② [C. 17, 'An act for reviving and continuance of several acts'. The reason given is that such poor persons at their first coming to a parish do commonly conceal themselves'. Nothing is said either here or in Burn's *Poor Law or Justice of the Peace* about parish officers bribing their poor to go to another parish.]

③ [3 W. and M., c. 11, § 3.]

据诉讼将该贫民遣回到他最后合法居住的教区去,①除非他已经租了年租金十镑以上的住房,或者向治安法官提供了担保放弃原属教区户籍的足额保证金。

据说针对此法令曾发生了很多弄虚作假的事情。有时候教区职员会贿赂本区贫民潜赴其他教区,并在其他教区匿居 40 天获得户簿,从而脱除原属教区的户籍。因此在詹姆斯二世一年②又做出规定:任何人在新教区获得户籍所必需的居住 40 天期限一律是从他以书面形式向当地教区委员或教区贫民管理员提高说明其新居住地址和家庭人口之日起。

詹姆斯二世二年法令规定新居民必须提出书面报告。

然而,教区官员对于他们自己的教区,却并不总像对其他教区那样公正地办事。有时他们对于那些闯进教区的人采取默许的态度,在接受书面报告之后并不采取任何适当措施。但由于教区内每个人为了切身利益都会尽可能阻止他们闯进本教区,所以在威廉三世三年③又颁布了如下的法令:那 40 天的居住期是从书面报告在教堂星期日做完礼拜后公布之日算起。

威廉三世的法令,根据威廉三年法这种书面报告应在教堂公布。

---

① 这个对有关户籍的法律规定的叙述尽管没错,但却违背了当初制定法律的意愿。序言中抱怨说,由于法律的漏洞,"穷人可以随意从一个教区到另一个教区,以便能在拥有最好资本的教区居住",所以法律给了治安法官权利,使他们可以"在任何这样的人来本郊区居住的 40 天内"有权命令他回到"他或他们最后作为本地人、房东、寄宿人、学徒或者雇工至少居住了 40 天以上而且拥有合法户籍的教区去"。"户籍"一词的使用,似乎就是从这项法律开始的。

② 第 17 号法令。"一个修正和延续几个法令的法律"它是基于"这些穷人首次来到一个教区时一般都会隐藏自己"。这里或者波恩的《贫民法》和《治安法官》都没有提到教区官员会贿赂他们教区的穷人到另一个教区。

③ 威廉和玛利三年第 11 号法令第 3 条。

| 国民财富的性质与原理

"After all," says Doctor Burn, "this kind of settlement, by "continuing forty days after publication of notice in writing, is very seldom "obtained; and the design of the acts is not so much for gaining of "settlements, as for the avoiding of them by persons coming into a" parish clandestinely: for the giving of notice is only putting a force "upon the parish to remove. But if a person's situation is such, that" it is doubtful whether he is actually removeable or not, he shall by "giving of notice compel the parish either to allow him a settlement" uncontested, by suffering him to continue forty days; or, by removing "him, to try the right."①

There were four other ways of gaining a settlement,

This statute, therefore, rendered it almost impracticable for a poor man to gain a new settlement in the old way, by forty days inhabitancy. But that it might not appear to preclude altogether the common people of one parish from ever establishing themselves with security in another, it appointed four other ways by which a settlement might be gained without any notice delivered or published. The first was, by being taxed to parish rates and paying them; the second, by being elected into an annual parish office, and serving in it a year; the third, by serving an apprenticeship in the parish; the fourth, by being hired into service there for a year, and continuing in the same service during the whole of it.②

two of which were impossible to all poor men.

Nobody can gain a settlement by either of the two first ways, but by the public deed of the whole parish, who are too well aware of the consequences to adopt any new-comer who has nothing but his labour to support him, either by taxing him to parish rates, or by electing him into a parish office.

and the other two to all married men,

No married man can well gain any settlement in either of the two last ways. An apprentice is scarce ever married; and it is expressly enacted, that no married servant shall gain any settlement by being hired for a year.③ The principal effect of introducing settlement by service, has been to put out in a great measure the old fashion of hiring

---

① [Richard Burn, *Justice of the Peace*, 1764, vol. ii., p. 253.]
② [§ §6, 8.]
③ [§ 7 confines settlement by service to unmarried persons without children.]

波恩博士说:"很少有人能通过在书面报告公布后继续居住40天的方式获得户籍。这项法令的目的不在于使人获得户籍,而在于避免潜往本教区者获得户籍。因为提交书面报告只是给教区一种驱逐的权利,如果一个人背景比较复杂,那么能否迫使其返回原教区就有了很大的问题。如果他提交书面报告的话,教区将不得不做出抉择,要么允许他继续居住40天并给他以户籍,要么利用该权利令其离开"。①

所以这项法令,就让穷人几乎不可能通过连续居住40天的老办法来获得新户籍。为了让一个教区的普通老百姓不会因为这项法律而根本无法在另一个教区取得居住权,法律又规定了其他四种不用提交或者公告任何报告来取得户籍的办法:第一,缴纳教区课征的税;第二,被选举担任一年任期的教区公职,并任职一年;第三,在教区当学徒;第四,在教区被雇用一年,并且在整个一年中从事同一工作。②〔有其他四种办法可以获得户籍,〕

除非由教区全体人民采取行动,谁都无法按照上述四种办法中的前两种办法来获得户籍。而教区人民却都非常清楚,把一个除了自身劳动力外一无所有的人通过课税或选为教区公职的办法收容进来的会产生什么样的后果。〔对于所有穷人来说其中两种方法是不可能的,〕

已经结婚的人都无法通过后两种办法来获得户籍。学徒一般都没有结婚。而法律又专门规定,凡是已经结婚的佣工不得因为受雇一年而获得户籍。③ 这个通过服务来获得户籍的办法产〔其他两种方法对于已经结婚的人来说也是不可能的。〕

---

① 理查德·波恩:《治安法官》,1764年,第2卷,第253页。
② 法律第6条、第8条。
③ 第7条规定,只有没有子女的未婚者才可以因为受雇用而获得户籍。

for a year, which before had been so customary in England, that even at this day, if no particular term is agreed upon, the law intends that every servant is hired for a year. But masters are not always willing to give their servants a settlement by hiring them in this manner; and servants are not always willing to be so hired, because, as every last settlement discharges all the foregoing, they might thereby lose their original settlement in the places of their nativity, the habitation of their parents and relations.

<small>and to all independent workmen.</small> No independent workman, it is evident, whether labourer or artificer, is likely to gain any new settlement either by apprenticeship or by service. When such a person, therefore, carried his industry to a new parish, he was liable to be removed, how healthy and industrious soever, at the caprice of any churchwarden or overseer, unless he either rented a tenement of ten pounds a year, a thing impossible for one who has nothing but his labour to live by; or could give such security for the discharge of the parish as two justices of the peace should judge sufficient. What security they shall require, indeed, is left altogether to their discretion; but they cannot well require less than thirty pounds, it having been enacted, that the purchase even of a freehold estate of less than thirty pounds value, shall not gain any person a settlement, as not being sufficient for the discharge of the parish. [1] But this is a security which scarce any man who lives by labour can give; and much greater security is frequently demanded.

In order to restore in some measure that free circulation of labour which those different statutes had almost entirely taken away, [2] the invention of certificates was fallen upon. By the 8th and 9th of William

---

[1] [By 9 Geo. I., c. 7.]

[2] [The Act, 13 & 14 Car. II., c. 12, giving the justices power to remove the immigrant within forty days was certainly obstructive to the free circulation of labour, but the other statutes referred to in the text, by making the attainment of a settlement more difficult, would appear to have made it less necessary for a parish to put in force the power of removal, and therefore to have assisted rather than obstructed the free circulation of labour. The poor law commissioners of 1834, long after the power of removal had been abolished in 1795, found the law of settlement a great obstruction to the free circulation of labour, because men were afraid of gaining a new settlement, not because a new settlement was denied them.]

生的主要结果就是在很大程度上取消了以前英格兰普遍采用的以一年为雇用期的老习惯,甚至目前对于没有专门规定期限的雇佣期限间还默认为一年。但雇主们未必都愿意因雇用佣工一年就给佣工户籍,而佣工也未必都愿意通过被雇一年来取得新户籍。因为获得新户籍就要取消以前的户籍,他们可能会因此失去他们的家乡即父母和亲属居住地的原有户籍。

显然,没有一个独立工人,无论他是普通劳动者还是技工,能够通过做学徒或被雇用而获得新的户籍。所以,无论一个人多么的健康和勤勉,当他带着他的技能来到一个新教区时,教区执事或者贫民管理员随时都可能令其离开,除非他已经租用每年租金10镑的土地,而这对于一个除了自身劳动力外一无所有的人是根本不可能的;或者能向两名治安法官提供足够的保证金来担保他们解除原属教区的户籍。保证金的数额完全由治安法官来决定,但这个数额必然会不少于30镑。因为法律规定,购买不到30镑的世袭不动产的人不准取得户籍,因为那不足以作为解除原户籍的担保。① 而靠劳动为生的人是根本无法支付这么大的数额的,而且实际中治安法官要求的数额比30镑往往还要大得多。

对于所有独立的工人也是不可能的。

为了在一定程度上恢复由于各种法律所几乎完全取消的劳动自由流动,当局推出了发证书的办法。根据威廉三世八年②

---

① 乔治一世九年第7号法令。
② 查理二世十三年和十四年的第12号法令,给了治安法官以权力,他们可以将40天内的迁入者驱逐出教区,这样毫无疑问有碍于劳动的自由流动。但此处提到的另外使得获得定居权更加困难的法律,这样看起来那种强制驱逐权就没有那么的必要了,这样它就是协助而不是限制劳动自由流动了。在1795年驱逐权被废除了,多年以后,在1834年贫民法委员们发现定居权构成对劳动自由流动的障碍的真正原因在于人民害怕获得一个新的定居权,而不是因为不能获得一个新的定居权。

国民财富的性质与原理

Certificates were invented to enable persons to reside in a parish without being immediately removable and without gaining a settlement.

III. ① it was enacted, that if any person should bring a certificate from the parish where he was last legally settled, subscribed by the churchwardens and overseers of the poor, and allowed by two justices of the peace, that every other parish should be obliged to receive him; that he should not be removeable merely upon account of his being likely to become chargeable, but only upon his becoming actually chargeable, and that then the parish which granted the certificate should be obliged to pay the expence both of his maintenance and of his removal. And in order to give the most perfect security to the parish where such certificated man should come to reside, it was further enacted by the same statute, ② that he should gain no settlement there by any means whatever, except either by renting a tenement of ten pounds a year, or by serving upon his own account in an annual parish office for one whole year; and consequently neither by notice, nor by service, nor by apprenticeship, nor by paying parish rates. By the 12th of Queen Anne too, stat. 1. c. 18. it was further enacted, that neither the servants nor apprentices of such certificated man should gain any settlement in the parish where he resided under such certificate, ③

Certificates were required by the new parish but refused by the old.

How far this invention has restored that free circulation of labour which the preceding statutes had almost entirely taken away, we may learn from the following very judicious observation of Doctor Burn. "It is obvious," says he, "that there are divers good reasons for" requiring certificates with persons coming to settle in any place; "namely, that persons residing under them can gain no settlement,"neither by apprenticeship, nor by service, nor by giving notice, "nor by paying

---

① [C. 30, 'An act for supplying some defects in the laws for the relief of the poor of this kingdom . The preamble recites,' Forasmuch as many poor persons chargeable to the parish, township or place where they live, merely for want of work, would in any other place when sufficient employment is to be had maintain themselves and families without being burdensome to any parish, township or place'. But certificates were invented long before this. The Act 13 & 14 Car. II. , c. 12, provides for their issue to persons going into another parish for harvest or any other kind of work, and the preamble of 8 & 9 W. III. , c. 30, shows that they were commonly given. Only temporary employment, however, was contemplated, and, on the expiration of the job, the certificated person became removable.]

② [Rather by the explanatory Act, 9 & 10 W. III. , c. II.]

③ [All these statutes are conveniently collected in Richard Burn's *History of the Poor Laws*, 1764, pp. 94-100.]

和九年的法令，①任何人如果持有他最后合法居住的教区授予的经该教区教会执事和贫民管理人签名和两名治安法官认可的申明任何教区都有收留他的义务的证书，他所移居的教区就不得以他可能被控诉为由令其离开。而只有当他实际上已经被控诉时，才可以被勒令遣返。此时签发证书的教区要负担其生活费和遣返费。为了保证持证者所要前来居住的教区能得到最大的安全保障，同一法令又进一步规定：②移居者只有租有年租金10镑的土地，或者免费为教区公职服务　年，才能取得户籍。这样，他就无法通过提交报告、被雇、做学徒或者缴纳教区税的方式来取得户籍了。而且，安妮女王十二年法令第一款第十八条又进一步规定，持有此证书的人的佣工或学徒不能据此在其所在的教区取得户籍。③

证书的发明，让人们可以在教区居住而不被立即驱逐，但还是没有户籍。

我们可以从波恩博士明智的言论中了解到这个授予证书的办法究竟在多大程度上恢复了被各种法令所几乎完全取消的劳动移动自由。他说："非常显然，教区有种种充分的理由要求来到任一地方定居的人持有证书。即持有证书而来定居的人，不能通

教区持证书而授证新要有书，原教拒绝。

---

① 第30号法令"一个补充减轻王国贫民法的几点缺陷的法令"。在厅言中叙述道："鉴于许多对于教区、城市或居所可控的贫民来说，他们仅仅是想在另外一处有足够的就业可以维持他们自己和他们的家庭而且不会给所在地带来负担的地方获得工作"。但证书在此以前已经就被发明出来了。查理二世十三年、十四年第12号法令允许人们可以进入另一个教区进行收割或者获得任何别的工作，而在威廉三世八年、九年第30号法令的序言中则表示这种证书已经被普遍授予了。只有那些临时工或者工作到期的人才会被驱逐。

② 更准确说是威廉三世九年和十年第11号解释性法令。

③ 所有这些法律都收集在理查德·波恩的《济贫法史》(1764年，第94～100页)中，查阅方便。

——— 323 ———

parish rates; that they can settle neither apprentices "nor servants; that if they become chargeable, it is certainly known "whither to remove them, and the parish shall be paid for the" removal, and for their maintenance in the mean time; and that if "they fall sick, and cannot be removed, the parish which gave the" certificate must maintain them: none of all which can be without "a certificate. Which reasons will hold proportionably for parishes" not granting certificates in ordinary cases; for it is far more than "an equal chance, but that they will have the certificated persons "again, and in a worse condition."① The moral of this observation seems to be, that certificates ought always to be required by the parish where any poor man comes to reside, and that they ought very seldom to be granted by that which he proposes to leave. "There is some"what of hardship in this matter of certificates, "says the same very intelligent Author, in his History of the Poor Laws," by putting it in "the power of a parish officer, to imprison a man as it were for life;" however inconvenient it may be for him to continue at that place "where he has had the misfortune to acquire what is called a settle ment," or whatever advantage he may propose to himself by living "elsewhere."②

The courts declined to force overseers to give a certificate.
Though a certificate carries along with it no testimonial of good behaviour, and certifies nothing but that the person belongs to the parish to which he really does belong, it is altogether discretionary in the parish officers either to grant or to refuse it. A mandamus was once moved for, says Doctor Burn, to compel the churchwardens and overseers to sign a certificate; but the court of King's Bench rejected the motion as a very strange attempt.③

The very unequal price of labour which we frequently find in England in places at no great distance from one another, is probably owing to the obstruction which the law of settlements gives to a poor man who would carry his industry from one parish to another without a

---

① [Burn, *Justice of the Peace*, 1764, vol. ii., p. 274.]
② [*Ibid.* 1764 pp .235,236.]
③ [*Ibid.* p. 209. The date given is 1730.]

过做学徒、被雇、提交报告或缴纳教区税而取得户籍。他们也不能为他们的学徒和雇工落户。一旦他们被控诉,教区就知道要把他们迁往哪个教区,而后一教区则要负担他们的遣返费和生活费。如果他们生病无法迁移,发证的教区必须负担他们的生活费。所有这些,没有证书是不行的。这也是为什么通常情况下教区不愿意颁发证书的原因。因为同样的道理,极有可能他们颁发的证书的持有人有被遣返的可能,而且当被遣返时情况要更糟。"①波恩博士这段话似乎意味着,一个教区穷人迁入时必须要持有证书,而贫民要迁出时教区则不要轻易授予证书。这个睿智的作家在他的著作《济贫法史》中又说:"授予证书这个办法,造就了一种困难的境地。它给予了教区官员权力通过它犹如将贫民终身监禁起来,不管该贫民在那个不幸获得户籍的地方继续居住是多么的不方便,也不管他想去移居的地方对他来说有多么的有利。"②

虽然证书并不证明持证者的品行良好,而只是说明他们所属的教区,但证书的是否发放却完全取决于教区官员的自由裁决。波恩博士说,曾经有人动议法院命令教区委员和贫民管理人签发证书,但高等法院认为这个建议太离奇了,就否决了该建议。③

我们常常会发现在英格兰境内,距离相隔不远的地方的劳动价格都极不均等,这可能是因为英格兰的居住法限制了没有证书的贫民带着他的技能从一个地方到另一地方劳动。的确,有时候

---

① 波恩:《治安法官》,1764 年,第 2 卷,第 274 页。
② 同上书,第 235、236 页。
③ 同上书,第 209 页。日期是 1730 年。

> This law is the cause of the very unequal price of labour in England,

certificate. A single man, indeed, who is healthy and industrious, may sometimes reside by sufferance without one; but a man with a wife and family who should attempt to do so, would in most parishes be sure of being removed, and if the single man should afterwards marry, he would generally be removed likewise. ① The scarcity of hands in one parish, therefore, cannot always be relieved by their superabundance in another, as it is constantly in Scotland, and, I believe, in all other countries where there is no difficulty of settlement. In such countries, though wages may sometimes rise a little in the neighbourhood of a great town, or wherever else there is an extraordinary demand for labour, and sink gradually as the distance from such places increases, till they fall back to the common rate of the country; yet we never meet with those sudden and unaccountable differences in the wages of neighbouring places which we sometimes find in England, where it is often more difficult for a poor man to pass the artificial boundary of a parish, than an arm of the sea or a ridge of high mountains, natural boundaries which sometimes separate very distinctly different rates of wages in other countries.

> and an evident violation of natural liberty, though tamely submitted to.

To remove a man who has committed no misdemeanour from the parish where he chuses to reside, is an evident violation of natural liberty and justice. The common people of England, however, so jealous of their liberty, but like the common people of most other countries never rightly understanding wherein it consists, have now for more than a century together suffered themselves to be exposed to this oppression without a remedy. Though men of reflection too have sometimes complained of the law of settlements as a public grievance; yet it has never been the object of any general popular clamour, such as that against general warrants, an abusive practice undoubtedly, but such a one as was not likely to occasion any general oppression. There is scarce a poor man in England of forty years of age, I will venture to say, who has not in some part of his life felt himself most cruelly oppressed by this ill-contrived law of settlements.

I shall conclude this long chapter with observing, that though

---

① [Since the fact of the father having no settlement would not free the parish from the danger of having at some future time to support the children.]

那些健康而且勤劳的独身者可能会受到宽容,没有证书也在其他教区居住了下来,但是对于那些有了家室的人来说如果试图这样做,一般情况下都会被大多数教区所驱逐。而且独身者如果后来结婚了,也将同样受到被驱逐的命运。① 所以,不像是苏格兰或者其他没有居住权问题的国家那样,英格兰一个教区劳动力的不足,往往无法由其他教区劳动力的过剩中得到弥补。在那些别的国家,虽然在大城市附近或者在对劳动力有特殊需求的地方工资可能会高点,但随着离这些地方越来越远,工资水平就越来越接近该国的普遍工资水平。像英格兰这样就如我们看到的在邻近地方的工资有时候会有突然的无法解释的差异,却是别处从来没有的现象。在英格兰,贫民要越过教区的人为界限,往往比越过国家之间由高山和海湾构成的自然界限还要困难得多,而这些自然界限有时就使这些国家的工资率相差很多了。

<small>这项法律造成英格兰劳动价格极不均等。</small>

强令一个没有犯过轻罪的人迁出他所选择定居的教区,这显然是违反天赋自由和公正的。虽然英格兰的普通民众羡慕自由,但也如别的大多数国家的普通民众一样,他们都没有真正理解到底什么是自由。一百多年以来,他们在承受着这种压迫而从未寻求解救之法。一些有思想的人有时也抱怨居住法为民众所不满,但它从来都有像一般搜查证那样成为民众高声反对的对象。虽然一般搜查证毫无疑问构成了滥用职权,但却不会像居住法那么产生普遍的压迫。我敢说,现在40岁的英格兰贫民几乎全都在其一生中受过这项设计错误的居住法的残酷压迫。

<small>这项法律是对自然公侵,虽然人们顺承,来地逆受它。</small>

我将通过下面的话来结束这冗长的一章:在过去,工资最初

---

① 因为一个没有户籍的父亲,就有让教区将来抚养其子女的危险。

anciently it was usual to rate wages, first by general laws extending over the whole kingdom, and afterwards by particular orders of the justices of peace in every particular county, both these practices have now gone entirely into disuse. "By the experience of above four "hundred years," says Doctor Burn, "it seems time to lay aside all "endeavours to bring under strict regulations, what in its own nature "seems incapable of minute limitation: for if all persons in the same "kind of work were to receive equal wages, there would be no emula-"tion, and no room left for industry or ingenuity."①

London tailors' wages are still rated by law.
Particular acts of parliament, however, still attempt sometimes to regulate wages in particular trades and in particular places. Thus the 8th of George Ⅲ. prohibits under heavy penalties all master taylors in London, and five miles round it, from giving, and their workmen from accepting, more than two shillings and sevenpence halfpenny a day, except in the case of a general mourning. Whenever the legislature attempts to regulate the differences between masters and their workmen, its counsellors are always the masters. When the regulation, therefore, is in favour of the workmen, it is always just and equitable; but it is sometimes otherwise when in favour of the masters. Thus the law which obliges the masters in several different trades to pay their workmen in money and not in goods, is quite just and equitable.② It imposes no real hardship upon the masters. It only obliges them to pay that value in money, which they pretended to pay, but did not always really pay, in goods. This law is in favour of the workmen; but the 8th of George Ⅲ. is in favour of the masters. When masters combine together in order to reduce the wages of their workmen, they commonly enter into a private bond or agreement, not to

① [*History of the Poor Laws*, p. 130, loosely quoted. After 'limitation' the passage runs, ' as thereby it leaves no room for industry or ingenuity; for if all persons in the same kind of work were to receive equal wages there would be no emulation.']

② [1 Ann., stat. 2, c. 18. applied to workmen in the woollen, linen, fustian, cotton and iron manufacture; 13 Geo. Ⅱ., c. 8, to manufacturers of gloves, boots, shoes and other leather wares. The second of these Acts only prohibits truck payments when made without the request and consent of the workmen.]

是由全国性的普通法律来予以规定的,后来则依据各州的治安法官的特殊命令来规定,而到现在这两种办法都已经完全不用了。波恩博士说:"根据四百多年来的经验,看来是时候把性质上不能详细限定的东西硬加以严格规定的做法废止的时候了。因为如果所有同行业的劳动者都拿到同样的报酬,那么所有的竞争都将停止,勤奋或才能也将无用武之地。"①

然而,时至今日国会的个别法令有时还试图规定个别行业个别地方的工资。乔治三世八年的法令就曾经规定,除国丧外,伦敦及其周边5英里以内的裁缝师傅每天为他们的工人不得支付超过两先令七便士的工资,而其工人也不得接受超过这个数额的工资,违者将处以重罚。无论何时当立法当局在规定雇主及工人们之间的关系时,总是以雇主为顾问。因此,当法规对于劳动者有利时,总是正当而又公平;但当对雇主有利时,则有时并非如此。例如,要求不同行业雇主必须以货币形式而不是以货物形式支付工资的法律,是完全正当而又公平的。② 它并没有给雇主们带来什么实际上的困难,它只是要求雇主们用货币支付他们试图用货物支付而实际上并没有这样执行的价值。这种法律对劳动者是有利的。但乔治三世八年的法令却对雇主有利。当雇主们试图联合起来降低劳动工资时,他们常常通过缔结秘密的同盟或

伦敦裁缝的工资还是受法律规定。

---

① 《济贫法史》,第130页,对原文做了宽松的引用。原文中有所有的同种工人都接受相同的报酬的话。
② 安妮女王一年的第2款第18号法令,适用于毛、麻、麻纱布、棉、铁制造业的工人;乔治二世十三年的第8号法令,则适用于手套、靴子、鞋及其他皮革制品的制造业。后者只禁止在没有得到工人的请求和同意时支付实物。

give more than a certain wage under a certain penalty. Were the workmen to enter into a contrary combination of the same kind, not to accept of a certain wage under a certain penalty, the law would punish them very severely; and if it dealt impartially, it would treat the masters in the same manner. But the 8th of George Ⅲ. enforces by law that very regulation which masters sometimes attempt to establish by such combinations. The complaint of the workmen, that it puts the ablest and most industrious upon the same footing with an ordinary workman, seems perfectly well founded.

<small>Attempts were also made to regulate profits by fixing prices, and the assize of bread still remains.</small> In ancient times too it was usual to attempt to regulate the profits of merchants and other dealers, by rating the price both of provisions and other goods. The assize of bread is, so far as I know, the only remnant of this ancient usage. Where there is an exclusive corporation, it may perhaps be proper to regulate the price of the first necessary of life. But where there is none, the competition will regulate it much better than any assize. The method of fixing the assize of bread established by the 31st of George Ⅱ. ①could not be put in practice in Scotland, on account of a defect in the law; its execution depending upon the office of clerk of the market, which does not exist there. This defect was not remedied till the 3d of George Ⅲ. ② The want of an assize occasioned no sensible inconveniency, and the establishment of one in the few places where it has yet taken place, has produced no sensible advantage. In the greater part of the towns of Scotland, however, there is an incorporation of bakers who claim exclusive privileges, though they are not very strictly guarded.

<small>The inequalities of wages and profits are not much affected by the advancing or declining state of the society.</small> The proportion between the different rates both of wages and profit in the different employments of labour and stock, seems not to be much affected, as has already been observed, by the riches or poverty, the advancing, stationary, or declining state of the society. Such revolutions in the public welfare, though they affect the general rates both of wages and profit, must in the end affect them equally in

---

① [C. 29.]

② [C. 6. The preamble relates the defect.]

协定,约定支付工资的上限,违者给予一定的处罚。如果工人也成立性质相反的联合,约定不许接受一定数额以下的工资,违者给予一定的处罚。那么法律就将严厉地制裁劳动者。法律要是公平的话,就得以同样的方式惩罚雇主。但乔治三世三年的法令却通过法律推行了雇主们有时试图通过联合才能来制定的规章。工人们常常抱怨说,这项法律将最有能力、最勤劳的工人和普通的工人同等对待,看来这种抱怨似乎是完全有根据的。

在古代,也常常通过规定食品和其他货物的价格来调节商人和其他买卖人的利润。据我所知,目前面包的法定价格就是这个古老习惯的唯一遗迹。在那些存在垄断的行业组织的地方规定生活首要必需品的价格或许正当的。但在没有行业组织的地方,竞争就要比任何法定价格调节物价的效果更好。由于法律上的缺陷,乔治二世三十一年制定的规定面包价格的做法在苏格兰没有得以实行。① 因为这个办法需要市场管理员来执行,但当时苏格兰却没有市场管理员。直到乔治三世三年这个法律上的缺陷才得以矫正。② 没有实行法定价格也没有什么明显的不便,而现在少数实施法定价格的地方却也没有看到什么明显的好处。不过,在苏格兰的大多数城市都有面包师的行业组织,他们要求垄断权,尽管他们并没有受到严格的保护。

正如前面已经指出的,用于不同用途的劳动和资本对应的不同的工资率和利润率之间的比例,似乎不受社会贫富、进步、停滞或者衰退状态的太多影响。虽然公共福利的变革会影响一般的

<small>经普通也曾试图通过定价的方式来调节面包利润,法定价格仍然存在。</small>

<small>和等的工资和利润均不受进者的影响,并不会或退太大响。</small>

---

① 第 29 号法令。
② 第 6 号法令。序言中讲述了这个缺陷。

all different employments. The proportion between them, therefore, must remain the same, and cannot well be altered, at least for any considerable time, by any such revolutions.

工资率和利润率,但最终会对所有不同的用途施以相同的影响。因此,至少在相当长的期间内用于不同用途的工资率和利润率之间的比例必然会保持不变,而不会因这些变革而发生改变。